D0267525

CIT

Sean Odom

CIT Exam Cram 2 (Exam 642-831)

International Standard Book Number: 0-789-73021-9

Library of Congress Catalog Card Number: 2003109243

Printed in the United States of America

First Printing: October 2003

06   05   04   03   4   3   2   1

Publisher
Paul Boger

Executive Editor
Jeff Riley

Acquisitions Editor
Carol Ackerman

Development Editor
Lorna Gentry

Managing Editor
Charlotte Clapp

Project Editor
Dan Knott

Production Editor
Benjamin Berg

Indexer
Larry Sweazy

Proofreader
Tracy Donhardt

Technical Editors
Jason Rader
Michael Ashton

Publishing Coordinator
Pamalee Nelson

Multimedia Developer
Dan Scherf

Interior Designer
Gary Adair

Cover Designer
Anne Jones

Trademarks

All terms mentioned in this book that are known to be trademarks or service marks have been appropriately capitalized. Que Publishing cannot attest to the accuracy of this information. Use of a term in this book should not be regarded as affecting the validity of any trademark or service mark.

Warning and Disclaimer

Every effort has been made to make this book as complete and as accurate as possible, but no warranty or fitness is implied. The information provided is on an "as is" basis. The author and the publisher shall have neither liability nor responsibility to any person or entity with respect to any loss or damages arising from the information contained in this book or from the use of the CD or programs accompanying it.

Bulk Sales

Que offers excellent discounts on this book when ordered in quantity for bulk purchases or special sales. For more information, please contact

U.S. Corporate and Government Sales

1-800-382-3419

corpsales@pearsontechgroup.com

For sales outside of the U.S., please contact

International Sales

1-317-428-3341

international@pearsontechgroup.com

CERTIFICATION

Que Certification • 201 West 103rd Street • Indianapolis, Indiana 46290

A Note from Series Editor Ed Tittel

You know better than to trust your certification preparation to just anybody. That's why you, and more than two million others, have purchased an Exam Cram book. As Series Editor for the new and improved Exam Cram 2 series, I have worked with the staff at Que Certification to ensure you won't be disappointed. That's why we've taken the world's best-selling certification product—a finalist for "Best Study Guide" in a CertCities reader poll in 2002—and made it even better.

As a "Favorite Study Guide Author" finalist in a 2002 poll of CertCities readers, I know the value of good books. You'll be impressed with Que Certification's stringent review process, which ensures the books are high-quality, relevant, and technically accurate. Rest assured that at least a dozen industry experts—including the panel of certification experts at CramSession—have reviewed this material, helping us deliver an excellent solution to your exam preparation needs.

Best Study Guides

We've also added a preview edition of PrepLogic's powerful, full-featured test engine, which is trusted by certification students throughout the world.

As a 20-year-plus veteran of the computing industry and the original creator and editor of the Exam Cram series, I've brought my IT experience to bear on these books. During my tenure at Novell from 1989 to 1994, I worked with and around its excellent education and certification department. This experience helped push my writing and teaching activities heavily in the certification direction. Since then, I've worked on more than 70 certification-related books, and I write about certification topics for numerous Web sites and for *Certification* magazine.

In 1996, while studying for various MCP exams, I became frustrated with the huge, unwieldy study guides that were the only preparation tools available. As an experienced IT professional and former instructor, I wanted "nothing but the facts" necessary to prepare for the exams. From this impetus, Exam Cram emerged in 1997. It quickly became the best-selling computer book series since "...*For Dummies*," and the best-selling certification book series ever. By maintaining an intense focus on subject matter, tracking errata and updates quickly, and following the certification market closely, Exam Cram was able to establish the dominant position in cert prep books.

You will not be disappointed in your decision to purchase this book. If you are, please contact me at etittel@jump.net. All suggestions, ideas, input, or constructive criticism are welcome!

Ed Tittel

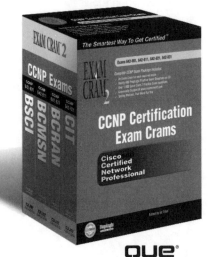

To Barbara Percox, who will be greatly missed by all who worked with her and knew her.

About the Author

Sean Odom has been in the IT industry for more than 14 years. In that time he has been an IT consultant for such companies as Network Design Associates, Wells Fargo Bank, CH2M Hill, Intel, Payne Webber, Lincoln National Life, and many more. He has written or coauthored more than 16 best-selling industry certification books. In addition, he has been a technical contributor to countless books and white papers. Sean has also been a Cisco instructor for Globalnet Training Solutions and is currently the president of the Sacramento/Placer County Cisco Users Group.

About the Technical Editors

Michael Ashton is a Corporate Systems Engineer for Altiris. He has worked in technology for 15 years in a wide variety of positions in technical presales, consulting, network administration, technical support, publishing, and telecommunications.

Michael has been a technical editor for Que Publishing and Cisco Press. In addition, he has written articles for *Microsoft Certified Professional Magazine*, *Smart Computing*, Earthweb's *Datamation*, *Y2K News*, *Computer Credible* and several other publications. He can be reached at hmashton@earthlink.net or michael_ashton@yahoo.com.

Jason Rader hails from the Sunshine State but sees very little of it. Security, telecom, and application/system development projects keep him quite busy. He owes all of his success to the patience of his wife, Julie, and the craziness of his boys, Chase and Zachary. Always looking for cool projects, Jason can be contacted at rader@raderlabs.com.

Acknowledgments

. . . .

There are many people I would like to thank. First, from my personal life: Mikayla, Trevor, Hillary, Macky, and most of all Erin. They have suffered from my working so much. Next I need to thank those I work with who keep my skills current and keep me in a real job. Those people include Frank Ono, Ernie Lopez, John Gilfillan, Jeff Wheeler, Kara Jane Taylor, Andrew Odom, David Green, Kris Pleschner, Cherrin Hosking, and Laurie Stark. Also two kids who have an unbelievable lust for technical knowledge, Zack and Travis Sweigart. There are also others at JTS: Jack Sweigart, Larry Carter, Victoria Sweigart, Jeff Sweigart, John Sweigart, Randy Sweigart, Daryl Whiteside, Tim Weir, Randy Ryan, Carol Martin, Cindy Moreno, and Karen Payne.

There is another group of people who have worked so hard and put so much faith in me, and those are the people from Que. Carol Ackerman, my acquisitions editor; my development editor, Lorna Gentry; Jason Rader and Michael Aston for finding my technical snafus; Dan Knott; Benjamin Berg; and Que publisher, Paul Boger.

There are several people who have influenced my life but may not know how much they have: Author Todd Lammle for all the tutoring and opportunities he has given me over the years, actor Ken Gregg for all his support and encouragement, acquisitions editor Jeff Kellum for my first writing opportunity, instructor John P. Turner for being a bright light to bounce technical problems off of, Kim Milroy for all she does for me and the Cisco users group behind the scenes, Sam Wheat for all his Microsoft help, Laury Sackman the owner of Network Design Associates, and to my parents—need I say more?

We Want to Hear from You!

As the reader of this book, *you* are our most important critic and commentator. We value your opinion and want to know what we're doing right, what we could do better, what areas you'd like to see us publish in, and any other words of wisdom you're willing to pass our way.

As an executive editor for Que, I welcome your comments. You can email or write me directly to let me know what you did or didn't like about this book—as well as what we can do to make our books better.

Please note that I cannot help you with technical problems related to the topic of this book. We do have a User Services group, however, where I will forward specific technical questions related to the book.

When you write, please be sure to include this book's title and author as well as your name, email address, and phone number. I will carefully review your comments and share them with the author and editors who worked on the book.

Email: feedback@quepublishing.com

Mail: Jeff Riley
           Executive Editor
           Que Certification
           800 East 96th Street
           Indianapolis, IN 46240 USA

For more information about this book or another Que title, visit our Web site at www.examcram2.com. Type the ISBN (excluding hyphens) or the title of a book in the Search field to find the page you're looking for.

Contents at a Glance

Table of Contents

. . . .

Introduction

. . . .

Welcome to the *CIT Exam Cram 2!* Whether this is your 1ˢᵗ or your 15ᵗʰ *Exam Cram 2* series book, you'll find information here that will help ensure your success as you pursue knowledge, experience, and certification. This introduction explains Cisco's certification programs in general and talks about how the *Exam Cram 2* series can help you prepare for Cisco Certified Network Professional (CCNP) exams. Chapter 1 discusses the basics of Cisco certification exams, including a description of the testing environment and a discussion of test-taking strategies. Chapters 2 through 12 are designed to remind you of everything you'll need to know in order to take—and pass—the 642-831 Cisco Support certification exam. The two sample tests at the end of the book should give you a reasonably accurate assessment of your knowledge—and, yes, we've provided the practice test answers and their explanations. Read the book and study the material, and you'll stand a very good chance of passing the test.

Exam Cram 2 books help you understand and appreciate the subjects and materials you need to pass Cisco certification exams. *Exam Cram 2* books are aimed strictly at test preparation and review. They do not teach you everything you need to know about a topic. Instead, I'll present and dissect the questions and problems I've found that you're likely to encounter on a test. I've worked to bring together as much information as possible about Cisco certification exams.

Nevertheless, to completely prepare yourself for any Cisco test, I recommend that you begin by taking the self-assessment that is included in this book, immediately following this introduction. The self-assessment tool will help you evaluate your knowledge base against the requirements for a CCNP under both ideal and real circumstances.

Based on what you learn from the self-assessment, you might decide to begin your studies with some classroom training, some practice with Cisco routers and switches, or some background reading. On the other hand, you might decide to pick up and read one of the many study guides available from Cisco or third-party vendors. I recommend that you supplement your study program with visits to www.examcram2.com to receive additional practice questions, get advice, and track the CCNP program.

I also strongly recommend that you install, configure, and play around with the Cisco technologies that you'll be tested on, because nothing beats hands-on experience and familiarity when it comes to understanding the questions you're likely to encounter on a certification test. Book learning is essential, but without a doubt, hands-on experience is the best teacher of all!

Included in this book is also a CD that contains the PrepLogic Practice Exams, Preview Edition exam simulation software. The preview edition exhibits most of the full functionality of the premium edition, but offers questions sufficient for only one practice exam. To get the complete set of practice questions and exam functionality, visit www.preplogic.com.

Taking a Certification Exam

After you've prepared for your exam, you need to register with a testing center. Each computer-based Cisco exam costs $125, and if you don't pass, you can retest for an additional $125 for each additional try. In the United States and Canada, tests are administered by Prometric and by VUE. Here's how you can contact them:

➤ **Prometric**—You can sign up for a test through the company's Web site at http://www.register.prometric.com. Within the United States and Canada, you can register by phone at 800-755-3926. If you live outside this region, you should check the Prometric Web site for the appropriate phone number.

➤ **VUE**—You can sign up for a test or get the phone numbers for local Cisco testing centers through the Web at www.vue.com, or by telephone at 800-404-EXAM (3926).

To sign up for a test, you must possess a valid credit card or contact either Prometric or VUE for mailing instructions to send a check (in the United States). Only when payment is verified or your check has cleared can you actually register for the test.

To schedule an exam, you need to call the number or visit either of the Web pages at least one day in advance. To cancel or reschedule an exam, you must call before 7 p.m. Pacific standard time the day before the scheduled test time (or you might be charged, even if you don't show up to take the test). When you want to schedule a test, you should have the following information ready:

➤ Your name, organization, and mailing address.

➤ Your Cisco test ID. (Inside the United States, this usually means your Social Security number; citizens of other nations should call ahead to find out what type of identification number is required to register for a test.)

➤ The name and number of the exam you want to take. For this book the Exam name is "Support 3.0" and the exam number is 642-831.

➤ A method of payment. (As mentioned previously, a credit card is the most convenient method, but alternate means can be arranged in advance, if necessary.)

After you sign up for a test, you are told when and where the test is scheduled. You should try to arrive at least 15 minutes early. You must supply two forms of identification—one of which must be a photo ID—and sign a nondisclosure agreement to be admitted into the testing room.

All Cisco exams are completely closed book. In fact, you are not permitted to take anything with you into the testing area, but you are given a blank sheet of paper and a pen (or in some cases an erasable plastic sheet and an erasable pen). We suggest that you immediately write down on that sheet of paper all the information you've memorized for the test. In *Exam Cram 2* books, this information appears on a tear-out sheet inside the front cover of each book. You are given some time to compose yourself, record this information, and take a sample orientation exam before you begin the real thing. I suggest that you take the orientation test before taking your first exam, but because all the certification exams are more or less identical in layout, behavior, and controls, you probably don't need to do this more than once.

When you complete a Cisco certification exam, the software tells you immediately whether you've passed or failed. If you need to retake an exam, you have to schedule a new test with Prometric or VUE and pay another $125.

The first time you fail a test, you can retake the test as soon as the next day. However, if you fail a second time, you must wait 14 days before retaking that test. The 14-day waiting period remains in effect for all retakes after the second failure.

Tracking CCNP Status

As soon as you pass any Cisco exam, you must complete a certification agreement. You will not be certified unless you agree to the terms outlined on the agreement.

The **Certification Tracking System** available at `https://www.certmanager.net/cisco` allows you to view your Cisco certification information. Cisco will contact you by email and explain how to use it. Once you are registered into one of the Cisco career certification tracks, you'll be given a login to the Web site.

Once you pass the necessary exams for any of Cisco's certifications and you complete the certification agreement, you'll be certified. About four to six weeks after you are certified, a package will arrive in the mail that contains your Cisco Welcome Kit, which contain a number of items, including

➤ A certificate that is suitable for framing, along with a laminated wallet card.

➤ Promotional items, which vary based on your certification.

Many people believe that the benefits of CCNP certification go well beyond the perks that Cisco provides to newly anointed members of this elite group. We're starting to see more job listings that request or require applicants to have CCNA, CCNP, CCDP, and so on, and many individuals who complete Cisco certification programs can qualify for increases in pay and/or responsibility. As an official recognition of hard work and broad knowledge, one of the CCNP credentials is a badge of honor in many IT organizations.

How to Prepare for an Exam

Preparing for any Cisco exam, including the Support related test (Exam 642-831), requires that you obtain and study materials designed to provide comprehensive information about the product that will appear on the specific exam for which you are preparing. The following list of materials can help you study and prepare:

➤ **Instructor-led training**—There is no substitute for expert hands-on instruction under professional supervision. There are several places to receive training, including Cisco Partners such as GeoTrain, Online partners such as Vlabs, and third-parties such as Globalnet Training Solutions.

➤ **Cisco Connection Online**—This is the name of Cisco's Web site at `www.cisco.com`. This is the best resource for updated Cisco training information.

> ➤ **Test preparation questions**—You can find test preparation questions in this book, on the book's CD, available online from Que at www.examcram2.com, or at other good resources such as www.boson.com.

> ➤ **Study guides**—Several publishers—including Que Publishing—offer certification exam preparation titles. Que Publishing offers the following:

>> ➤ The *Exam Cram 2* series—These books give you information about the material you need to know to pass the tests.

What This Book Will Not Do

This book will *not* teach you everything you need to know about computers, or even about a given topic. Nor is this book an introduction to computer technology. If you're new to Cisco routing or switching and looking for an initial preparation guide, check out www.quepublishing.com, where you will find a whole section dedicated to the CCNP certifications. This book will review what you need to know before you take the test, with the fundamental purpose dedicated to reviewing the information needed on the Cisco 642-831 certification exam.

This book uses a variety of teaching and memorization techniques to analyze the exam-related topics and to provide you with ways to input, index, and retrieve everything you'll need to know in order to pass the test. Once again, it is *not* an introduction to network support techniques.

What This Book Is Designed to Do

This book is designed to be read as a pointer to the areas of knowledge you will be tested on. In other words, you may want to read the book one time, just to get an insight into how comprehensive your knowledge of Cisco devices is. The book is also designed to be read shortly before you go for the actual test and to give you a distillation of the entire field of supporting Cisco routers and switches in as few pages as possible. We think you can use this book to get a sense of the underlying context of any topic in the chapters—or to skim-read for exam alerts, bulleted points, summaries, and topic headings.

I've drawn on material from Cisco's own listing of knowledge requirements, from other preparation guides, and from the exams themselves. I've also drawn from a battery of third-party test-preparation tools and technical Web sites, as well as from my own experience with Cisco technologies and the exam. My aim is to walk you through the knowledge you will need—looking over your shoulder, so to speak—and point out those things that are important for the exam (exam alerts, practice questions, and so on).

The 642-831 exam makes a basic assumption that you already have a strong background of experience with the Cisco technologies and network terminology. I've tried to demystify the jargon, acronyms, terms, and concepts. Also, wherever I think you're likely to blur past an important concept, I've defined the assumptions and premises behind that concept.

About This Book

I've structured the topics in this book to build upon one another. Therefore, the topics covered in later chapters might refer to previous discussions in earlier chapters.

I suggest you read this book from front to back. You won't be wasting your time, because nothing I've written is a guess about an unknown exam. I've had to explain certain underlying information on such a regular basis that I've included those explanations here.

Once you've read the book, you can brush up on a certain area by using the index or the table of contents to go straight to the topics and questions you want to reexamine. I've tried to use the headings and subheadings to provide outline information about each given topic. After you've been certified, I think you'll find this book useful as a tightly focused reference and an essential foundation to help you support Cisco technologies.

Chapter Formats

Each *Exam Cram 2* chapter follows a regular structure, along with graphical cues about especially important or useful material. The structure of a typical chapter is as follows:

➤ **Opening hotlists**—Each chapter begins with lists of the terms you'll need to understand and the concepts you'll need to master before you can be fully conversant with the chapter's subject matter. I follow the hotlists with a few introductory paragraphs, setting the stage for the rest of the chapter.

➤ **Topical coverage**—After the opening hotlists, each chapter covers the topics related to the chapter's subject.

➤ **Alerts**—Throughout the topical coverage section, I highlight material most likely to appear on the exam by using a special Exam Alert layout that looks like this:

This is what an exam alert looks like. An exam alert stresses concepts, terms, software, or activities that will most likely appear in one or more certification exam questions. For that reason, I think any information found offset in exam alert format is worthy of unusual attentiveness on your part.

Even if material isn't flagged as an exam alert, *all* the content in this book is associated in some way with test-related material. What appears in the chapter content is critical knowledge.

➤ **Notes**—This book is an overall examination of computers. As such, I'll dip into many aspects of supporting Cisco technologies. Where a body of knowledge is deeper than the scope of the book, I use notes to indicate areas of concern or specialty training.

Cramming for an exam will get you through a test, but it won't make you a competent IT professional. Although you can memorize just the facts you need in order to become certified, your daily work in the field will rapidly put you in water over your head if you don't understand the technologies you are troubleshooting, supporting, or configuring.

➤ **Tips**—I provide tips that will help you to build a better foundation of knowledge or to focus your attention on an important concept that will reappear later in the book. Tips provide a helpful way to remind you of the context surrounding a particular area of a topic under discussion.

You should also read Chapter 1, "Overview of Cisco Certification," for helpful strategies used in taking a test. The introduction to Sample Test #1 in Chapter 13 contains additional tips on how to figure out the correct response to a question and what to do if you draw a complete blank.

➤ **Practice questions**—This section presents a short list of test questions related to the specific chapter topic. Each question has a following explanation of both correct and incorrect answers. The practice questions highlight the areas we found to be most important on the exam.

➤ **Need To Know More?**—Every chapter ends with a section titled "Need To Know More?" This section provides pointers to resources that we found to be helpful in offering further details on the chapter's subject matter. If you find a resource you like in this collection, use it, but don't feel compelled to use all these resources. I use this section to recommend resources that I have used on a regular basis, so none of the recommendations will be a waste of your time or money. These resources may go out of print or be taken down (in the case of Web sites), so I've tried to reference widely accepted resources.

The bulk of the book follows this chapter structure, but there are a few other elements that we would like to point out:

> **Practice exams**—The practice exams, which appear in Chapters 13 and 15 (with answer keys in Chapters 14 and 16), are very close approximations of the types of questions you are likely to see on the current 642-831 exam.

> **Answer keys**—These provide the answers to the practice exams, complete with explanations of both the correct responses and the incorrect responses.

> **Glossary**—This is an extensive glossary of important terms used in this book.

> **The Cram Sheet**—This appears as a tear-away sheet inside the front cover of this *Exam Cram 2* book. It is a valuable tool that represents a collection of the most difficult-to-remember facts and numbers we think you should memorize before taking the test. Remember, you can dump this information out of your head onto a piece of paper as soon as you enter the testing room. These are usually facts that we've found require brute-force memorization. You only need to remember this information long enough to write it down when you walk into the test room. Be advised that you will be asked to surrender all personal belongings before you enter the exam room itself.

You might want to look at the Cram Sheet in your car or in the lobby of the testing center just before you walk into the testing center. The Cram Sheet is divided under headings, so you can review the appropriate parts just before each test.

> **The CD**—The CD includes many helpful code samples that demonstrate all of the topics on the exam. If you work through the samples on the CD, you'll understand the techniques that you're likely to be tested on. The CD also contains the PrepLogic Practice Exams, Preview Edition exam simulation software. The preview edition exhibits most of the full functionality of the premium edition, but offers questions sufficient for only one practice exam. To get the complete set of practice questions and exam functionality, visit www.preplogic.com.

Code and Commands

Limitations of printed pages will, many times, require me to write code with smaller margins than I might use in practice. In these cases, I've indented the following line to indicate the output line is an extension of the previous line. This is so that the code you see on the printed page is syntactically correct.

Contacting the Author

This book is only one of many Cisco and networking related books I have written. I also work to support Cisco technologies every day of my life. Along with consulting and writing, I am a part-time instructor of Cisco courseware. All these hobbies and day-to-day activities helped me in creating a real-world tool that you can use to prepare for and pass the 642-831 certification exam. I'm interested in any feedback you would care to share about the book, especially if you have ideas about how I can improve it for future test-takers. I'll consider everything you say carefully and will respond to all reasonable suggestions and comments. You can reach me via email at `Sean@DigitalCrawlSpaces.com`.

Let me know if you found this book to be helpful in your preparation efforts. I'd also like to know how you felt about your chances of passing the exam *before* you read the book and then *after* you read the book. Of course, I'd love to hear that you passed the exam—and even if you just want to share your triumph, I'd be happy to hear from you.

Thanks for choosing me as your personal trainer, and enjoy the book. I would wish you luck on the exam, but I know that if you read through all the chapters and work with the product, you won't need luck—you'll pass the test on the strength of real knowledge!

Self-Assessment

I've included a self-assessment in this *Exam Cram* to help you evaluate your readiness to tackle the Cisco Certified Network Professional (CCNP) certification. It should also help you understand what you need to master the topic of this book: namely, Exam 642-831, "Support 3.0." Before you tackle this self-assessment, however, I'll talk about the concerns you might face when pursuing a CCNP certification and what an ideal candidate might look like.

A CCNP in the Real World

In the next section, I describe an ideal CCNP candidate, knowing full well that only a few certification candidates meet this ideal. In fact, my description of that ideal candidate might seem downright scary. But take heart; although the requirements to obtain a CCNP certification may seem formidable, they are by no means impossible to meet. However, you should be keenly aware that it does take time, requires some expense, and calls for a substantial effort.

You can get all the real-world motivation you need from knowing that many others have gone before you. You can follow in their footsteps. If you're willing to tackle the process seriously and do what it takes to gain the necessary experience and knowledge, you can take and pass the certification tests. In fact, the *Exam Crams* and the companion CCNP *Exam Preps* are designed to make it as easy as possible for you to prepare for these exams, but prepare you must!

The same, of course, for other Cisco career certifications, including

➤ Cisco Certified Network Associate (CCNA), which certifies candidates in the basics of networking, Cisco component configuration, and Cisco network troubleshooting.

➤ Cisco Certified Design Associate (CCDA), which is a basic certification for those who design high-level networks.

➤ Cisco Certified Design Professional (CCDP), which is the equivalent of a CCNP certification for those who design advanced and complex networks. Some of the exams needed for the CCNP exam are the same needed for the CCDP certification.

➤ Cisco Certified Internetwork Expert (CCIE), which is known as the black belt in networking today. This exam is famous for its difficulty; those who obtain this certification easily find employment in the industry today.

The Ideal CCNP Candidate

Just to give you some idea of what an ideal CCNP candidate is like, here are some relevant statistics about the background and experience such an individual might have. Don't worry if you don't meet these qualifications (or, indeed, if you don't even come close) because this world is far from ideal. Where your qualifications fall short, simply be aware that you have more work to do.

That said, the ideal candidate for the 642-831 certification exam will have the following:

➤ Professional or academic training in network theory, concepts, and operations. This training includes areas such as networking media, Cisco switch and router configuration, troubleshooting, LAN and WAN transmission techniques, networking terminology, networking protocols, network operating systems, services, and applications.

➤ Three-plus years of professional networking experience, including experience with Ethernet, token ring, modems, and other networking media. This experience must include installation, configuration, upgrades, and troubleshooting experience.

➤ A good knowledge of the OSI Reference model, IPX suite of protocols, and the TCP/IP suite of protocols. This knowledge should include a thorough understanding of name resolution and subnetting.

The length of time needed to prepare for the exam can always be decreased by a good instructor, mentor, and a good self-learner. The preceding qualifications may seem overwhelming, but there have been many people before you who have overcome the challenge. You can too.

Put Yourself to the Test

The following series of questions and observations is designed to help you figure out how much work you'll face in pursuing Cisco career certification and what kinds of resources you can consult on your quest. Be absolutely honest in this self-assessment, or you'll end up wasting money on exams you're not ready to take. There are no right or wrong answers, only steps along the path to certification. Only you can decide where you really belong in the broad spectrum of aspiring candidates.

Two things should be clear from the outset, however:

➤ Even a modest background in computer science will be helpful.

➤ Hands-on experience with Cisco switches, routers, and technologies is an essential ingredient for certification success.

Educational Background

1. Have you ever taken any computer-related classes? (Yes or No)

   If yes, proceed to question 2; if no, proceed to question 4.

2. Have you taken any classes in the Cisco curriculum? (Yes or No)

   If yes, you will probably be able to handle the discussions relating to the Cisco product configuration and troubleshooting. If you're rusty, brush up on the basic concepts and networking. If the answer is no, consider some basic reading in this area. I strongly recommend *CCNA Exam Cram 2*, Que, James Jones and Sheldon Barry, ISBN: 0-7897-3019-7 2003. If this title doesn't appeal to you, check out reviews for other, similar titles at your favorite online bookstore. You can expect to see a long list.

3. Have you taken any networking concepts or technologies classes? (Yes or No)

   If yes, you will probably be able to handle the networking terminology, concepts, and technologies (but brace yourself for frequent departures from normal usage). If you're rusty, brush up on basic networking concepts and terminology. If your answer is no, you might want to check out some titles on the Transport Communication Protocol/Internet Protocol (TCP/IP), subnetting, LAN and WAN transmission methodology, as well as the OSI Reference Model.

4. Have you done any reading on routing or routed protocols? (Yes or No)

If yes, review the requirements from questions 2 and 3. If you meet them, move to the next section, "Hands-On Experience." If you answered no, consult the recommended reading for both topics. This kind of strong background will be of great help in preparing for the CCNP exams.

Hands-On Experience

Another important key to success on all the CCNP tests is hands-on experience. If I leave you with only one realization after taking this self-assessment, it should be that there's no substitute for time spent installing, configuring, and troubleshooting Cisco technologies.

5. Have you installed, configured, and worked with a Cisco switch or router? (Yes or No)

If yes, make sure you understand the basic concepts covered in Exam 642-831.

If you haven't worked with Cisco routers or switches, you need to find a way to get hands-on experience or the equivalent thereof. There are several router simulation programs available from Cisco or other third parties if you do not have the funds or access to the physical equipment. If you or your employer can afford to pay for training, Cisco's official class curriculum is offered through Cisco Training Partners.

 You can obtain the exam objectives, practice questions, and other information about Cisco exams from the Cisco's Training and Certification page on the Web at **http://www.cisco.com/training**.

Before you even think about taking any Cisco exam, make sure you've spent enough time with Cisco products. You should understand how Cisco routers and switches are installed and configured, how to maintain such an installation, and how to troubleshoot when things go wrong. This will help you in the exam as well as in real life.

Testing Your Exam-Readiness

Whether you attend a formal class on a specific topic to get ready for an exam or use written materials to study on your own, some preparation for the

Cisco certification exams is essential. At $125 a try, pass or fail, you want to do everything you can to pass on your first try. That's where studying comes in.

I have included in this book several practice exam questions for each chapter and two practice exams, so if you don't score well on the chapter questions, you can study more and then tackle the practice exams at the end of the book. If you don't earn a score of at least 66% on Practice Exam 1 and 70% on Practice Exam 2, you'll want to investigate the other practice test resources available via the Web. (Locate them by using your favorite search engine.)

For any given subject, consider taking a class if you've tackled self-study materials, taken the test, and failed anyway. If you can afford the privilege, the opportunity to interact with an instructor and fellow students can make all the difference in the world. For information about Cisco classes, visit the Certification Program page at http://www.cisco.com.

If you can't afford to take a class, visit the Certification Program page anyway because it also includes pointers and additional resources. Even if you can't afford to spend much at all, you should still invest in some low-cost practice exams from commercial vendors because they can help you assess your readiness to pass a test better than any other tool. Check with the http://www.boson.com Web site for other available resources.

6. Have you taken a practice exam on your chosen test subject? (Yes or No)

If yes, and you scored 70% or better, you're probably ready to tackle the real thing. If your score isn't above that crucial threshold, keep at it until you break that barrier. If you answered no, obtain all the free and low-budget practice tests you can find (or afford) and get to work. Keep at it until you can comfortably break the passing threshold.

 There is no better way to assess your test readiness than to take a good-quality practice exam and pass with a score of 70% or better.

Assessing Your Readiness for the CCNP Support Exam

In addition to the general exam-readiness information in the previous section, other resources are available from some of the country's best Cisco Users Groups to help you prepare for the exams. Two Web sites come to mind: `http://dfw.cisco-users.org/study_groups.htm` and `http://www.dcug.` `org/cugs.htm.` One of my favorite troubleshooting websites is `http://www.experts-exchange.com.` Experts in virtually every field of computers are there to answer your questions and an easy to use search engine is available to search for previously asked questions. This is one of my favorite Web sites for researching hard to solve problems.

One last note: I hope it makes sense to stress the importance of hands-on experience in the context of the exams. As you review the material for the exams, you'll realize that hands-on experience with Cisco IOS commands, tools, and utilities is invaluable.

Onward, Through the Fog!

After you've assessed your readiness, undertaken the right background studies, obtained the hands-on experience that will help you understand the products and technologies at work, and reviewed the many sources of information to help you prepare for a test, you'll be ready to take a round of practice tests. When your scores come back positive enough to get you through the exam, you're ready to go after the real thing. If you follow my assessment regimen, you'll not only know what you need to study, but also know when you're ready to make a test date at Prometric or Vue. Good luck!

Overview of Cisco Certification

. . . .

Terms you'll need to understand:

✓ Radio button
✓ Check box
✓ Careful reading
✓ Exhibits
✓ Multiple-choice question formats
✓ Simulation questions
✓ Process of elimination

Techniques you'll need to master:

✓ Preparing to take a certification exam
✓ Practicing to take a certification exam
✓ Making the best use of the testing software
✓ Budgeting your time
✓ Guessing (as a last resort)

It doesn't matter how well prepared a person might be, nearly everyone is nervous when taking a certification exam, especially since a certain amount of money is on the line. A familiarity with the exam always helps to relieve your test anxiety. You probably won't be as nervous when you take your second or third Cisco certification exam as you will be when you take your first one.

Whether it is your second exam or your tenth, understanding the finer points of exam taking (how much time to spend on questions, the setting you will be in, and so on) and the exam software will help you concentrate on the questions at hand rather than on the surroundings. Mastering some basic exam-taking skills should help you recognize some of the tricks and traps you are bound to find in several of the exam questions.

This chapter describes some proven exam-taking strategies you should be able to use to your advantage when preparing for and taking the exam.

The Exam Situation

When you arrive at the testing center where you scheduled your exam, you will need to sign in with an exam proctor. He or she will ask you to show two forms of identification, one of which must be a government-issued photo ID. After you have signed in, you will be asked to deposit any books, bags, cell phones, pagers, or other items you brought with you. Then you'll be escorted into the closed room that houses the exam seats.

All exams are completely closed book. In fact, you won't be permitted to take anything with you into the testing area except a pen or pencil, and a blank piece of paper handed to you by the exam proctor. In many testing centers a small white board and erasable felt-tip pen are given to you. These items are to help you write down notes from exam questions or do mathematics that may be required of subnetting issues. You must return all the paper and items given to you by the exam proctor at the end of the exam.

Most test rooms feature a wall with a large picture window, a camera, or both. This permits the exam proctor to monitor the room, prevent exam takers from talking to one another, and observe anything out of the ordinary that might go on. The exam proctor will have preloaded the appropriate Cisco certification exam—for the readers of this book, that's the Cisco Support Certification Exam 642-831—and you'll be permitted to start as soon as you are seated in front of the computer. At the beginning of each test is a tutorial you can go through if you are unfamiliar with the testing environment.

All Cisco certification exams allow a predetermined, maximum amount of time in which to complete your work. (This time is indicated on the exam by an onscreen counter/clock in the upper-right corner of the screen, so you can check the time remaining whenever you like.) All exams are computer generated and use primarily a multiple-choice format and simulation questions. Simulation questions test your real-world experience in the actual Cisco interface. You will be required to submit the proper series of commands to accomplish a particular configuration based on the given scenario or diagram. Whenever possible, the complete output from the router or switch is used in this book. Commands and syntaxes typed in by the administrator of the switch or router are highlighted in bold.

You will also encounter questions that demand a fill-in-the-blank answer that represents the proper Cisco command. The Cisco Support exam consists of 55 to 65 randomly selected questions from a pool of several hundred questions. You can take up to 75 minutes to complete the exam.

Although this might sound quite simple, the questions are formulated to thoroughly check your mastery of the material. Cisco exam questions are also very adept at testing you on more than one area of knowledge with a single question—for example, testing your knowledge of the command syntax, as well as the proper command mode. Often, you will be asked to provide more than one answer to a question. Likewise, you might be asked to select the best or most effective solution to a problem from a range of choices, all of which technically are correct. Taking the exam is quite an adventure, and it involves real thinking as well as skill and an ability to manage your time. This book shows you what to expect and how to deal with potential problems, puzzles, and predicaments you are likely to encounter.

When you complete a Cisco certification exam, the software will tell you whether you have passed or failed. The results are then broken down into several main objectives or domain areas. You will be shown the percentage that you got correct for each individual domain. Even if you fail, you should ask for (and keep) the detailed report the test proctor prints for you. You can use this report to help you prepare for another go-round, if necessary. If you need to retake an exam, you will have to schedule a new test with Prometric or VUE and pay for another exam. Keep in mind that, because the questions come from a pool, you will receive different questions the second time around. Cisco also has a retake policy, which is that you must wait 72 hours between exam attempts.

In the following section, you will learn more about how Cisco test questions look and how they must be answered.

Exam Layout and Design

Some exam questions require you to select a single answer, whereas others ask you to select multiple correct answers. The following multiple-choice question requires you to select a single correct answer. Following the question is a brief summary of each answer selection and why it is either correct or incorrect.

Question 1

The Catalyst 1900 and 2820 switches support 1,005 VLANs, of which how many can be configured to support Spanning Tree Protocol?

○ A. 1005 VLANs

○ B. 10 VLANs

○ C. 512 VLANs

○ D. 64 VLANs

○ E. 128 VLANs

Answer D is correct. On a Catalyst 1900 or 2820 series switch, Spanning Tree Protocol can be configured on only 64 VLANs. You can have up to 1,005 VLANs, but STP must be disabled on all but 64. By default, STP is enabled on VLANs 1 through 64.

This sample question format corresponds closely to the Cisco Support Certification Exam format. The only difference on the exam is that questions are not followed by answer keys. To select an answer, position the cursor over the radio button next to the answer and then click the mouse button to select the answer. See the practice exam CD that comes with this book for a general idea of what the questions will look like.

Next, we examine a question that requires choosing multiple answers. This type of question provides check boxes rather than radio buttons for marking all appropriate selections. These types of questions can either specify how many answers to choose or instruct you to choose all the appropriate answers.

Question 2

> What are the two basic methods for implementing VLAN boundaries? (Choose two.)
>
> ❑ A. WAN topology
>
> ❑ B. End-to-end VLANs
>
> ❑ C. Local VLANs
>
> ❑ D. LAN wire speeds

Answers B and C are correct. End-to-end and local VLANs are both basic methods for implementing VLAN boundaries. A WAN Topology is the mapping of an entire Wide Area Network, and LAN wire speeds are the speed of the physical wire in the local network.

For this type of question, more than one answer is required. Such questions are scored as wrong unless all the required selections are chosen. In other words, a partially correct answer does not result in partial credit when the test is scored. If you are required to provide multiple answers and do not provide the number of answers the question asks for, the testing software indicates that you did not complete that question. For Question 2, you have to check the boxes next to answers C and B to obtain credit for this question. Realize that choosing the correct answers also means knowing why the other answers are incorrect!

Although these two basic types of questions can appear in many forms, they are the foundation on which most of the Support Certification Exam questions are based. Some other complex questions might include exhibits, simple fill-in-the-blank questions, as well as simulation questions. For some of these questions, you will be asked to make a selection by clicking the portion of the exhibit that answers the question or by typing the correct answer(s) in the testing interface. Your knowledge and expertise of router configuration must go well beyond merely memorizing the purpose of various commands. The Support exam tests your ability to configure a router in a variety of scenarios and configurations.

 Do not rely simply on your success at answering traditional multiple-choice questions. Although these represent the core of the exam, your failure to answer the many fill-in-the-blank, simulator, and configuration scenario type questions will lead to an unsuccessful testing session.

Other questions involving exhibits use charts or diagrams to help document a network scenario you'll be asked to configure or troubleshoot. Careful attention to such exhibits is the key to success. In these instances, you might have to toggle between the exhibit and the question to absorb all the information being shown and properly answer the question.

You also might see a question or two where you must enter a simple command into an input box. You will be presented a long list of available commands as part of the testing interface. You will also encounter from two to five simulation questions. You will be given a simulated scenario involving a procedure you must complete in the Cisco IOS environment. This generally involves performing a series of steps at the command line or possibly dragging and dropping the correct order of a certain procedure. Therefore, actual experience with the Cisco operating system interface and real-world practice are critical to success on the Support exam.

Exam-Taking Techniques

A well-known principle when taking certification exams is to first read over the entire exam from start to finish while answering only those questions you feel absolutely sure of. The next time around, you can delve into the more complex questions. Knowing how many such questions you have left helps you spend your exam time wisely. Although this is good overall testing advice, this capability is not available to you on the Support exam 642-831. To protect the integrity of the certifications, Cisco does not allow you to mark and go back to review a previously answered question.

 It is critical on a Cisco exam that you read each question thoroughly. After you input your answer and move on to the next question, you cannot go back!

 As you approach the end of your allotted testing time of 75 minutes, you are better off guessing than leaving a question unanswered.

The most important advice about taking any exam is this: *Read each question carefully.* Some questions are deliberately ambiguous, some use double negatives, and others use terminology in incredibly precise ways. The authors have taken numerous exams—both practice and live—and in nearly every one have missed at least one question because they didn't read it closely or carefully enough.

Here are some suggestions on how to deal with the tendency to jump to an answer too quickly:

➤ Make sure you read every word in the question very carefully, even if it means reading it several times.

➤ As you read, try to reformulate the question in your own words. If you can do this, you should be able to pick the correct answer(s) much more easily.

➤ Sometimes, rereading a question enables you to see something you might have missed the first time you read it.

➤ If you still do not understand the question, ask yourself what you don't understand about the question, why the answers don't appear to make sense, or what appears to be missing. If you think about the subject for a while, your subconscious might provide the details that are lacking or you might notice a "trick" that will point to the correct answer.

Above all, try to deal with each question by thinking through what you know about supporting and troubleshooting networks. Use the OSI reference model and your knowledge of middle- and lower-layer protocols that are where a majority of your questions will come from. By reviewing what you know (and what you have written down on your information sheet), you will often recall or understand enough to be able to deduce the answer to the question.

Question-Handling Strategies

Based on exams I have taken in the past, for questions that take only a single answer, usually two or three of the answers will be obviously incorrect, and two of the answers will appear to have a possibility of being correct. Of course, only one can be correct. Unless the answer leaps out at you, begin the process of answering by eliminating those answers that are most obviously wrong.

A word of caution: If the answer seems too obvious, reread the question to look for a trick. Often those are the ones you are most likely to get wrong. If you have done your homework for an exam, no valid information should be completely new to you. In that case, unfamiliar or bizarre terminology most likely indicates a bogus answer. Of course there are times when they throw in a simple question, such as a CCNA-level question. In any event, knowing the material should help you to pass this exam.

As you work your way through the exam, budget your time by making sure you have completed one quarter of the questions one quarter of the way through the exam period and three quarters of them three quarters of the way through the exam. This ensures that you will have time to go through all of the questions. As you know, there will be 55 to 65 questions to answer in a 75-minute time frame. That gives you, on average, less than a minute-and-a-half to answer each question. The simulation questions will probably take longer than the multiple-choice questions, so give yourself ample time.

If you are not finished when 95% of the time has elapsed, use the last few minutes to guess your way through the remaining questions. Remember that guessing is potentially more valuable than not answering because blank answers are always wrong, but a guess might turn out to be right. If you don't have a clue about any of the remaining questions, quickly eliminate the answers you know are not correct and guess from the remaining selections. The important thing is to submit an exam for scoring that has an answer for every question, even if some of answers are simply guesses.

Statistically, even if you can eliminate all but three of the possible answers to a multiple-choice question, you have a one-in-three chance of getting the answer correct.

Mastering the Inner Game

If you study the information in this book carefully and review all the practice questions at the end of each chapter, you should become aware of those areas where you need additional learning and studying.

Follow up by reading some or all of the materials recommended in the "Need to Know More?" section at the end of each chapter. Don't hesitate to look for more resources online. Remember that the idea is to become familiar enough with the concepts and situations you find in the sample questions that you can reason your way through similar scenarios on a real exam. If you know the material, you have every right to be confident that you can pass the exam.

After you have worked your way through the book, take the sample tests in Chapter 13, "Practice Exam 1," and Chapter 15, "Practice Exam 2." This will provide a reality check and help you identify areas you need to study further. Answer keys to these exams can be found in Chapter 14, "Answer Key 1," and Chapter 16, "Answer Key 2."

Make sure you follow up and review materials related to the questions you miss on the practice exam before scheduling a real exam. The key is to know why and how the answers are correct or incorrect. If you memorize the answers, you do yourself a great injustice and might not pass the exam. Memorizing answers will not benefit you because you are unlikely to see the identical question on the exam. Only when you have covered all the ground and feel comfortable with the whole scope of the practice exam should you take a real one.

 If you take the practice exam and do not score at least 90% correct, you should practice further. When you practice, remember that it is important to know *why* the answer is correct or incorrect. If you memorize the answers instead, it will trip you up when taking the exam.

With the information in this book and the determination to supplement your knowledge, you should be able to pass the certification exam. However, you need to work at it. Otherwise, you will have to pay for the exam more than once before you finally pass. As long as you get a good night's sleep and pre-pare thoroughly, you should do just fine. Good luck!

Additional Resources

A good source of information about Cisco certification exams comes from Cisco itself. The best place to go for exam-related information is online. The Cisco CCNP Certification home page, which includes a link to Support information, resides at `www.cisco.com/warp/public/10/wwtraining/certprog/` `lan/programs/ccnp.html`.

Coping with Change on the Web

Sooner or later, all the information we have shared about Web-based resources mentioned throughout this book might go stale or be replaced by newer information. However, there is always a way to find what you want on the Web if you are willing to invest some time and ener-gy. Cisco's site has a site map to help you find your way around, and most large or complex Web sites offer search engines. Finally, feel free to use general search tools to search for relat-ed information.

Networking Principles

Terms you'll need to understand:

✓ Open Systems Interconnection (OSI) Reference model.
✓ Connectionless protocol
✓ Connection-oriented protocol
✓ Encapsulation
✓ Framing
✓ Latency
✓ Static route

Techniques you'll need to master:

✓ The responsibilities of each layer of the OSI Reference model
✓ The responsibilities of the three layers of the Cisco Hierarchical model and the types of device found at each layer
✓ The steps involved in the Internetwork Troubleshooting model

Network Models

In this second chapter in this Exam Cram, you learn about the basics of inter-networking. This chapter also introduces you to the different network models used to maintain, organize, and troubleshoot Cisco systems.

 In this chapter, you learn about three network models, the OSI Reference model, the Troubleshooting model, and the Cisco Hierarchical model. You need to know about one other model, the TCP/IP Internetworking Model. That model is covered extensively in the next chapter.

Reference models provide many advantages to system engineers by dividing the complexities of network operations into a more manageable set of individual layers. Reference models also allow changes to occur in one layer without having an impact on, or disabling the responsibilities of, other layers. This enables specialization in development for equipment and application developers by allowing new features for old products and new products to be developed. As a result, using reference models allows you to conceptually take a part from one vendor and replace it with a part from another vendor. In a way, a network model defines standard interfaces for "plug and play" multivendor integration.

The Open Systems Interconnection (OSI) model is the primary architectural model used in creating standards in today's networks. This model has seven hierarchical layers. Each of the layers help companies in the industry create a standard method to communicate between disparate systems.

Cisco also supplemented the OSI model with its own three-layer hierarchical network model that should be used to build, implement, troubleshoot, and maintain any size network that uses Cisco equipment. This model allows you to effectively build, maintain, and troubleshoot any size network.

OSI Reference Model

Late in the 1970s the OSI Reference model was created to help facilitate data transfer between disparate hosts using different operating systems. The OSI Reference model is a set of guidelines that application developers can use for creating and implementing applications to run on a network. This model provides guidelines or a framework for creating and implementing networking standards, devices, and internetworking schemes.

The OSI Reference model has seven individual layers, each with its own responsibility and rules. The OSI Reference model layers are as follows:

➤ Application layer

➤ Presentation layer

➤ Session layer

➤ Transport layer

➤ Network layer

➤ Data Link layer

➤ Physical layer

These seven OSI layers can be divided into two different groups (see Figure 2.1). The top three layers define how the applications within the end stations will communicate with each other and with users. The bottom four layers define how data is transmitted from one point to another. The Application, Presentation, and Session layers know nothing about networking or network addresses—that is the responsibility of the four bottom layers. The Transport, Network, Data Link, and Physical layers define how data is transferred through a physical wire, and through switches and routers. These layers also build a data stream from a transmitting host to a destination host's application.

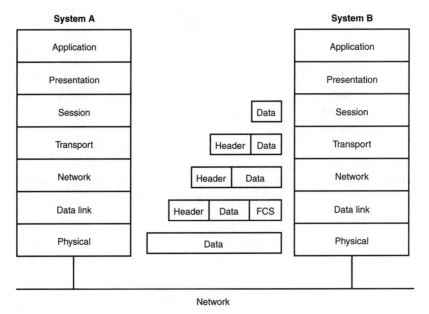

Figure 2.1   The division of the OSI Reference model into upper and lower layers.

In Figure 2.1, you can see two different computer systems. In this example, each layer communicates with its peer layer on the other system. The data starts at the Application layer, which is the layer where the user interacts with the machine and the installed software. The following sections of this chapter describe how each layer encapsulates the data so the same layer can be retranslated at the receiving system. The upper layers are responsible for applications communicating between hosts.

The following sections describe each of the seven layers of the OSI Reference model in detail.

The Application Layer

As you have learned, the Application layer of the OSI model can be remembered as the layer where users communicate with the computer. The Application layer identifies and establishes the availability of the intended communication partner as well as determining what resources are needed for the intended communication and whether those needed resources exist.

In some cases, computer applications may require only desktop resources, or applications may unite communicating components from more than one network application. Examples of this include file transfers, email using Simple Mail Transfer Protocol (SMTP), remote access, network management activities, Web browsers, Telnet, and File Transfer Protocol (FTP).

The Presentation Layer

The Presentation layer presents data to the Application layer, and as such, functions as a translator providing coding and conversion functions. By providing translation services, the Presentation layer ensures that the data transferred from the Application layer of one host can then be read by the Application layer of another host. This layer of the OSI Reference model has protocol standards that define how data should be formatted. Tasks such as data compression, decompression, encryption, and decryption are associated with this layer.

Other Presentation layer protocols provide standards for multimedia and visual image presentation. The following protocols are a few examples of those included in this group:

➤ Tagged Image File Format (TIFF) is a standard graphics format for high resolution pictures.

➤ Joint Photographic Experts Group (JPEG) standards give us a compression method that allows us the ability to transfer images as very small file sizes.

➤ Musical Instrument Digital Interface (MIDI) is used for digitized music.

➤ Motion Picture Experts Group's (MPEG) standard for the compression and coding of motion video for CDs is increasingly popular.

The Session Layer

The Session layer is responsible for setting up, managing, and then tearing down sessions between the Presentation layer entities. The Session layer is used to coordinate communication between different disparate systems.

Some examples of Session protocols and interfaces are Structured Query Language (SQL), which provides a simple way of defining information requirements on both local and remote systems, and Remote Procedure Call (RPC), which is a broad client/server redirection tool. RPC's procedures are created on clients and performed on servers.

There are many more examples of protocols used at this layer, which you learn about when studying for the CCNA Exam (those examples appear in *CCNA Exam Cram 2*). Readers of this book have most likely already passed the CCNA Exam.

The Transport Layer

The Transport layer is the demarcation point between the upper layers and the lower layers. This layer is known for using segments, and shields the upper-layer applications from having to learn anything about the lower layers. This layer assembles and disassembles information from the upper and lower layers into a data stream also known as a session or virtual circuit.

Common examples of protocols used at this layer are Transmission Control Protocol (TCP) and User Datagram Protocol (UDP), which both work at the Transport layer and are used by TCP/IP. TCP is a reliable service and UDP is not. TCP is an example of a *connection-oriented protocol*. It is the equivalent of sending certified mail. The packet is sent and the receiving device sends an acknowledgement that it received the entire packet. UDP is an example of *connectionless* or best-effort protocol. The packet is sent on the physical wire without a confirmation of delivery. The sending device sends the data and never knows whether the destination device received the packet. Application developers have their choice of the two protocols when working with TCP/IP protocols. Also used at this layer is Novell's Sequenced Packet Exchange (SPX).

You should remember the Transport layer's primary functions, which are

➤ To establish and tear down sessions or virtual circuits

➤ Flow Control, which controls the speed at which packets are sent

➤ Providing connection-oriented communication through acknowledgments.

The Network Layer

The Network layer uses packets and is responsible for routing through an internetwork and handling network addressing. Routers work at this layer. Simply put, this is the layer that handles network data between devices that are not locally attached in the same network or subnet.

When a router receives a packet on a network attached interface (port), the destination IP address is checked against the router's routing table. The router's routing table is a list of all the routes to other networks. If the router knows where the destination network is located, an exit interface is chosen and the packet is sent to the interface to be framed and sent out on the local network. *Framing* is the process of placing header and footer information in a layer 2 frame. Alternatively, the packet is sent out through an exit interface to the next router, which is commonly called the next hop.

If the entry for the destination network is not found in the routing table, the router will send the packet to the gateway of last resort (if there is one configured). The *gateway of last resort* is usually the exit to the Internet or another gateway to an upper-level network. The router uses this gateway by default for any destination the router has not yet learned about. If no gateway of last resort is configured, the router drops the packet.

Routing tables are also collected and used on the router. Routes called static routes are manually configured on the router. A *static route* is a route manually entered into a device to route data from one device to another. A route learned by a device on its own is called a *dynamic route*. Routes are learned dynamically by using a routing protocol. *Routing protocols* are protocols that dynamically update routes in a router's routing table and send route update packets. A routing protocol uses route update packets to notify neighboring routers about networks that are connected to the routers, as well as networks the router knows about in the internetwork. Some examples of routing protocols are

➤ Routing Information Protocol (RIP), or a later version called RIPv2

➤ Enhanced Interior Gateway Routing Protocol (EIGRP)

➤ Open Shortest Path First (OSPF)

These are the primary routing protocols used in today's networks and the ones you should know thoroughly to pass the exam.

NOTE   IP addressing is covered in depth in Chapter 4, "Troubleshooting TCP/IP." Routing protocols and troubleshooting are covered in more detail in Chapter 11, "Troubleshooting Routing Protocol."

The Data Link Layer

In the preceding section you learned about the Network layer and how routers use addressing to route packets. Routers do not care where a host is located. A router tracks where networks are located and the number of paths to get to that network so they can decide the best way to reach it. The Data Link layer uses frames and is responsible for uniquely identifying each device on a local network.

The Institute of Electronics and Electrical Engineers (IEEE) standard provides two Data Link layer sublayers. The most commonly used in today's networks is called the Media Access Control (MAC) sublayer of the IEEE 802.3 standard. Physical addressing uses six hexadecimal octets to make up a MAC address; the address is assigned to the network interface card (NIC), which connects to the network. The first three octets make up a vendor-assigned number and the last three are similar to a serial number, giving every manufactured NIC card a unique address.

The second sublayer of the Data Link Layer is the Logical Link Control (LLC) or the IEEE 802.2 standard. This sublayer is responsible for identifying Network layer protocols and using *encapsulation* to get frames to the correct destination. Encapsulation is the process of placing header information in a packet.

The LLC can provides flow control and sequencing of control bits. This layer adds additional functionality to the Data Link layer itself.

There are many IEEE 802 standards; you learn more about them in Chapter 3, "LAN Technologies."

Switches and bridges both work at the Data Link layer. These devices filter data traversing the network, using MAC addresses. Layer two switching is considered hardware-based bridging since it uses specialized hardware called Application Specific Integrated Circuits (ASICs). ASICs are small chips that use hardware to route data. ASICs can run up to gigabit speeds with very low latency. *Latency* is the term used to describe the time required for a network device to receive a frame or packet and make a forwarding decision, and then for the frame or packet to completely exit the device. A device with a switch that requires a considerable amount of time to decide through which port the data should exit is called a *high-latency device*.

The Physical Layer

The Physical layer converts upper-layer data, headers, and footers to bits. Bits are values of ones and zeros. The Physical layer communicates directly with various types of physical media, such as Unshielded Twisted Pair (UTP), coax, or fiber cabling.

The Physical layer is responsible for defining the physical, electrical, mechanical, and procedural functions for activating, maintaining, and deactivating a signal on the actual network cabling.

 Ethernet and other physical media are covered in more detail in Chapter 3.

Internetwork Troubleshooting Model

As you will read many times in this book, networks can grow to be very complex. Effective troubleshooting of these complex networks requires a systematic approach, such as the Internetwork Troubleshooting model you learn about in this section. The Internetwork Troubleshooting model assumes that you are in a large company that uses helpdesk software. The model is illustrated in Figure 2.2.

You should remember that just because a user in your network reports a problem, you can't assume that the problem is in your network. Instead, you need to obtain more information to determine if the issue affects only the user reporting the problem, or if it affects many other system users. In some cases, you may determine that user error or lack of training is causing the problem, and that a technical problem never really existed.

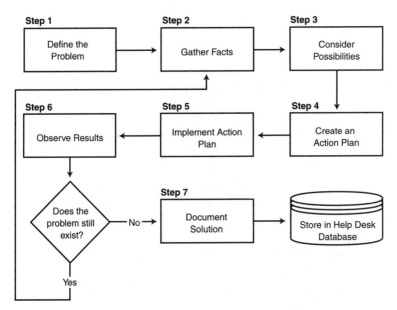

Figure 2.2   The process map of a typical Internetwork Troubleshooting Model.

The model in Figure 2.2 is called a process map, which illustrates the steps used to troubleshoot typical problems in a representative network. The Internetwork Troubleshooting model takes a step-by-step approach to troubleshooting network problems. The steps are as follows:

1. Define the problem.

2. Gather the facts.

3. Review and evaluate the possibilities.

4. Design a plan of action.

5. Implement the action plan.

6. Evaluate and observe the solution.

7. Document the solution.

You should know these steps for the exam. The following sections discuss these steps in detail.

NOTE   An eighth step sometimes noted in Cisco texts is called "Iterate the Process." If the results of the first seven steps do not resolve the problem or issue, redo the steps. *Iterate* by definition means to redo or repeat the process.

The following sections describe each of these steps in detail.

Step 1: Define the Problem

Most of the time, you, as the network administrator, will receive a ticket from the help desk, indicating that a problem needs to be resolved. You cannot always accept the information on the ticket at face value. The help desk person who could not resolve the issue over the phone may exaggerate, overestimate, or misinterpret the problem in his or her description on the ticket. If, for example, you get a call or a ticket from the helpdesk that says "Nobody can connect to the Internet," you have to question whether everyone in the building is truly unable to connect to the Internet. Does that mean that the user calling in the problem truly asked everyone in the building if they could access the Internet? You get the point. In defining the problem, you clear away any mistakes or misconceptions about the issue you must deal with.

The ticket should be used only as a notification that a problem exists. In defining the problem, you need to investigate the information you received with the ticket and verify its accuracy. It is usually necessary to contact those who are having the problem to get a clear explanation of what the problem is and what is being affected by the problem. Occasionally, you may have to visit the user and have the user demonstrate what he or she is seeing.

Step 2: Gather the Facts

Gathering facts may be more than just talking to the users who are reporting that an issue or problem in the network exists. Sometimes the issues reported may indicate a problem with a Cisco switch or router; you may need to use show or debug commands on the switch or router to determine if the issue or problem is being caused by the hardware or software used by the switch or router. If more than one person has a problem, you might want to ask questions to determine what are common symptoms, what devices are affected, and what network services are affected.

Step 3: Review and Evaluate the Possibilities

At this point you should have accumulated a mountain of information within an appropriate timeframe. After reviewing the information you have gathered about the problem, you should start to list the possible cause or causes, and how you can eliminate multiple possibilities. If you need to, consult with your peers and other network administrators, do research on the Web, or look at closed helpdesk tickets to review past issues the network has had.

Step 4: Design a Plan of Action

Once you have narrowed down the possibilities to a short list of potential causes for the problem, you can create a plan for resolving the problem. When you have some ideas as to what the problem might be, you can outline the steps you must take to resolve the issue; these steps form your plan of action. The plan may require reconfigurations of network devices or the resolution of a major outage, or it could be as small as rebooting a single device in the network. Your plan must anticipate how the resolution will affect the users on the network. Your plan of action may need to include notifying users of outages or other interruptions that will occur during the resolution of the problem.

Step 5: Implement the Action Plan

You have an idea of what the problem is; you have a plan to resolve it. Whether this is a hardware change or a software or operating system reconfiguration, now is when you need to follow your action plan and implement the resolution. Carefully document the process of implementing your plan, so you can use the information should the process fail or further problems arise.

Step 6: Evaluate and Observe the Solution

Did your action plan and implementation resolve the issue? If it didn't, you need to go back to step 2, and gather more facts. Even if your plan of action didn't resolve the issue, during the attempt you may have gathered more information to make a more informed decision.

Sometimes solving one issue actually creates new problems. Once you think you have resolved the issue, you should test and make sure that the problem has truly been addressed and no new problems now exist, creating an error-free solution. If a new problem exists, it becomes step 1 of a new troubleshooting phase. You need to start with step 1 of the process and add your resolution here to your gathering of facts. You should always remember to document everything that you have tried in resolving the issue in case you need to go back and reevaluate your troubleshooting steps.

Step 7: Document the Solution

Once you are sure you have resolved the issue, the next and final step is to make sure that the trouble ticket you opened is closed with a very detailed explanation of what was done to resolve the issue. This documentation may help you or another network administrator resolve the same issue if it happens again. If your solution created a secondary issue, your careful documentation may help you or another administrator back-track to resolve the secondary issue.

Cisco Three-Layer Hierarchical Model

Cisco has its own networking model made up of three layers—the Core layer, the Distribution layer, and the Access layer. Together, these three layers are called the Cisco Hierarchical model.

Large networks are extremely complicated and use multiple protocols, large configurations, and very diverse technologies. A hierarchical model helps to summarize a complex collection of equipment into an understandable model. When you place equipment properly in a network design, the network will function more efficiently. The Cisco Hierarchical model is used to design, implement, and maintain a scalable, reliable, cost-effective hierarchical internetwork. Each of the layers has specific responsibilities, and the layers are logical and not necessarily physical. Sometimes a single device can be placed in multiple layers, as well.

At the top of the Cisco Hierarchical model is the Core layer; at the bottom of the model is the Access layer; these layers are separated by the Distribution layer. Cisco classifies switches and routers the same way it classifies networks. The better the device functions and the more features the device has, the higher the layer in which it gets placed. Figure 2.3 illustrates the three layers of the Cisco Hierarchical model.

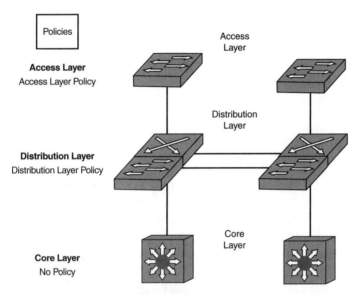

Figure 2.3. The Cisco Hierarchical model.

A hierarchy offers the benefits of helping you position certain routers and switches in identifiable logical places in your network. For example, a very popular router is the Cisco 1700 series, which is used in small offices and can't support more than about 50 or so users. In a large organization you would put that type of router at the Access layer in the Cisco Hierarchical Model. You wouldn't want to place that router as the core router for a company with 40 locations, for example, because the processing required for just a few locations alone would overwhelm that size router.

The Core Layer

The Core layer is the heart of the network. This layer is responsible for transporting the largest amount of data and sometimes voice traffic. The Core layer needs to be reliable, have the lowest latency possible, and work as quickly as possible. A failure or routing problem at the Core layer means that multiple locations and most users are affected. Placing fault tolerant devices at this layer is critical to network operations.

You should never have the devices in the Core layer assigned to anything that might slow down network traffic. You should avoid, for example, configuring a router to use access lists or packet filtering, route between virtual local area networks (VLANs), or allow support for workgroup access at the Core layer. As the network grows larger, you also should avoid expanding by adding additional routers or switches at the Core layer. Instead, upgrade or replace the devices at this layer to accommodate network growth.

The Core layer should facilitate speed and redundancy. It is common to find Gigabit Ethernet and Fast Ethernet (with redundant links) or Asynchronous Transfer Mode (ATM) interfaces at this layer. By using routing protocols with lower convergence times, you can increase the speed of data traveling at this layer as well.

The Distribution Layer

The Distribution layer is commonly referred to as the *workgroup layer*. This layer is responsible for serving as the communication point between the Access layer and the Core layer. This layer of the network is kind of like the network's post office. Access lists and route maps used with routing protocols act as the postman in the Distribution layer, deciding whether the packets traversing the network are valid or junk mail, and determining the route that packets will take. If the Distribution layer determines that the packet is junk, the packet is not allowed to go to another point in the network block and is returned. You need to remember that this layer provides routing, filtering, packet access to the Core layer, and WAN access to other locations or the Internet. The Distribution layer also is the layer where access lists, packet filtering, and access policies for the network should be enforced. An organized and maintained security plan and firewalls should be placed at this layer. Routing protocol redistribution, VLAN routing, and static routing also should be located in this layer.

The Access Layer

The Access layer is where the local users reside; this layer is sometimes referred to as the *desktop layer*. The network resources that most users need will be available locally. Any data or voice traffic destined for remote locations are handled by the distribution layer.

Access control policies, such as access lists on the router, can still be implemented here in this layer, as well as the creation of separate collision domains. Frequently, static routing is used instead of dynamic routing protocols at this layer.

Chapter Summary

Network models help to simplify complexities of the network and facilitate the process of troubleshooting network problems. In this chapter you learned about the different hierarchical network models that Cisco expects you to know for the exam.

The OSI Reference model is used to maintain standards for networking products. This model spans from the Application layer, where the user inputs data, to the Physical layer, which places the bits onto the physical media for transmission.

The Internetwork Troubleshooting model helps to simplify the complexities of troubleshooting network problems, including complex situations where many possible problems exist. By using the model's seven-step process map, you can quickly narrow down the possibilities, formulate and implement a plan for resolving the problem, and document the solution in case the problem recurs or another problem was created by your solution.

The Cisco Hierarchical model organizes the network in three layers to help you in the placement of different types of equipment in the network. You should have a good understanding of the types of equipment that should be found at the Core, Distribution, and Access layers.

Exam Prep Practice Questions

Question 1

Data formatting, such as encryption and decryption, are found at which layer of the OSI Reference model?

- ○ A. The Core layer
- ○ B. The Documentation layer
- ○ C. The Formatting layer
- ○ D. The Presentation layer
- ○ E. The Application layer

Answer: **D.** The Presentation layer of the OSI Reference model defines data formatting, including the formatting for encryption and decryption.

Question 2

Which layer of the Cisco Hierarchical model should not have access lists controlling policies in the network?

- ○ A. The Access layer
- ○ B. The Core layer
- ○ C. The Distribution layer
- ○ D. The non-policy layer
- ○ E. The speed layer
- ○ F. The Physical layer

Answer: **B.** The Core layer of the Cisco Hierarchical model should route data as quickly as possible. Access lists or policies require processing that slows down devices handling heavy network traffic. Therefore, these lists shouldn't be included in the Core layer.

Question 3

Hierarchical network models provide which of the following? (Choose all that apply.)

☐ A. A way to identify placement of devices in the network

☐ B. Simplification of complexities in networks

☐ C. Compatibility between computer vendors

☐ D. All of the above

Answer: **D.** All of the above are true. Hierarchical network models help us to decide where equipment and policies are placed, simplify the complexities of networks, and make sure that one vendor's hardware operating at one layer will not affect hardware operating at another layer.

Question 4

The Physical layer is part of which hierarchical model?

○ A. Peer-to-Peer Networking model

○ B. Troubleshooting model

○ C. Internetwork Cabling model

○ D. Internetwork Troubleshooting model

○ E. OSI Reference model

Answer: **E.** The Physical layer is the layer that transmits and receives data in 1s and 0s and is the last layer in the OSI Reference model.

Question 5

Which step of the Cisco Internetwork Troubleshooting model is used for collecting additional information from devices and users experiencing a reported network problem or issue?

○ A. Define the problem in the network

○ B. Review and evaluate possibilities

○ C. Gather facts

○ D. All of the above

○ E. None of the above

Answer: **C.** By gathering facts you can collect information from the users having problems, as well as collect information on your own from prior problem tickets. You can also use show and debug commands on Cisco equipment to locate and retrieve information to add to your facts.

Question 6

If you add a new workgroup-class switch to the network, in which layer of the Cisco Hierarchical Model would you place that switch?

○ A. Core Layer

○ B. Network layer

○ C. Distribution layer

○ D. Access layer

○ E. Primary layer

Answer: **D.** The Access layer is where users and workgroups should be placed in the network.

Question 7

Which layer of the OSI Reference model is where users interact with applications?

○ A. The Access layer

○ B. The Core layer

○ C. The Distribution layer

○ D. The non-policy layer

○ E. The Application layer

○ F. The Physical layer

Answer: **E.** The Application layer is the layer where users interact with the applications in the OSI Reference model.

Question 8

In which layer of the OSI Reference Model would IP addresses be found?

○ A.   The TCP layer

○ B.   The Core layer

○ C.   The Network layer

○ D.   The IP layer

○ E.   The Application layer

○ F.   The Physical layer

Answer: **C.** The Network layer of the OSI Reference model is where network addressing using IP addresses are defined.

Need to Know More?

 Black, Uyless D. *OSI: A Model for Computer Communications Standards.* Prentice Hall Publishing, Indianapolis, IN 1991. ISBN: 0136371337.

 Jones, Jim. *CCNA Exam Cram 2.* Que Publishing, Indianapolis, IN. ISBN: 0789730197.

 Network Basics For Execs, "How This Stuff Works" on Cisco's CCO Web site, http://business.cisco.com/prod/tree. taf%3Fasset_id=103205&MagID=103167&public_view=true&kbns=1. html

 How ThisStuffWorks.Com http://computer.howstuffworks.com/ osi.htm

LAN Technologies

Terms you'll need to understand:

✓ Active Monitor
✓ autonegotiation
✓ broadcast domain
✓ collision domain
✓ network diameter
✓ network sniffer
✓ network topology
✓ bus topology
✓ ring topology
✓ star topology

Techniques you'll need to master:

✓ Know and identify different LAN topologies
✓ Understand different LAN devices in a network
✓ Understand Ethernet technology
✓ Identify a star topology, and know its speeds and capabilities
✓ Understand Token Ring and the ring topology
✓ Understand the capabilities of ATM and its advantages
✓ Understand the advantages of segmenting

The focus of this book is to prepare for an exam that covers supporting and troubleshooting Cisco networks. In order to prepare for this exam, you need to understand some of the principles and media types used in today's networks in order to begin troubleshooting. You should have a good knowledge of different topologies and how certain media standards operate. The IEEE media standards you should know for the exam are the Ethernet, Fast Ethernet, Gigabit Ethernet, ATM, Token Ring, and wireless standards.

For the exam, Cisco expects you to know many aspects of the network. You should understand how hubs, bridges, switches, and routers segment the networks, as well as how they divide broadcast and collision domains. In this chapter, I give you an overview of the different LAN topologies and the IEEE LAN media standards you need to know in order to do well on the CCNP exam.

LAN Topology Types

In the next three sections I will explain the three different network topologies you need to know for the exam. A network topology is all the combined physical, logical, or virtual components that make up the network or network segment. Although there are many topologies, we will focus on those necessary for the exam, which include the bus, ring, and star topologies.

Bus

A bus topology is a local area network (LAN) where each of the networked devices are attached to a single cable or link, as shown in Figure 3.1. In a bus topology, stations are attached to a linear multiport medium where only half-duplex operations exist between a station and a bus.

 Half-duplex is where communication occurs bi-directionally on one cable. This means that a device sending data cannot receive data at the same time. Full-duplex uses two individual cables, one to send and another to receive. This allows a device to send at the same time it receives data.

Frames that are transmitted to the bus provide the address of the frame's destination. If the frame gets to the end of the link and the frame has not found its intended destination, then the frame is lost. In a bus topology, there is no security; every node attached to the line can see the conversations of the other nodes on the link.

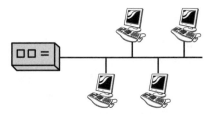

Figure 3.1   A bus topology LAN. Notice that all the workstations are connected by a single cable.

Ring

In a ring topology LAN (shown in Figure 3.2), as in a bus topology LAN, all the nodes or devices in the network are attached to the network on the same cable or link. The difference is that a ring topology makes a complete circle. Both Token Ring/IEEE and Fiber Distributed Data Interface (FDDI) use a ring topology. FDDI is an American National Standard Institute (ANSI) X3T9.5 standard cable, which now supports up to Gigabit speeds using fiber-optic cabling. It can use a single ring for half-duplex operations or a dual–ring architecture for full-duplex operations.

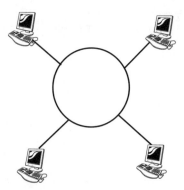

Figure 3.2   A ring topology LAN. Notice that all of the nodes connect to the ring. Data for most implementations travels in one direction on the ring. However, many technologies, including Token Ring, allow for a second ring which allows for full-duplex operations.

When a break in the ring occurs, such as a cut cable or other cabling problem, it affects all the stations. This means that none of the stations connected can receive or transmit data. The longer the cable or link and the more attached stations, the more repeaters that are needed. However, due to timing distortions within signals, a limited number of repeaters can be used in the same network. In a ring-topology network, centralized access means that faults are easy to detect and isolate. Multiple rings are sometimes used to make a very robust and reliable network.

Star

The star topology is the most common topology in today's networks, and includes Ethernet, Fast Ethernet, and Gigabit Ethernet. Each node in a star topology connects to a dedicated link where the other end connects to a switch or hub. In the star-topology network shown in Figure 3.3, multiple devices are connected to a switch or hub.

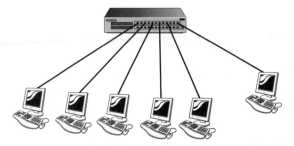

Figure 3.3   A Star topology LAN. Notice that each workstation is directly connected to a hub or switch.

One of the best reasons to use a star topology is that a loss of any node will not disrupt network operations. It is also easy to add or remove a node from the network. From wiring to installation, it is particularly easy to set up a star topology network.

Ethernet

Ethernet is a LAN standard that has become one of the most used LAN media today for many reasons. Ethernet is one of the cheapest and most widely available LAN media, and it has the ability to carry high-speed transmission. One of the most important reasons Ethernet is the most popular LAN medium is that there is a large platoon of skilled network administrators that know how to implement, administer, and troubleshoot Ethernet networks.

When you connect devices to an IEEE 802.3 Ethernet network, you attach one end of the cable to either a hub or switch. For this exam, therefore, an understanding of hubs and switches and their functions is essential. I explain each device throughout this chapter. In the following sections, you take a look at the differences between switches and hubs, and between collision and broadcast domains; you also learn how to troubleshoot problems in Ethernet networks.

Collision and Broadcast Domains

In a network, a *collision domain* is defined as all the interfaces on a single segment that can send data on the same physical wire, where a collision of the data being sent can occur. When you use a hub, all the nodes connected to the hub are in the same collision domain. A *hub* is basically a repeater that resends any signal it receives out each one of its ports. This means that, when a network uses a hub, every frame sent on the wire is seen by every node on the network.

If a node sends out a broadcast, all the nodes that can receive that broadcast on the physical wire are in the same *broadcast domain*. Since an Ethernet hub repeats the same signal it received out all of its ports, all the nodes that are in the same collision domain are also in the same broadcast domain.

Even if the frame is not destined for the node that receives the frame, the frame must still be checked to see what the destination address is. This in turn uses valuable processing power on the device receiving the frame.

 For the exam, you must know the differences between a broadcast and a collision domain, as they occur in Ethernet networks. Remember that a broadcast copies and sends a transmission to every destination node on the network.

In networks that use hubs, every frame that traverses the broadcast domain must be processed by every node. When the nodes are processing broadcasts and frames for 100 devices, they can accomplish little else. Switches were designed to overcome the handicaps of a hub.

A switch looks similar to a hub but each port on a switch is in its own collision domain. Only the devices on ports assigned to the same Virtual Local Area Network (VLAN) receive broadcasts from one another. An administrator can assign certain devices to a VLAN as a way of creating smaller broadcast domains. A broadcast from a device connected to a port on VLAN 10 will only be seen by devices connected to ports assigned to VLAN 10. By default, Cisco switches are usually assigned to VLAN 1.

When a transmission is sent over an Ethernet network, if the switch knows the port of the destination node, the switch directs the frame to that node without the use of a broadcast to learn where the node is located. This greatly reduces the processing required by the nodes on the network, since the frames are received only by the destination device.

Ethernet Elements

In the late 1970s, Xerox created the first Ethernet standard. In 1984, a consortium of Digital, Intel, and Xerox, calling themselves DIX, created the Ethernet_II standard. Around the same time, the IEEE created its own standard, with three groups providing input. The first group was called The High Level Interface (HILI), and was responsible for developing high-level internetworking protocols. This group later became the IEEE 802.1 Committee.

The second group was called The Logical Link Control Group, which focused on end-to-end connectivity. This group later became the IEEE 802.2 Committee.

The last group, called the Data Link and Medium Access Control (DLMAC) group, was responsible for developing medium access protocols. This group later formed committees for Ethernet (802.3), Token Bus (802.4), and Token Ring (802.5).

When the 802.3 group finished their Ethernet standard, it was almost identical to the Ethernet_II standard. The major difference was their descriptions of the Media Access Control (MAC) layer and the Logical Link Control (LLC) layer's responsibilities.

Ethernet consists of three basic elements: the physical medium, a set of medium access control rules, and the Ethernet frame. The physical medium is used to carry Ethernet signals devices. The network uses a set of medium access control rules, which allow multiple computers to share the available bandwidth. Each Ethernet frame that is sent on the physical medium consists of a set of bits understandable by the devices connected to the LAN.

Ethernet takes packets from upper-layer protocols, and places header and footer information around the data before it traverses the network. This process is called *data encapsulation* or *framing*. Ethernet frames travel at the Data Link layer of the OSI model and must be a minimum of 64 bytes and a maximum of 1518 bytes.

Figure 3.4 shows an Ethernet IEEE 802.3 frame and an Ethernet frame.

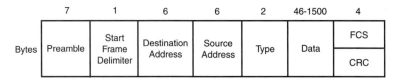

Figure 3.4   An IEEE 802.3 frame and an Ethernet frame.

Here is a brief description of each field in an IEEE 802.3 frame and an Ethernet frame:

➤ *Preamble*—An alternating pattern of ones and zeros that is used by the receiver to establish bit synchronization. Bit synchronization is like helping each device speak the same dialect of a language. Both Ethernet and IEEE 802.3 frames begin with a preamble.

➤ *Start frame delimiter*—Indicates where the frame starts, and is the byte before the destination address in both the Ethernet and IEEE 802.3 frame.

➤ *Destination Address and Source Address*—Are each six bytes long in both Ethernet and IEEE 802.3 frames, and are contained in hardware on the Ethernet and IEEE 802.3 interface cards. The IEEE standards committee specifies the first three bytes of the address to a specific vendor. The source address is always a *unicast* (single-node) address, whereas the destination address may be unicast, *multicast* (group), or *broadcast* (all nodes).

➤ *Type Field*—In Ethernet frames, this is the two-byte field after the source address. After Ethernet processing, the type field specifies the upper-layer protocol to receive the data.

➤ *Length Field*—In IEEE 802.3 frames, the Length Field is a two-byte field following the source address. The length field indicates the number of bytes of data that follow this field and precede the frame check sequence field.

➤ *Data Field*—Is the actual data contained in the frame and follows the type and length fields. After Physical-layer and Link-layer processes are complete, this data is sent to an upper-layer protocol. With Ethernet, the upper-layer protocol is identified in the type field. With IEEE 802.3, the upper-layer protocol must be defined within the data portion of the frame. If the data of the frame is not large enough to fill the frame to its minimum size of 64 bytes, padding bytes are inserted to ensure at least a 64-byte frame.

➤ *FCS (Frame Check Sequence) or CRC (Cyclic Redundancy Check) fields*—Are at the end of the frame. The frame check sequence recalculates the number of frames to make sure that none are missing or damaged. The CRC applies to all fields except the first, second, and last.

CSMA/CD (Carrier Sense Multiple Access with Collision Detection) Protocol

Ethernet uses a communication concept called *datagrams* to get messages across the network. The *Carrier Sense Multiple Access with Collision Detection (CSMA/CD)* protocol makes sure that two datagrams aren't sent out at the same time, and if they are, it acts as a mediator to retransmit. A good analogy to CSMA/CD is that of a police radio system. If you are on the correct channel, you can hear everything, but if you try to talk when another person is speaking, one or both of you won't be heard clearly. You must wait for a break in communication to speak and be heard. The CSMA/CD communication control method works in a similar manner; if a channel is busy on the network, other stations cannot transmit. CSMA/CD, therefore, can slow the communication process in a network environment.

A datagram is a packet or a frame sent on the physical wire from one host to another.

The IEEE committee finalized a specification for running Ethernet-type signaling over unshielded twisted-pair (UTP) wiring. The IEEE calls the 10Mbps UTP standard *10Base-T*, which indicates that networks using this standard use a signaling speed of ten megabits per second, a baseband signaling scheme, and twisted-pair wiring. 10Base-T isn't always fast enough; Transmission speeds of 100Base-T and Gigabit speeds are needed for today's typical networks to remain in a healthy state without significant latency. Although many smaller companies still use 10Base-T technology because it meets their needs, many notice that their newer applications are more demanding of resources. The next few sections a look at both 10Base-T and 100Base-T Ethernet technologies and how Ethernet adapted to increase LAN speeds.

Baseband, also known as *narrowband*, is a feature of a technology, such as Ethernet, that uses a single carrier frequency.

Fast Ethernet

Fast Ethernet (or 100Base-T) uses the CSMA/CD protocol and has 10 times the performance of 10Base-T. Because 100Base-T uses the same protocol as

10Base-T (CSMA/CD), you can integrate 100Base-T into existing 10Base-T networks. 100Base-T technology uses the same network wiring and equipment as does 10Base-T, provided the wiring and equipment supports both 10Base-T and 100Base-T. Some Ethernet standards, such as Category 1, 2, or 3 cabling, cannot support 100Base-T. However, the biggest issue that a network administrator will face in upgrading to Fast Ethernet 100Base-T technology is at the workstation. To allow the workstation to transmit and receive at either 10Mbps or 100Mbps, the PCs need a NIC (network interface card) that is 10/100 capable (as you learn in the next section of this chapter, many networks today use 10/100/1000 NICs). Older Ethernet NICs allow only 4 to 10Mbps.

In addition to replacing NICs in every workstation, the actual implementation of 100Base-T in the network is another challenge. 10Base-T uses a larger collision domain diameter than 100Base-T and thus has a different signaling system. The *network diameter* is the cabling distance between the two farthest points in the network. The diameter between two devices would be the cabling distance between the two devices. The PC in your office may only be 250 feet from the wiring closet. However, if you were to wire from the switch in the wiring closet, up the wall, through the ceiling, back down through the wall in your office, and add another 10 foot cable from the wall to the PC desk, you may have over extended the available distance diameter for the cabling you are using.

The collision domain diameter of 100Base-T is 205 meters, which is approximately ten times smaller than that of 10Base-T. What does this mean? Because 100Base-T uses the same collision-detection mechanism as 10Base-T, the network diameter has to be reduced for 100Base-T. Think of it in terms of time slots. Each station gets its turn or time slot to transmit all of its data before another station can transmit its data. For 100Base-T networks to transmit in the same time slots as 10Base-T, the distance must be reduced (because 100Base-T travels at a faster rate; 100Base-T moves 10 times as fast, so it can only go one-tenth as far).

Autonegotiation

A 100Base-T network also supports an optional feature called *autonegotiation*, which allows a hub or switch and a network device to communicate their compatibilities and to agree upon an optimal communication speed and duplex. Autonegotiation can detect speed matching for 10 and 100Mbps, full-duplex, and automatic signaling configurations for 100Base-T4 and 100Base-TX stations. Autonegotiation can be enabled or disabled on hubs or switch ports.

Devices usually have autonegotiation on by default to automatically negotiate a mutual speed for both devices for communication. Such autonegotiation is a nice feature now that most networks use multiple speeds and duplexes.

Duplexing

A switch can provide dedicated point-to-point bandwidth availability from the switch port to the attached device. This means that a 10Mbps network interface card can provide 10Mbps, rather than sharing that bandwidth with all other stations. A small 12-port Ethernet switch provides a theoretical 120Mbit of bandwidth, compared to the 10Mbit provided by an Ethernet hub.

Full-duplex Ethernet is another advancing technology for Ethernet. Full duplex allows data to be sent and received simultaneously over a link. You may find full-duplex capabilities in autonegotiation hubs and interfaces. In a half-duplex link, data can either be sent or received, but not both at the same time. In theory, with full duplex, you can have twice the bandwidth of normal (half-duplex) Ethernet. The full-duplex mode requires that each end of the link connect to only a single device, such as a workstation, server, or a switched hub port. The devices also have to be running at the same speed, such as at 10Mbps, 100Mbps, or 1000Mbps.

Gigabit Ethernet

Gigabit Ethernet is another addition to the IEEE 802.3 Ethernet standards. Gigabit Ethernet is 10 times faster than 100Base-T, with speeds up to 1000Mbps or 1Gbps (gigabit per second). This has been a welcome addition to many database and heavy process intensive networks; pushing large files across a network using standard Ethernet was nearly impossible, due to slow transfer speeds. Gigabit Ethernet allows for more resources to be shared throughout a network. It can run in half-duplex or full-duplex mode. Most products that use gigabit technology use fiber-optic cable. Ethnernet allows you to use Category 5 or 6 UTP and use distances of approximately 25 meters. Using fiber optics can greatly extend this distance. Implementing Gigabit Ethernet in your network increases its bandwidth and capacity, improves Layer 2 performance, and can eliminate Layer 2 bottlenecks.

Gigabit Ethernet looks identical to Ethernet from the Data Link layer upward. The physical layer is defined in the IEEE 802.3z 1000BASE-T standard, which is the standard for Gigabit Ethernet over the Category 5 or 6 cabling. Cisco recommends that it be installed according to the specifications of ANSI/TIA/EIA-568A. 1000BASE-T works by using all four of the Category 5 or 6 pairs to achieve 1000 Mbps operation. This means that each pair sends 250Mbps of data, and is capable of sending and receiving data over each of the four pairs simultaneously. 100BASE-TX (Fast Ethernet) uses two pairs, one to transmit and one to receive.

In early March 2002, Cisco agreed to support the IEEE 802.3ae 10 Gigabit Ethernet standard. This new standard preserves the 802.3 Ethernet frame format and continues to use *MAC (Media Access Control)* addresses embedded on the NIC card. The new standard allows for distances of up to 40km using multimode fiber cabling.

Cisco joined with six other companies to establish the 10 Gigabit Ethernet Alliance. The 10 Gigabit Ethernet standards began in March 1999 with a group called the Higher Speed Study Group (HSSG). This study group is now called the IEEE 803.3ae 10 Gigabit Ethernet Task Force.

Gigabit Media Types

Switch vendors offer different media types for switch interfaces needing to use Gigabit Ethernet. The three types of media for Gigabit Ethernet are longwave, shortwave, and copper medium:

➤ Longwave (LW) laser can use single-mode and multimode fiber. This specification is referred to as 1000BaseLX. The 1000BaseLX GigaBit Interface Converter (GBIC) interfaces can pass data up to 1.8 miles (three kilometers).

➤ Shortwave (SW) laser uses multimode fiber. This specification is generally referred to as 1000BaseSX. With the GBIC interfaces, 1000BaseSX gives the option for multimode fiber-optic cable connections with a 1,800 foot distance limitation.

➤ A provision within the IEEE 802.3z specification defines Gigabit Ethernet over coaxial copper (1000BaseCX) using shielded 150-ohm copper. This can be used only for short distances because this cabling method has a distance limitation under 25 meters.

Unicast, Broadcasts, and Multicast

Sometimes different types of broadcasts can bring your network to its knees because of the sheer size or the large numbers of the datagrams. As a network administrator, you must understand these different types of broadcasts so that you can identify what they are and where they are coming from. Sometimes using a device called a sniffer on the network while the network is slow can be very helpful. A sniffer is a device that connects to the network to monitor the traffic on the network, including the broadcasts and who is sending them. This monitoring can be helpful in diagnosing whether there is a problem in the network. The three types of LAN data transmissions are unicast, multicast, and broadcast.

A Unicast transmission is a single packet that is sent from the source node to the destination node on a network. The source node sends a packet by sending it to the address of the destination node, and the packet is then sent on the network to find the address of the destination node.

A Multicast transmission is a single data packet that is copied and sent to a specific set of nodes on the network. The source node uses a multicast address to send a single packet addressed to several nodes. The packet is then sent on to the network where it's copied and sent to each destination node that is part of the multicast address.

A Broadcast transmission is a single data packet that is copied and sent to all nodes on the network. In this transmission, the source node sends a packet addressed to all destination nodes on the network. The packet is then sent on the network where it's copied and sent to every destination node on that network.

 Broadcast transmissions can be very taxing on the network. You may want to segment your network into smaller sections to reduce the broadcast domain.

ATM (Asynchronous Transfer Mode)

Asynchronous Transfer Mode (ATM) is an adaptable technology that can be used in LANs and WANs (Wide-Area Networks). ATM is based on the efforts of the ITU-T Broadcast Integrated Services Digital Network (BISDN) standard.

ATM uses both switching and multiplexing, and it can provide very high bandwidth with few delays. Instead of using frames like Ethernet uses, ATM uses 53-byte, fixed-size cells. The first five bytes contain cell-header information, and the remaining 48 bytes contain the *payload* (user information). It was originally conceived as a high-speed transfer technology for voice, video, and data over public networks. Small fixed-length cells are best suited for transferring voice and video traffic because they are intolerant of delays that result from having to wait for a large data packet to download (among other network activities). Although ATM is not dependent on a Physical-layer implementation, it does require a medium such as fiber optic to support the amount of bandwidth that's needed to run ATM.

ATM's chief advantage is its capability to create a seamless and fast network reaching from the desktop out across a wide area. Ultimately, ATM could do away with routers, allocate bandwidth, and be able to run high-end applications. Although ATM's potential certainly sounds like a dream for networks, the technology also has disadvantages. ATM uses a great deal of overhead and carries many additional expenses. Because most organizations are only pushing data through their network with a few higher-end applications, the need for millisecond synchronization is not a necessity. ATM has a large overhead, and most companies—those with networks that usually push data and very little video—may not even notice the difference, making the overhead and expense of ATM an unwise investment.

ATM appeals mainly to companies that need to deliver synchronized video and sound. The companies that benefit from ATM are movie and entertainment players, such as Time-Warner, that want to deliver on-demand video and sound to your home. At this point, ATM is overkill for most companies passing data, but it has continued to gain popularity over the years and may continue to do so in the future. Some phone companies have adapted the technology and use it over Digital Subscriber Line (DSL) with a technology called ATM over DSL.

Token Ring

After Ethernet, Token Ring is the second most widely used LAN technology, and its second rank is due mostly to its cost factor. Ethernet technology is simply cheaper to implement than is Token Ring. Token Ring is a ring topology created by IBM in the 1970s. The IEEE 802.5 subcommittee—with help from IBM representatives—developed a set of standards that described a token-passing network in a ring topology.

Token-passing networks move a stream of data, called a token, around the network. Any station with a message or data to transmit waits until it receives a free token. It then changes the free token to a busy token and transmits a block of data called a frame. The frame contains the data that needs to be sent to the rest of the network. The token circulates around the ring, passing through as many as three stations at a time until it finds the receiving station.

The receiving station copies the data from the frame, and the frame continues around the ring, making a complete round trip back to the original transmitting station. The transmitting station now knows the frame has been received, and the station then purges the busy token it has been keeping and inserts a new free token on the ring for others to use.

The use of token-passing prevents messages from interfering with one another by guaranteeing that only one station at a time is transmitting. Therefore, collisions cannot occur on the network. Unlike Ethernet, token passing ensures the delivery of the frame.

The Token Ring topology runs at the Physical and Data Link layers of the OSI model, and it is modeled as a star topology using STP wiring. Each station is connected to a central hub called a *multistation access unit (MSAU)* that houses electromechanical relays to make the physical star into a logical ring. The *logical ring* is where each station receives signals from its *nearest active upstream neighbor (NAUN)* and repeats these signals to its downstream neighbors.

Token Ring networks use a priority system that permits certain user-designated, high-priority stations to use the network more frequently. Priority levels are configured by the network administrator. A Token Ring network has two fields inside the frame of the token, as shown in Figure 3.5, that control priority: the *priority field* and the *reservation field*. When a priority token is transmitted, it can be seized by only those stations with a priority that is equal to or higher than the priority value contained in that token. The station then seizes the token and changes it to an information frame, and only stations with a priority value higher than that of the transmitting station can reserve the token for the next pass around the network. When the next token is generated, it includes the higher priority of the reserving station. Stations that raise a token's priority level must reinstate the previous priority after the transmission is complete.

The original IBM Token Ring product ran at speeds of 4Mbps. In 1989, IBM released a faster version of Token Ring, which ran at 16Mbps. Over time, a high-speed Token Ring (HSTR) was released that operated at 100Mbps and led to 1Gbps Token Ring. The speed has maintained with the evolving technology and makes Token Ring topology a serious contender against Ethernet.

Frame Format of Token Ring

Token Ring is similar to FDDI frames, in that they both support token formats, as well as data. Figure 3.5 illustrates the frame format of both the token being passed and a frame sent from a node on the ring during a Token Ring network communication.

Here is a brief explanation of each field in a Token Ring frame as shown in Figure 3.5.

➤ *Start Delimiter*—Alerts each station of a token and uses a unique coding for the frame.

➤ *Access-Control Byte*—Contains a series of bits that circulate throughout the ring and are used by the active monitor to ensure delivery: a *Priority bit* indicates the priority of the frame or token; a *Reservation bit* indicates the priority required for the next token to gain access to the ring; a *Token bit* differentiates a token from a data or command frame; and a *Monitor bit* determines whether a frame is circling the ring endlessly. Active monitor employs a mechanism for detecting and compensating for network fault.

➤ *Frame Control*—Indicates the frame type and contains the Frame type bit, the Reserved bit, and the Control bits.

➤ *Destination Address*—Indicates the address of the receiver.

➤ *Source Address*—Identifies the address of the sender.

➤ *Data*—Indicates the actual data being sent from the upper layers.

➤ *Frame Control Sequence*—Ensures that all the frames are delivered without damage.

➤ *End Delimiter*—Defines the end of the token or frame and contains bits to indicate if a frame is damaged.

➤ *Frame Status*—Terminates the frame and ensures that the frame has been copied to the destination address.

Data Frame Format

Preamble	Start Delimiter	Frame Control	Destination Address	Source Address	Date	FCS	End Delimiter	Frame Status

Token Frame Format

Preamble	Start Delimiter	Frame Control	End Delimiter

Figure 3.5   The Token Ring Frame formats.

Active Monitor

Token Ring networks employ a mechanism for detecting and compensating for network faults. Any station on a Token Ring network can be selected to be the active monitor. This active monitor station acts as a centralized source of timing information for the Token Ring stations and makes sure that there isn't more than one token on the ring at any given time. Also, when a sending device fails, its frame may continue to circle the ring. This can prevent other stations from transmitting their frames, which may lock up the network. The active monitor can detect such frames, remove them from the ring, and generate a new token. The active monitor also has several standby monitors that act as backups in case the active monitor goes offline.

Wireless

Wireless LANs are an evolving technology that many companies find worth watching. Although such networks aren't totally wireless, they do primarily use radio or infrared technology to connect subnets to the main body of a network. Although wireless networks are extensions of cabled networks, they cannot replace them. Technically, a few laptops joined together could constitute a wireless network, but, for our purposes, we will consider wireless networks that are connected to wired networks.

Without a doubt, wireless networks have more constrictions, usually related to the data transmission rates. However the convenience of turning on your PC and having an instant connection anywhere in a building sometimes outweighs the hassle of installing cables.

Most wireless LANs have an access point or wireless router that is connected to a wired network via a coax cable, Universal Serial Bus (USB), or Ethernet connection. Because most wireless LANs are extensions of a wired LAN, the access point is usually placed up high or in a similar location without many objects around it to obstruct the signal. The devices you want to connect to the wireless LAN must have a peripheral component to communicate with the access point. For laptops, this component is usually just a card to fit in the PCMCIA slot; for PCs, the card fits like a standard NIC or an attached USB dongle and antenna.

802.11a and 802.11b

The IEEE 802.11 committee established a standard in 1997 with a data rate of only 2Mbps. The standards supporting wireless are known as IEEE 802.11a, 802.11b, and 802.11g. Both 802.11a and 802.11b have distance limitations of 100 feet from the wireless access point or wireless router. 802.11b uses the 2.4GHz band, and currently supports data rates up to 11 Mbps.

Cisco wireless products, such as the Aironet series, integrate seamlessly into an existing network as a wireless overlay, or create freestanding all-wireless networks, enabling mobility quickly and cost effectively. These products are compliant with IEEE 802.11a and 802.11b standards using both single and dual band configurations.

IEEE 802.11g

A new wireless technology allowing speeds of up to 54Mbps is now available, and most companies provide legacy support of the older 802.11a and 802.11b technologies. This wireless technology is known as IEEE 802.11g, Wireless-G, or 54g, and continues to use the 2.4 GHz band.

Segmentation

A network's congestion problems cannot always be corrected simply by increasing bandwidth. When troubleshooting congestion problems, one thing to look into is the source of all the traffic. Examining broadcasts traversing the network using a network *sniffer* can yield important insight into the problem of network congestion. A network sniffer is software that uses a promiscuous NIC card to collect data frames and packets from the network to view and diagnose what's happening in the network. Sometimes bad NICs can send out tons of broadcasts onto your network, without your knowledge. These faulty NICs are sometimes referred to as *jabbering NICs*. Servers also send broadcasts. The sniffer can uncover such unnecessary broadcasts. Once you have isolated the issue of network congestion, you can implement devices that are designed to alleviate unnecessary traffic, increase the bandwidth, and correct network bottlenecks.

One way of solving congestion problems and increasing performance on a LAN is to divide a single Ethernet segment into multiple network segments—a process called *segmentation*. Network segmentation reduces the size of the collision domain. This helps maximize available bandwidth by reducing the number of users in the collision domain or broadcast domain. Fortunately, you have at your disposal a few tried-and-true devices to segment a LAN and help relieve Ethernet congestion: bridges, routers, and LAN switches. The following sections discuss these devices in detail.

Segmenting a Network with Bridges

A bridge can connect several LANs together and provide more bandwidth to the user. Bridges also reduce collisions by making smaller collision domains. Bridges operate on the Data Link layer (or Layer 2), and they dynamically build a *forwarding table*, which is a table of information that contains the learned MAC addresses and their corresponding port information based on the source address the device learned from incoming data frames. A bridge uses the destination address in a frame to make a forwarding decision. One disadvantage of using a bridge is its inability to filter broadcasts; as a result, it sends the broadcast on all the segments. Occasionally, broadcasts use up all or a majority of the available bandwidth, a situation referred to as a *broadcast storm*.

Segmentation Using LAN Switches

Switches are Layer 2 devices, similar to bridges in that they learn the topology dynamically and forward, as well as filter, data traffic. Switches read the destination Layer 2 MAC address and often begin to forward the frames before the entire packet is received. This ability results in lower latency. Switches also give you a higher port density than bridges do, and they cost less than a bridge. In some ways, a switch is really a multiport bridge, because the switch can filter to the port via MAC addresses and each port on the switch is in its own collision domain.

Using a LAN switch offers some advantages over using a bridge, including full-duplex communication, media rate adaptation, and easy migration. Also, implementing LAN switches usually doesn't require many changes to the network. You can use the existing wiring, and simply replace hubs with switches or slowly migrate by replacing one hub at a time.

Segmenting with a Router

Routers can connect networks that use different media types. Switches and bridges filter and route data at the Data Link layer by MAC addresses. Routers operate at the Network layer and filter by logical addresses. A *logical address* is a Layer 3 address assigned by a protocol such as IP or IPX addresses.

Routers keep a table that records where devices are located on the network. The difference between a router and a bridge, however, is that a bridge keeps track of the hosts or addresses on the network, whereas the router keeps track of networks, not hosts. Using the routing tables, the router can make an informed routing decision on where to send incoming data.

 By default, routers won't forward broadcasts to the rest of the network, which alleviates unnecessary traffic on the network caused by broadcasts.

Chapter Summary

In this chapter we learned the differences between ring, star, and LAN topologies. You should know how each is used in the network, and that Token Ring uses a ring topology, while Ethernet uses a star topology when using CAT 5 cabling.

Remember that some of the advantages of LAN segmentation are achieved by separating the network using various devices. You can create smaller broadcast domains by using *routers* throughout the network. Also, using *switching* in the network can drastically reduce the number of collisions and create smaller collision and broadcast domains. Switching allows for high-end devices or demanding applications to be placed on the network with dedicated circuits and less congestion. You can see that it's important to know which devices help you best utilize a network's bandwidth.

A variety of LAN topologies are available to fit any network:

➤ *Ethernet* technology is most widely used because of its efficiency and its cost. Ethernet technology is constantly evolving to maintain its status and to stay ahead of the network demands. Ethernet is fairly easy to install because of the wide variety of equipment on the market and the standards that accompany it. Ethernet speed ranges from 10Mbps to 10,000Mbps, for a wide variety of networks.

➤ *Token Ring* is the second most widely used technology in today's networks. Token Ring uses a ring topology and a Token-passing method to access the physical medium, which consist of a virtual ring.

➤ *ATM* is great for high-speed technologies, such as video and voice. Most companies, however, do not pass large amounts of video or sound, sending mainly straight data. Because of ATM's large overhead, these companies don't need to pay the extra money for ATM simply because they won't fully utilize its capabilities.

➤ *Wireless LANs* are very convenient and will likely be highly considered for short-distance WANs and LANs. Wireless LANs will almost always be connected to a wired network. Although wireless technology boast speeds as high as 11Mbps, they are probably running at a speed of 5Mbps to 7Mbps in reality.

Exam Prep Practice Questions

Question 1

The IEEE 802 defines Ethernet as which IEEE standard?

- ○ A. 802.3
- ○ B. 802.5
- ○ C. 802.11
- ○ D. 802.9
- ○ E. 802.3ae
- ○ F. 802.11b

Answer: **A.** The 802.3 IEEE standard describes Ethernet and CSMA/CD.

Question 2

What does *UTP* stand for?

- ○ A. Unknown twisted pair
- ○ B. Unusual twisted pair
- ○ C. Unshielded twisted pair
- ○ D. Usual token protocol

Answer: **C.** UTP, or unshielded twisted pair, is the term used to describe Category 3, 5, 6, and 7 cabling made without shielding.

Question 3

What is the minimum frame size for an Ethernet Frame?

- ○ A. 45 bytes
- ○ B. 100 bytes
- ○ C. 48 bytes
- ○ D. 64 bytes
- ○ E. 12 bytes
- ○ F. 1518 bytes

Answer: **D.** The minimum frame size for Ethernet is 64 bytes.

Question 4

Ethernet LAN technology employs which protocol to detect collisions in LAN transmissions?

- O A. FDDI
- O B. CSMA/CD
- O C. CSMA
- O D. RIP
- O E. BGP

Answers: **B.** Ethernet technology employs the Carrier Sense Multiple Access with Collision Detection protocol (CSMA/CD).

Question 5

Token Ring uses a _____ to pass a stream of data in a network.

- O A. Full duplex
- O B. Broadcast
- O C. Baton
- O D. Token
- O E. Terabit
- O F. CSMA/CD

Answer: **D.** Token Ring uses a token to circulate the ring, and stations wait for the token in order to transmit data. If the token is busy, stations must wait until the token is free.

Question 6

When segmenting a LAN, what device reduces the size of a broadcast domain?

- O A. Hub
- O B. Layer 2 Switch
- O C. Layer 3 Router
- O D. LAN Extender
- O E. Bridge

Answer: **C.** A router can reduce the size of the broadcast domain because routers create a smaller network, thus creating a smaller broadcast domain.

Some switches use Virtual LANs at Layer 3 to create smaller broadcast domains as well.

Question 7

> When segmenting a LAN, what device cannot be used to reduce the collision domain?
>
> O a. Bridge
> O b. Switch
> O c. Hub
> O d. Router

Answer: **C.** A hub can't reduce the size of the collision domain because hubs use a shared environment.

Question 8

> Token Ring employs this mechanism for detecting and compensating for network faults and multiple tokens in a Token Ring network.
>
> O A. Multicast
> O B. FDDI
> O C. Active monitor
> O D. Ethernet
> O E. MAU
> O F. Token

Answer: **C.** Active monitor is the mechanism for detecting and compensating network faults. One station is selected to be active monitor.

Question 9

> If used to segment the LAN, what device decreases the size of segments and can connect several LANs?
>
> ○ A. Switch
> ○ B. Hub
> ○ C. Bridge
> ○ D. Router
> ○ E. FDDI
> ○ F. Token Ring

Answer: **C.** A bridge will decrease the size of the segment and can connect several LANs.

Question 10

> A _____ copies and sends a transmission to every destination node on the network.
>
> ○ A. Unicast
> ○ B. Broadcast
> ○ C. Full duplex
> ○ D. FDDI
> ○ E. Multicast

Answer: **B.** A broadcast sends a copy of a transmission to all nodes on the network.

Need to Know More?

 Spurgeon, Charles E. *Ethernet, The Definitive Guide*. O'Reilly & Associates, 2000. ISBN: 1565926609.

 Nassar, Daniel J. *Ethernet and Token Ring Optimization*. iUniverse.com, 2000. ISBN: 1583482199.

 McDysan, David E. and Darren L. Spohn. *ATM Theory and Applications*, McGraw-Hill Osborne Media, 1998. ISBN: 0070453462

 Cisco CCO Web site, Ethernet Protocols, `http://www.cisco.com/ en/US/customer/tech/tk389/tk214/tech_protocols_list.html`

4

Troubleshooting TCP/IP

. . . .

Terms you'll need to understand:

✓ Address Resolution Protocol (ARP)
✓ IP address
✓ Transmission Control Protocol (TCP)
✓ User Datagram Protocol (UDP)
✓ Well-known Port Numbers
✓ Ephemeral Port Numbers

Techniques you'll need to master:

✓ ICMP Protocol Commands and the meanings of the characters displayed by the trace command output
✓ How to find the valid subnets, valid hosts, and the broadcast address for each subnet
✓ **show ip** commands and syntaxes
✓ How and when to use Debug ip commands

TCP/IP (*Transmission Control Protocol/Internet Protocol*) addressing is the foundation of almost every modern network today. IP Addresses are used to route data across the Internet and the world. Virtually every PC connected to the Internet is assigned an IP address; even the Palm Pilot I have in my backpack has an IP address. Although you can use a number of other protocols on your Cisco router, most likely it is TCP/IP problems you will face when troubleshooting your Cisco router or switch problems.

This chapter begins with an overview of the TCP/IP suite and its applications, and follows with troubleshooting issues regarding those protocols. The LAN protocols covered in the Support Exam include TCP/IP and Novell IPX. The following sections give an overview of the TCP/IP protocol and what you need to know for the exam to troubleshoot this protocol suite.

This chapter covers a great deal of information, and it's critically important in your preparation for the CCNP Exam. You can expect that what you learn in this chapter will account for twenty five percent or more of the exam.

TCP/IP Overview

The name TCP/IP represents a suite of protocols designed for wide area networks (WANs). The U.S. Department of Defense Advanced Research Projects Agency began development of TCP/IP in 1969 for a resource-sharing experiment called ARPANET. The primary purpose behind the project was to provide high-speed communication to various government agencies. TCP/IP provides communication in heterogeneous environments. TCP is a connection-oriented protocol found at the Host-to-Host layer of the DoD (Department of Defense) Reference model. This protocol verifies the receipt of sent packets with acknowledgement packets. The IP address is a network address assigned to a node on a network to allow it to send and receive packets through an IP based network.

You should have already learned the basics of the DoD Reference model while studying for the CCNA Exam, which is a prerequisite to the Support exam. On the CCNP exam, you are expected to know how to troubleshoot TCP/IP. This means you need to have a good understanding of the differences between *UDP (User Datagram Protocol)* and TCP, and *ARP (Address Resolution Protocol)*. The following sections provide an overview of this information. You also must understand subnetting and know the commands used on a Cisco router to configure and troubleshoot TCP/IP and its related protocols, as described in later sections of the chapter.

DoD Model

In previous chapters, we have discussed the seven layers of the OSI Reference model. The DoD model, with four layers, is a condensed version of the OSI Reference Model's seven layers (see Figure 4.1). These four layers of the DoD model are as follows:

➤ The Application layer, sometimes called the Process layer

➤ The Host-to-Host layer

➤ The Internet layer

➤ The Network Access layer.

These layers match up to the OSI Reference Layer as shown in Figure 4.1.

Layer	OSI Reference Model	DoD Reference Model
7	Application	Application/Process Layer FTP
6	Presentation	TELNET SMTP
5	Session	SNMP
4	Transport	Host to Host Layer TCP UDP
3	Network	Internetwork Layer IP ICMP
2	Data Link	Network Layer ARP/RARP
1	Physical	

Figure 4.1   The four-layer DoD Model compared to the seven-layer OSI Reference Model.

IP is a routed protocol using Layer 3 addresses with hierarchical addressing to get data from one point to another. Routers also use routing protocols to help map the network so the router knows where different networks reside. Although these protocols work with TCP/IP, they are covered later in this book.

TCP Versus UDP

Let's start with Transmission Control Protocol (TCP) which, in combination with UDP, is defined at the DoD model's Host-To-Host layer. TCP is a reliable, connection-oriented transfer protocol residing at the Transport layer of the OSI model. TCP breaks down large blocks of data into segments; it numbers and sequences the segments so that they can be reassembled by TCP running at the receiving end. Before a device starts transmitting information, it contacts the TCP protocol of the receiving host and establishes a connection. After this virtual circuit is established, both parties start negotiating the reliability factors, such as the amount of data that will be sent before receiving an acknowledgement from the destination host's TCP protocol. After sending the agreed-upon number of segments, TCP waits for the acknowledgement that states the segments have arrived and are intact. Missing segments (by number) will be re-sent.

All of this error-checking and re-sending (if necessary) causes this full-duplex transport protocol to have a large overhead; therefore, TCP should not be used for transmissions such as broadcasts, that don't require an acknowledgement. If every broadcast received were acknowledged back to the sender, the network would be clogged very quickly. Today's networks are much more reliable than networks used to be, which means the use of acknowledgements is not as important.

UDP is an unreliable, connectionless transport protocol running on top of IP. It does not make a connection with the destination host before it delivers a datagram, nor does it require an acknowledgement that the message has been received at the other end (the message may get lost). UDP receives blocks of data from the upper layers and breaks them down into segments, numbering them for reassembly. However, UDP itself is not responsible for putting the segments back into sequence. UDP simply leaves this task to the upper layers.

TCP Port Numbers

TCP uses port numbers to identify connections to hosts. TCP has what are known as *well-known port numbers* from 1 through 1023. Well-known port numbers are those port numbers assigned to protocols certain applications and services required by TCP/IP. Some good examples of TCP port numbers are port 80 for World Wide Web (WWW) browser access, ports 20 and 21 for File Transfer Protocol (FTP), port 25 for Simple Mail Transfer Protocol (SMTP), and port 23 for Telnet.

Ephemeral port numbers are known as ports that can be used as *host ports* and are selected for a particular connection on a temporary basis. These ports are reused after the connection is freed. These ports typically are numbered higher than the well-known port numbers, but not always. When the host tries to initiate the connection to the server, the host uses an ephemeral port. The host and the server will continue to exchange data on these two ports for the entirety of their session. If you are using TCP/IP for your connection to the Internet, your host connection will use this combination of source IP address and source port to connect to the destination IP address and destination port.

You may find many other connections originating from other source IP addresses to this same destination IP and destination port, but that host will have a different source IP address and probably a different source port. When you open two different Internet windows on the same host connecting to the same Web server, the ephemeral source ports involved keep the communications separated.

Troubleshooting and Configuring Address Resolution Protocol (ARP)

ARP is used by the Cisco IOS software to provide dynamic mapping of 32-bit IP addresses and 48-bit MAC (hardware) addresses. The *ARP cache* is a table of these listings and is checked every time communication is initiated between machines (you learn more about the ARP cache and its purpose in the later section of this chapter titled "show ip arp Command"). If the required hardware address cannot be found in the cache, a broadcast is sent out to resolve it. The broadcast address (FFFFFFFF) is already stored, although not visible in the table. After the previously unknown address is found, it is entered in the cache and is readily available the next time around. No broadcast will be necessary, which saves bandwidth. Every listing in the cache has a timestamp and a *time-to-live (TTL)*. When this time expires, the entry is deleted from the table.

Sometimes you may find the need to *statically define* an ARP cache. This means that you are making permanent entries to the table of listings. You can do so globally by using the arp ip-address hardware-address type command. The router will then use the entries you've added to resolve the IP address to the associated hardware address. Let's walk through the process of using this command and the options available for each syntax.

First, type the `arp` command followed by a question mark, which will display the possible syntaxes. The question mark tells the router that you would like a list of the available syntaxes:

```
RTR(config)#arp ?
  A.B.C.D  IP address of ARP entry
  vrf      Configure static ARP for a VPN Routing/Forwarding instance
```

The output above shows the required syntaxes available for the `arp` command. Next, type in the IP address that you want to map, followed by a question mark (used to find out the next syntax to enter):

```
RTR(config)#arp 10.1.1.1 ?
  H.H.H  48-bit hardware address of ARP entry
RTR(config)#arp 10.1.1.1  0000.8029.5981 ?
  arpa    ARP type ARPA
  sap     ARP type SAP (HP's ARP type)
  smds    ARP type SMDS
  snap    ARP type SNAP (FDDI and TokenRing)
  srp-a   ARP type SRP (side A)
  srp-b   ARP type SRP (side B)
```

The output above shows the available syntaxes for the `arp 10.1.1.1` command. Now, statically map the IP address of 10.1.1.1 to the MAC address of 0000.8029.5981 and put in the interface type. Then, use the question mark again to ask the router for the available syntaxes:

```
RTR(config)#arp 10.1.1.1 0000.8029.5981 arpa ?
  Async             Async interface
  BVI               Bridge-Group Virtual Interface
  CTunnel           CTunnel interface
  Dialer            Dialer interface
  Ethernet          IEEE 802.3
  FastEthernet      FastEthernet IEEE 802.3
  Lex               Lex interface
  Loopback          Loopback interface
  MFR               Multilink Frame Relay bundle interface
  Multilink         Multilink-group interface
  Null              Null interface
  Tunnel            Tunnel interface
  Vif               PGM Multicast Host interface
  Virtual-Template  Virtual Template interface
  Virtual-TokenRing Virtual TokenRing
  alias             Respond to ARP requests for the IP address
  <cr>
```

The output above shows the available syntaxes for the `arp 10.1.1.1 arpa` command.

The next syntax binds the mapping to the Interface connected to the device by creating a static mapping of the IP address to the MAC address. In this case it is the Fast Ethernet 0 interface.

```
RTR(config)#arp 10.1.1.1 0000.8029.5981 arpa fastEthernet ?
  <0-0>  FastEthernet interface number
```

```
RTR(config)#arp 10.1.1.1 0000.8029.5981 arpa fastEthernet 0
RTR(config)#
```

The above output shows that the IP address was mapped successfully to the network interface using the MAC address of 0000.8029.5981.

To learn the encapsulation type and the current timeout value, you can use the show interfaces command. Here is an example of using the command on a Cisco 1720 router's Ethernet interface:

```
RTR#show interfaces
Ethernet0 is up, line protocol is up
  Hardware is PQUICC Ethernet, address is 0007.eb32.d6a3
                              (bia 0007.eb32.d6a3)
  Internet address is 207.212.78.110/29
  MTU 1500 bytes, BW 10000 Kbit, DLY 1000 usec,
     reliability 255/255, txload 1/255, rxload 1/255
  Encapsulation ARPA, loopback not set
  Keepalive set (10 sec)
  Half-duplex, 10BaseT
  ARP type: ARPA, ARP Timeout 04:00:00
  Last input 00:00:00, output 00:00:00, output hang never
  Last clearing of "show interface" counters never
  Queueing strategy: fifo
  Output queue 0/40, 0 drops; input queue 0/75, 51 drops
  5 minute input rate 12000 bits/sec, 4 packets/sec
  5 minute output rate 2000 bits/sec, 4 packets/sec
     5759966 packets input, 4271546097 bytes, 0 no buffer
     Received 186 broadcasts, 0 runts, 0 giants, 0 throttles
     0 input errors, 0 CRC, 0 frame, 0 overrun, 0 ignored
     0 input packets with dribble condition detected
     5493207 packets output, 775247573 bytes, 0 underruns
     2213 output errors, 3551 collisions, 2 interface resets
     0 babbles, 0 late collision, 0 deferred
     0 lost carrier, 0 no carrier
     0 output buffer failures, 0 output buffers swapped out
```

The above output shows that the interface is up and the layer 3 protocol and addressing assigned to the interface are also working correctly. It also shows that the interface is running at 10Mbps, and that there have been 2,213 output errors, 3,551 collisions, and 2 interface resets.

To see the current view of what is currently in the routers ARP table, use the show arp command. Here is an example of that command used on a Cisco 3725 router:

```
RTR#show arp
Protocol  Address          Age (min)  Hardware Addr   Type  Interface
Internet  10.1.2.10                4  0030.4851.cee0  ARPA  FastEthernet0
Internet  10.1.1.2                 -  0007.eb32.d6a2  ARPA  FastEthernet0
Internet  10.1.1.1                 -  0000.8029.5981  ARPA  FastEthernet0
```

The above output shows that the router is aware of three addresses and all of them are accessible out of the FastEthernet 0 interface.

The show ip arp displays all IP to MAC address entries in the ARP table with a similar output to the show arp command. Let's take a look at the output:

```
RTR#show ip arp
Protocol  Address          Age (min)  Hardware Addr   Type   Interface
Internet  10.1.2.10                2  0030.4851.cee0  ARPA   FastEthernet0
Internet  10.1.2.1                 0  0002.a5ab.06b3  ARPA   FastEthernet0
Internet  10.1.1.2                 -  0007.eb32.d6a2  ARPA   FastEthernet0
Internet  10.1.1.1                 -  0000.8029.5981  ARPA   FastEthernet0
```

The above is similar to the show arp command. However, this time the router knows about four addresses accessible on the FastEthernet 0 interface.

Sometimes the router needs to have the ARP cache cleared in order to rediscover a reconfigured device or to allow for newer devices to enter the cache. Use clear arp-cache to remove all non-static entries from the ARP cache:

```
RTR#clear arp-cache
RTR#
```

Static ARP cache entries are not removed.

IP Addressing and Subnetting

IP addresses are four 8-bit(1 byte) octets that make up a 32-bit address. These addresses are usually shown in a dotted-decimal form, as in 10.1.2.25. These addresses are sometimes shown as hexadecimal or binary addresses as well. But for this exam you will need to be familiar with these addresses in dotted-decimal form.

This hierarchical addressing scheme allows for about 4.3 billion addresses. IP addresses use a hierarchical addressing scheme that is structured by network and host. In larger networks it is structured by network, subnet, and host.

Every device on the same network shares the same network address but a unique host address. In the sample address 207.212.78.106, the network address is 207.212.78 and the device's unique node address is 106.

Classes of networks are created based on different network sizes. Three classes, Classes A, B, and C, are used to address network nodes in today's networks using TCP/IP. Two other classes also exist; Class D is used for Multicast and Class E addresses are used for research and development of the IP protocol and associated applications.

Class A network addresses use only the first octet to assign the network address; the first octet will contain a number between 1 and 126. The three remaining octets are used for the node addressing. Addresses are displayed as network.node.node.node. The address 10.1.1.1 would be an example of a Class A IP address.

> There are several specialized addresses that you should know. The address 127.0.0.1 is reserved for loopback tests, which are used to test connectivity and problems on the local devices interface. The address 0.0.0.0 is used by Cisco routers to designate a default route. The address 255.255.255.255 is used to broadcast to all nodes on the local network. A network broadcast to all the nodes on the Class A network 10.0.0.0 would be addressed as 10.255.255.255.

A Class B network uses the first two octets to assign the network address. The other two octets are used for node addresses. The format of a Class B address is network.network.node.node. The first octet of a Class B address contains a number between 128 through 191; the second octet contains a number between 0 and 255. Some implementations of TCP/IP allow for the use of zero and 255 in the second octet. The IP address 175.1.1.1 is an example of a Class B IP address.

A Class C network address uses the first three octets to identify the network. The first octet contains a value between 192 and 224. The second and third octets can contain any value from 0 to 255. The format of a Class C address is network.network.network.node. An example of a Class C address would be 195.1.1.1.

There has been some disagreement that using 255 or zero is not allowed on the Internet. However, as I point out to my students, if you try pinging the real IP addresses of 207.212.0.1 or 207.212.255.1, both get a reply from valid hosts on the Internet as shown in the output below as an address from pac-bell.net:

```
C:\>tracert 207.212.255.1
Tracing route to 207-212-255-1.ded.pacbell.net [207.212.255.1]
```

The output above shows an example of using Trace Route, an ICMP utility, to verify the route to the IP address of 207.212.255.1.

Subnetting IP

You should have covered subnetting thoroughly in your CCNA book or class. Many mistakes made in networks today involve incorrect subnetting. Why? Because subnetting requires mathematical accuracy.

> You will not need to know how to subnet a Class A network on the exam. Properly troubleshooting a subnetted Class B or Class C network may be on the exam.

Subnet Masks

Every machine on the network must be configured with a minimum of an IP address, a default gateway, and a subnet mask to be able to route data between networks. Subnet masks allow network devices using IP addresses to know which part of the IP address will be used as the network address and which part is used for the host address. Table 4.1 shows the default subnet masks for Classes A, B, and C.

Table 4.1 The Default Subnet Mask for Class A, B, and C Networks	
Class	Default Subnet Mask
Class A	255.0.0.0
Class B	255.255.0.0
Class C	255.255.255.0

Subnetting Class C Network Addresses

When subnetting a Class C network address, only the last 8-bit octet is available for defining the hosts. Subnet bits are read from left to right. A Class C subnet mask would be shown as 255.255.255.x. The x would represent the octet that defines the host. This means the subnet mask can be one of these values, depending on the number of node addresses you need in each subnet:

00000000 = 0 for 254 nodes in each subnet.

10000000 = 128 for 126 nodes in each subnet.

11000000 = 192 for 62 nodes in each subnet.

11100000 = 224 for 30 nodes in each subnet.

11110000 = 240 for 14 nodes in each subnet.

11111000 = 248 for 6 nodes in each subnet.

11111100 = 252 for 2 nodes in each subnet.

11111110 = 254 is not valid for any host addresses.

Because you need at least two bits for defining hosts, the Request For Comments (RFCs) provide a rule that the first subnet mask that you can legally use is 192, and the last one is 252.

The Magic Number

You can use the magic number of 256 to help determine the number of hosts in a subnet, the valid host addresses for each network, or the broadcast address. In the previous section you read about the different subnet masks you can use in a Class C network. If you take the magic number of 256 minus the subnet mask, you produce a numerical value. Subtract from that value the network address (subnet) and broadcast address; the remainder will be available for hosts. For example, if you have a 252 mask, you would subtract the subnet mask number 252 from the magic number 256; the result is the number 4, which is your first subnet. Each subnet after that is formed by doubling the one before it; therefore, the number 8 would be your second subnet, the number 12 would be your third, and so on until you reach the value of the subnet mask of 252. Three numbers separate each of these subnets. The first two numbers following a subnet (in our example, 5 and 6, 9 and 10, and so on) represent the valid hosts. The fourth number—which is the last number before the next subnet address—would be the broadcast address for all the hosts in your subnet. Table 4.2 shows the first three subnet addresses you could calculate based on the previous magic number example. This table should help to clarify any confusion you may have from this paragraph.

Table 4.2 The First Three Subnets using a 255.255.255.252 Mask		
Subnet Address	Valid Hosts	Broadcast Address
4	5, 6	7
8	9, 10	11
12	13, 14	15

To put the magic number into action, consider an example using the network address 207.212.78.x and the 252 subnet mask. If you were to address the hosts in the first network, the hosts addresses would be 207.212.78.5 and 207.212.78.6. A broadcast to the hosts would be addressed as 207.212.78.7.

Class B Subnetting

If you have mastered the Class C network subnetting using the fourth octet, subnetting a class B network using the third octet is relatively easy. Simply take the same magic number 256 and the third octet of the IP address and apply the same process as you used for the Class C network. The only difference is that you now have all the addresses in the fourth octet to use for hosts, and that will be a lot more hosts. A Class B network address has 16 bits available for host addressing. Fourteen bits are available for subnetting, since we must leave at least two bits for host addresses. Let's take a look at the available subnets for a Class B network:

➤ 255.255.128.0

➤ 255.255.192.0

➤ 255.255.224.0

➤ 255.255.240.0

➤ 255.255.248.0

➤ 255.255.252.0

➤ 255.255.254.0

➤ 255.255.255.0

➤ 255.255.255.128

➤ 255.255.255.192

➤ 255.255.255.224

➤ 255.255.255.240

➤ 255.255.255.248

➤ 255.255.255.252

The process for subnetting a Class B network is similar to the process used to subnet Class C networks. Use the same subnet numbers you used with Class C, but add a zero to the network portion and a 255 to the broadcast section in the fourth octet. Table 4.3 shows an example of subnetting using a Class B 255.255.252.0 subnet mask:

Table 4.3 Class B Subnetting for the 255.255.255.252 Mask			
Subnet	First Host	Last Host	Broadcast Address
4.0	4.1	7.254	7.255
8.0	8.1	11.254	11.255

This means if we were using the Class B network of 133.1.x.x, our first host address would be addressed as 133.1.4.1 and the last 133.1.7.254. Broadcasts to the subnet would be addressed to 133.1.7.255.

Configuring IP Addresses on Interfaces

The IP address and subnet mask are required on each network interface in a TCP/IP network. The default gateway is not necessary on a router as it is the default gateway to those switches and devices directly attached to the routers interfaces. A Cisco switch, however, can be configured with a default gateway. The example that follows walks you through configuring an IP address on a Fast Ethernet interface.

When you first connect to the router—whether from a console cable or a Telnet session—you are automatically at the User EXEC level, as indicated by a > symbol. Use the `enable` command to enter the Privilege Exec Mode, which is identified with a # symbol as shown below:

```
RTR>enable
RTR#
```

Privilege Exec mode is where you would use most `show` and `debug` commands for troubleshooting. The User Exec Mode does have a very limited number of `show` commands available. The config terminal commands bring you in to Global Configuration Mode, identified by a `(config)#` added to the router's prompt. Changes made here affect every interface on the router.

```
RTR#config terminal
```

Next we need to go into Interface Configuration Mode. You do this by using the `interface` command, followed by the type of interface, then the number of the interface you need to configure. In this case we are configuring the first of two Fast Ethernet Interfaces. On a Cisco router, the first interface is always identified by a zero, the second a one, and so on.

```
RTR(config)#interface fastethernet0
```

Above we see the command to select the interface. Once in Interface Configuration Mode, you will notice the prompt now shows a `(config-if)#` identifying the new mode. You now need to assign the IP address and subnet mask. To do so, apply the 192.16.1.254 IP address, which becomes the default gateway for the hosts on the network attached to the interface and the Class C subnet mask as shown below.

```
RTR(config-if)#ip address 192.16.1.254 255.255.255.0
```

Above we see the IP address now configured on the interface as 192.16.1.254 with a 24-bit subnet mask. The `no shutdown` command brings up the interface as shown.

```
RTR(config-if)#no shutdown
1w5d: %LINK-5-CHANGED: Interface FastEthernet0,
    changed state to administratively down
1w5d: %LINEPROTO-5-UPDOWN: Line protocol on Interface FastEthernet0,
    changed state to down
1w5d: %LINK-3-UPDOWN: Interface FastEthernet0, changed state to up
1w5d: %LINEPROTO-5-UPDOWN: Line protocol on Interface FastEthernet0,
    changed state to up
```

The output above shows that the IP address configuration was successful, that the interface and the protocols running on the interface have changed states to "up", and that the interface is operating properly.

DNS (Domain Name System)

DNS is a name resolution protocol that converts hostnames to IP addresses, and vice versa. Its structure is that of a hierarchical database, much like the directory structure of a file system. DNS is the reason you don't have to remember the IP address of every Web site. The DNS database consists of the *root domain* (".") residing at the top of the hierarchy, and *top-level domains* directly underneath it (such as .com and .edu). Subdomains follow (*example.com*), which in turn can have other subdomains (*specifics.example.com*). Hostnames are based on this system, where each level is separated by a dot.

DNS servers provide the service for name resolution. When a host needs to resolve a domain name, the DNS server receives a request from the host. If the DNS server has the domain name listed in its table, the server simply replies to the host with the IP address of the domain name. If the domain name is a name outside of your network, the DNS server simply needs to know the address of the root name server on the Internet to which it will forward the request. The root server then filters the request through the appropriate domain beneath it, and so on, until the correct name server is reached and the information about the host is available.

Configuring a Router with DNS Servers

A router can use the services of DNS, as well. Configuring the router with DNS servers is easier than having to set up a table of hostnames. By default, the ip domain lookup command is enabled. When the router can't resolve a hostname, it generates a broadcast to look for a DNS server. This can cost you valuable time when you're in a hurry. To terminate this process rather than wait for the broadcast timeout, you can press Ctrl+Shift+6. When setting up the router to use specific DNS servers for name resolution, use the ip name-server *ip-address* command. In the following example, using a Cisco

3725, we are assigning three DNS servers; you can see that adding a space and an additional DNS server's IP address allows you to add multiple DNS servers:

```
RTR(config)#ip name-server ?
  A.B.C.D     Domain server IP address (maximum of 6)
  X:X:X:X::X  Domain server IP address (maximum of 6)
RTR(config)#ip name-server 206.13.31.12 ?
  A.B.C.D     Domain server IP address (maximum of 6)
  X:X:X:X::X  Domain server IP address (maximum of 6)
  <cr>
RTR(config)#ip name-server 206.13.31.12 206.13.28.12 ?
  A.B.C.D     Domain server IP address (maximum of 6)
  X:X:X:X::X  Domain server IP address (maximum of 6)
  <cr>
RTR(config)#ip name-server 206.13.31.12 206.13.28.12 10.1.2.25
RTR(config)#
```

The above output shows the successful configuration of three DNS servers on the router. The search order for domain name resolutions is the same order that they are entered.

If you decide to use a hostname table, you have to disable the ip domain lookup command by using the no ip domain lookup command. You must then use the ip host hostname ip-address command to build your hostname table. You can have up to eight IP addresses for a hostname. Depending on the size of your network, making all of these entries may take a fair amount of time. To view the hostnames in the table and their corresponding IP addresses, use the show hosts command as shown:

```
RTR#show hosts
Default domain is not set
Name/address lookup uses domain service
Name servers are 206.13.31.12, 206.13.28.12, 10.1.2.25
Codes: u - unknown, e - expired, * - OK, ? - revalidate
       t - temporary, p - permanent
   Host                    Age  Type   Address(es)
*p ns2.cwie.net            **   IP     64.38.192.11
*p ns1.cwie.net            **   IP     64.38.192.10
*t digitalcrawlspaces.com  0    IP     64.38.192.188
*t yahoo.com               0    IP     64.58.79.230  66.218.71.198
RTR#
```

This output shows the known NS resolved hosts in the routers host table.

DNS Caching and Default Gateways

DNS caching saves time and bandwidth and is, therefore, a process of great value. After a DNS server has resolved a name, it stores this mapping in its *cache*, making it available the next time the server receives a query for one of the already stored mappings. This means that if a query for a host address has already been resolved, the mapping is already stored and, thus, a query does not need to be made across the network a second time.

The expiration of an entry is set by the time-to-live (TTL) value, which is entered in the domain Start of Authority (SOA) record. This ensures room for new mappings and updates. Information about a particular name might change if the old mapping stayed in the cache too long. As a result, the DNS server would provide the wrong information when queries are made.

Part of a router's job is to send packets to remote networks. The default gateway is utilized when a host needs to send a packet to a host on a network other than its own, for which the router does not have a specific route in its routing table. This manually entered route is also known as the *gateway of last resort*. If a router has no known route to a destination and no gateway of last resort is configured, the router has no other choice but to drop the packet and notify the sending device that it doesn't know where to send the packet.

Once a packet has been directed to the gateway of last resort, the next router can direct the packet to other gateways, and so on, until it reaches its final destination. The default gateway parameter is an IP address specifying the router interface, on which the gateway is configured.

For hosts to communicate with each other on a TCP/IP network, they have to be configured with several IP addresses, one IP address and subnet mask representing the host itself, a default gateway, DNS servers, and occasionally a Windows Internet Naming Server (WINS). On small networks, having static addresses assigned manually at each workstation or server is no big deal, and coping with those changes on the network that will affect every single machine, such as the default gateway, is relatively easy.

Internet Control Message Protocol (ICMP)

ICMP is one of the most important management protocols and one of the most used in today's TCP/IP networks for troubleshooting problems. ICMP is TCP/IP's delivery service for error messages in the form of IP datagrams. ICMP is even simpler than UDP, because it doesn't contain any port numbers in its header. Port numbers are not needed when directing an ICMP message.

There are many times when a router or switch may need to deliver a message to a sending device in order to deliver bad news. ICMP is used to deliver such messages in the following situations:

➤ If a datagram reaches the maximum number of hops assigned to it before reaching its destination, it will be deleted by the router on its last hop. This router then uses ICMP to send a time-exceeded message informing the sender of the deleted datagram.

NOTE

An in-depth discussion of how ICMP works is found in Chapter 5, "Windows Troubleshooting," under the "Ping Command" section.

➤ When a router receives a datagram with a destination network that is unknown to it—meaning that it is not listed in its routing table—the router will send a message to the sender via ICMP stating "Destination unreachable." In this situation, a default gateway is not configured, as we discussed in the last section.

➤ A router's memory buffer can hold only a certain amount of data, and when this limit is reached, the router uses ICMP to send a source quench message.

Routers advertise addresses of their interfaces periodically with router advertisements. An ICMP router discovery message is independent of a specific routing protocol. Routers become aware of their neighboring routers simply by listening to these advertisements. A router that just started up may also send a router solicitation, which forces immediate router advertisements. Routers that are not being advertised because a link is down will eventually be discovered when the link comes back up, because routers also send unsolicited periodic advertisements.

ping and trace Commands

The `ping` and `trace` commands are tools that use the ICMP protocol to test for node connectivity. These two tools work together. When you suspect there is a problem with a connection, you can ping the IP address of the device to see if that device exists. If you are resolving NetBIOS names or Fully Qualified Domain Names (FQDN), either through a static entry or a configured DNS server, there is a good chance that you can ping the host name or FQDN name in the place of the IP address.

Let's look at the results of trying a ping using an IP address, host name, and an FQDN. We'll also look at an example of a failed ping. This first example is the results of the ping command using an IP address.

```
RTR>enable
Password: ******
```

```
RTR#ping 10.1.2.7
Type escape sequence to abort.
Sending 5, 100-byte ICMP Echos to 10.1.2.7, timeout is 2 seconds:
!!!!!
Success rate is 100 percent (5/5), round-trip min/avg/max = 1/2/4 ms
RTR#
```

The exclamation marks in the preceding example indicate a successful ping. Here's an example of using the Ping command with a FQDN:

```
RTR#ping data6.digitalcrawlspaces.com
Type escape sequence to abort.
Sending 5, 100-byte ICMP Echos to 10.1.2.1, timeout is 2 seconds:
!!!!!
Success rate is 100 percent (5/5), round-trip min/avg/max = 1/1/4 ms
RTR#
```

The above shows an example of pinging the FQDN address of data6.digital-crawlspaces.com, which is a real Web server on the Internet. Next, take a look at an example of a ping using a statically entered host name. In this example, I first configure the host name of DataServer1 in Global Configuration mode before I ping the node.

```
RTR(config)#ip host dataserver1 10.1.2.1 ?
  A.B.C.D  Host IP address
  <cr>
RTR(config)#ip host jtscom1 10.1.2.1
RTR(config)#exit
RTR#ping dataserver1
Type escape sequence to abort.
Sending 5, 100-byte ICMP Echos to 10.1.2.1, timeout is 2 seconds:
!!!!!
Success rate is 100 percent (5/5), round-trip min/avg/max = 1/1/1 ms
RTR#
```

The above shows the hostname of Dataserver1 configured on the router and the process of pinging the address by the host name configured on the router. The ping to Dataserver1 was successful, as shown by the exclamation marks. For the exam you may need to know what a failed ping looks like. Let's take a look at the following output:

```
RTR#ping dataserver1
Translating "dataserver1"...domain server (10.1.2.25) (206.13.31.12)
% Unrecognized host or address, or protocol not running.
RTR#
```

In the output above we see that the router has no listing in its host table and tries contacting the DNS servers configured for a resolution that never came. What happens is resolvable through DNS servers or is listed in the router's host table. Let's look at the output below:

```
RTR#ping dataserver1
Type escape sequence to abort.
Sending 5, 100-byte ICMP Echos to 10.2.2.200, timeout is 2 seconds:
```

. . . . .
```
Success rate is 0 percent (0/5)
RTR#
```

In the output above we see the failure indicated by periods, which indicates 5 attempts to send ICMP packets that failed to return. Successfully pinging a device does not indicate that there is not a problem with the network. The path that a packet takes to its destination may not be the most optimal path. Many times there are more than one path or link to a destination. One may be a high speed link, the other a slower path. Frequently, there are ISDN lines or other more expensive slower links to a destination used as a backup in case the high speed path is not functioning. You may also want to see where a failure occurs in the transit of a packet. The trace command allows you to see each hop to a destination device. This allows you to see the path the ICMP packets take and the latency of the packet in milliseconds. If there is a link down in the path to the destination, the output will stop with the last device that successfully replied with an ICMP reply. Let's take a look at the output from the router.

```
RTR#trace 10.2.2.1
Type escape sequence to abort.
Tracing the route to 10.2.2.1
  1 10.1.1.1 4 msec 4 msec 4 msec
  2 10.2.1.1 4 msec 4 msec 8 msec
  3 10.2.2.1 4 msec 4 msec 4 msec
RTR#
```

The above output was a successful trace to the target IP address. Here is a result of a trace that was able to go one hop to the default gateway but unable to complete the trace after that. The astrisks indicate a failure uncovered by the trace command.

```
RTR#trace 10.4.1.1
Type escape sequence to abort.
Tracing the route to 172.16.50.2
  1 10.1.1.1 4 msec 4 msec 4 msec
  2 * * *
  3 * * *
  ^C
RTR#
```

Notice in the above output that the trace command stopped after the first hop and displayed only asterisks. This is because the trace failed and no reply was sent from the second hop device. For the exam you should know the following characters which may appear in the trace command output:

➤ msec—The round trip time in milliseconds.

➤ *—A timed out request.

➤ ?—An Unknown packet type.

➤ Q—A source quench message was received.

➤ P—The protocol is unreachable.

➤ N—The network is not reachable.

➤ U—The port is not reachable.

➤ H—A designated host is not reachable.

The Default Route

As you learned earlier, the default route is known as the gateway of last resort. This route is normally the address of an organization's core network router or the address out of the network to an Internet router. If a router receives a packet and does not know the route to the packet's destination network, the router has two choices: The router can forward the packet out the interface designated by the default route, or it can drop the packet and notify the source device that the packet could not be delivered.

To see if a default route has been configured, use the show ip route command as shown below.

```
RTR#show ip route
Codes: C - connected, S - static, I - IGRP, R - RIP, M - mobile, B - BGP
       D - EIGRP, EX - EIGRP external, O - OSPF, IA - OSPF inter area
       N1 - OSPF NSSA external type 1, N2 - OSPF NSSA external type 2
       E1 - OSPF external type 1, E2 - OSPF external type 2, E - EGP
       i - IS-IS, L1 - IS-IS level-1, L2 - IS-IS level-2, ia - IS-IS inter area
       * - candidate default, U - per-user static route, o - ODR
       P - periodic downloaded static route
Gateway of last resort is 207.212.78.105 to network 0.0.0.0
     207.212.78.0/29 is subnetted, 1 subnets
C       207.212.78.104 is directly connected, Ethernet0
     10.0.0.0/8 is variably subnetted, 5 subnets, 2 masks
R       10.2.0.0/16 [120/2] via 10.1.1.1, 00:00:10, FastEthernet0
R       10.3.0.0/16 [120/2] via 10.1.1.1, 00:00:10, FastEthernet0
C       10.1.0.0/16 is directly connected, FastEthernet0
R       10.4.0.0/16 [120/3] via 10.1.1.1, 00:00:10, FastEthernet0
S       10.1.2.25/32 is directly connected, FastEthernet0
C    192.168.1.0/24 is directly connected, Loopback0
S*   0.0.0.0/0 [1/0] via 207.212.78.105
RTR#
```

Notice the two lines in bold in the above output which show the gateway of last resort. The route shows up as both a static route and as the gateway of last resort. Now let's look at the same router with the gateway of last resort not configured as shown in the following output.

```
RTR#show ip route
Codes: C - connected, S - static, I - IGRP, R - RIP, M - mobile, B - BGP
   D - EIGRP, EX - EIGRP external, O - OSPF, IA - OSPF inter area
   N1 - OSPF NSSA external type 1, N2 - OSPF NSSA external type 2
   E1 - OSPF external type 1, E2 - OSPF external type 2, E - EGP
   i - IS-IS, L1 - IS-IS level-1, L2 - IS-IS level-2, ia - IS-IS inter area
   * - candidate default, U - per-user static route, o - ODR
   P - periodic downloaded static route
Gateway of last resort is not set
     207.212.78.0/29 is subnetted, 1 subnets
C       207.212.78.104 is directly connected, Ethernet0
     10.0.0.0/8 is variably subnetted, 5 subnets, 2 masks
R       10.2.0.0/16 [120/2] via 10.1.1.1, 00:00:10, FastEthernet0
R       10.3.0.0/16 [120/2] via 10.1.1.1, 00:00:10, FastEthernet0
C       10.1.0.0/16 is directly connected, FastEthernet0
R       10.4.0.0/16 [120/3] via 10.1.1.1, 00:00:10, FastEthernet0
S       10.1.2.25/32 is directly connected, FastEthernet0
C    192.168.1.0/24 is directly connected, Loopback0
RTR#
```

If you need to configure the Gateway of Last Resort, use the `ip route` command as shown below. In this example, the IP address 207.212.78.254 is the router belonging to the ISP. The 0.0.0.0 0.0.0.0 IP address indicates to the router that if the routing table doesn't list any IP address with any subnet mask, the router is to forward the packet to that IP address. That action signals the end of the router's responsibility for routing the packet.

```
RTR#ip route 0.0.0.0 0.0.0.0 207.212.78.254
RTR#
```

Show Commands for Troubleshooting TCP/IP

For the exam you should know the `show` commands that you can use to troubleshoot problems with TCP/IP. You should know the following commands:

➤ show ip access-list

➤ show ip arp

➤ show controllers

➤ show ip interface

➤ show ip protocols

➤ show ip route

➤ show ip traffic

The following sections explain the use of these commands.

show ip access-list Command

The show ip access-list command provides information regarding a specific access list or all standard or extended access lists. In the following example, we look at an extended access list from a Cisco 3725 router.

```
RTR#show ip access-lists 101
Extended IP access list 101
    deny ip 10.1.0.0 0.0.255.255 216.136.0.0 0.0.255.255 (4042 matches)
    deny ip host 10.1.4.200 66.163.0.0 0.0.255.255 (9 matches)
    deny ip host 10.1.4.200 64.58.0.0 0.0.255.255 (95 matches)
    deny ip host 10.1.4.200 204.71.0.0 0.0.255.255
    deny tcp any any eq www
    deny tcp any any eq 5418 (5 matches)
    permit ip any any (560764 matches)
```

The output above shows an IP extended access list numbered 101, configured on a Cisco 3725.

show ip arp Command

The show ip arp command provides information from the router's ARP cache. The ARP cache is responsible for keeping records of the known IP addresses and their learned MAC address. The ARP cache also keeps information on the encapsulation type, as well as the interface that learned the MAC to IP information. The following is an example of the ARP cache from a Cisco 1720.

```
RTR#show ip arp
Protocol  Address       Age (min)  Hardware Addr   Type   Interface
Internet  10.1.2.10          0     0030.4851.cee0  ARPA   FastEthernet0
Internet  10.1.1.2           -     0007.eb32.d6a2  ARPA   FastEthernet0
Internet  10.1.2.1           0     0002.a5ab.06b3  ARPA   FastEthernet0
Internet  10.1.1.1          24     0000.8029.5981  ARPA   FastEthernet0
```

show controllers Command

The show controllers command's output shows the current state of the network's physical interface. This includes the number of transmitting errors and collisions. The following output is from a Cisco 1720 router's Fast Ethernet interface.

```
RTR#show controllers fa0
Interface FastEthernet0
Hardware is PQUICC MPC855T ADDR: 8130A608, FASTSEND: 800117F8
DIST ROUTE ENABLED: 0
Route Cache Flag: 0
 ADDR_LOW =0x0007EB32, ADDR_HIGH =0x0000D6A2,
                HASH_HIGH =0x00200100, HASH_LOW =0
x00000000
```

```
 R_DES_ST  =0x01C4AB20, X_DES_ST  =0x01C4AD60,
                        R_BUFF_SIZ=0x00000600, ECNTRL   =0
xF0000006
 IEVENT   =0x00000000, IMASK     =0x0A000000,
                        IVEC      =0xC0000000, R_DES_ACT=0
x01000000
 X_DES_ACT=0x00000000, MII_DATA  =0x60524732,
                        MII_SPEED =0x00000014, R_BOUND  =0
x00000600
 R_FSTART =0x00000500, X_FSTART  =0x00000440,
                        FUN_CODE  =0x7F000000, R_CNTRL  =0
x00000006
 R_HASH   =0xEF0005F2
 X_CNTRL  =0x00000000
HW filtering information:
 Promiscuous Mode Disabled
Software MAC address filter(hash:length/addr/mask/hits):
pquicc_fec_instance=0x8130C318
rx ring entries=64, tx ring entries=32
rxring=0x1C4AB20, rxr shadow=0x8130C508, rx_head=27, rx_tail=0
txring=0x1C4AD60, txr shadow=0x8130C634, tx_head=2, tx_tail=2, tx_count=0
throttled=0, enabled=0, disabled=0
rx_framing_err=0, rx_overflow_err=0, rx_buffer_err=0
rx_no_enp=0, rx_discard=0
tx_one_col_err=41336, tx_more_col_err=84470, tx_no_enp=0, tx_deferred_err=0
tx_underrun_err=0, tx_late_collision_err=0, tx_loss_carrier_err=7
tx_exc_collision_err=0, tx_buff_err=0, fatal_tx_err=0
...Output cut off
```

 The output for the **show controllers** command is low-level memory information and error counters for every interface processor. Usually this output is only requested when receiving technical support from Cisco, where configuration settings for the IOS iteslf are neded.

show ip interface Command

The show ip interface command provides information on the selected interfaces status, the IP address configured, the subnet mask, broadcast address, any access lists that are applied to an interface, and any interface-specific rules configured on the network. If you do not specify an interface, all the interfaces on the router are displayed. The following output is from a Cisco 1720 router's Fast Ethernet interface.

```
RTR#show ip interface fa0
FastEthernet0 is up, line protocol is up
  Internet address is 10.1.1.2/16
  Broadcast address is 255.255.255.255
  Address determined by non-volatile memory
  MTU is 1500 bytes
  Helper address is not set
  Directed broadcast forwarding is disabled
  Multicast reserved groups joined: 224.0.0.9
  Outgoing access list is not set
  Inbound  access list is not set
```

```
Proxy ARP is enabled
Security level is default
Split horizon is enabled
ICMP redirects are always sent
ICMP unreachables are always sent
ICMP mask replies are never sent
IP fast switching is disabled
IP fast switching on the same interface is disabled
IP Flow switching is disabled
IP Null turbo vector
IP multicast fast switching is disabled
IP multicast distributed fast switching is disabled
IP route-cache flags are None
Router Discovery is disabled
IP output packet accounting is disabled
IP access violation accounting is disabled
TCP/IP header compression is disabled
RTP/IP header compression is disabled
Probe proxy name replies are disabled
Policy routing is disabled
Network address translation is enabled, interface in domain inside
WCCP Redirect outbound is disabled
WCCP Redirect inbound is disabled
WCCP Redirect exclude is disabled
BGP Policy Mapping is disabled
RTR#
```

The above output shows the Fast Ethernet 0 interface's configuration on a
Cisco 3725 router that is functioning correctly.

show ip protocols

You need to remember that the show ip protocols command provides information about the IP routing protocols that run on the router. The following
output shows Routing Information Protocol (RIP), which is the routing protocol configured on the Cisco 1720 router this output came from.

```
RTR#show ip protocols
Routing Protocol is "rip"
  Sending updates every 30 seconds, next due in 16 seconds
  Invalid after 180 seconds, hold down 180, flushed after 240
  Outgoing update filter list for all interfaces is not set
  Incoming update filter list for all interfaces is not set
  Redistributing: rip
  Default version control: send version 1, receive version 1
    Interface          Send  Recv  Triggered RIP  Key-chain
    Ethernet0           1     1
    FastEthernet0       1     1
  Automatic network summarization is in effect
  Maximum path: 4
  Routing for Networks:
    10.0.0.0
    207.212.78.0
  Routing Information Sources:
    Gateway         Distance       Last Update
    10.1.1.1            120         00:00:03
  Distance: (default is 120)
```

The above output shows the interfaces and protocols that are running on the Cisco 1710 router. Also shown are the networks for which the router's routing protocols are configured and the default gateway used for unknown hosts.

show ip route Command

The show ip route command displays information from the router's IP route table. The command shows all routes the router's routing table contains.

```
RTR#show ip route
Codes: C - connected, S - static, I - IGRP, R - RIP, M - mobile, B - BGP
   D - EIGRP, EX - EIGRP external, O - OSPF, IA - OSPF     inter area
   N1 - OSPF NSSA external type 1, N2 - OSPF NSSA     external type 2
   E1 - OSPF external type 1, E2 - OSPF external type 2,     E - EGP
   i - IS-IS, L1 - IS-IS level-1, L2 - IS-IS level-2, * -candidate default
U - per-user static route, o - ODR
Gateway of last resort is not set
     10.0.0.0/0 is variably subnetted, 2 subnets, 2 masks
D       10.1.0.0/16 [90/6541002] via 10.1.1.1, 00:00:23, Serial0
C       10.2.0.0/16 is directly connected, Serial1
RTR#
```

The above output shows all the routers that are manually configured or that the router has learned about. When a network is specified, the results of the show ip route command are displayed in more detail. The following output is from the same router, with the same configuration as the original output, but results from using the command with a specified network.

```
RTR#show ip route 10.0.0.0
Routing entry for 10.0.0.0/8, 5 known subnets
  Attached (2 connections)
  Variably subnetted with 2 masks
  Redistributing via rip
R       10.2.0.0/16 [120/2] via 10.1.1.1, 00:00:11, FastEthernet0
R       10.3.0.0/16 [120/2] via 10.1.1.1, 00:00:11, FastEthernet0
C       10.1.0.0/16 is directly connected, FastEthernet0
R       10.4.0.0/16 [120/3] via 10.1.1.1, 00:00:11, FastEthernet0
S       10.1.2.25/32 is directly connected, FastEthernet0
RTR#
```

Notice that the output above only shows the addresses learned or manually configured for the 10.0.0.0 network. The "S" character shows that the route is a static route, meaning it was manually configured.

You should know how to properly configure a static route as well as the gateway of last resort. This is covered in Chapter 11, " Troubleshooting Routing Protocols," in the section called "Static Routes."

show ip traffic Command

The show ip traffic command returns output regarding the router's IP traffic statistics, as sequenced by IP protocol. The following is output from a Cisco 1720 production router at Digital Crawl Spaces.

```
RTR#show ip traffic
IP statistics:
  Rcvd:  7549856 total, 67433 local destination
         0 format errors, 0 checksum errors, 0 bad hop count
         13 unknown protocol, 0 not a gateway
         0 security failures, 0 bad options, 13 with options
  Opts:  0 end, 0 nop, 0 basic security, 0 loose source route
         0 timestamp, 0 extended security, 0 record route
         0 stream ID, 0 strict source route, 13 alert, 0 cipso, 0 ump
         0 other
  Frags: 12 reassembled, 0 timeouts, 0 couldn't reassemble
         36 fragmented, 0 couldn't fragment
  Bcast: 62529 received, 26572 sent
  Mcast: 80 received, 0 sent
  Sent:  35930 generated, 7455695 forwarded
  Drop:  337 encapsulation failed, 0 unresolved, 0 no adjacency
         12 no route, 0 unicast RPF, 0 forced drop
ICMP statistics:
  Rcvd: 0 format errors, 0 checksum errors, 0 redirects, 8 unreachable
        481 echo, 5 echo reply, 0 mask requests, 0 mask replies, 0 quench
        0 parameter, 0 timestamp, 0 info request, 0 other
        0 irdp solicitations, 765 irdp advertisements
  Sent: 9 redirects, 7079 unreachable, 5 echo, 481 echo reply
        0 mask requests, 0 mask replies, 0 quench, 0 timestamp
        0 info reply, 0 time exceeded, 0 parameter problem
        0 irdp solicitations, 0 irdp advertisements
IGRP statistics:
  Rcvd: 0 total, 0 checksum errors
  Sent: 0 total
IP-IGRP2 statistics:
  Rcvd: 0 total
  Sent: 0 total
UDP statistics:
  Rcvd: 64118 total, 0 checksum errors, 64019 no port
  Sent: 26617 total, 0 forwarded broadcasts
TCP statistics:
  Rcvd: 2040 total, 0 checksum errors, 221 no port
  Sent: 1745 total
Probe statistics:
  Rcvd: 0 address requests, 0 address replies
        0 proxy name requests, 0 where-is requests, 0 other
  Sent: 0 address requests, 0 address replies (0 proxy)
        0 proxy name replies, 0 where-is replies
OSPF statistics:
  Rcvd: 0 total, 0 checksum errors
        0 hello, 0 database desc, 0 link state req
        0 link state updates, 0 link state acks
  Sent: 0 total
PIMv2 statistics: Sent/Received
  Total: 0/0, 0 checksum errors, 0 format errors
  Registers: 0/0, Register Stops: 0/0,  Hellos: 0/0
  Join/Prunes: 0/0, Asserts: 0/0, grafts: 0/0
  Bootstraps: 0/0, Candidate_RP_Advertisements: 0/0
```

```
  State-Refresh: 0/0
IGMP statistics: Sent/Received
  Total: 0/0, Format errors: 0/0, Checksum errors: 0/0
  Host Queries: 0/0, Host Reports: 0/0, Host Leaves: 0/0
  DVMRP: 0/0, PIM: 0/0
ARP statistics:
  Rcvd: 136349 requests, 264 replies, 2 reverse, 0 other
  Sent: 785 requests, 5953 replies (78 proxy), 0 reverse
RTR#
```

The above output is great when you need general information for the IP protocols running on the router. Its provided statistics include the ARP and ICMP protocol statistics, as well.

IP debug Commands

Debug commands can be used to provide you with a great deal of troubleshooting information. Using these commands comes at a price, namely the loss of processing power on the router. By using debug commands you can actually make the router so slow that no data is routed through the network. These commands should be used as a last-resort troubleshooting tool and not for monitoring day-to-day operations. The following output from a Cisco 1720 shows all of the syntaxes available to the debug ip command.

```
RTR#debug ip ?
  audit        IDS audit events
  auth-proxy   Authentication proxy debug
  bgp          BGP information
  cache        IP cache operations
  cef          IP CEF operations
  cgmp         CGMP protocol activity
  dhcp         Dynamic Host Configuration Protocol
  dvmrp        DVMRP protocol activity
  eigrp        IP-EIGRP information
  error        IP error debugging
  flow         IP Flow switching operations
  ftp          FTP dialogue
  html         HTML connections
  http         HTTP connections
  icmp         ICMP transactions
  igmp         IGMP protocol activity
  igrp         IGRP information
  inspect      Stateful inspection events
  interface    IP interface configuration changes
  mbgp         MBGP information
  mcache       IP multicast cache operations
  mhbeat       IP multicast heartbeat monitoring
  mpacket      IP multicast packet debugging
  mrm          IP Multicast Routing Monitor
  mrouting     IP multicast routing table activity
  msdp         Multicast Source Discovery Protocol (MSDP)
  mtag         IP multicast tagswitching activity
  nat          NAT events
```

```
nbar        StILE - traffic classification Engine
ospf        OSPF information
packet      General IP debugging and IPSO security transactions
peer        IP peer address activity
pgm         PGM Reliable Transport Protocol
pim         PIM protocol activity
policy      Policy routing
postoffice  PostOffice audit events
rgmp        RGMP protocol activity
rip         RIP protocol transactions
routing     Routing table events
rsvp        RSVP protocol activity
rtp         RTP information
scp         Secure Copy
sd          Session Directory (SD)
security    IP security options
socket      Socket event
ssh         Incoming ssh connections
tcp         TCP information
tempacl     IP temporary ACL
udp         UDP based transactions
urd         URL RenDezvous (URD)
wccp        WCCP information
```

Although there are many syntaxes for the `debug ip` command, the most important syntaxes used for troubleshooting TCP/IP are shown in Table 4.4.

> **NOTE**
>
> The **debug ip** commands related to routing protocols will be discussed in Chapter 11.

Table 4.4	Important IP Debug Syntaxes to Know
Syntax	**Description**
arp	IP ARP and HP Probe transactions
cache	IP cache debugging
error	IP error debugging
flow	IP flow switching operations
ftp	FTP operations debugging
http	HTTP connection debugging
icmp	ICMP debugging
igmp	Internet Group Management Protocol debugging
igrp	Internet Gateway Routing Protocol debugging
mcache	IP multicast cache debugging
mds	IP distributed multicast debugging

(continued)

Table 4.4 Important IP Debug Syntaxes to Know *(continued)*	
mobile	Mobility protocols debugging
mpacket	IP multicast packet debugging
mrouting	IP multicast routing table activity
msdp	Multicast Source Discovery Protocol (MSDP) debugging
mtag	IP multicast tag switching activity
nat	Network Address Translation debugging
packet	IP debugging and security debugging
peer	IP peer address activity
pim	Protocol Independent Multicast debugging
policy	Policy routing debugging
sd	Session Directory (SD) debugging
security	IP security debugging
socket	Socket event debugging
tcp	TCP information debugging
udp	UDP information debugging

The **debug ip packets** command provides an option for an access list to narrow the scope of information this command provides. In order to properly use the **debug ip packets** command, the packets must be process-switched. All other switching types must be turned off.

Configuring DHCP and the IP Helper Command

On a large network, keeping up with network changes and the necessary manual configurations creates a lot of work for the administrator. Many administrators don't realize that their Cisco routers can also be DHCP servers and distribute and track host addressing.

Manually configuring host IP information and changes is time-consuming and potentially prone to errors. If the network changes frequently and has limited address space, assigning a static address to a machine that accesses the network infrequently, such as a remote user's laptop or workstation that is used only a few hours a day, is a waste of time.

This is where a DHCP server works well in the network. DHCP is a protocol developed from BOOTP (Boot Protocol), with a few modifications, such as the BOOTP relay agent. BOOTP was used (or may still be used) to allow diskless workstations to be configured with the necessary TCP/IP parameters to communicate on the network. DHCP dynamically assigns the IP address, subnet mask, DNS server, and WINS information. All information is only valid until the lease time assigned by an administrator expires or the host is manually released before the expiration period.

It is not necessary to have a DHCP server on each subnet, because DHCP can work across Cisco routers (as discussed in the next section of this chapter), or function with the help of BOOTP relay agents that listen to the DHCP messages and then forward them. Certain addresses have to remain the same with every reboot of a host and thus need to be configured as *address reservations* on the DHCP server. This ensures the correct address assignment for default gateways, DNS servers, and so forth.

In Global Configurations mode on a Cisco router, you can configure DHCP. The following is an example of a configuration on a Cisco 1720 using the IP-PLUS version of the Cisco IOS.

```
RTR(config)#ip dhcp pool 0
RTR(config)#network 10.1.0.0 /16
RTR(config)#domain-name digitalcrawlspaces.com
RTR(config)#dns-server 206.13.31.12 10.1.2.25
RTR(config)#default-router 10.1.1.1
RTR(config)#netbios-name-server 10.1.2.1 10.2.2.3
RTR(config)#netbios-node-type h-node
RTR(config)#lease 30
RTR(config)#ip dhcp excluded-address 10.1.2.1 10.1.2.25
```

The output above will successfully configure DHCP on the router. It will begin distributing IP addresses for any DHCP requests that come in on the interface configured for the same subnet that was configured with the network command. For security purposes you may want to create a *manual binding* for a DHCP client. With a manual binding in place, the NIC card must have the specified MAC address before it can receive a DHCP configuration. Let's look at an example of binding an IP address with a MAC address:

```
RTR(config)#ip dhcp pool Sean
RTR(config)#host 10.1.2.99
RTR(config)#hardware-address 1c33.ab45.89cd ieee802
RTR(config)#client-name SeansLaptop
```

The above output shows that the IP address 10.1.2.99 will be assigned to the client each time using the 1c33.ab45.89cd MAC address. In a network environment, routers are commonly placed between two segments to prevent broadcasts from being forwarded between them. This design keeps local traffic local on the network segment and forwards only unicast traffic. When a DHCP server and DHCP client are implemented into a network, all requests are broadcast within that segment. But what happens if you have a client in a different segment of the network that needs access to its resources? How do you allow DHCP to send broadcasts across the router and still keep other broadcasts local on the segment?

IP Helper Addresses

The *IP Helper Address* is a specialized address-translation command that converts broadcast messages into directed broadcast or unicast messages. The `ip helper-address` command is used on a router to instruct the router to convert the messages accordingly.

If the IP Helper Address is specified and UDP forwarding is enabled, broadcast packets destined for the following eight protocols and their associated port numbers are forwarded by default:

➤ TFTP (port 69)

➤ DNS (port 53)

➤ Time (port 37)

➤ TACACS (Terminal Access Controller Access Control System) (port 49)

➤ BOOTP client (port 68)

➤ BOOTP server (port 67)

➤ NetBIOS name server (port 137)

➤ NetBIOS datagram service (port 138)

If only one server is located on a remote segment, the IP Helper Address is configured with the address of that server. Any broadcast traffic of the type just listed is forwarded to that server. If several servers are located on a remote segment, the IP Helper Address is configured with the broadcast address for that segment. Broadcast traffic of the type in the preceding list is sent in the form of a directed broadcast to all the servers on the segment. This helps in many ways. For example, let's say that you have a DHCP server distributing addresses in a remote segment. The broadcast forwarding from that server will allow clients on the remote segment to obtain the DHCP information to configure their machine.

Before you use this setting, make sure you consider all the other broadcast issues you might unleash on your network. Just imagine what the impact would be if you were to have 30 subnets' worth of broadcast traffic hitting the same segment.

Chapter Summary

This chapter has offered a lot to learn, but the information covered here is among the most important you'll need to know if you are to pass the exam. You can expect that what you learned in this chapter will account for twenty five percent or more of the exam. From this chapter you should have learned about the DoD Reference model, which is a four-layer model that parallels the seven levels in the OSI Reference model.

This chapter also covered almost every aspect of configuring TCP/IP networks on a Cisco router. You learned everything from the basic steps for configuring an IP address on an interface, to how to configure a Gateway of Last Resort, to how to work with DNS servers, to how to subnet IP addresses, and how to configure DHCP server services on a router.

You need to remember the TCP/IP diagnostic commands, such as `ping` and `trace`, to isolate connectivity problems. There are many syntaxes that you can use with the `debug` and the `show ip` commands. You should know which syntaxes will help you diagnose protocol problems or narrow the scope of possible problems.

Exam Prep Practice Questions

Question 1

> When you use the **trace** command, one line in the output displays an N charac-
> ter; what is the meaning of that character?
>
> ○ A. Node has a newer version of TCP/IP
>
> ○ B. The network is unreachable
>
> ○ C. The network protocol is unreachable
>
> ○ D. Not a valid port number

Answer: **B.** The `trace` command returns an "N" character when the network is not reachable. A "P" character would indicate the protocol is unreachable and a "U" character indicates that the port is unreachable.

Question 2

> Which **show** command would be used to find out if there is a gateway of last
> resort configured on the router?
>
> ○ A. **show ip route**
>
> ○ B. **show ip protocol**
>
> ○ C. **show ip gateway**
>
> ○ D. **show ip default**

Answer: **A.** The `show ip route` command is used to determine whether a router has a gateway of last resort configured. The `show running-config` or `show startup-config` commands both display the configuration on the router and also display a configured default route. However, the proper way to troubleshoot if a default route is configured is to use the `show ip route` command.

Question 3

The Time-Exceeded message indicating that a hop count limit has been exceeded is sent by which of the following protocols?

○ A. ARP
○ B. ICMP
○ C. UDP
○ D. IP

Answer: **B.** An ICMP response with a "Time-exceeded" message is sent when the maximum hop count is exceeded and there is no additional routing information available.

Question 4

Which of the following is a broadcast sent by ARP when it is unable to locate a host on the network?

○ A. 224.255.255.255
○ B. FFFFFFFF
○ C. 11111111
○ D. 00000000

Answer: **B.** FFFFFFFF is equal to the broadcast address of 255.255.255.255, which is the address ARP uses to broadcast over a LAN.

Question 5

Which of the following will resolve a hostname to an IP address?

○ A. DHCP
○ B. Windows
○ C. DNS
○ D. NetBIOS

Answer: **C.** A Domain Name Service (DNS) is used to resolve a hostname to an IP address.

Question 6

> When configuring a network client to access the Internet from a LAN, you need an IP address, subnet mask, and default gateway.
>
> ○ A. True
> ○ B. False

Answer: **A.** An IP address, subnet mask, and a default gateway are all required to access the Internet from a LAN using a network client. A DNS server address will also allow the client to make FQDN and hostname resolutions.

Question 7

> What command must be configured on a local Cisco router to allow DHCP clients to get a DHCP IP Address and DHCP configuration from a remote router?
>
> ○ A. **ip dhcp pool**
> ○ B. **ip dhcp distribution**
> ○ C. **ip helper-address**
> ○ D. **ip broadcast-helper**

Answer: **C.** The `ip helper-address` command is the command used to allow broadcasts for certain protocols, including DHCP, to traverse routers in the network. The `ip dhcp pool` command is a valid command but would be used to define the DHCP pool on the remote Cisco router providing DHCP server services.

Question 8

> Which of the following addresses indicates a default route address?
>
> ○ A. 255.255.255.255
> ○ B. 255.255.0.0
> ○ C. 10.255.255.255
> ○ D. 0.0.0.0

Answer: **D.** The address of 0.0.0.0 indicates a default route or the gateway of last resort. 255.255.255.255 and 10.255.255.255 are broadcast addresses and the address of 255.255.0.0 is a Class B subnet address.

Question 9

> When are ARP entries removed from the ARP Cache table? [Choose the three best answers.]
>
> ❏ A. Whenever a new static entry is made, the cache clears.
> ❏ B. They must be manually removed.
> ❏ C. When the Time-To-Live(TTL) expires.
> ❏ D. When the **clear arp-cache** command is used.
> ❏ E. If you reboot the router

Answer. **C, D, E.** Cache entries are removed when the TTL expires, the routers is rebooted, or when the command clear arp-cache is executed.

Question 10

> Which of the following best describes a ping?
>
> ○ A. Ping is an end-to-end test of connectivity using ICMP.
> ○ B. Ping uses UDP to test for WINS compatibility.
> ○ C. Ping can be used to test for MX records in DNS.
> ○ D. Ping can be used to verify connectivity to an FQDN.

Answer: **A.** The characteristics of a ping are to determine reachability from end-to-end using the ICMP protocol. Ping does not check MX records in DNS or WINS. Ping can be used to verify connectivity to an FQDN by checking a DNS server for the IP address of an FQDN. Static entries can also be made in the routers configuration for FQDN and NetBIOS names. Another ICMP tool called using the trace command provides hop-by-hop information connectivity information.

Need to Know More?

 Shannon, Michael. *CCNP Routing Exam Cram 2*. Que, 2003. ISBN: 0789730170

 Stevens, W. Richard. *The Protocols (TCP/IP Illustrated, Volume 1)*. Adison-Wesley Publishing Co., 1994, ISBN: 0201633469

 Library Noi Net, Introduction Into Internetworking and TCP/IP, http://library.n0i.net/networking/protocols/ro-routing-refg/ch1-intr.html

 Cisco CCO Web site, IP Routing Frequently Asked Questions, http://www.cisco.com/en/US/customer/tech/tk365/tk80/technologies_q_and_a_item09186a008012d8f7.shtml

Windows Troubleshooting

Terms you'll need to understand:

✓ ARP (Address Resolution Protocol)
✓ ipconfig
✓ winipcfg
✓ ping
✓ tracert
✓ telnet

Techniques you'll need to master:

✓ Troubleshooting connectivity issues in the network using the commands **ping**, **pathping**, and **tracert**, and using the appropriate syntaxes with each of these commands.

✓ Using the **ipconfig** and **winipcfg** commands to add, remove, and troubleshoot Dynamic Host Configuration Protocol (DHCP) information on a hosts interface.

✓ Understanding the **nslookup** command and its modes and syntaxes in order to troubleshoot and resolve DNS query problems.

✓ Understanding the **route** command, its syntaxes, and its subcommands in order to use them to statically add, change, and remove known routes through the network on the local host.

✓ Using **nbtstat** and **netstat** command syntaxes in order to troubleshoot many problems in your network and on the local host.

Windows clients not only are configured to work in the network, they have a large array of troubleshooting tools to aid in testing connectivity issues and other problems in the network. Cisco has also made Windows troubleshooting a large part of the exam. That's why this chapter deals with Windows troubleshooting techniques.

You need to remember that a Cisco switch or router has to work correctly with different traffic types. Data may be sent from a number of networking protocols from Windows 95/98/NT/XP/2000/2003 clients or servers. Cisco router configurations must change, depending on what data traffic types the routers need to support. Some examples of traffic types include TCP/IP, NetBEUI, NetBIOS, transparent bridging, and source route bridging.

In this chapter, you learn about the following commands, their syntaxes, and how they're used in troubleshooting Windows issues:

➤ ipconfig

➤ winipcfg

➤ ping

➤ tracert

➤ pathping

➤ nslookup

➤ nbtstat

➤ netstat

➤ route

➤ arp

➤ ftp

➤ telnet

We'll take a look at each one of these commands and some of their most important syntaxes used in troubleshooting. At the end of this chapter, we look at troubleshooting common problems from Windows clients.

ipconfig Command

The ipconfig command is used by Windows clients and servers to display current TCP/IP network configuration parameter values. Windows 95 and

98 clients use a similar command called `winipcfg`. The command can be used on systems running DHCP to determine the TCP/IP configuration values that have been configured by DHCP (Dynamic Host Configuration Protocol). Here are the syntaxes for the commands:

```
C:\>ipconfig /?
USAGE:
    ipconfig [/? ¦ /all ¦ /release [adapter] ¦ /renew [adapter]
             ¦ /flushdns ¦ /registerdns
             ¦ /showclassid adapter
             ¦ /setclassid adapter [classidtoset] ]
    adapter    Full name or pattern with '*' and '?' to 'match',
               * matches any character, ? matches one character.
    Options
        /?              Display this help message.
        /all            Display full configuration information.
        /release        Release the IP address for the specified adapter.
        /renew          Renew the IP address for the specified adapter.
        /flushdns       Purges the DNS Resolver cache.
        /registerdns    Refreshes all DHCP leases and re-registers DNS names
        /displaydns     Display the contents of the DNS Resolver Cache.
        /showclassid    Displays all the dhcp class IDs allowed for adapter.
        /setclassid     Modifies the dhcp class id.
```

The /all syntax shows all parameters configured on the device. If this switch is not used, only the IP address, subnet mask, and default gateway are displayed. In the output that follows, I added the ¦ more syntax which allows the output to be displayed one page at a time.

```
C:\>ipconfig /all ¦ more
Windows 2000 IP Configuration
    Host Name . . . . . . . . . . . . : Laptop101009
    Primary DNS Suffix  . . . . . . . :
    Node Type . . . . . . . . . . . . : Hybrid
    IP Routing Enabled. . . . . . . . : No
    WINS Proxy Enabled. . . . . . . . : No
Ethernet adapter Local Area Connection 2:
    Connection-specific DNS Suffix  . :
    Description . . . . . . . . . . . : Sierra Wireless GPRS Adapter
    Physical Address. . . . . . . . . : 00-A0-D5-FF-FF-83
    DHCP Enabled. . . . . . . . . . . : Yes
    Autoconfiguration Enabled . . . . : Yes
    IP Address. . . . . . . . . . . . : 10.88.72.78
    Subnet Mask . . . . . . . . . . . : 255.0.0.0
    Default Gateway . . . . . . . . . : 10.88.72.254
    DHCP Server . . . . . . . . . . . : 10.88.72.253
    DNS Servers . . . . . . . . . . . : 10.250.1.10
    Primary WINS Server . . . . . . . : 10.1.2.1
    Secondary WINS Server . . . . . . : 10.2.2.3
    Lease Obtained. . . . . . . . . . : Monday, April 21, 2003 8:19:09 PM
    Lease Expires . . . . . . . . . . : Thursday, April 24, 2003 8:19:09 PM
Ethernet adapter Local Area Connection:
    Media State . . . . . . . . . . . : Cable Disconnected
    Description . . . . . . . . . . . : Intel(R) PRO/100 VE Network Connection
    Physical Address. . . . . . . . . : 00-08-02-63-D4-54
C:\>
```

The output shown next uses the /renew syntax. This syntax reloads the DHCP configuration parameters and can only be used on devices using DHCP:

```
C:\>ipconfig /renew
Windows 2000 IP Configuration
Ethernet adapter Local Area Connection 5:
        Connection-specific DNS Suffix  . : gateway.2wire.net
        IP Address. . . . . . . . . . . . : 172.16.1.33
        Subnet Mask . . . . . . . . . . . : 255.255.0.0
        Default Gateway . . . . . . . . . : 172.16.0.1
Ethernet adapter Local Area Connection:
        Media State . . . . . . . . . . . : Cable Disconnected
C:\>
```

The /release syntax releases the current DHCP configuration for DHCP clients. You can use this syntax to force the client to give up an address that you want to assign to another adapter:

```
C:\>ipconfig /release
Windows 2000 IP Configuration
IP address successfully released for adapter "Local Area Connection 5"
C:\>
```

The /flushdns syntax clears the local DNS cache of all the entries, as shown here:

```
C:\>ipconfig /flushdns
Windows 2000 IP Configuration
 Successfully flushed the DNS Resolver Cache.
        /registerdns Refreshes all DHCP leases and re-registers DNS names
C:\>ipconfig /registerdns
Windows 2000 IP Configuration
 Registration of the DNS resource records for all adapters of this computer
has been initiated. Any errors will be reported in the Event Viewer in 15
minutes.
        /displaydns  Display the contents of the DNS Resolver Cache.
```

The /registerdns syntax initiates a client registration with all the DNS servers configured on each interface. This forces the client to reregister with the DNS servers, guaranteeing updated and current DNS information. Failures will be reported to the Windows Event Viewer fifteen minutes after the registration attempt. Here is the syntax:

```
C:\>ipconfig /registerdns
Windows 2000 IP Configuration
 Registration of the DNS resource records for all adapters of this computer
has been initiated. Any errors will be reported in the Event Viewer in 15
minutes.
C:\>
```

The /displaydns syntax displays the records in the local DNS currently in the DNS cache:

```
C:\>ipconfig /displaydns
Windows 2000 IP Configuration
    localhost.
        Record Name . . . . . : localhost
        Record Type . . . . . : 1
        Time To Live  . . . . : 31530398
        Data Length . . . . . : 4
        Section . . . . . . . : Answer
        A (Host) Record . . . :
                            127.0.0.1
    ns2.cwie.net.
        Record Name . . . . . : ns2.cwie.net
        Record Type . . . . . : 1
        Time To Live  . . . . : 86394
        Data Length . . . . . : 4
        Section . . . . . . . : Answer
        A (Host) Record . . . :
                            64.38.192.11
    1.0.0.127.in-addr.arpa.
        Record Name . . . . . : 1.0.0.127.in-addr.arpa
        Record Type . . . . . : 12
        Time To Live  . . . . : 31530398
        Data Length . . . . . : 4
        Section . . . . . . . : Answer
        PTR Record  . . . . . :
        localhost   digitalcrawlspaces.com.
        Record Name . . . . . : digitalcrawlspaces.com
        Record Type . . . . . : 1
        Time To Live  . . . . : 86394
        Data Length . . . . . : 4
        Section . . . . . . . : Answer
        A (Host) Record . . . :
                            64.38.192.188
```

The /showclassid syntax lists the allowable DHCP class IDs for the adapter. The DHCP class ID string identifies the DHCP client as a member of a specific user or vendor options class when it obtains its address lease from the DHCP server. You can use an asterisk to see the DHCP class ID for all the host's configured adapters as shown here:

```
C:\>ipconfig /showclassid *
Windows 2000 IP Configuration
DHCP Class ID for Adapter "Local Area Connection":
 DHCP ClassID Name . . . . . . . . : Default Routing and Remote Access Class
 DHCP ClassID Description  . . . . : User class for remote access clients
 DHCP ClassID Name . . . . . . . . : Default BOOTP Class
 DHCP ClassID Description  . . . . : User class for BOOTP Clients
There are no DHCP classes for adapter {CAB41D6B-41A7-40DE-AA45-4DF9CE172AD7}
C:\>
```

The /setclassid syntax can be used to modify the DHCP class ID on a configured adapter. You can set the DHCP class ID for all the configured adapters by using the asterisk in place of the network adapter name. This parameter is available only on computers with adapters that are configured to obtain an IP address by DHCP. In this output, I am setting the wireless adapter called Connection 5 to the Class ID of Test:

```
C:\>ipconfig /setclassid "Local Area Connection 5" TEST
Windows 2000 IP Configuration
   DHCP ClassId successfully modified for adapter "Local Area Connection 5"
C:\>
```

After setting the adapter, I can use the ipconfig command to verify the setting has taken place:

```
C:\>ipconfig
Windows 2000 IP Configuration
Ethernet adapter Local Area Connection 5:
        Connection-specific DNS Suffix: digitalcrawlspaces.com
        IP Address. . . . . . . . . . . : 10.1.2.173
        Subnet Mask . . . . . . . . . . : 255.255.0.0
        Default Gateway . . . . . . . . : 10.1.1.1
        DHCP Class ID . . . . . . . . . : TEST
```

The ipconfig command is one of the most powerful tools in diagnosing local client configuration and hardware problems. The most common syntax you will use is /all, which displays all the configuration information for the local NIC cards. Don't forget that you need to use this command at a DOS prompt. To help view the information, you should use the ¦ all syntax, which allows you to view the output one full screen at a time.

winipcfg Command

The winipcfg command used on Windows 95 and 98 clients is similar to the ipconfig command. With the winipcfg command, however, you get to see the DHCP information configured on the host in a GUI form, as shown in Figure 5.1.

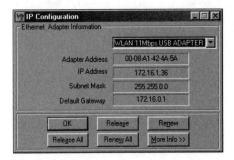

Figure 5.1 The winipcfg command GUI.

The initial screen gives you the MAC address of the adapter, the IP address, subnet mask, default gateway, and the adapter type.

If you choose the More Info button, you can see a more complete list of the advanced settings, including the DNS and WINS server configured and other advanced DHCP settings. The More Info screen is shown in Figure 5.2.

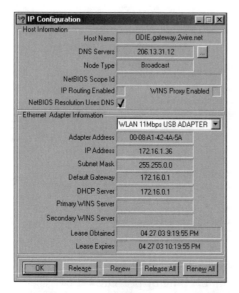

Figure 5.2   The advanced DHCP configuration information shown by using the More Info button.

Three elements need to be verified when troubleshooting TCP/IP problems in Windows 95/98: the host, the router, and the server. If you have network connectivity and you can ping the default gateway but you cannot resolve an FQDN, then you should verify your DNS server settings (you learn more about pinging in the next section of this chapter).

 For the exam, remember that the **winipcfg** command is used only on Windows 95 and 98 clients. The **ipconfig** command, however, works on all Windows 95,98, NT, XP, 2000, and 2003 clients.

The remainder of buttons at the bottom of the GUI allow you to release or renew your DHCP settings.

ping Command

The ping *(packet internet groper)* command issued from a Windows command prompt is used for diagnostic purposes to verify host-to-host connectivity.

The `ping` command sends an ICMP echo-request datagram. The destination receives this datagram and replies with an ICMP echo-reply packet. The following displays the syntaxes that can be used with the `ping` command from a Windows 2000 workstation:

```
C:\>ping
Usage: ping [-t] [-a] [-n count] [-l size] [-f] [-i TTL] [-v TOS]
            [-r count] [-s count] [[-j host-list] ¦ [-k host-list]]
            [-w timeout] destination-list
Options:
    -t              Ping the specified host until stopped.
                    To see statistics and continue - type Control-Break;
                    To stop - type Control-C.
    -a              Resolve addresses to hostnames.
    -n count        Number of echo requests to send.
    -l size         Send buffer size.
    -f              Set Don't Fragment flag in packet.
    -i TTL          Time To Live.
    -v TOS          Type Of Service.
    -r count        Record route for count hops.
    -s count        Timestamp for count hops.
    -j host-list    Loose source route along host-list.
    -k host-list    Strict source route along host-list.
    -w timeout      Timeout in milliseconds to wait for each reply.
C:\>
```

You can continuously send ICMP ECHO packets to a remote host using the `-t` syntax as shown below. You can stop the ping by pressing CTRL+C.

```
C:\>ping -t 207.212.78.107
Pinging 207.212.78.107 with 32 bytes of data:
Reply from 207.212.78.107: bytes=32 time=30ms TTL=251
Reply from 207.212.78.107: bytes=32 time=20ms TTL=251
Reply from 207.212.78.107: bytes=32 time=50ms TTL=251
^C
C:\>
```

In Chapter 4, "Troubleshooting TCP/IP," you learned about DNS. DNS maps an IP address to a host name or FQDN. These names are separated into zones and kept in what is called *zone tables*. A *forward lookup zone* searches by the host name or FQDN until it either finds an entry that matches or reaches the end of the zone table. When a user knows the IP address of a host and wants the associated name, the user can employ a *reverse lookup*; a reverse lookup occurs when you use `ping` with the `-a` switch. This tells `ping` to display the host name along with the ICMP Echo Reply, like this:

```
C:\>ping -a 207.212.78.107
Pinging web1.digitalcrawlspaces.com [207.212.78.107] with 32 bytes of data:
Reply from 207.212.78.107: bytes=32 time=20ms TTL=251
Reply from 207.212.78.107: bytes=32 time=20ms TTL=251
Reply from 207.212.78.107: bytes=32 time=20ms TTL=251
Ping statistics for 207.212.78.107:
    Packets: Sent = 4, Received = 4, Lost = 0 (0% loss),
Approximate round trip times in milli-seconds:
```

```
    Minimum = 20ms, Maximum =  20ms, Average =  20ms
C:\>
```

The output above shows that the reply from the device was successful and that it took a total of 20ms for all three replies.

The -n syntax sends ICMP ECHO packets a specified number of times as shown below; in this example, the 5 specifies the number of ICMP ECHO packets. The default number of packets is 4.

```
C:\>ping -n 5 10.1.1.1
Pinging 10.1.1.1 with 32 bytes of data:
Reply from 10.1.1.1: bytes=32 time<10ms TTL=30
Reply from 10.1.1.1: bytes=32 time<10ms TTL=30
Reply from 10.1.1.1: bytes=32 time<10ms TTL=30
Reply from 10.1.1.1: bytes=32 time<10ms TTL=30
Reply from 10.1.1.1: bytes=32 time<10ms TTL=30
Ping statistics for 10.1.1.1:
    Packets: Sent = 5, Received = 5, Lost = 0 (0% loss),
Approximate round trip times in milli-seconds:
    Minimum = 0ms, Maximum =  0ms, Average =  0ms
Persistent Routes:   None
```

The -l syntax sends ICMP ECHO packets with data padded in the packet to a specific length consisting of a repeated string of the letters *a* through *w*. By padding the packet, you can increase the size of the sent packet, allowing you to increase or decrease the amount of bandwidth used. If you are trying to test the amount of bandwidth available on a higher end link, you could pad the ICMP ECHO packet, creating a larger packet size for each packet traversing the link you are testing. The ping sent below is set to a length of 128 bytes. The default packet length is 64 bytes, and the maximum is 8192 bytes.

```
C:\>ping -l 128 207.212.78.107
Pinging 207.212.78.107 with 128 bytes of data:
Reply from 207.212.78.107: bytes=128 time=40ms TTL=251
Reply from 207.212.78.107: bytes=128 time=40ms TTL=251
Reply from 207.212.78.107: bytes=128 time=30ms TTL=251
Ping statistics for 207.212.78.107:
    Packets: Sent = 4, Received = 4, Lost = 0 (0% loss),
Approximate round trip times in milli-seconds:
    Minimum = 30ms, Maximum =  40ms, Average =  35ms
C:\>
```

NOTE On an Ethernet network, specifying a length of more than 1,500 bytes causes the datagram to become fragmented. When that occurs, the data in the original packet is divided and sent in more than one packet.

Occasionally, gateways will fragment data along a route. Using the -f syntax sends a Do Not Fragment flag in the IP datagram packet, and ensures the ICMP ECHO-Request and ECHO-Reply datagrams are not fragmented. If you use the -l option and specify more than 1,500 bytes, the ICMP ECHO request will not be sent.

```
C:\>ping -f 207.212.78.107
Pinging 207.212.78.107 with 32 bytes of data:
Reply from 207.212.78.107: bytes=32 time=30ms TTL=251
Reply from 207.212.78.107: bytes=32 time=21ms TTL=251
Reply from 207.212.78.107: bytes=32 time=30ms TTL=251
```

The -i syntax can be used to specify a Time To Live (TTL) field in the IP datagram. The TTL value is the number of hops the ICMP ECHO packet can take before it expires. Values can range from 1 to 255. In the output below a TTL value is specified.

```
C:\>ping -i 5 207.212.78.107
Pinging 207.212.78.107 with 32 bytes of data:
Reply from 207.212.78.107: bytes=32 time=31ms TTL=251
Reply from 207.212.78.107: bytes=32 time=20ms TTL=251
Reply from 207.212.78.107: bytes=32 time=20ms TTL=251
```

When the number of hops to a destination device is greater than the allowed number of hops specified, the number of hops is illegal. This will cause you to receive an error such as the one below. Note that our host is three hops away and only one hop is specified.

```
C:\>ping -i 1 207.212.78.107
Pinging 207.212.78.107 with 32 bytes of data:
Reply from 172.16.0.1: TTL expired in transit.
Reply from 172.16.0.1: TTL expired in transit.
Reply from 172.16.0.1: TTL expired in transit.
```

NOTE

The **-v** syntax is rarely used in Unix and stands for Verbose Mode. This command can be used to specify the value of the Type Of Service (TOS) field in an ICMP ECHO packet.

The -r syntax allows you to set the number of hosts along a route to display for an ICMP ECHO request and the ICMP ECHO reply packets. The number of hosts can be set between 1 and 9 and must be specified after the syntax is used. The output below sets the number of hosts to 3.

```
C:>ping -r 3 207.212.78.107
Pinging 207.212.78.107 with 32 bytes of data:
Reply from 207.212.78.107: bytes=32 time=40ms TTL=251
    Route: 64.164.37.70 ->
           64.171.152.66 ->
           207.212.78.110
```

The -s syntax specifies the timestamp for the number of hops specified by the value of count, with a maximum of 4. The output below specifies a count of 3.

```
C:\>ping -s 3 207.212.78.107
Pinging 207.212.78.107 with 32 bytes of data:
Reply from 207.212.78.107: bytes=32 time=30ms TTL=251
    Timestamp: 64.164.37.70 : 2225911648 ->
                64.171.152.66 : 3097738496 ->
                207.212.78.110 : 4101167234
Reply from 207.212.78.107: bytes=32 time=30ms TTL=251
    Timestamp: 64.164.37.70 : 2225912648 ->
                64.171.152.66 : 2577906944 ->
                207.212.78.110 : 3598112898
Reply from 207.212.78.107: bytes=32 time=20ms TTL=251
    Timestamp: 64.164.37.70 : 2225913648 ->
                64.171.152.66 : 2209070336 ->
                207.212.78.110 : 3229276290
Reply from 207.212.78.107: bytes=32 time=30ms TTL=251
    Timestamp: 64.164.37.70 : 2225914648 ->
                64.171.152.66 : 2024783104 ->
                207.212.78.110 : 3044989058
Ping statistics for 207.212.78.107:
    Packets: Sent = 4, Received = 4, Lost = 0 (0% loss),
Approximate round trip times in milli-seconds:
    Minimum = 20ms, Maximum =  30ms, Average =  27ms
```

Using an illegal count will return an error as specified below.

```
C:\>ping -s 10 207.212.78.107
Bad value for option -s, valid range is from 1 to 4.
C:\>
```

The **-j** specifies loose source routing, where a list of hosts on the path are specified by host-list. The maximum number of hosts allowed by IP is 9. The **-k** specifies strict source routing. Consecutively displayed hosts cannot be separated by intermediate routers. The maximum number of hosts is 9. These two syntaxes are out of the scope of this exam so no output will be shown.

The -w syntax specifies a timeout interval in milliseconds as shown below. The timeout value is set to 30 milliseconds.

```
C:\>ping -w 30 207.212.78.107
Pinging 207.212.78.107 with 32 bytes of data:
Reply from 207.212.78.107: bytes=32 time=30ms TTL=251
Reply from 207.212.78.107: bytes=32 time=20ms TTL=251
Reply from 207.212.78.107: bytes=32 time=20ms TTL=251
Reply from 207.212.78.107: bytes=32 time=20ms TTL=251
Ping statistics for 207.212.78.107:
    Packets: Sent = 4, Received = 4, Lost = 0 (0% loss),
Approximate round trip times in milli-seconds:
    Minimum = 20ms, Maximum =  30ms, Average =  22ms
```

The **tracert** Command

The tracert command utility is similar to the Unix traceroute or a Cisco routers trace command. The tracert command output reports the IP address and sometimes the host name of each device in the path between the client and the target. This is a great troubleshooting tool; if the `ping` command fails, this command allows you to see a point of origin for the failure. Like the `trace` command used on a Cisco router, the `tracert` command sends a series of ICMP Echo Requests to the destination host, similar to the `ping` command, except that `Tracert` controls the *Time-To-Live (TTL)* value in the ICMP packet.

By default the `tracert` command sends the first ICMP ECHO Request with a TTL of 1. The second ICMP Echo Request has a TTL of 2, then 3, and so on until the destination host finally responds. Each request is repeated three times. The reason a host name is sometimes present is that by default, a reverse DNS query is made to get the name associated with each IP address. The following shows an example:

```
C:\>tracert 64.38.215.244
Tracing route to www.itdreamteam.com [64.38.215.244]
over a maximum of 30 hops:
  1    10 ms   <10 ms <10 ms  homeportal.gateway.2wire.net [172.16.0.1]
  2    20 ms    20 ms   20 ms  dsl.scrm01.pacbell.net [64.164.39.254]
  3    30 ms    20 ms   20 ms  dist1-vlan50.scrm01.pbi.net [64.171.152.66]
  4    20 ms    20 ms   20 ms  bb1-g6-0.scrm01.pbi.net [64.171.152.247]
  5    30 ms    30 ms   20 ms  sntc01.sbcglobal.net [151.164.188.121]
  6    20 ms    30 ms   20 ms  sprintlink.net [144.228.44.41]
  7    30 ms    20 ms   30 ms  sprintlink.net [144.232.3.145]
  8    20 ms    30 ms   20 ms  sprintlink.net [144.232.3.165]
  9    30 ms    30 ms   30 ms  sprintlink.net [144.232.20.66]
 10    20 ms    30 ms   30 ms  SanJose1.Level3.net [209.245.146.245]
 11    30 ms    20 ms   30 ms  gar2.SanJose1.level3.net [209.244.3.141]
 12    20 ms    20 ms   20 ms  mp2.SanJose1.Level3.net [64.159.1.77]
 13    50 ms    40 ms   50 ms  mp2.Phoenix1.level3.net [209.247.8.122]
 14    50 ms    50 ms   41 ms  hsipaccess1.Phoenix1.Level3.net [64.159.3.110]
 15    40 ms    50 ms   50 ms  bgp-cwie-cust.level3.net [63.214.160.130]
 16    50 ms    50 ms   50 ms  kyst.com [64.38.215.244]
Trace complete.
C:\>
```

`tracert` uses a number of syntaxes. The `-d` syntax turns off host name lookups, significantly speeding up traces, as shown in this example:

```
C:\>tracert -d 207.212.78.107
Tracing route to 207.212.78.107 over a maximum of 30 hops
  1    10 ms   <10 ms   <10 ms   172.16.0.1
  2    20 ms    10 ms    10 ms   64.164.39.254
  3    10 ms    20 ms    20 ms   64.171.152.66
  4    20 ms    20 ms    20 ms   64.171.152.70
  5    30 ms    30 ms    30 ms   207.212.78.107
Trace complete.
C:\>
```

The `-h` syntax can be used to increase the maximum hop count, which is 30 hops by default. The following output changes the hop count to 50.

```
C:\>tracert -h 50 207.212.78.107
```

```
Tracing route to web1.digitalcrawlspaces.com[207.212.78.107]
                  over a maximum of 50 hops:
  1   <10 ms   <10 ms    <10 ms   homeportal.gateway.2wire.net [172.16.0.1]
  2    20 ms    20 ms     20 ms   dsl.scrm01.pacbell.net [64.164.39.254]
  3    20 ms    20 ms     20 ms   dist1-vlan50.scrm01.pbi.net [64.171.152.66]
  4    20 ms    20 ms     20 ms   rback1-fe2-0.scrm01.pbi.net [64.171.152.70]
  5    30 ms    30 ms     30 ms   web1.digitalcrawlspaces.com [207.212.78.107]
Trace complete.
C:\>
```

The -w syntax increases the maximum timeout in milliseconds. The output below sets the timeout to 30 milliseconds.

```
C:\>tracert -w 30 207.212.78.107
Tracing route to web1.digitalcrawlspaces.com[207.212.78.107]
                  over a maximum of 50 hops:
  1   <10 ms   <10 ms    <10 ms   homeportal.gateway.2wire.net [172.16.0.1]
  2    20 ms    20 ms     20 ms   dsl.scrm01.pacbell.net [64.164.39.254]
  3    20 ms    20 ms     20 ms   dist1-vlan50.scrm01.pbi.net [64.171.152.66]
  4    20 ms    20 ms     20 ms   rback1-fe2-0.scrm01.pbi.net [64.171.152.70]
  5    30 ms    30 ms     30 ms   web1.digitalcrawlspaces.com [207.212.78.107]
Trace complete.
```

pathping Command

Windows 2000 and 2003 has a fast trace diagnostic command called pathping. When you use the tracert command, statistical information is not displayed on the screen until the last hop has finished its reply. The pathping command sends out a series of ICMP Echo Requests with incremented TTLs, just as the tracert command does. The difference is that the pathping command results display the statistical calculations after the hop identifiers are displayed and all the replies from hops have been received.

In the following output you see the /? syntax being used to obtain the available syntaxes for the command.

```
C:\>pathping /?
Usage: Pathping [-n] [-h maximum_hops] [-g host-list] [-p period]
                [-q num_queries] [-w timeout] [-t] [-R] [-r] target_name

Options:
-n                  Do not resolve addresses to hostnames.
-h maximum_hops     Maximum number of hops to search for target.
-g host-list        Loose source route along host-list.
-p period           Wait period milliseconds between Pings.
-q num_queries      Number of queries per hop.
-w timeout          Wait timeout milliseconds for each reply.
-T                  Test connectivity to each hop with Layer-2 priority tags.
-R                  Test if each hop is RSVP aware.
C:\>
```

As you can see, the syntaxes are similar to those used with the tracert command. In the next output, you see the pathping command in use to display the route to 10.1.2.1:

```
D:\>pathping 10.1.2.1
Tracing route to Web1 [10.1.2.1]
over a maximum of 30 hops:
  0  DataServer [10.1.2.7]
  1  Web1 [10.1.2.1]
Computing statistics for 25 seconds...
               Source to Here   This Node/Link
Hop  RTT    Lost/Sent = Pct  Lost/Sent = Pct  Address
  0                                            DataServer1 [10.1.2.7]
                                 0/ 100 =  0%   |
  1    0ms    0/ 100 =  0%      0/ 100 =  0%  Web1 [10.1.2.1]
Trace complete.
D:\>
```

The results above show that the Web1 server is only one hop away and that the server replied successfully.

The **nslookup** Command

The nslookup command is the tool of choice for finding problems with DNS. This command enables you to examine resource records in the zone table. The nslookup command can be used to verify that a DNS server exists, to find out what zone tables it manages, and to verify that the DNS server has a particular resource record, as well as allowing you to browse the resource records.

The nslookup command has many syntaxes and command-line prompts. In this section, you look at only a few. For the exam, you need only a brief overview of the nslookup command. To see the IP address for www.digital-crawlspaces.net and the name servers that are authoritative for that zone, use the nslookup command followed by the name of the DNS server as shown below.

```
C:\>nslookup www.digitalcrawlspaces.com homeportal.gateway.2wire.net
Server:   homeportal.gateway.2wire.net
Address:  172.16.0.1
Name:     www.digitalcrawlspaces.com
Address:  64.38.192.188
```

To use the interactive mode, enter the nslookup command with no parameters. When you enter interactive mode, you get a listing of the default name server followed by a command prompt, >:

```
c:\>nslookup
Default Server:  dns.digitalcrawlspaces.com
Address:  207.212.78.106
>
```

Let's take a look at the available syntaxes for the `nslookup` command and a brief description of each syntax in the following output.

```
> ?
Commands:   (identifiers are shown in uppercase, [] means optional)
NAME            - print info about the host/domain NAME using default server
NAME1 NAME2     - as above, but use NAME2 as server
help or ?       - print info on common commands
set OPTION      - set an option
 all          - print options, current server and host
 [no]debug    - print debugging information
 [no]d2       - print exhaustive debugging information
 [no]defname  - append domain name to each query
 [no]recurse  - ask for recursive answer to query
 [no]search   - use domain search list
 [no]vc       - always use a virtual circuit
 domain=NAME  - set default domain name to NAME
 srchlist=N1[/N2/.../N6] - set domain to N1 and search list to N1,N2, etc.
 root=NAME    - set root server to NAME
 retry=X      - set number of retries to X
 timeout=X    - set initial time-out interval to X seconds
 querytype=X  - set query type, e.g., A,ANY,CNAME,MX,NS,PTR,SOA
 type=X       - synonym for querytype
 class=X      - set query class to one of IN (Internet), CHAOS, HESIOD or ANY
server NAME     - set default server to NAME, using current default server
lserver NAME    - set default server to NAME, using initial server
finger [USER]   - finger the optional NAME at the current default host
root            - set current default server to the root
ls [opt] DOMAIN [>FILE] - list addresses in DOMAIN(optional:output to FILE)
 -a           - list canonical names and aliases
 -d           - list all records
 -t TYPE      - list records of the given type (e.g. A,CNAME,MX,NS,PTR etc.)
view FILE       - sort an 'ls' output file and view it with pg
exit            - exit the program
```

If you want to see the default settings for NSLOOKUP, use the `set all` command in interactive mode, as shown below.

```
> set all
Default Server:  homeportal.gateway.2wire.net
Address:  172.16.0.1
Set options:
  nodebug
  defname
  search
  recurse
  nod2
  novc
  noignoretc
  port=53
  type=A
  class=IN
  timeout=2
  retry=1
  root=A.ROOT-SERVERS.NET.
  domain=gateway.2wire.net
  MSxfr
  IXFRversion=1
  srchlist=gateway.2wire.net/2wire.net
>
```

The following sections review the most common `nslookup` interactive commands and set parameters.

The **server** Command

This command can be used to change the name of the DNS server that fields `nslookup` command queries. Be sure to use FQDNs with a trailing dot. The following output identifies the DNS server that fields queries to ns1.digitalgear.com.

```
> server ns1.digitalgear.com.
Default Server:  ns1.digitalgear.com
Address:  64.57.105.6
>
```

The **root** Command

The `root` command selects the name of the DNS server from the top of the server list in the CACHE.DNS file. This command would then set the DNS queries to either an InterNIC root server or a private root server. In the following output, the DNS server resolving DNS queries has been returned to `a.root-servers.net from ns1.digitalgear.com`.

```
C:\>nslookup
Default Server:  homeportal.gateway.2wire.net
Address:  172.16.0.1
> root
Default Server:  A.ROOT-SERVERS.NET
Address:  198.41.0.4
>
```

ls

The `ls` command lists the resource records in a particular zone. In essence, `ls` does a zone transfer of the selected record type. You can limit the scope of the transfer by specifying a record type using the -t switch. Here is an example showing the host records (A records) in the company.com zone:

```
> ls -t a digitalcrawlspaces.com.
[web1.digitalcrawlspaces.com]
 digitalcrawlspaces.com.    A        10.1.1.1
```

Using the **–d** syntax with **ls** command, you can display the entire zone table. But be aware that this can be quite a long list depending on the DNS server providing the information.

set debug Command

Using the set debug command is somewhat like using the DEBUG command on a router. The command displays real-time information and shows the results of a query and the DNS servers included in the search. The following example is the result of a query for digitalcrawlspaces.com that started at an InterNIC root server and worked its way down to find the associated IP address.

```
> set debug
> digitalcrawlspaces.com
Server:  homeportal.gateway.2wire.net
Address:  172.16.0.1
Got answer:
    HEADER:
        opcode = QUERY, id = 8, rcode = REFUSED
        header flags:  response, auth. answer, want recursion
        questions = 1,  answers = 0,  authority records = 0,  additional = 0
    QUESTIONS:
        digitalcrawlspaces.com.gateway.2wire.net, type = A, class = IN
Got answer:
    HEADER:
        opcode = QUERY, id = 9, rcode = NOERROR
        header flags:  response, auth. answer, want recursion
        questions = 1,  answers = 1,  authority records = 2,  additional = 2
    QUESTIONS:
        digitalcrawlspaces.com, type = A, class = IN
    ANSWERS:
    ->  digitalcrawlspaces.com
        internet address = 64.38.192.188
        ttl = 86400 (1 day)
    AUTHORITY RECORDS:
    ->  digitalcrawlspaces.com
        nameserver = ns1.cwie.net
        ttl = 86400 (1 day)
    ->  digitalcrawlspaces.com
        nameserver = ns2.cwie.net
        ttl = 86400 (1 day)
    ADDITIONAL RECORDS:
    ->  ns1.cwie.net
        internet address = 64.38.192.10
        ttl = 86400 (1 day)
    ->  ns2.cwie.net
        internet address = 64.38.192.11
        ttl = 86400 (1 day)
------------
Name:   digitalcrawlspaces.com
Address:  64.38.192.188
```

In the above output the DNS server was queried on the digitalcrawlspaces.com domain. The DNS servers with entries have replied with the domain's known information.

The **set type** Command

You can limit the scope of a query to a DNS server by setting a query to look only for a certain record type. In the example that follows, I am querying for mail Mail Exchange (MX) records on a name server:

```
> set type=mx
> digitalcrawlspaces.com
Server:  homeportal.gateway.2wire.net
Address:  172.16.0.1
   QUESTIONS:
       digitalcrawlspaces.com, type = MX, class = IN
   ANSWERS:
   ->  digitalcrawlspaces.com
       MX preference = 10, mail exchanger = mail.digitalcrawlspaces.com
       ttl = 86400 (1 day)
   AUTHORITY RECORDS:
   ->  digitalcrawlspaces.com
       nameserver = ns2.cwie.net
       ttl = 86400 (1 day)
   ->  digitalcrawlspaces.com
       nameserver = ns1.cwie.net
       ttl = 86400 (1 day)
   ADDITIONAL RECORDS:
   ->  mail.digitalcrawlspaces.com
       internet address = 64.38.212.71
```

The above output shows only the MX record entries on the DNS servers queried. The only known entry found is for mail.digitalcrawlspaces.com.

The **nslookup** Command

Windows TCP/IP clients resolve NetBIOS names and store the results in a NetBIOS Name Cache table, which was the way Windows resolved host names before IP and DNS. However, it is still used today in our LANs. An entry entered into the cache stays for 600 seconds (10 minutes) by default. You can use the nbtstat command to view and manipulate the contents of NetBIOS name cache.

The following bulleted list displays the syntaxes available for the NBTSTAT command and the syntaxes function. Please note that the syntaxes are case sensitive.

➤ -a. This syntax displays the name cache for a remote node by using its NetBIOS name. This option also displays the MAC address of the remote network devices NIC.

➤ -A. This switch displays the name cache of a remote node by using the nodes IP address. The output also displays the MAC address of the remote network adapter. Example syntax: nbtstat -A 10.1.1.1.

➤ -n. This syntax displays information about the local computer, including the computer name, the locally logged-on user, the workgroup or domain of the computer, and any browser services running.

```
Node IpAddress: [10.1.1.27] Scope Id: []
            NetBIOS Local Name Table
    Name                    Type        Status
- - - - - - - - - - - - - - - - - - - - - - - - - - - - - -
DCSWRK1      <00>    UNIQUE      Registered
DCSGRP       <00>    GROUP       Registered
DCSWRK1      <03>    UNIQUE      Registered
DCSWRK1      <20>    UNIQUE      Registered
DCSGRP       <1E>    GROUP       Registered
..__ __.     <01>    GROUP       Registered
```

➤ -r. This syntax lists the statistics of the DNS name cache and how they were resolved. This syntax also resolves the names resolved by WINS. You need to remember that you use this syntax when you are trying to determine whether a computer used a broadcast or WINS to resolve a host name to an IP address.

```
C:\>nbtstat -r
    NetBIOS Names Resolution and Registration Statistics
    Resolved By Broadcast     = 0
    Resolved By Name Server   = 0
    Registered By Broadcast   = 9
    Registered By Name Server = 0
C:\>
```

➤ -R. This syntax clears the name cache and loads any preload (#PRE) items out of a local machine LMHOSTS file. The LMHOSTS file is a text file with static mapPings of IP addresses matched with their associated host addresses.

➤ -s. This syntax displays the current sessions on the local machine, showing the IP addresses of the connected machines. This is very useful when you want a quick display of the services that have active connections:

```
NetBIOS Connection Table
Local Name              State   In/Out  Remote Host   Input   Output
DCSWRK1      <03>       Listening
DCSWRK1                 Connected   In   10.1.1.1      2KB     3KB
ADMINISTRATOR <03>      Listening
```

➤ -s. This output is virtually identical to the uppercase syntax, with the exception that the remote host is listed. The output lists the host name of the remote host instead of the IP address, as shown below.

```
NetBIOS Connection Table
Local Name              State   In/Out  Remote Host   Input   Output
DCSWRK1      <03>       Listening
DCSWRK1                 Connected   In              WEB1    2KB     3KB
ADMINISTRATOR <03>      Listening
```

➤ -RR. This syntax helps to resolve WINS errors by reregistering the host with the WINS Server. This is good for getting an immediate registration when you change the IP address or host name.

The **nbtstat** Command

The netstat command utility is a great tool for finding what ports are open and what services may be causing certain ports to become unusable. This utility can also be used to help determine whether there are outside attacks on your network and obtain network statistics by protocol. Let's look at the syntaxes for the netstat command.

➤ -a. Displays the established TCP and UDP sessions as an interface. One of the best uses of this syntax is to identify potential teardrop attacks or other possible problems that could cause a server to accumulate excessive TCP listens or initiated sessions.

```
C:\>netstat -a
Active Connections
  Proto  Local Address              Foreign Address          State
  TCP    Laptop101009:echo          .:0                      LISTENING
  TCP    Laptop101009:discard       .:0                      LISTENING
  TCP    Laptop101009:daytime       .:0                      LISTENING
  TCP    Laptop101009:epmap         .:0                      LISTENING
  TCP    Laptop101009:microsoft-ds  .:0                      LISTENING
  TCP    Laptop101009:38292         .:0                      LISTENING
  TCP    Laptop101009:pop3          .:0                      LISTENING
  TCP    Laptop101009:1031          .:0                      LISTENING
  TCP    Laptop101009:netbios-ssn   .:0                      LISTENING
  TCP    Laptop101009:1984          webmail.surewest.net:http ESTABLISHED
```

➤ -e. This syntax displays Ethernet interface statistics, including error and discarded packets, as shown below.

```
Interface Statistics
                          Received      Sent
Bytes                     646455        9735466
Unicast packets           8763          29846
Non-unicast packets       3242          467
Discards                  0             0
Errors                    1             2
Unknown protocols         0
```

➤ -n. This syntax displays local addresses and protocol port numbers for the various sessions and listens, as well as the current state of each session.

```
C:\>netstat -n
Active Connections
  Proto  Local Address         Foreign Address       State
  TCP    172.16.1.33:2187      64.236.44.71:80       ESTABLISHED
```

```
TCP    172.16.1.33:2188    64.236.44.71:80    ESTABLISHED
TCP    172.16.1.33:2189    64.236.44.71:80    ESTABLISHED
TCP    172.16.1.33:2190    64.236.44.71:80    ESTABLISHED
TCP    172.16.1.33:2191    64.236.44.71:80    ESTABLISHED
TCP    172.16.1.33:2192    64.236.44.71:80    ESTABLISHED
TCP    172.16.1.33:2193    64.236.44.71:80    ESTABLISHED
```

➤ -p [tcp] [udp] [ip]. This syntax followed by a protocol is similar to -n syntax, but lists the host name instead of the IP Address.

```
C:\>netstat -p tcp
Active Connections
   Proto   Local Address    Foreign Address                     State
   TCP     Laptop101009:1224 web3.digitalcrawlspaces.com:5631 ESTABLISHED
```

➤ netstat -r. Displays the contents of the local routing table. The listing also includes the active ports: -r displays the IP routing table and active connections. -p replaces *protocol* with the name of the protocol for which connection statistics will be seen. You can combine this option with the -s option to see active connections on the protocol.

```
C:\>netstat -r
Route Table
Interface List
0x1 ......................... MS TCP Loopback interface
0x1000003 ...00 08 02 63 d4 54 ......
                    Intel 8255x-based Integrated Fast Ethernet
0x1000004 ...00 08 a1 42 3c 0e ...... WLAN 11Mbps PCMCIA ADAPTER(5V)
Active Routes:
Network Destination        Netmask          Gateway       Interface  Metric
          0.0.0.0          0.0.0.0         10.1.1.1      10.1.2.173      1
         10.1.0.0      255.255.0.0         10.1.2.173    10.1.2.173      1
       10.1.2.173  255.255.255.255         127.0.0.1      127.0.0.1      1
         10.2.0.0      255.255.0.0         10.1.1.1      10.1.2.173      3
         10.3.0.0      255.255.0.0         10.1.1.1      10.1.2.173      3
         10.4.0.0      255.255.0.0         10.1.1.1      10.1.2.173      4
   10.255.255.255  255.255.255.255         10.1.2.173    10.1.2.173      1
        127.0.0.0        255.0.0.0         127.0.0.1      127.0.0.1      1
        224.0.0.0        224.0.0.0         10.1.2.173    10.1.2.173      1
  255.255.255.255  255.255.255.255         10.1.2.173      1000003       1
Default Gateway:           10.1.1.1
```

➤ -s. This syntax displays statistics for each protocol. The -p syntax can be used in conjunction with this syntax to select a particular protocol statistics for TCP, UDP, ICMP, or IP.

```
C:\>netstat -s
IP Statistics
   Packets Received               = 8893
   Received Header Errors         = 0
   Received Address Errors        = 9
   Datagrams Forwarded            = 0
   Unknown Protocols Received     = 0
   Received Packets Discarded     = 0
   Received Packets Delivered     = 8890
   Output Requests                = 8160
```

```
      Routing Discards                    = 0
      Discarded Output Packets            = 0
      Output Packet No Route              = 0
      Reassembly Required                 = 0
      Reassembly Successful               = 0
      Reassembly Failures                 = 0
      Datagrams Successfully Fragmented   = 0
      Datagrams Failing Fragmentation     = 0
      Fragments Created                   = 0
ICMP Statistics
                             Received        Sent
      Messages               179             184
      Errors                 0               0
      Destination Unreachable 0              5
      Time Exceeded          0               0
      Parameter Problems     0               0
      Source Quenches        0               0
      Redirects              0               0
      Echos                  179             0
      Echo Replies           0               179
      Timestamps             0               0
      Timestamp Replies      0               0
      Address Masks          0               0
      Address Mask Replies   0               0
TCP Statistics
      Active Opens                        = 124
      Passive Opens                       = 0
      Failed Connection Attempts          = 16
      Reset Connections                   = 38
      Current Connections                 = 1
      Segments Received                   = 8022
      Segments Sent                       = 7282
      Segments Retransmitted              = 40
UDP Statistics
      Datagrams Received     = 670
      No Ports               = 19
      Receive Errors         = 0
      Datagrams Sent         = 648
C:\>
```

The above output shows the sent packets, received packets, messages, and open connections for each protocol being used by the LAN connection to the PC.

The route Command

The route command is used to display the hosts routing table or to make static changes to the table. With this command you can specify a local router to use to reach a specific remote network or individual host.

 Cisco expects you to have a good understanding of the syntaxes to the **route** command. Make sure you also understand how you add or delete a route using the route command.

The route command has subcommands called the print, add, delete, or change commands. These commands are used to print, add, delete, or change route table entries, respectively. Output from the route printcommand is shown below.

```
C:\>route print
Interface List
0x1 ......................... MS TCP Loopback interface
0x1000003 ...00 08 02 63 d4 54 .. Intel 8255x-based Integrated Fast Ethernet
0x1000004 ...00 08 a1 42 3c 0e .. WLAN 11Mbps PCMCIA ADAPTER(5V)
Active Routes:
Network Destination        Netmask          Gateway       Interface  Metric
          0.0.0.0          0.0.0.0        10.1.1.1       10.1.2.173       1
         10.1.0.0      255.255.0.0      10.1.2.173       10.1.2.173       1
       10.1.2.173  255.255.255.255       127.0.0.1        127.0.0.1       1
         10.2.0.0  255.255.255.255        10.1.1.1       10.1.2.173       3
      66.209.77.34  255.255.255.255        10.1.1.2       10.1.2.173       1
        127.0.0.0        255.0.0.0       127.0.0.1        127.0.0.1       1
    168.143.113.20  255.255.255.255        10.1.1.2       10.1.2.173       1
    216.200.14.151  255.255.255.255        10.1.1.2       10.1.2.173       1
          224.0.0.0         224.0.0.0      10.1.2.173       10.1.2.173       1
  255.255.255.255  255.255.255.255      10.1.2.173         1000003       1
Default Gateway:           10.1.1.1
Persistent Routes: None
C:\>
```

The above output displays all the routes to different networks and devices known by the PC. If you want to display routes only for a specific network, specify the network number. In the following output, the Class A network of 10 is displayed.

```
C:\>route print 10*
Interface List
0x1 ......................... MS TCP Loopback interface
0x1000003 ...00 08 02 63 d4 54....Intel 8255x-based Integrated Fast Ethernet
0x1000004 ...00 08 a1 42 3c 0e....WLAN 11Mbps PCMCIA ADAPTER(5V)
Active Routes:
Network Destination        Netmask          Gateway       Interface  Metric
         10.1.0.0      255.255.0.0      10.1.2.179       10.1.2.179       1
       10.1.2.179  255.255.255.255       127.0.0.1        127.0.0.1       1
         10.2.0.0      255.255.0.0      10.2.2.207       10.2.2.207       1
         10.2.0.0      255.255.0.0        10.1.1.1       10.1.2.179       3
       10.2.2.207  255.255.255.255       127.0.0.1        127.0.0.1       1
         10.3.0.0      255.255.0.0        10.1.1.1       10.1.2.179       3
         10.4.0.0      255.255.0.0        10.1.1.1       10.1.2.179       4
  10.255.255.255  255.255.255.255      10.1.2.179       10.1.2.179       1
  255.255.255.255  255.255.255.255      10.2.2.207       10.2.2.207       1
Default Gateway:           10.1.1.1
Persistent Routes:   None
C:\>
```

You can add a route or delete a route using the add or delete subcommands. The following output shows how to add a route to reach the subnetwork 192.16.1.0 through the router at IP address 10.1.1.2. In this example, the subnetwork has a subnet mask of 255.255.255.0. To delete the route, you can use the same command, but replace the subcommand add with the subcommand delete.

```
> route add 192.16.1.0 mask 255.255.255.0 10.1.1.2.
```

> **NOTE** You can make an added route a persistent route by specifying the **-p** syntax. A persistent route is a route that will remain in the routing table even after the dynamically learned routes have expired. By using a persistent route, you ensure that a route to another network will not be removed from the routing table after the normal expiration time for non-persistent routes has expired.

The arp Command

The arp command is similar to the show arp command on a Cisco Internetwork Operating System (IOS) based router. This command can be used to display or edit the Address Resolution Protocol (ARP) cache on a Windows computer. arp is used for mapping IP addresses to the hardware address of a network interface. TCP/IP transmissions on a Layer 2 network are preceded by an ARP request that is used to discover the hardware address (MAC address) of the destination device using a particular IP address. Let's look at the syntaxes for the ARP command that you should know for the exam.

The -a syntax displays all the entries in the ARP Cache. Only the IP address and physical addresses for the computer are displayed.

```
C:\>arp -a
Interface: 172.16.1.33 on Interface 0x1000004
  Internet Address      Physical Address      Type
  172.16.0.1            00-d0-9e-58-94-71     dynamic
C:\>
```

The -d syntax is used to delete an entry specified by the IP address given. The following output shows the router at 172.16.0.1 being removed from the ARP Cache.

```
C:\>arp -d 172.16.0.1
C:\>
```

To statically map an IP address to a MAC address in the ARP cache, you can use the -s syntax. You must manually enter the host's IP address and MAC address; the MAC address is specified as six hexadecimal bytes separated by hyphens. The IP address is specified in the standard dotted decimal notation. In the cache table, the new entry is shown as a static entry and set to never time-out. The following output shows the IP address 10.1.1.212 being mapped to the MAC address of 00.dd.03.62.c3.aa.

```
C:\arp -s 10.1.1.212    00-dd-03-62-c3-aa
```

The **ftp** Command

The File Transfer Protocol (ftp) command is used to start an interactive session to transfer files to and from two nodes using TCP ports 20 and 21. When using the ftp command from a DOS prompt, you are acting as an FTP client. The other end of your connection, with which FTP creates a session, is considered an FTP server providing FTP Server services.

One important point to remember is that every layer of the OSI Reference Model needs to be working correctly to make a connection to a remote host. If you can use FTP to connect to a remote host and transfer files, the local machine and remote nodes' TCP/IP stack are functioning correctly. Although you can purchase third-party FTP software, I will only explain the general syntaxes for the FTP client provided by the Windows operating system and used at the command prompt.

```
C:\>ftp 207.212.78.106
Connected to 207.212.78.106.
220-Welcome to Digital Crawl Spaces.
Please e-mail Sean Odom (sean@digitalcrawlspaces.com)
for help or login problems.  Thank you.
User (207.212.78.106:(none)): sean
331 User sean Ok, password please
Password:*****
230 Password Ok, User logged in
ftp>
```

The ftp command has several syntaxes. I will briefly explain each and then the most common commands used to find and transfer files.

```
ftp [-v] [-d] [-i] [-n] [-g] [-s: filename] [host]
```

➤ -v. This syntax suppresses the display of responses from the remote FTP server.

➤ -n. This syntax suppresses auto-login during the initial connection.

➤ -i. This syntax disables interactive prompting during multiple file transfers, using the FTP commands mget and mput, which are used to upload and download multiple files.

➤ -d. This syntax enables debugging which displays all ftp commands between the FTP client and the FTP server.

➤ -g. This syntax can be used to disable filename *globbing*. Globbing is a term that refers to the use of wildcard characters in file names and path names.

➤ -s. This syntax specifies that the file name is a text file that contains the commands that run when ftp starts.

➤ host. This is the host name or the IP address of FTP server.

Once an FTP client has connected to an FTP server, a completely different set of commands are used; the most used commands are as follows:

➤ dir. Display the directory of the current folder.

➤ cd. This is the change directory command. This command followed by a folder name will change the current folder. To return to a previous folder, use a single period. To return to the root folder, use the cd command followed by two periods.

➤ md. This is the make directory command. This command followed by a folder name will create that folder in the current directory.

➤ put. This command followed by a file name will upload that file in the current folder. This is the folder that is displayed by a single dir command.

➤ get. This command followed by a file name in the current folder that can be displayed by the dir command will download the file to the local host.

The **telnet** Command

The telnet command is another client tool for terminal emulation, remotely connecting or managing a remote computer or device through the use of a telnet daemon that must be running on the remote computer. The following line shows the general syntaxes of this command:

```
telnet host [port]
```

The *host* syntax specifies the host name or IP address of the remote computer. The *port* specifies the TCP port to which the remote computer connects. The default value for this port is 23.

NOTE
You can identify alternate port numbers with the **telnet** command to connect to special services running on a remote computer at the specified port address. This allows you to verify that a particular port on a remote device is listening and available.

The following output shows the telnet command used to connect to a Cisco 1720 at Digital Crawl Spaces.

```
C:\>telnet 207.212.78.111
User Access Verification
Password: *******
RTR1>enable
```

```
Password: *******
RTR1#
```

You can also use `telnet` to connect to another Cisco router or switch from a Privilege Mode prompt. In the output, `telnet` is connecting from the Cisco 1720 to a Cisco 4506 switch.

```
RTR1#telnet 10.1.10.1
Trying 10.1.10.1 ... Open
User Access Verification
Password: ****
DCS-SW1>enable
Password: ****
```

Chapter Summary

You learned about a number of commands, subcommands, and syntaxes in this chapter. You need to know these for the exam, and you should know when to use each of them in troubleshooting your network from a Windows host. Pay attention to the commands and what is displayed by the output of each one. If you don't, it may come back to haunt you on the exam.

You need to remember that the `ping`, `ipconfig`, `tracert`, and `pathping` commands use ICMP ECHO messages to test for connectivity. These commands have many syntaxes and you need to know what each syntax does.

The `nslookup` command is used to diagnose and correct DNS query problems. This command operates in two modes which have unique commands and syntaxes.

You also need to remember the following commands, what they're used for, and each of their subcommands and syntaxes:

➤ The `netstat` command and syntaxes are used to troubleshoot port listening and session problems.

➤ The `nbtstat` command and syntaxes are used to troubleshoot NetBIOS issues.

➤ The `arp` command and it syntaxes are used to troubleshoot and display IP-to-MAC-address mappings on a local host.

➤ The `route` command, its subcommands, and syntaxes are used to view, add, or change local host route mappings.

➤ The `telnet` command is used for terminal emulation and creating a session between two hosts to communicate.

➤ The `ftp` command allows two hosts to communicate and share files.

Exam Prep Practice Questions

Question 1

You are using a Windows 2000 Workstation PC and have just changed the name of the PC. You want to initiate a client registration with both the WINS servers and DNS Servers that have already been configured. Which two commands should be used at a command prompt?

❑ A. **ipconfig -renew**

❑ B. **ipconfig -flushdns**

❑ C. **ipconfig /registerdns**

❑ D. **nbtstat -RR**

❑ E. **nbtstat /registerwins**

Answers: **C, D.** The first thing to remember is that the ipconfig command can register your machine with DNS. The ipconfig command uses no dashes in its syntaxes. The nbtstat command uses no forward slashes, and the RR indicates that the client should reregister with WINS.

Question 2

Which of the following will allow you to continuously send ICMP ECHO messages to a host until it is manually stopped?

○ A. **ping –l 128 10.1.2.1**

○ B. **ping –a 10.1.2.1**

○ C. **ping –t 10.1.2.1**

○ D. **ping /c 10.1.2.1**

○ E. **ping /t 10.1.2.1**

○ F. **ping /l 10.1.2.1**

Answer: **C.** The -t syntax allows you to send continuous ICMP ECHO messages to a host. You can interrupt the sending of messages by using CTRL+C. The -1 syntax indicates a packet length, and the -a syntax forces a forward DNS lookup. Using forward slashes with the ping command is not valid.

Question 3

You are trying to diagnose a connectivity issue between you and a host at another company. Both your PC and remote hosts can ping their default gateways successfully and you are not relying on DNS to make any resolutions. You want to know if the problem is in your network, either of the ISP's networks, or the remote hosts network. Which of the following commands would best be used to isolate the point of failure?

○ A. **nslookup**

○ B. **route diagnose**

○ C. **route map**

○ D. **ping –l 1500**

○ E. **tracert**

Answer: **E.** The tracert command displays the IP address and sometimes the host name of each device in the path between the client and the target. If there is a failure in the path, the last device displayed is the last device to return with connectivity to return an ICMP ECHO-Reply.

Question 4

While using the **tracert** command, you cannot trace the entire path because the maximum hop count of 30 has been reached. Which of the following **tracert** syntaxes will allow you to increase the hop count to 75?

○ A. **-w 75**

○ B. **-d 75**

○ C. **-h 75**

○ D. **/hopcount 75**

Answer: **C.** The -h syntax followed by a hop count value will increase the hop count. The -w syntax increases the maximum timeout period in milliseconds, and the -d syntax turns off hostname lookups. There is no /hopcount 75 syntax with the tracert command.

Question 5

Which of the following commands and syntaxes allows you to manually map an
IP address to a hardware address?

- ○ A. **nslookup -s 10.1.1.1 08-cc-91-34-da-fd**
- ○ B. **arp –s 10.1.1.1 08-cc-91-34-da-fd**
- ○ C. **ipconfig /s 10.1.1.1 08-cc-91-34-da-fd**
- ○ D. **route –s 10.1.1.1 08-cc-91-34-da-fd**
- ○ E. **winipcfg /s 10.1.1.1 08-cc-91-34-da-fd**

Answer: **B.** The arp command using the -s syntax followed by the IP address
and the MAC address allows you to make a static IP address to hardware
address entry in to the ARP Cache. The other commands are all invalid commands as listed.

Question 6

Which of the following requires all seven layers of the OSI Reference model to
be functioning correctly?

- ○ A. **NSLookup**
- ○ B. **ping**
- ○ C. **tracert**
- ○ D. **ftp**
- ○ E. **arp**

Answer: **D.** FTP is an application and requires all the OSI Reference Layers
from the Application layer to the Physical layer to be functioning correctly.
The other commands need only the bottom half of the OSI Reference model
to be functioning correctly.

Question 7

> Which of the following commands would be used to reload the DHCP information on a Windows 2000 Professional Host?
>
> ○ A. **ipconfig /renew**
>
> ○ B. **winipcfg /renew**
>
> ○ C. **ipconfig /reload**
>
> ○ D. **ipconfig -renew**
>
> ○ E. **arp –refresh**

Answer: **A.** `ipconfig /renew` would be used to reload or refresh the DHCP settings when using Windows NT, 2000, or 2003. The other commands and syntaxes are invalid.

Question 8

> Which of the following would display a statically configured route to an alternate default gateway?
>
> ○ A. **ipconfig /routeview**
>
> ○ B. **ipconfig /showiproute**
>
> ○ C. **route print**
>
> ○ D. **nslookup**
>
> ○ E. **ipconfig –showregistrations**

Answer: **C.** The `route print` command allows you to view all the dynamically learned or statically configured routes on a host. The only other valid command is the `nslookup` command that helps you troubleshoot and resolve DNS issues.

Need to Know More?

Joyce, Jerry, and Marianne Moon. *Troubleshooting Microsoft Windows 2000 Professional*, Microsoft Press, ISBN: 0735611653.

Doyle, Jeff, and Jennifer DeHaven Carroll. *Routing TCP/IP, Volume II (CCIE Professional Development)*, Cisco Press. ISBN: 1578700892.

Siyan, Karanjit. *Windows 2000 TCP/IP*, New Riders. ISBN: 0735709920.

IPX/SPX

Terms you'll need to understand:

✓ Get Nearest Server (GNS)
✓ IPX EIGRP (Enhanced Interior Gateway Protocol)
✓ Internetwork packet exchange (IPX)
✓ IPX Routing Information Protocol (IPX RIP)
✓ IPX/SPX (IPX/sequenced packet exchange)
✓ NetWare Link Services Protocol (NLSP)
✓ Service Advertising Protocol (SAP)

Techniques you'll need to master:

✓ Recognize problem symptoms that relate to IPX.
✓ Know the inner workings of Novell IPX.
✓ Understand and know how to troubleshoot SAP.
✓ Know how GNS messages work and when they are used.
✓ Configure and troubleshoot IPX access lists.
✓ Know the advantages and disadvantages of RIP and NLSP.
✓ Know how to use IPX troubleshooting commands.

There are many legacy technologies that linger in today's networks, and you need to know how to manage and troubleshoot them. Novell's IPX/SPX protocols are some of those protocols. For the CCNP exam, you need to know more about troubleshooting commands than you do about the commands used to configure NetWare protocols. This chapter will give you an overview of NetWare's routing protocols, and the connection sequences and the diagnostic tools that relate to troubleshooting in an IPX (internetwork packet exchange) environment.

Protocol Overview

IPX/SPX (internetwork packet exchange/sequenced packet exchange) is an OSI Reference model Layer 3 protocol suite used with Novell NetWare for transferring data from servers to clients (you learned about the OSI Reference model in Chapter 2, "Networking Principles"). Like TCP/IP, IPX/SPX is a suite of protocols used for network interactions, such as data transport and routing. IPX/SPX (was developed by Novell for use with the NetWare operating system (version 4 and earlier).

NetWare's IPX/SPX network protocols removed many of the client-configuration issues that were inherent with other legacy protocols. Because of this, the release of version 3.11 quickly earned market share and a great reputation for stability, quick installation, and very low maintenance. In NetWare 5 and 6, IPX no longer is required, but rather is an option. TCP/IP is now the default communications protocol.

In this chapter, you learn about the following protocols:

➤ IPX

➤ SAP and GNS

➤ IPX EIGRP

➤ RIP

➤ NLSP

IPX

The IPX protocol operates at Layer 3 of the OSI Reference model and can share addressing schemes with the IP protocol. This sharing capability makes IPX easy to configure and administer in the network. Just like an IP address, an IPX address is divided into a network identifier (which is 4 octets) and a node (host) address. The node address is combined with the physical

MAC address of the network interface card (NIC) located inside the node. Figure 6.1 shows how Novell NetWare protocols including IPX match up to the OSI Reference model.

Netware					OSI
Applications		NCP	RPC Applications	LU 62 Support	Application
Net Bios Emulator	Netware Shell (client)				Presentation
			RPC		Session
SPX					Transport
IPX					Network
Physical Cabling					Link
					Physical

Figure 6.1   The Novell NetWare protocol stack compared to the seven-layer OSI Reference model.

IPX addresses can be found in several formats, but hexadecimal is the most common format. A hexadecimal address of 0000018A.0000.834A.AD66, for example, can be broken down into two parts. The first part consists of the 8 hexadecimal digits, 0000018A, and indicates the network the node resides in. The other 12 hexadecimal digits, 0000.834A.AD66, indicate the node address. Most of the time, when you see the network portion of the address, the 0s preceding the network number are dropped. Therefore, the full IPX network address, including the network and node, would appear as 18A.0000.834A.AD66.

NOTE   Hexadecimal is a number representation using the digits 0-9, with their usual meaning, plus the letters A-F, which represent hexadecimal digits with values of (decimal) 10 to 15. The rightmost digit counts ones, the next counts multiples of 16, then multiples of 256, and so on.

IPX Encapsulation

NetWare uses encapsulation, as well as a framing method, to add an IPX datagram at Layer 3 to an appropriate Layer 2 frame. An important piece of knowledge in troubleshooting Novell is the framing process and how it relates to Ethernet, token ring, and *Fiber Distributed Data Interface (FDDI)* physical topologies.

There are several different IPX frame types and it is possible to set the wrong frame types for the network. When an IPX frame type mismatch exists in the network, the IPX networked components cannot communicate, because this situation is somewhat similar to two people trying to communicate in two different languages without a translator. The following are the five Ethernet IPX frame types (the Cisco identifier name that is used to set the frame type is in parentheses):

➤ *Ethernet_802.3 (novell-ether)*—The default IPX frame type up to NetWare version 3.11. This version supports only IPX and the Ethernet physical media.

➤ *Ethernet_802.2 (sap or iso1)*—The default IPX frame type beginning in NetWare version 3.12. This frame type is supported on multiple physical media types, including Ethernet, FDDI, and token ring, and is recommended for networks with multiple media types.

➤ *Ethernet_II (arpa)*—This frame type supports TCP/IP and IPX. An ether type value is placed after the source MAC address to identify the protocol. The ether value for IPX is 8137, and IP is 0800.

➤ *Ethernet_SNAP (snap)*—This frame type supports AppleTalk, IPX, and TCP/IP on multiple physical media types, which are token ring, Ethernet, and FDDI, using a SNAP header.

➤ *Token Ring (token)*—This frame type supports only token ring traffic for IP, IPX, or Novell Layer 3 traffic.

Depending on the Cisco IOS you are using, you can view the configuration and frame types configured on the router by using the following commands:

➤ `write terminal` (IOS version 11.1 or later)

➤ `show running-config` (IOS version 11.2 or later)

SAP and GNS

To connect to a local Novell server, a client must be able to locate the server. The Get Nearest Server (GNS) protocol and the Service Advertising Protocol (SAP) are used to handle this task. Novell NetWare clients use GNS to request information on the nearest active server of a given type. GNS uses broadcasts that are answered by all IPX servers on the network, accepting the first broadcast for the initialization process. The first server that responds is not always the preferred server identified in the client's configuration file.

Novell clients can't also be a server. A server is a server, and a client uses resources from the server. IPX assigns a GNS listener to each IPX network. The router contains an SAP table that can respond to a GNS request. Both routers and servers can reply to a GNS request. GNS request broadcasts are not forwarded by a router, and a Cisco router will not respond to a GNS request if a NetWare server is on the segment.

If the router must respond to a GNS request because a server is on another segment, a client will request routing information from the router. The router will provide this information to the client to establish a direct connection to the server. IPX Routing Information Protocol (IPX RIP) is a dynamic routing protocol used with Novell NetWare to locate networks and devices in the internetwork. This protocol uses a hop count as a routing metric.

The following are the steps used to resolve a GNS request when the server resides on another segment and a router must handle the request:

1. The Novell client sends a GNS request.

2. No server resides on the segment, so the router responds with a GNS reply.

3. The client responds with an IPX RIP request to get the routing information to the server.

4. The client sends a *NetWare Control Protocol (NCP)* request, which is a connection-oriented protocol used for primary Novell functions. After the client and server establish an NCP session, the client proceeds to the login phase after an IPX NCP reply.

Understanding SAP

By default, every 60 seconds, NetWare servers use SAP to advertise their services to other servers and routers. *SAP* is a protocol used in Novell NetWare to notify network clients of available resources in the network. It's through these advertisements that Novell clients find the servers that they need. The nearest server needs to have an entry in its SAP table for that resource. Unless the router has a security policy using access lists, all the servers and routers become aware of all the NetWare resources in the internetwork. This enables any client to obtain the network topology information from any server in the network.

All the services that are learned from SAP are entered into the server's or router's topology tables. These tables summarize a list of where resources reside in the network. This information is then re-sent out to each interface on the router or server to help inform all the other routers and servers in the network of the existence of other resources. If a problem arises when forwarding or storing the SAP table on any server or router, the problem can cause services to become unavailable. If a new service is introduced, it is automatically broadcast and added to local SAP tables and added to new SAP advertisements to populate the other servers' and routers' SAP tables.

Troubleshooting SAP

Troubleshooting SAP is not that difficult if you make a small checklist of the most common issues. You can narrow down the source of an SAP-related problem by doing the following:

➤ Check the frame types and the client configuration. This includes checking the frame type and hardware settings (including the IRQ [interrupt request] and DMA [Direct Memory Access] settings). This check also involves making sure the client has the proper drivers for the NIC and physical connectivity to the network. All the network servers and routers need to have their external IPX network numbers set to the same value.

 A good indicator of a misconfigured network number is an error that is similar to "00:50:60:2A:94:AD claims network 200 should be 300."

➤ Check the local Cisco router configuration. This includes checking the configured network numbers especially for duplicates, encapsulation type, access lists, frame types, and SAP table sizes.

 The NetWare servers, routers, and clients on the same physical cable segments using a common frame type must share the same network address. All devices on a common network must also use the same frame type.

➤ Check for non-IPX protocol–related problems. This includes over-loaded segments, down links, processor overloads on the routers, IP configuration, and AppleTalk issues.

➤ Check for incorrectly set timers.

Managing IPX and SAP on Virtual Circuits

A NetWare file server and other network resources can be located on a remote segment of the network. You can also configure the routers to dial a server remotely over a *switched virtual connection (SVC)* or a *permanent virtual connection (PVC)* connecting across a WAN link.

When setting up an SVC connection (which is an interface that is set to dial only when traffic is present), remember to turn off IPX RIP routing or the connection will not terminate, because the routing updates will keep the link active. (IPX RIP is discussed in detail in the next section of this chapter.)

A PVC is a permanent, always-on communication connection. As an IPX network begins to grow, the sheer volume of IPX RIP traffic and SAP traffic also grows. Eventually, a WAN connection will be overwhelmed with RIP and SAP updates where data cannot be sent successfully over the links without high latency. In some medium to large networks, a T1 line can easily be saturated, causing difficulty sending RIP messages, SAP messages, and data. That saturation occurs even without including any other protocols, such as IP and AppleTalk, that may be running in the network.

 Always remember that very few networks in existence today have only Novell NetWare's IPX protocol running on them.

In an SVC where the router must dial when data traffic is queued to be sent, the router must respond when a server is not present. The time it takes a router to dial and make a connection may cause GNS queries sent by a client to fail due to timeouts or other unforeseen issues. In these situations, you can use debugging commands to find the problem, but use them with caution—and don't rely on them. The debugging commands can actually cause a time-out issue, because the commands are given a high priority on the processor and are processor-intensive.

The `ipx gns-round-robin` command provides a form of load balancing between the servers, making sure no one server is overburdened with data traffic. This command can be helpful for the router when the servers are overloaded. This command can be used if multiple servers are an equal distance from the router. Although such a problem is rare, you can use another command to set a delay if a problem occurs in the network whereby the router responds to a client more quickly than the client can handle a return request. The default delay is 0 milliseconds (ms), but this can be changed by using the `ipx gns-response-delay` command.

If your network consists of just a few locations connected by three routers using T1 WAN lines, and not too many servers, RIP and SAP can probably run successfully in your network. The reason is that SAP and RIP broadcast everything that they know every 60 seconds throughout the network. In a small network, SAP and RIP tables are pretty small and don't use up a lot of bandwidth. But imagine that you manage a network that has 100 servers and 50 locations. This may sound far-fetched to some, but chances are good that if you're administering a Novell network, it is going to be at least this size.

Now, imagine that SAP updates advertising all of those servers are crossing your WAN connections every 60 seconds. You probably realize that you might need to implement some flow control or buffering, or perhaps you need a lot more than that. You have to leave some bandwidth for data traffic, too.

In this situation you might have a very lengthy *convergence time*, the amount of time required to update IPX network addresses and services in a router's SAP tables if a link or server problem exists in the network. If you are using IPX RIP, the convergence time compared to newer more efficient routing protocols is a lot longer. IPX RIP doesn't notify other servers and routers until it is time for their regularly scheduled 60 second spaced broadcast. If you have more than one hop (you can have up to 15 with RIP), you can add up to an extra minute to that convergence time per hop.

IPX RIP and SAP just don't scale well in larger networks. Even if nothing else but the convergence time or redundancy is important to you, you should consider IPX Enhanced Interior Gateway Routing Protocol (EIGRP) and NetWare Link State Protocol (NLSP), discussed in later sections of this chapter.

Configuring IPX RIP

Configuring IPX RIP is rather simple. Use the `ipx router rip` command at the global configuration prompt and identify the network numbers running in the network. The following is an example of configuring IPX RIP:

```
DCS2514(config)#ipx router rip
DCS2514(config-ipx-router)#network 100
```

```
DCS2514(config-ipx-router)#network 200
DCS2514(config-ipx-router)#network 300
DCS2514(config-ipx-router)#^Z
DCS2514#
```

IPX EIGRP

In a total Cisco routed environment, a better choice than IPX RIP is Cisco's *Enhanced Interior Gateway Routing Protocol (EIGRP)*. IPX EIGRP is a routing protocol for a growing network.

IPX EIGRP is better for a number of reasons. First, it scales better in larger networks. The protocol has a 224-hop count limitation as opposed to the 15-hop limit for IPX RIP. The convergence time is also much faster, so routers learn of problems in the network much faster than with IPX RIP. Updates between routers are only sent out when they are needed, which saves a considerable amount of bandwidth.

Configuring EIGRP

To configure IPX EIGRP, you must use the `ipx router eigrp` command and identify both an autonomous system number and the network numbers in the network. You must have IPX routing enabled, and all the interfaces must be configured with an IPX network number and encapsulation type. The following shows an example of configuring IPX EIGRP:

```
DCS2514# config terminal
DCS2514(config)# ipx router eigrp 10
DCS2514(config-ipx-router)# network 100
DCS2514(config-ipx-router)# network 200
DCS2514(config-ipx-router)# network 300
```

Troubleshooting IPX EIGRP

There are several commands that you should know for troubleshooting IPX EIGRP problems and configurations. `show ipx eigrp` is one of the main commands used to help troubleshoot problems with EIGRP. The following are the available syntaxes for the command:

```
DCS12514# show ipx eigrp ?
 interfaces IPX EIGRP Interfaces
 neighbors  IPX EIGRP Neighbors
 topology   IPX EIGRP Topology Table
 traffic    IPX EIGRP Traffic Statistics
```

The above output shows the syntaxes available for the command. The interfaces syntax displays all the interfaces using IPX EIGRP. The neighbors syntax displays all the one hop away devices running the IPX EIGRP protocol. The topology syntax displays the known networks and routes learned with the IPX EIGRP protocol. The traffic syntax displays the current statistic counters relating to the IPX EIGRP protocols.

To successfully troubleshoot IPX EIGRP, you also need to have a good understanding of the commands that will allow you to see the known routes through the network, and whether the routing table is updating correctly. The show ipx eigrp neighbors, show ipx eigrp topology, and show ipx route commands are used to troubleshoot these. The following sections take a look at these commands in detail.

show ipx eigrp neighbors

The show ipx eigrp neighbors command displays information that can be used to find the directly connected neighbors or to identify routes that are going up and down, which can be identified by an increase in the sequence numbers on an interface.

The following output shows the first EIGRP neighbor the router learned about a little more than 22 hours ago on the Ethernet1 interface. Since learning the route, 2,614 updates have been received on that interface. The Smooth Round TripTime (SRTT) is set to 15 seconds and the Retransmission TimeOut (RTO) is set to 30 seconds.

```
DCS2514# show ipx eigrp neighbors
IPX EIGRP Neighbors for process 10
H   Address              Interface   Hold   Uptime    Q   Seq   SRTT   RTO
1   100.0000.604a.3d7d  Ethernet1    12    06:12:43   0   2614   15    30
0   300.0000.604a.5a4b  Ethernet0    12    06:12:46   0   2617   15    30
```

show ipx eigrp topology

The following output from the use of the show ipx eigrp topology command shows that for IPX EIGRP process 10, networks 100, 200, and 300 are connected to the Ethernet 0 interface on the router:

```
DCS2514# show ipx eigrp topology
Topology Table for process 10
Codes: P-Passive, A-Active, U-Update, Q-Query, R-Reply, r-Reply status
P 100, 1 successors, FD is 225488
     via 300.0000.604a.5a4b (225488/274200), Ethernet0
P 200, 1 successors, FD is 265486
     via 300.0000.604a.5a4b (265486/302430), Ethernet0
P 300, 1 successors, FD is 211852
     via Connected, Ethernet0
```

show ipx route

The following output from the `show ipx route` command provides information on static and IPX routing protocols, including RIP, EIGRP, and NLSP discovered routes:

```
DCS2514# show ipx routes
Codes: C - Connected primary network, c - Connected secondary network,
S - Static, F - Floating static, L - Local (internal), W - IPXWAN, R - RIP
, E - EIGRP, N - NLSP, X - External, A - Aggregate, s - seconds,  u - uses
4 Total IPX routes. Up to 1 parallel paths and 16 hops allowed.
No default route known.
L 400 is the internal network
C 300 (NOVELL-ETHER), Ethernet0
C 200 (NOVELL-ETHER), Ethernet1
E 100 [284228/0] via 300.0000.604a.5a4b, age 2w5d, 1u, E0
```

The preceding output shows that network 400 is the internal network, Ethernet 0 is directly attached to network 300, Ethernet 1 is attached to network 200, and network 100 can be reached through the same interface as network 300 by using the Ethernet 0 interface.

NLSP

The NetWare Link Services Protocol (NLSP) is an advanced link-state routing protocol developed by Novell for use in Novell NetWare. NLSP has several advantages over IPX RIP. NLSP enables you to remove IPX SAP advertisements from an identified network segment. NLSP then handles network updates. The protocol reduces both IPX RIP and SAP advertisements by sending updates on changes to a database, rather than by sending the complete table every 60 seconds. This is another routing protocol that sends an update only if a change in the network topology has occurred, unless no activity takes place for two hours, after which time the NLSP-enabled interface will send an update to all of its neighbors.

Enabling NLSP

To enable NLSP, use the `ipx nlsp enable` command on each interface connecting to segments that need to have NLSP enabled. You must then identify the NLSP area address.

You need to configure a couple of prerequisites when using NLSP. The `area-address area mask` command is used to define which IPX addresses are part of a particular area. You can use zero for area address and zero for the mask. Using zeros indicates that all area addresses are to be included in this area.

NLSP requires use of the `ipx internal-network` command to identify the IPX internal network.

When configuring NLSP, we must first enable IPX routing by using the `ipx internal-network` command to identify the IPX internal network for the router. Next, configure both active the default encapsulation (HDLC on Serial 0, novell-ether on Ethernet 0) on the interface, and identify the networks connected to each interface. The following shows an example:

```
DCS2514#config terminal
DCS2514(config)# ipx routing
DCS2514(config)# ipx internal-network d
DCS2514(config)# ipx router nlsp
DCS2514(config-ipx-router)# area-address 0 0
DCS2514(config)# interface serial0
DCS2514 (config-if)# ipx network 100
DCS2514(config-if)# ipx nlsp enable
DCS2514 (config-if)# interface ethernet0
DCS2514 (config-if)# ipx network 300
DCS2514(config-if)# exit
DCS2514(config)#
```

NLSP Troubleshooting Commands

In order to troubleshoot the NLSP protocol, you can use the following `show` commands to verify the configuration is correct and that NLSP is functioning correctly:

➤ `show ipx route`

➤ `show ipx servers`

➤ `show ipx nlsp neighbors`

➤ `show ipx nlsp database`

In the next sections, let's take a look at each command and its output.

show ipx route Command

When you configure NLSP, the routing table output produced by using the `show ipx route` command shows a serial route, as in this example:

```
DCS2514# show ipx route
Codes: C - Connected primary network,
       c - Connected secondary network
       S - Static, F - Floating static, L - Local
       (internal), W - IPXWAN
       R - RIP, E - EIGRP, N - NLSP, X - External,
       A - Aggregate
       s - seconds, u - uses
3 Total IPX routes. Up to 1 parallel paths and 16 hops allowed.
No default route known.
```

```
L 400 is the internal network
C 500 (HDLC), Serial0
C 200 (NOVELL-ETHER), Ethernet0
```

show ipx servers Command

You can use the show ipx servers command to view all the known routes to the servers learned by the router. The following is an example of using the show ipx servers command:

```
DCS2514# show ipx servers
Codes: S - Static, P - Periodic, E - EIGRP, N - NLSP,
       H -Holddown, + = detail
2 Total IPX Servers
Table ordering is based on routing and server info
     Type  Name       Net Address            Port Route  Hops Itf
N    4     File&Print1 100.0000.0000.0001:0000 12/02  2    Se0
N    4     CAD1        100.0000.0000.0002:0000 12/02  2    Se0
```

show ipx nlsp neighbors Command

The show ipx nlsp neighbors command can be used to display all the known NLSP neighbors, which are NLSP resources that are directly connected to the router's interfaces. The following is an example of using the show ipx nlsp neighbors command as well as the output.

```
DCS2621# show ipx nlsp neighbors
NLSP Level-1 Neighbors: Tag Identifier = notag
System Id Interface State Holdtime Priority  Circuit Id
DCS2514 Se0        Up    55       0         04
DCS2621 has one NLSP neighbor, DCS2514. By adding the detail command, the
output includes the IPX internal network number and the uptime.

DCS2621# show ipx nlsp neighbors detail
NLSP Level-1 Neighbors: Tag Identifier = notag
System Id Interface State Holdtime Priority  Circuit Id
DCS2514 Se0        Up    43       0         04
IPX Address: 100.0000.0000.0001
IPX Areas: 00000000/00000000
Uptime: 01:13:09
```

show ipx nlsp database Command

The show ipx nlsp database command provides information on the NLSP processes, as in the following example:

```
DCS2514#show ipx nlsp database
NLSP Level-1 Link State Database
LSPID             LSP Seq       Num LSP      Checksum LSP Holdtime ATT/P/OL
DCS2501.00-00 *  0x0000043B    0x2C77       203              0/0/0
DCS2514.04-00 *  0x000001D2    0x1A2D       440              0/0/0
DCS2514.00-00    0x00000023    0x1CAA       2311             0/0/0
DCS2621.03-00    0x00000A22    0x9DE9       892              0/0/0
DCS2621.00-00    0x00000342    0xCD9B       821              0/0/0
RSM1.00-00       0x00000221    0x2C99       16               0/0/0
RSM.02-00        0x00000361    0x235B       16               0/0/0
```

The preceding output shows each entry in the NLSP database that is using a link state protocol identifier (LSPID). This column contains a value including a system identifier, a pseudonode circuit identifier, and a fragment number. The link state protocol (LSP) is the foundation of NLSP, and the show ipx nlsp database command reports significant information, including the last sequence number, the checksum, and the LSP holdtime. The holdtime indicates when the information will be flushed from the database, if a Hello packet or update is not received. The ATT/P/OL field is used by the Cisco Technical Assistance Center (TAC) for troubleshooting. This field is used to describe the Layer 2 attachments and the overload bits. The P bit (partition) indicates whether or not a partition is used.

IPX Access Lists

Cisco routers use *access lists* to enable security and to control the types of traffic passed between interfaces. One of the options of access lists is the ability to control SAP advertisements coming into or leaving the router's interfaces. In addition to management of SAP advertisement traffic, an administrator may use access lists to filter certain IPX packets for network security.

IPX access lists are similar to IP access lists. Both protocols use standard and extended access lists in their configurations. Standard IPX access lists are numbered from 800 to 899, and extended access lists are numbered from 900 to 999.

To apply a completed access list to an interface, you use the access-group command followed by the access list number and code that indicates whether the access list should filter data going in or out of the interface. The following sample shows the access list command and the available syntaxes for the command:

```
access-list access-list-number [deny ¦ permit] source-network[.source-node
  [source-node-mask]] [destination-network[.destination-node
  [destination-node-mask]]
```

With IPX standard access lists, a packet can be filtered based only on the source and destination address information contained in a packet header. To add filtering capabilities for IPX traffic based on socket numbers, protocol, or other IPX identifiers, an extended access lists must be used. The following are the syntaxes for the access-list command using an extended access list:

```
access-list access-list-number [deny¦permit] protocol [source-network]
[[[.source-node] source-node-mask] ¦ [.source-node source-network-mask.
source-node-mask]] [source- spocket][destination.network][[[.destination-
```

```
node] destination-  node-mask] ¦ [.destination-node destination-network-
mask.destination-nodemask]] [destination-socket]
```

The output above shows the syntaxes required for the access-list command. In the next few sections, you will see examples of using this command and the required syntaxes being used for each type of access list.

> At the end of every access list is an implied "deny all." You can't see it in the output when displaying a configured access list. This means that any traffic you want to permit must be configured in the access list.

An example can help explain the access-list command syntaxes. The following output shows an example of a simple extended access list. This example lists the syntax fields and then the output. Here is a look at the command and the syntaxes required:

```
access-list [number] [permit¦deny] [protocol] [source] [socket][destination]
[socket number].
```

Now let's look at an example of the command with each syntax configured and applied to the Ethernet 0 interface:

```
DCS2514(config)#access-list 900 deny -1 100 0 200 0
DCS2514(config)#interface ethernet0
DCS2514(config-if)#ipx access-group 900 in
DCS2514(config-if)#exit
```

> You can substitute the **any** syntax for **–1**, which is the wildcard **all** syntax (if your IOS supports this syntax). The extended access list 900 is configured to deny all IPX protocols from network 100 that are sent to network 200 through the Ethernet0 interface.

Controlling SAP Advertisements with Access Lists

The service advertisements generated by SAP can send a significant amount of traffic in medium-scale networks. In larger networks, SAP can cause high processor utilization and overall degradation of the network because of the amount of bandwidth being used from the large number of sent advertisements.

Standard and extended IPX access lists are used to control traffic between IPX network interfaces. You use SAP access lists to control SAP traffic between network interfaces on a router using access list numbers in the range of 1000 to 1099. The following lists the syntaxes used to configure IPX SAP access lists:

```
access-list [number] [permit/deny] [source] [service type]
```

This type of access list is relatively simple to use. The following output lists an example of denying SAP traffic from any server from network 100 on Ethernet0:

```
DCS2514# config terminal
Enter configuration commands, one per line. End with CNTL/Z.
DCS2514(config)# access-list 1000 deny 100.0000.0000.0001 0
DCS2514(config)# interface ethernet0
DCS2514(config-if)# ipx input-sap-filter 1000
DCS2514(config-if)# exit
```

In the output above, the service type 0 represents all service types. You can use service type 4 to identify file servers, and type 7 to identify only print servers. Instead of using the access-group command to apply this to an interface, you must use the ipx input-sap-filter command on an inbound interface, or the ipx output-sap-filter command to filter on an outbound interface. The command must be followed by the configured access list number.

To disable IPX access lists for troubleshooting purposes, use the following commands:

```
DCS2514(config-if)# no ipx access-group access-group number
DCS2514(config-if)# no ipx input-sap-filter access-list number
DCS2514(config-if)# no ipx output-sap-filter access-list number
```

IPX General Troubleshooting Commands

A wide variety of commands can be used to aid in troubleshooting Novell protocols, including the configuration, statistics, IPX, and SAP protocols. The Cisco router's show commands provide a wealth of information regarding IPX. The following bulleted list reviews the output from the most commonly used IPX troubleshooting commands, which include the following:

➤ debug ipx routing. This command displays the IPX routing protocol processes running on the router. These processes include the IPX routing protocols IPX RIP, IPX-EIGRP, and NLSP. An example of the output follows:

```
*Sep 30 03:14:47.301 UTC: IPXRIP: Deleting network 101
*Sep 30 03:14:47.303 UTC: IPX: cache flush
```

```
*Sep 30 03:14:47.304 UTC: IPX: Setting state of E0:300 to [up]:[up]
*Sep 30 03:14:47.304 UTC: IPX: cache flush
*Sep 30 03:38:47.304 UTC: IPXRIP: Marking network 100 for Flash Update
```

➤ `debug ipx packet`. This command is used to display all the IPX traffic either entering or exiting the router.

The **debug ipx packet** command should be used with caution because the debug command is assigned a high priority on the router's processor and can actually render the router inoperable.

The **debug ipx packet** command doesn't display IPX packets that are fast-switched. If you need to view all packets, including those that are fast-switched, use the **no ipx route-cache** command on each interface that you wish to include in the debug capture. The following is an example of the output. It shows the entry of a packet destined for a server on the 200 network, with the response sent to the gateway on network 200:

```
IPX: src=253.0000.604c.12bf, dst=200.0000.0000.0001, packet
                    ➥received
IPX: src=253.0000.604c.12bf, dst=200.0000.0000.0001,
                    ➥gw=200.0000.80a5.abd1, sending packet
```

➤ `debug ipx sap activity`. This command allows you to view the SAP traffic, which provides information regarding whether or not the SAP processes are functioning correctly. If SAP is not functioning properly, you can prevent access to services and cause other connectivity issues in your network. An example of the output follows:

```
DCS2514# debug ipx sap activity
IPX service debugging is on
Oct 30 10:06:31.424:type 0x30C, "PTR_1",800.0006.0d86.5380(401C), 4 hops
Oct 30 10:06:31.424:type 0x30C, "PTR_2",800.0006.0d6e.1a65(400C), 4 hops
Oct 30 10:06:31.618:type 0x44C, "AR3", 300.0000.0000.0001(8600), 3 hops
Oct 30 10:06:31.618:type 0x23F, "SRL03",300.0000.0000.0001(907B), 3 hops
Oct 30 10:06:31.704: IPXSAP: at 690465B4:
I SAP Response type 0x2 len 480 src:800.0060.837b.4a19
    dest:200.ffff.ffff.ffff(452)
```

The highlighted line represents an SAP packet received. The "PTR 1" indicates the name of the server being advertised. The address of 800.0006.0d86.5380(401C) indicates the address and socket number in parenthesis. The last line indicates the number of hops to the server from the router.

➤ `ping ipx`. Just like in IP where the `ping` command uses the ICMP protocol and an IP address, you can use the `ping ipx` command and an IPX address to verify connectivity with another device. By using this utility for troubleshooting IPX connectivity problems, you can verify that the routing tables are being updated correctly and that connectivity to other networks and devices is taking place. The following shows an example of using the ping ipx command to ping a Cisco router's interface assigned to the 18a network:

```
DCS2621# ping ipx 18a.0000.834a.3d51
Type escape sequence to abort.
Sending 5, 100-byte IPX cisco Echoes to 18a.0000.834a.3d51,
                                         timeout is 2 seconds
!!!!!
Success rate is 100 percent (5/5), round-trip min/avg/max =  16/19/31 ms
```

➤ show ipx route. This command can be useful when you need to know the state of a NetWare network. You can use this command to verify that certain paths exist through the network. Using this command, you can view the routes learned; path decisions made by IPX RIP, NLSP, IPX-EIGRP, and IPXWAN; and the static routes that are configured on the interface. The following shows an example of using this command:

```
DCS2514# show ipx route
Codes: C - Connected primary network c - Connected secondary network,
S - Static, F - Floating static, L - Local (internal), W - IPXWAN
R -RIP, E - EIGRP, N - NLSP, X - External, A - Aggregate   s - seconds,
u - uses
1 Total IPX routes. Up to 3 parallel paths and 16 hops allowed.
No default route known.
R    1  [03/02] via   300.0060.602a.1d4c,  8s, Hs3/0
```

The above output shows that the router has learned of one network via the IPX RIP routing protocol and that the router has no default gateway.

➤ show ipx servers. This command displays all servers known to the router that have been learned from SAP advertisements. If servers are missing, there may be an access list misconfiguration, duplicate network numbers, a downed link or interface, network congestion, or misconfigured frame types. The following is the output from the command, followed by an explanation of the fields that are listed:

```
DCS2514#show ipx servers
Codes: S - Static, P - Periodic, E - EIGRP, N - NLSP,  H - Holddown,
      + = detail
2 Total IPX Servers
Table ordering is based on routing and server info
Type Name          Net Address      Port   Route   Hop  Itf
N  4 File&Print1  100.0000.0000.0001:0451  727/03  2    E1
N+ 4 EmailSAC     200.0000.0000.0001:0451  729/03  2    E1
```

➤ `show ipx traffic`. This command displays information regarding IPX packets that have been transmitted or received. An example of the output from this command follows:

```
DCS 2514# show ipx traffic
System Traffic for 300.0000.0000.0001 System-Name: DCS2514
 Rcvd:    3298322 total, 158 format errors, 0 checksum errors,
          0 bad hop count, 6 packets pitched
          65955970 local destination, 0 multicast
Bcast:    3287985 received, 139078 sent
Sent:     1324204 generated, 4 forwarded
          0 encapsulation failed, 0 no route
SAP:      0 SAP requests, 0 SAP replies, 2 servers
          0 SAP advertisements received, 8 sent
          5 SAP flash updates sent, 0 SAP format errors
RIP:      0 RIP requests, 0 RIP replies, 6 routes
          0 RIP advertisements received, 0 sent
          0 RIP flash updates sent, 0 RIP format errors
Echo:     Rcvd 0 requests, 0 replies
          Sent 0 requests, 0 replies
          0 unknown: 0 no socket, 0 filtered, 0 no helper
          0 SAPs throttled, freed NDB len 0
Watchdog:
          0 packets received, 0 replies spoofed
Queue lengths:
    IPX input: 0, SAP 0, RIP 0, GNS 0
    SAP throttling length: 0/(no limit), 0 nets pending lost route reply
    Delayed process creation: 0
EIGRP: Total received 4413, sent 1784
    Updates received 58, sent 128
    Queries received 32, sent 17
    Replies received 17, sent 32
    SAPs received 0, sent 0
NLSP: Level-1 Hellos received 0, sent 0
    PTP Hello received 0, sent 0
    Level-1 LSPs received 0, sent 0
    LSP Retransmissions: 0
    LSP checksum errors received: 0
    LSP HT=0 checksum errors received: 0
    Level-1 CSNPs received 0, sent 0
    Level-1 PSNPs received 0, sent 0
    Level-1 DR Elections: 0
    Level-1 SPF Calculations: 0
    Level-1 Partial Route Calculations: 0
```

The above output is great for getting a detailed description of how IPX is working. The output shows that there are 158 format errors from received servers. The output also shows that the router has learned about two servers through SAP.

You should be aware that some of these commands are not available on certain IOS versions, and some versions support additional syntaxes that are not displayed here. You should always use the `show ipx ?` command to see the available syntaxes.

Chapter Summary

The latest NetWare versions, 5.0 and 6.0, no longer rely on the IPX and SPX protocols. NetWare now supports TCP/IP. Even though the newest versions center around TCP/IP, many legacy applications and networks still use the IPX protocol, so legacy-protocol support is still included in version 5.0. This chapter focused on the configuration and troubleshooting commands associated with NetWare. It also looked at the connection sequences and the diagnostic tools that can be reliably used to troubleshoot problems in an IPX environment.

The Net Address field shows the MAC address as 0000.0000.0001. This is the internal IPX network address indicator. The output shows the SAP type, number of known servers, how the information was learned, the number of hops to the server, and the server name.

This chapter also included common NetWare network problems and a list of troubleshooting commands that can be used to resolve those issues. The most important IPX configuration and IPX routing protocol troubleshooting commands were covered, including the show, debug, and the ping ipx commands.

Exam Prep Practice Questions

Question 1

> Which of the following commands would provide an administrator with a list of
> known Novell servers on the network?
>
> ○ A. **debug ipx ipxwan**
> ○ B. **show ipx servers**
> ○ C. **show ipx traffic**
> ○ D. **show ipx all**

Answer: **B.** The show ipx servers command would show all the known servers
in the network.

Question 2

> Which of the following commands was used to produce this output?
>
> ```
> IPX EIGRP Topology Table for process 20
> Codes: P - Passive, A - Active, U - Update, Q - Query,
> R - Reply, r - Reply status
> P A, 1 successors, FD is 342217
>      via 20.0060.3a7b.ab21 (342217/307200), s0
> P D, 1 successors, FD is 152221
>      via Connected, s1
> ```
>
> ○ A. **show ipx eigrp topology**
> ○ B. **show ipx eigrp events**
> ○ C. **show ipx eigrp detail**
> ○ D. **show ipx eigrp neighbors**

Answer: **A.** This output is from the show ipx eigrp topology command. The
first line indicates the table.

You can expect the exam to have obvious questions just like Question 2.

Question 3

An IPX extended access list can filter based on which of the following?

❑ A. IPX socket number

❑ B. IPX protocol

❑ C. Source network/node

❑ D. Destination network/node

❑ E. All of the above

Answer: **E.** All the items listed are valid criteria for filtering with an extended IPX access list.

Question 4

Which of the following number ranges can be used to number an IPX standard access list?

○ A. 1-99

○ B. 800-899

○ C. 900-999

○ D. 1000-1099

Answer: **B.** The valid range of numbers for an IPX standard access list is 800-899.

Question 5

Which of the following is the default encapsulation type for Novell NetWare 5.0 or 6.0 clients and servers?

○ A. ARPA

○ B. Ethernet_II

○ C. NOVELL-ETHER

○ D. Ethernet_802.3

○ E. None of the above

Answer: **E.** IP is the default for Novell clients and servers running NetWare 5.0 and 6.0, so an encapsulation type would not be needed. Options C and D would be correct for the default encapsulation type for Novell clients and servers that are not running NetWare 5.0 or later.

Question 6

A Novell client is using Ethernet II. Which of the following frame types can be used? [Choose the two best answers.]

❑ A. Ethernet II

❑ B. 802.3

❑ C. ARPA

❑ D. 802.5

Answers: **A, B.** This is a trick question. Ethernet II and ARPA are the same thing. You need to remember that Novell calls the encapsulation type Ethernet II and Cisco calls it ARPA, so both answers are correct.

Question 7

Which of the following is a valid IPX network address?

○ A. 20.0000.0000.0001

○ B. FileServer.0000.0000.0001

○ C. 132.16.4.0

○ D. 6.0000.0G24.1211

Answer: **A.** An IPX address requires four octets in hexadecimal format that specify both the network and the node.

Question 8

By default, SAP packets are sent how often?

○ A. 120 seconds

○ B. 30 seconds

○ C. 60 seconds

○ D. You must manually specify the default

Answer: **C.** The default setting for SAP packet advertisements is 60 seconds.

Question 9

What is the maximum number of hops supported by IPX RIP?

○ A. 7

○ B. 15

○ C. 64

○ D. Unlimited

Answer: **B.** IPX RIP has the same hop count maximum as IP RIP, which is 15. This means that no more than 15 routers can exist between any two given points in the network.

Question 10

Which of the following commands was used to display this output?

```
S/0 is up, line protocol is up
IPX address is 20.0060.1a30.289a [up] line-up,
            RIPPQ: 0, SAPPQ: 0
Delay of this IPX network, in ticks is 1
            throughput 0 link delay 0
 IPXWAN processing not enabled on this interface.
 IPX SAP update interval is 1 minute(s)
 IPX type 20 propagation packet forwarding is disabled
 Incoming access list is not set
 Outgoing access list is not set
 IPX helper access list is not set
 SAP GNS processing enabled, delay 0 ms, output filter
            list  is not set
 SAP Input filter list is not set
 SAP Output filter list is not set
 SAP Router filter list is not set
 Input filter list is not set
 Output filter list is not set
 Router filter list is not set
```

○ A. **show interface s0**

○ B. **show ipx protocol interface s0**

○ C. **show ipx interface s0**

○ D. **debug ipx interface s0**

Answer: **C.** The `show ipx interface s0` command was used to produce the output.

Need to Know More?

 Chappell, Laura. *Novell's Guide To LAN/WAN Analysis*, Hungry Minds Publishers, 1998. ISBN: 0764545086.

 Cisco Systems, Inc., and Riva Technologies. *Cisco IOS 12.0 Solution Network Protocols Volume II: IPX, Apple Talk, and More*, Cisco Press, 1999. ISBN: 1578701643.

Troubleshooting the
Physical Layer

. . . .

Terms you'll need to understand:

✓ bandwidth

✓ buffer

✓ Cisco Discovery Protocol (CDP)

✓ collision

✓ cyclic redundancy check (CRC)

✓ Network Management Systems (NMS)

✓ optical time domain reflector (OTDR)

Techniques you'll need to master:

✓ Know the show commands that can be used to view the configuration, and to monitor and view the statistics of Cisco interfaces.

✓ Understand the need for Network Monitoring Systems.

✓ Know what SNMP is and how it works with Network Monitoring Systems.

✓ Know the different types of cable testers and how they can help you resolve Physical layer problems.

✓ Know Cisco Discovery Protocol and how it can help you in troubleshooting.

Troubleshooting at the Physical layer is one of the most important parts of network troubleshooting. If your network is properly configured and stops working without any notice, most likely it will relate to a hardware issue, an issue with the physical layer cabling, or an issue with the interfaces the physical cabling connects to.

In this chapter, you learn how to utilize tools and commands that can help you identify problems with a Cisco router or switch, network cabling, or other network problems affecting the Physical layer of the network. When you are done with this chapter you should have a good knowledge of the basics of troubleshooting the network's Physical layer. These basics include using the show commands, physical tools (such as cable testers), management system software, and protocol analyzers (sniffers).

Equipment Used to Troubleshoot the Physical Layer

Many problems that are encountered occur at the bottom of the OSI Reference model at the Physical layer. This is the layer where you convert the data to bits and place them on the physical wire in the network. Problems at the Physical layer can be some of the simplest to solve; for example, by seeing a break in the cable or a cable not plugged in.

 When the network's Physical layer is intact, the Data Link layer will be where you next want to start looking for your problem.

Physical layer problems can be extremely difficult to solve, however, especially if the problems reside in the hardware. These problems can include things such as a NIC card connecting to the network or bad cabling in the wall. You also have those pesky rodents who like to chew on your sweet tasting cabling in the roof and walls. So many factors can contribute to errors and loss of connectivity that isolating the exact problem may be hard at times. Tools are available that can help in testing the physical infrastructure of a network. You should know the different types of troubleshooting equipment available to you, and how and when to use each type; this knowledge can alleviate a lot of headaches associated with network troubleshooting. The next few sections take a look at some of the tools available to test the physical layer of the network, including its cabling.

Basic Cable Testers

Noise levels, heat, insects, animals, seismic events, static, or humidity can all make subtle changes that affect cabling or devices. Some of the tools used to test network cabling are volt-ohm and digital meter. These devices measure parameters such as AC and DC voltage, currents, resistance, and cable continuity. Time domain reflectors (TDRs) are another type of cable tester; they can isolate a break in the cabling.

A cable tester is a must for anyone who works with the infrastructure in the network. Since there are so many potential Layer 1 problems, you need to be able to isolate such problems and fix them quickly. Cable testers can be used to test for physical connectivity on the existing wiring. Different types of cable testers exist; some are for general use, while others focus on a specific type of cabling.

One of the most common types of cable testers focuses on 10BaseT or 100BaseT UTP for Ethernet networks. Specific testers are made for fiber-optic cabling, but they're expensive, and so they are used mainly by companies that install fiber. Using a cable tester for Ethernet, you can find problems with physical connectivity, test the wire mapping, and report cable conditions, including near-end crosstalk (NEXT), attenuation, and noise.

If you are using an advanced cable tester, you can configure the tester with an IP address to test for LAN connectivity, as well as display MAC addresses, provide information about LAN traffic, and provide a generic look at network utilization. You also can perform tests such as ping and arp to test the LAN connectivity; these tests report the time a packet takes to reach a destination. In a large campus environment, cable tester devices are helpful in testing the basic equipment, such as data jacks and connectivity.

One of my favorite cable testers is the Pentascanner 350 shown in Figure 7.1. This tester uses multiple automated tests and displays a very clear picture of the cable's continuity and problems. By connecting two ends of a copper cable such as CAT 3, 4, 5 or 6 cable to both parts of the tester and pressing Test, the cable will be tested and the scanner will display the results. The results can also be saved and labeled for later viewing or porting to a spreadsheet.

Time Domain Reflectors (TDRs)

Time Domain Reflectors, or TDRs, are sophisticated and complex cable testers. Some of the problems TDRs look for are open circuits, short circuits, crimped wires, and anything that may inhibit the connectivity on the wire.

TDRs not only report problems with a cable, but also can isolate the location of the problem on the cable.

Figure 7.1 A Pentascanner 350 cable tester.

TDRs work with a principle similar to ping. A TDR sends an electronic signal down the physical wire, then waits until the same signal returns to the device, reporting the time intervals from sending and receiving. When the TDR receives the signal back, it looks at the signal for any abnormalities with the signal strength or other possible errors. If the TDR detects a problem, it attempts to determine where the problem could be located. Depending on the signal, the TDR reports whether the problem is a short, a crimp, open cabling, or other cabling issue. The TDR reviews the time factor of the received signal to determine where on the cable the signal may be failing. TDRs usually can determine within a foot or two the location of the problem on the cable. This type of equipment is imperative to have when you are looking at thousands of wires, each of which may be 100 to 200 feet long.

Optical Time Domain Reflectors (OTDRs)

OTDRs, or *Optical Time Domain Reflectors*, are advanced cable testers that analyze fiber by sending pulses. OTDRs test exclusively for fiber-optic cabling using optical pulses rather than electronic signals. OTDRs use the same testing principle used by TDRs; after sending and receiving a pulse, the testers analyze the pulse for possible problems.

Protocol Analyzers

A protocol analyzer, sometimes called a sniffer, is a software-based application that works to find faults in the network, as well as test the performance. This software enables a network administrator to capture data packets, review the contents of a data packet, decode data from the captured packets, and collect and view network traffic statistics. More advanced protocol analyzers can include features, such as traffic generators, to create traffic flows to test the network, can perform fault analysis, can provide network isolation tools, and have the ability to add remote management interfaces.

Troubleshooting with the **show** Commands

The show commands are used to troubleshoot the Physical layer of the network. The following sections discuss each of the commonly used show commands in more detail. These sections also display and explain the show command's output.

For the exam it is important that you understand the Physical layer troubleshooting commands and when to use those commands. You also need to know how to interpret each command output.

The **show interfaces** Command

One of the most common show commands that you will use is show interfaces, which enables you to see what is happening on all the interfaces on the router. It gives you a quick glance at an interface; the show interfaces command indicates whether the network is up or down, provides a bit of information on network configuration, and provides a look at the packets on the network. The following is example output from show interfaces:

```
DCSRootRTR#show interfaces
Async1 is down, line protocol is down
  Hardware is Async Serial
  MTU 1500 bytes, BW 9 Kbit, DLY 100000 usec,
     reliability 255/255, txload 1/255, rxload 1/255
  Encapsulation SLIP, loopback not set
Ethernet2/1 is up, line protocol is up
  Hardware is cxBus Ethernet, address is 1203.ef12.1d41 (bia 1203.ef12.1d41)
  Description: Subnet 211 for Pismo Beach Site
  Internet address is 192.16.32.254/24
  MTU 1500 bytes, BW 10000 Kbit, DLY 1000 usec,
     reliability 255/255, txload 4/255, rxload 1/255
```

```
   Encapsulation ARPA, loopback not set
   Keepalive set (10 sec)
   ARP type: ARPA, ARP Timeout 04:00:00
   Last input 00:00:00, output 00:00:05, output hang never
   Last clearing of "show interface" counters never
   Queueing strategy: fifo
   Output queue 0/40, 22591 drops; input queue 0/75, 929 drops
   5 minute input rate 44000 bits/sec, 25 packets/sec
   5 minute output rate 174000 bits/sec, 23 packets/sec
      293110943 packets input, 4194038437 bytes, 0 no buffer
      Received 42837453 broadcasts, 0 runts, 0 giants, 71 throttles
      0 input errors, 0 CRC, 0 frame, 0 overrun, 25 ignored
      0 input packets with dribble condition detected
      264542130 packets output, 1810892381 bytes, 0 underruns
      0 output errors, 31586499 collisions, 2 interface resets
      0 babbles, 0 late collision, 0 deferred
      0 lost carrier, 0 no carrier
      0 output buffer failures, 0 output buffers swapped out
Ethernet2/2 is administratively down, line protocol is down
   Hardware is cxBus Ethernet, address is 1203.ef12.1d42 (bia 1203.ef12.1d42)
   Description: Subnet 212 Monterey Site
   Internet address is 198.132.212.254/24
   MTU 1500 bytes, BW 10000 Kbit, DLY 1000 usec,
      reliability 255/255, txload 1/255, rxload 1/255
   Encapsulation ARPA, loopback not set
   Keepalive set (10 sec)
   ARP type: ARPA, ARP Timeout 04:00:00
   Last input never, output never, output hang never
   Last clearing of "show interface" counters never
   Queueing strategy: fifo
   Output queue 0/40, 0 drops; input queue 0/75, 0 drops
   5 minute input rate 0 bits/sec, 0 packets/sec
   5 minute output rate 0 bits/sec, 0 packets/sec
DCSRootRTR#
```

The output above shows a serial interface on a Cisco 3725 router. By looking at the second line, you get a picture of an unhealthy interface. The interface will not connect and the Layer 3 protocols running on the interface are
not receiving keepalives. Keepalive packets are sent by Layer 3 protocols at
specific intervals and whenever there is a topology change in the network to
verify that the interface is still active and functioning correctly. You know this
because both the line and protocol identifiers are showing they are down. If
you look at the line in bold you will also note that there was a very large
number of collisions, which could signal either a hardware problem or a
problem with the link itself.

 It's a lot easier to find current problems in the output of the **show interfaces** command if you erase the legacy statistics. You can reset all the counters on the **show
interfaces** command output to zeros by using the **clear counters** command on the
interface. This will also update the field that displays when the counters were last
cleared.

The show interfaces ethernet Command

Unfortunately, you can't just type in the show interfaces ethernet command and see all the Ethernet interfaces on the router. You have to identify the interface you want to view after the command. This command allows you to examine the status of an Ethernet and get in-depth information on that interface's problems (if there are any). The following example shows the first Ethernet interface on the router indicated by the zero at the end of the show interfaces ethernet command:

```
DCSRoot# show interfaces ethernet 0
Ethernet0 is up, line protocol is up
  Hardware is PQUICC Ethernet,address is 0007.eb32.d6a3 (bia 0007.eb32.d6a3)
  Internet address is 207.212.78.110/29
  MTU 1500 bytes, BW 10000 Kbit, DLY 1000 usec,
     reliability 255/255, txload 1/255, rxload 1/255
  Encapsulation ARPA, loopback not set
  Keepalive set (10 sec)
  Half-duplex, 10BaseT
  ARP type: ARPA, ARP Timeout 04:00:00
  Last input 00:00:00, output 00:00:00, output hang never
  Last clearing of "show interface" counters never
  Queueing strategy: fifo
  Output queue 0/40, 0 drops; input queue 0/75, 329 drops
  5 minute input rate 44000 bits/sec, 7 packets/sec
  5 minute output rate 4000 bits/sec, 7 packets/sec
     8812047 packets input, 539578735 bytes, 0 no buffer
     Received 15611 broadcasts, 0 runts, 0 giants, 0 throttles
     475 input errors, 0 CRC, 1 frame, 0 overrun, 474 ignored
     0 input packets with dribble condition detected
     7040396 packets output, 1116153898 bytes, 0 underruns
     55169 output errors, 71884 collisions, 8 interface resets
     0 babbles, 0 late collision, 0 deferred
     474 lost carrier, 0 no carrier
```

Let's go line by line and break down the preceding output to see what each line is telling us:

➤ Ethernet 0 is {up ¦ down ¦ administratively down}—This line indicates whether the physical port that connects to the network is active or whether it has been taken down by an administrator. The "Up" descriptor indicates the link is connected and is live, the "down" descriptor indicates that the link is not connected to another functioning device or there is a problem with the interface or cabling, and the "Disabled" descriptor indicates that the router has received more than 5,000 errors in a keepalive interval, which is 10 seconds by default. The "administratively down" descriptor means that the shutdown command was used on the interface.

➤ Line protocol is {up ¦ down}—This indicates whether keepalives are successful and that the software controller for the interface believes the interface is usable.

➤ Hardware type—Indicates the cable types used on the interface.

➤ Internet address—The IP address which is followed by the subnet mask.

➤ MTU (Maximum Transmission Unit)—This is the maximum size (in bytes) of data that can be sent out through this interface.

➤ BW (Bandwidth)—Shows the bandwidth of the interface which is displayed in kilobits per second. *Bandwidth* is the rated throughput capacity of a given network protocol or medium.

➤ DLY (Delay)—This displays the delay of the interface, shown in microseconds.

➤ Rely (Reliability)—This is the reliability of the interface, shown as a fraction of 255. A 255 out of 255 indicates 100% reliability. This number is shown as an average of packets sent during the last 5 minutes prior to the output on the screen.

➤ Load—This is the average load on the interface during the 5 minutes prior to the output being displayed. This average is shown as a fraction of 255. A 255 out of 255 (255/255) result indicates that the interface is completely saturated.

➤ Encapsulation—This is the type of encapsulation that is being used on the interface.

➤ Loopback—This indicates whether a loopback is being used on the interface. A loopback is usually used for testing the interface.

➤ Keepalive—This indicates whether keepalives are set or not.

➤ ARP type—This is the type of Address Resolution Protocol which is assigned to the interface.

➤ Half-duplex—Indicates that the interface is using half-duplex. The differences between half-duplex and full duplex are discussed in Chapter 3, "LAN Technologies."

➤ 10BaseT—Indicates that the interface is using 10Mbps Ethernet.

➤ Last input—Indicates in hours, minutes, and seconds the time when the last packet was received successfully. If the time indicated is more that 24 hours, the value is displayed in days and hours.

➤ Output—Indicates in hours, minutes, and seconds when the last packet was transmitted successfully. If the time indicated is more that 24 hours, the value is displayed in days and hours.

➤ `Output hang`—Indicates in hours, minutes, and seconds since the interface was last reset or timed out. If the time indicated is more that 24 hours, the value is displayed in days and hours.

➤ `Last Clearing Time of "show interface" counters`—Shows when the interface counters were last cleared using the clear counters command.

➤ `Output queue`—The first number indicates the current output queue size; the second number following the slash is the maximum output queue size.

➤ `Input queue`—The first number indicates the current input queue size; the second number following the slash is the maximum input queue size.

➤ `Drops`—The number of packets dropped from the queue because packets arrived faster than they could be processed or buffered.

A *buffer* is a storage area used to receive/store data waiting to be processed. Buffers are mainly used by devices that receive and store data from faster processing devices; buffers allow the device to process the data as fast as the processing speeds allow.

➤ `5 minute input rate`—This displays the average number of bits received by the interface during the five minutes prior to the output being displayed.

➤ `5 minute output rate`—This displays the average number of bits transmitted by the interface during the five minutes prior to the output being displayed.

➤ `Packets input`—This is the total number of packets received by the interface which were checked and determined to have no errors. The following value displays the total bytes which those error-free packets totaled.

➤ `No buffers`—This is the total number of received packets which were lost because there was no buffer space available in the main system. A large number in this field might be the indicator of a broadcast storm in the network.

➤ `Received broadcasts`—The total number of broadcast or multicast packets received by the interface.

➤ `Received runts`—The total of packets received that are smaller than the physical medium's minimum packet size. Ethernet's minimum packet size is 64 bytes.

➤ Received `giants`—Total number of packets that were received and discarded because they exceed the physical medium's maximum packet size. Ethernet's maximum packet size is 1518 bytes.

> One exception applies to the Received Giants rule: When you use IEEE 802.1q Trunking, giant frames that are more than 1518 bytes are calculated as giants but they are not discarded.

➤ Received `throttles`—This is the total number of times the interface fails to buffer an incoming packet. This counter is also the same as the "misses" counter output obtained by using the `show buffers` command.

➤ Received `input Errors`—The total number of received error packets including runts, giants, no buffer, bad CRC, bad frames, overruns, and ignored counts.

> CRC, or *Cyclic Redundancy Checksum*, is a method that is used to check for errors in packets that have been transferred across a network. A computation bit is added to the packet and recalculated at the destination to determine whether the entire packet contents have been transferred correctly.

➤ Received `CRC`—This totals the number of frames received where the cyclic redundancy checksum (CRC) does not match the checksum calculated from the data received. The CRC is a mathematical value of the packet calculated by the sending device. The receiving device makes its own calculation once the frame or packet is received. If it matches the receiving device, it knows that it received the packet or frame without failure.

➤ Received `frame`—You receive this error usually as a result of a collision on the physical medium (a *collision* is the result of two frames transmitted simultaneously; when these two frames collide in an Ethernet network, both frames are destroyed). This number increases by one when you receive a frame with a bad CRC or indifference in the size of each data field in the frame.

➤ Received `overrun`—This is the total number of times the received packet or frame rate exceeded the rate at which the interface could successfully send the data to the buffer.

➤ Received `ignored`—This is the total number of times the system's internal buffers ran low on storage space because of high volume in processes or receive rates. The internal buffers should not be confused with the system buffers. Increases in number here can be another indicator of a broadcast storm or bursts in the network.

➤ `Received input packets with dribble condition detected`—Dribble bit error indicates that a frame is slightly too long but the router accepted the frame.

➤ `Packets output`—This is the total number of packets or frames sent by the router's interface.

➤ `Bytes`—This is the total bytes sent out the interface on the router.

➤ `Underruns`—This is the total number of times the transmitter has run faster than the router itself. This is usually never reported by the interface.

➤ `Output errors`—This is the total of all detected errors that prevented a successful transmission.

➤ `Collisions`—This is the number of times the interface retransmitted a frame because of a collision of data on the physical wire.

➤ `Interface resets`—This is the total number of times the interface has reset since the router was started or the `clear counters` command was issued.

➤ `Babbles`—This is the number of times that the transmitter has used the interface for longer than the time needed to transmit the largest frame being sent.

➤ `Late collision`—This is the total number of late collisions that were detected on the physical wire. This means that while the router was sending data out of the interface, another device stated sending data.

➤ `Deferred`—The number of frames or packets that had to be held before transmission because of data being sent on the physical wires.

➤ `Lost carrier`—This is the total number of times the router lost contact with the destination device during a transmittal process.

➤ `No carrier`—This is the total number of times the router was unable to detect a device at the other end of the physical interface.

Good Documentation

One small, but very critical piece of troubleshooting is documentation. If your network is documented, troubleshooting is much easier. Documentation includes labeling devices, using descriptions on the router interfaces, and having a router topology with the networks defined. By having good documentation, you know all the components and devices that exist in the network, as well as what devices might be causing a problem in the network. You also can determine addressing problems much easier, and you can much more easily determine the tools necessary to resolve a problem.

It is a very tedious job, but putting labels on fiber and ports will ease the pain in finding where the cabling is connected when a problem arises. If you are in a large campus environment, the network operations center (NOC) may have 30 to 40 pieces of fiber strung across the racks. When you need to find a particular fiber belonging to a network you believe to be down, you will be thankful that you put labels on the port of the device and on the fiber.

Placing a description of the network on the router interfaces will ensure less time being spent scrolling for the correct interface. If an interface only shows an IP address, you will have to correlate it with the correct network and, sometimes, that can be stressful and time-consuming. Taking the time to provide a description will alleviate a lot of headaches in the end, especially when you are in a panic.

The **show interfaces tokenring** Command

The show interfaces tokenring command is used to show the status of a Token Ring interface. Just like in the show interfaces ethernet command, this command must be followed by the interface number as shown below:

```
DCSRouter2#show interface tokenring 0
TokenRing0 is up, line protocol is down
  Hardware is TMS380, address is 0002.cda1.26ac (bia    0002.cda1.26ac)
  Internet address is 172.16.21.254, subnet mask is    255.255.255.0
  MTU 4464 bytes, BW 4000 Kbit, DLY 630 usec, rely 255/255, load 1/255
  Encapsulation SNAP, loopback not set, keepalive set (10 sec)
  ARP type: SNAP, ARP Timeout 04:00:00
  Ring speed: 4 Mbps
  Single ring node, Source Route Transparent Bridge capable
  Ethernet Transit OUI: 0x000000
  Last input never, output never, output hang never
  Last clearing of "show interface" counters never
  Queueing strategy: fifo
  Output queue 0/40, 0 drops; input queue 0/75, 0 drops
  5 minute input rate 0 bits/sec, 0 packets/sec
  5 minute output rate 0 bits/sec, 0 packets/sec
     0 packets input, 0 bytes, 0 no buffer
     Received 0 broadcasts, 0 runts, 0 giants
     0 input errors, 0 CRC, 0 frame, 0 overrun, 0 ignored, 0 abort
     0 packets output, 0 bytes, 0 underruns
     0 output errors, 0 collisions, 0 interface resets
     0 output buffer failures, 0 output buffers swapped out
     1 transition
```

The preceding output is very similar to the Ethernet output and has many of the same fields. Let's take a look at only the fields that are different from the show interfaces ethernet command:

➤ Token Ring is {up ¦ down ¦disabled ¦ reset ¦ initializing ¦ administratively down}—When "up" is displayed it indicates there is a connection to the ring, the "down" indicates that there is a problem with the connection to the ring, and "disabled" indicates the router has received more than 5,000 detected errors during the router's keepalive interval. The keepalive interval is 10 seconds by default. If "reset" is displayed, a hardware error has occurred; if "initializing" appears, the connection is in the process of attaching to the ring; and if the interface states "administratively down" it has been taken down using the `shutdown` command.

> `Ring Speed`—The ring speed should list 4 or 16 Mbps.

> `Single ring¦multiring node`—Indicates whether a single ring is being used or more than one. It is also an indicator that the interface can use Source Route Bridging (SRB).

 Token Ring places data on the ring in one direction and only one station can transmit at each time. If collisions are registered on the interface, it is an indication that there is a major hardware problem.

The **show controllers** Command

The `show controllers` command output shows information on all of the router's controllers. You can specify the type of controller when using this command, as shown below:

```
DCSSacramento#show controllers ?
  Ethernet      IEEE 802.3
  FastEthernet  FastEthernet IEEE 802.3
  ¦             Output modifiers
  <cr>
```

Although the preceding output only lists Ethernet and FastEthernet interfaces, routers with other types of interfaces, such as serial, BRI, CBus, FDDI, Lex, MCI, PCBus, serial, T1, T3, Token, or VGAnylan controllers, can also be specified.

This is the command you want to use if you want to view the versions of firmware being used, types of memory management, or another view of the errors detected on interfaces on the router. Much of the information displayed here is unusable, but in between is information that can be used to troubleshoot Physical layer interface problems. Let's take a look at the output from the Ethernet 0 interface on a Cisco 1720 router shown below:

```
RTR#show controllers ethernet0
PQUICC Ethernet unit 0 using SCC1, Microcode ver 0
Current station address 0007.eb32.d6a3, default address 8167.0210.8107
idb at 0x81310358, driver data structure at 0x81312140
SCC Registers:
```

```
General [GSMR]=0x0:0x1088003C, Protocol-specific [PSMR]=0x80A
Events [SCCE]=0x0000, Mask [SCCM]=0x001F, Status [SCCS]=0x0002
Transmit on Demand [TODR]=0x0, Data Sync [DSR]=0xD555
Interrupt Registers:
Config [CICR]=0x00365F80, Pending [CIPR]=0x0400C000
Mask    [CIMR]=0x40200000, In-srv  [CISR]=0x00000000
Command register [CR]=0x600
Port A [PADIR]=0x0000, [PAPAR]=0x0903
       [PAODR]=0x0000, [PADAT]=0xF7FF
Port B [PBDIR]=0x0000100F, [PBPAR]=0x0000100E
       [PBODR]=0x00000000, [PBDAT]=0x0003EDFC
Port C [PCDIR]=0x0000, [PCPAR]=0x0000
       [PCSO]=0x0030,  [PCDAT]=0x0FCC, [PCINT]=0x0000
IPM_SYS_REGS->tecr is0x11
SCC GENERAL PARAMETER RAM (at 0xFF003C00)
Rx BD Base [RBASE]=0x2230, Fn Code [RFCR]=0x18
Tx BD Base [TBASE]=0x22B0, Fn Code [TFCR]=0x18
Max Rx Buff Len [MRBLR]=1520
Rx State [RSTATE]=0x18000000, BD Ptr [RBPTR]=0x2258
Tx State [TSTATE]=0x18000AE3, BD Ptr [TBPTR]=0x22C0
SCC ETHERNET PARAMETER RAM (at 0xFF003C30)
CRC Preset [C_PRES]=0xFFFFFFFF, Mask [C_MASK]=0xDEBB20E3
Errors: CRC [CRCEC]=0, Alignment [ALEC]=1, Discards [DISFC]=0
PAD Char [PADS]=0x0
Retry Limit [RET_LIM]=15, Count [RET_CNT]=15
Frame Lengths: [MAXFLR]=1518, [MINFLR]=64
Max DMA Lengths: [MAXD1]=1518, [MAXD2]=1518
Group Address Filter [GADDRn]=0000:0000:0020:0100
Indiv Address Filter [IADDRn]=0000:0000:0000:0000
Physical Address [PADDR1]=A3D6.32EB.0700
Last Address Set in Filter [TADDR]=CCCC.CC0C.0001
Persistence [P_Per]=0, Backoff Cnt [BOFF_CNT]=65535
BD Pointers:
First Rx [RFBD]=0x0, First Tx [TFBD]=0x22C0, Last Tx [TLBD]=0x22B8
Receive Ring
        rmd(FF002230): status 9000 length 4D4 address 1CA0CA4
        rmd(FF002238): status 9000 length 262 address 1CA26A4
        rmd(FF002240): status 9000 length 3B6 address 1C9C524
        rmd(FF002248): status 9000 length 5EE address 1CA3A24
        rmd(FF002250): status 9000 length 5EE address 1C9DF24
        rmd(FF002258): status 9000 length 4EC address 1C9FFA4
        rmd(FF002260): status 9000 length 8A address 1C9AB24
        rmd(FF002268): status 9000 length 5EE address 1C9FFA4
        rmd(FF002270): status 9000 length 5EE address 1C9E5A4
        rmd(FF002278): status 9000 length 5EE address 1C97724
        rmd(FF002280): status 9000 length 5EE address 1CA40A4
        rmd(FF002288): status 9000 length 1F3 address 1CA2024
        rmd(FF002290): status 9000 length 5EE address 1C9A4A4
        rmd(FF002298): status 9000 length 5EE address 1CA2D24
        rmd(FF0022A0): status 9000 length 48A address 1C9F924
        rmd(FF0022A8): status B000 length 5EE address 1C99E24
Transmit Ring
        tmd(FF0022B0): status 5C00 length 3C address 1B343CA
        tmd(FF0022B8): status 5C00 length 3C address 1B343CA
        tmd(FF0022C0): status 5C00 length 3C address 1B343CA
        tmd(FF0022C8): status 5C00 length 3C address 1B343CA
        tmd(FF0022D0): status 5C00 length 159 address 1B35DCA
        tmd(FF0022D8): status 5E00 length 3C address 1B343CA
        tmd(FF0022E0): status 5C00 length 3C address 1B343CA
        tmd(FF0022E8): status 5C00 length 3C address 1B343CA
        tmd(FF0022F0): status 5C00 length 3C address 1B343CA
```

```
tmd(FF0022F8): status 5C00 length 3C address 1B343CA
tmd(FF002300): status 5C00 length 15D address 1B35DCA
tmd(FF002308): status 5C00 length 15C address 1B35DCA
tmd(FF002310): status 5E00 length 3C address 1B343CA
tmd(FF002318): status 5C00 length 151 address 1B3748A
tmd(FF002320): status 5C00 length 3C address 1CD9C8A
tmd(FF002328): status 7C00 length 3C address 1CD9C8A
```
483 missed datagrams, 0 overruns
0 transmitter underruns, 0 excessive collisions
44446 single collisions, 35471 multiple collisions
0 dma memory errors, 0 CRC errors
1 alignment errors, 0 runts, 0 giants
QUICC SCC specific errors:
483 buffer errors, 0 overflow errors
0 input aborts on late collisions
0 throttles, 0 enables

Most of the output above is only useful to the Cisco TAC that can decifer it. However, the bolded lines at the end show a tremendous amount of useful information about the errors received on the interface. The same information, however, can be learned by other troubleshooting commands, such as the show interfaces command.

The **show ip traffic** Command

The show ip traffic command is used to display traffic statistics showing the numbers of IP packets that were sent and received for each IP protocol. It also shows the numbers of errors detected, numbers of multicasts, and the number of broadcasts sent and received by the interface. This command is useful because it reveals protocol problems on the interface that are not shown by the show ip interfaces command. An example of the command is shown below:

```
DCSRTR#show ip traffic
IP statistics:
  Rcvd:  169054310 total, 1038115 local destination
         0 format errors, 0 checksum errors, 21202 bad hop count
         559 unknown protocol, 1 not a gateway
         0 security failures, 0 bad options, 789 with options
  Opts:  0 end, 0 nop, 0 basic security, 0 loose source route
         230 timestamp, 0 extended security, 0 record route
         0 stream ID, 0 strict source route, 559 alert, 0 cipso, 0 ump
         0 other
  Frags: 5 reassembled, 13 timeouts, 0 couldn't reassemble
         1336 fragmented, 0 couldn't fragment
  Bcast: 953104 received, 305351 sent
  Mcast: 1147 received, 0 sent
  Sent:  581960 generated, 167783917 forwarded
  Drop:  185754 encapsulation failed, 0 unresolved, 0 no adjacency
         20594 no route, 0 unicast RPF, 0 forced drop

ICMP statistics:
  Rcvd: 0 format errors, 1 checksum errors, 14 redirects, 19615 unreachable
        1036 echo, 40 echo reply, 0 mask requests, 0 mask replies, 2 quench
```

```
            0 parameter, 0 timestamp, 0 info request, 0 other
            0 irdp solicitations, 5882 irdp advertisements
      Sent: 162077 redirects, 36604 unreachable, 850 echo, 1036 echo reply
            0 mask requests, 0 mask replies, 0 quench, 0 timestamp
            0 info reply, 21214 time exceeded, 0 parameter problem
            0 irdp solicitations, 0 irdp advertisements

   TCP statistics:
     Rcvd: 37767 total, 2 checksum errors, 7018 no port
     Sent: 25963 total

   UDP statistics:
     Rcvd: 973075 total, 0 checksum errors, 972367 no port
     Sent: 335235 total, 0 forwarded broadcasts

   BGP statistics:
     Rcvd: 0 total, 0 opens, 0 notifications, 0 updates
           0 keepalives, 0 route-refresh, 0 unrecognized
     Sent: 0 total, 0 opens, 0 notifications, 0 updates
           0 keepalives, 0 route-refresh

   OSPF statistics:
     Rcvd: 0 total, 0 checksum errors
           0 hello, 0 database desc, 0 link state req
           0 link state updates, 0 link state acks

     Sent: 0 total

   IP-EIGRP statistics:
     Rcvd: 0 total
     Sent: 0 total

   PIMv2 statistics: Sent/Received
     Total: 0/0, 0 checksum errors, 0 format errors
     Registers: 0/0, Register Stops: 0/0,  Hellos: 0/0
     Join/Prunes: 0/0, Asserts: 0/0, grafts: 0/0
     Bootstraps: 0/0, Candidate_RP_Advertisements: 0/0
     State-Refresh: 0/0

   IGMP statistics: Sent/Received
     Total: 0/0, Format errors: 0/0, Checksum errors: 0/0
     Host Queries: 0/0, Host Reports: 0/0, Host Leaves: 0/0
     DVMRP: 0/0, PIM: 0/0

   ARP statistics:
     Rcvd: 1177966 requests, 1050 replies, 110 reverse, 0 other
     Sent: 181941 requests, 96748 replies (441 proxy), 0 reverse
   DCSRTR#
```

The above output is helpful because it separates the network statistics, including errors by protocol. This enables you to rule out certain protocols as being problems during troubleshooting.

Statistics for AppleTalk and Novell can be displayed by using the **show appletalk traffic** or **show novell traffic** commands.

show arp

Another show command that may be useful is the show arp command, which is very helpful when you're trying to locate a particular device on your network. The ARP cache records all the devices that have traversed the router. The ARP cache lasts only for a short time after the device is no longer on the network, so this command is time-sensitive. By using this command, you can find the MAC address and associate it to an IP address on the network, enabling you to see how long the device was on the network. The show arp command also identifies which interface the devices are using. The following is example output from show arp:

```
DCSRootRTR#show arp
Protocol  Address         Age (min)  Hardware Addr  Type  Interface
Internet  192.16.33.254              0083.12eb.1dd5  ARPA  Ethernet2/1
Internet  192.16.34.224          3  00a0.b8be.9512  ARPA  Ethernet2/4
Internet  192.16.35.65          63  0080.5abc.55b4  ARPA  Ethernet2/5
```

The above output shows the ARP table from the router, which shows the MAC address to IP resolutions the router has made, as well as the interface to reach each host.

Cisco Discovery Protocol (CDP)

Cisco Discovery Protocol (CDP) is a Cisco proprietary Layer 2 (Data Link layer) protocol that was added to version 10.3 and later. CDP gathers and stores information regarding other neighboring devices on the network. It can be used in Ethernet, Token Ring, Serial, and FDDI media types. All Cisco devices, including hubs, support CDP. CDP runs on most Cisco manufactured devices that include Cisco routers, switches, hubs, bridges, and communication servers. CDP collects such information as the device name, device capabilities, hardware platform type, port type, and the port number through which CDP information is being sent out.

CDP periodically sends multicasts using 0100.0ccc.cccc as the destination address on the frame header. Information about the router itself is sent on all the router's interfaces every 60 seconds by default. Any neighboring Cisco device that is directly connected adds the learned CDP information to a table called the CDP table. CDP-enabled neighboring devices then hold this information for the specified CDP hold-time (180 seconds, by default). The CDP command has several syntaxes which display different collected information. Let's take a look at each one of the syntaxes:

```
DCSRTR#show cdp ?
  entry      Information for specific neighbor entry
  interface  CDP interface status and configuration
```

```
neighbors   CDP neighbor entries
traffic     CDP statistics
|           Output modifiers
<cr>
```

The output above shows all the syntaxes available for the show cdp command.

The **show cdp entry** Command

This command shows all the entries learned from all the interfaces on the router or switch. The following display shows that the router is directly attached to a Cisco 2950 switch as shown in Figure 7.2. An asterisk after the show cdp entry command indicates "all" devices.

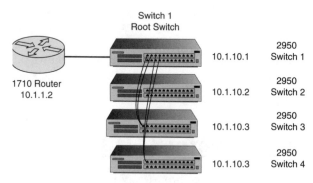

Switch 1
Root Switch

1710 Router
10.1.1.2

10.1.10.1   2950
            Switch 1

10.1.10.2   2950
            Switch 2

10.1.10.3   2950
            Switch 3

10.1.10.3   2950
            Switch 4

Figure 7.2   The configuration shown by the **show cdp entry** command.

```
DCSRTR#show cdp entry *
Device ID: DCS-SAC-Sw1
Entry address(es):
  IP address: 10.1.10.1
Platform: cisco WS-C2950-24,  Capabilities: Trans-Bridge Switch
Interface: FastEthernet0,  Port ID (outgoing port): FastEthernet0/1
Holdtime : 140 sec
Version :
Cisco Internetwork Operating System Software
IOS (tm) C2950 Software (C2950-C3H2S-M), Version 12.0(5.3)WC(1),
          MAINTENANCE INT
ERIM SOFTWARE
Copyright (c) 1986-2001 by cisco Systems, Inc.
Compiled Mon 30-Apr-01 07:56 by devgoyal
advertisement version: 2
Protocol Hello:  OUI=0x00000C, Protocol ID=0x0112; payload len=27,
          value=0000000
0FFFFFFFF010121FF00000000000000006525ACD80FF0001
VTP Management Domain: ''
```

This is the same command viewed from the attached 2950 switch. This output shows that the switch is directly attached to the Cisco router that the preceding output came from:

```
DCS-SAC-Sw1#show cdp entry *
Device ID: DCSRTR
Entry address(es):
  IP address: 10.1.1.2
Platform: cisco 1710,  Capabilities: Router
Interface: FastEthernet0/1,  Port ID (outgoing port): FastEthernet0
Holdtime : 149 sec
Version :
Cisco Internetwork Operating System Software
IOS (tm) C1700 Software (C1710-K9O3SY-M), Version 12.2(4)XL,
            EARLY DEPLOYMENT RE
LEASE SOFTWARE (fc1)
TAC Support: http://www.cisco.com/tac
Copyright (c) 1986-2001 by cisco Systems, Inc.
Compiled Thu 15-Nov-01 18:45 by ealyon
advertisement version: 2
```

The show cdp interface Command

The show cdp interface command shows all the interfaces on the router or switch that are using the CDP protocol, the status of the interface, the encapsulation type, how often CDP packets are sent on the interface, and how long entries are held. The following output shows the interfaces on a Cisco 1710 router and displays the default settings on the interface.

```
CSRTR#show cdp interface
Ethernet0 is up, line protocol is up
  Encapsulation ARPA
  Sending CDP packets every 60 seconds
  Holdtime is 180 seconds
FastEthernet0 is up, line protocol is up
  Encapsulation ARPA
  Sending CDP packets every 60 seconds
  Holdtime is 180 seconds
DCSRTR#
```

The show cdp neighbors Command

The show cdp neighbors command displays all the connected neighbors, the Device ID, the interface connecting to the device, the device's capabilities, the type of device, and the port ID on the remote device that is connected to the switch. Here is an example of this command in use:

```
DCSRTR#show cdp neighbors
Capability Codes: R - Router, T - Trans Bridge, B - Source Route Bridge
                  S - Switch, H - Host, I - IGMP, r - Repeater

Device ID      Local Intrfce    Holdtme    Capability Platform  Port ID
DCS-SAC-Sw1    Fas 0            158         T S        WS-C2950-2Fas 0/1
DCSRTR#
```

The `show cdp neighbors` command has many syntaxes. For the exam you should be familiar with the output from the `detail` syntax, which is all shown below:

```
DCSRTR#show cdp neighbors ?
  Async               Async interface
  BVI                 Bridge-Group Virtual Interface
  CTunnel             CTunnel interface
  Dialer              Dialer interface
  Ethernet            IEEE 802.3
  FastEthernet        FastEthernet IEEE 802.3
  Lex                 Lex interface
  MFR                 Multilink Frame Relay bundle interface
  Multilink           Multilink-group interface
  Tunnel              Tunnel interface
  Vif                 PGM Multicast Host interface
  Virtual-Template    Virtual Template interface
  Virtual-TokenRing   Virtual TokenRing
  detail              Show detailed information
  |                   Output modifiers
  <cr>
DCSRTR#show cdp neighbors detail
Device ID: DCS-SAC-Sw1
Entry address(es):
  IP address: 10.1.10.1
Platform: cisco WS-C2950-24,  Capabilities: Trans-Bridge Switch
Interface: FastEthernet0,  Port ID (outgoing port): FastEthernet0/1
Holdtime : 172 sec
Version :
Cisco Internetwork Operating System Software
IOS (tm) C2950 Software (C2950-C3H2S-M), Version 12.0(5.3)WC(1),
              MAINTENANCE INT
ERIM SOFTWARE
Copyright (c) 1986-2001 by cisco Systems, Inc.
Compiled Mon 30-Apr-01 07:56 by devgoyal
advertisement version: 2
Protocol Hello:  OUI=0x00000C, Protocol ID=0x0112; payload len=27,
              value=0000000
0FFFFFFFF010121FF0000000000000006525ACD80FF0001
VTP Management Domain: ''
DCSRTR#
```

Notice that in the output from the `detail` syntax above, the Platform, Device ID, the interface on the device being used, the IP address of the device, the device type, and the version of the IOS the attached device is using are all displayed.

The show cdp traffic Command

The output of this command shows the total CDP packets sent, CDP packets received, CDP version type, memory errors, and any CDP packet problems that were detected. An example of the output follows:

```
CSRTR#show cdp traffic
CDP counters :
```

```
          Total packets output: 45984, Input: 23303
          Hdr syntax: 0, Chksum error: 0, Encaps failed: 0
          No memory: 0, Invalid packet: 0, Fragmented: 0
          CDP version 1 advertisements output: 0, Input: 0
          CDP version 2 advertisements output: 45984, Input: 23303
DCSRTR#
```

Configuring CDP

The CDP protocol can be disabled on all the routers' interfaces by using no cdp run command. It can be re-enabled by using the cdp run command as shown below:

```
Password:
DCSRTR>enable
Password:
DCSRTR#config terminal
Enter configuration commands, one per line.  End with CNTL/Z.
DCSRTR(config)#no cdp run
DCSRTR(config)#cdp run
```

If you would like to disable CDP on a particular interface, use the no cdp enable command. To re-enable CDP, use the cdp enable command as shown below:

```
Password:
DCSRTR>enable
Password:
DCSRTR#config terminal
Enter configuration commands, one per line.  End with CNTL/Z.
DCSRTR(config)#interface fastethernet0
DCSRTR(config-if)#no cdp enable
DCSRTR(config-if)#cdp enable
```

Both the CDP timer and holddown values are controlled at the global configuration interface. To set the CDP timer—which controls how often CDP packets are sent—use the cdp timer command and indicate how often in seconds you want CDP packets to be sent, as shown below:

```
Password:
DCSRTR>enable
Password:
DCSRTR#config terminal
Enter configuration commands, one per line.  End with CNTL/Z.
DCSRTR(config)#cdp timer 150
DCSRTR(config)#
```

The CDP hold-time timer also needs to be configured in Global configuration mode using the cdp holddown command follows by the hold-time that is indicated in seconds. The configured CDP timers should be configured the same on neighboring Cisco devices as the current router. An example of the command is shown below, setting the hold time to 300 seconds:

```
Password:
DCSRTR>enable
Password:
DCSRTR#config terminal
Enter configuration commands, one per line.  End with CNTL/Z.
DCSRTR(config)#cdp holddown 300
DCSRTR(config)#
```

The above output shows the CDP hold down timer being set to 300 seconds. This means that learned entries will not expire for 5 minutes.

Configuration and Fault Management

As networks have grown larger over the years, so has the need for a better monitoring system. As the number of devices you have on your network increases, the complexity, monitoring responsibilities, and possible number of network failures also increase. Network management has been defined by the International Organization for Standardization (ISO) as having five key areas: accounting management, configuration and name management, fault management, performance management, and security management. Fault management and configuration management are the two areas of network management that deal with troubleshooting.

Configuration management relies on the initial configuration of devices with agents so the devices are capable of being seen, of communicating on the network, and of reporting to a central monitoring system. The network is configured centrally to interact with the devices and respond to network upgrades the administrator may implement. The centrally monitored network will also be able to respond to failures and recover quickly. This is where fault management comes into play.

Fault management is described as the tracking and logging of an abnormal network event, which is usually defined as failing components or an excessive amount of errors. With early treatment of any network faults, the network downtime is minimal to none.

To find faults in the network, Network Management Systems (NMSs) use different methods to discover the network. An NMS is a complete package of hardware and software for monitoring a network and gathering information on system performance and security. The NMS begins by utilizing a central device to slowly discover anything that is configured for the central device to see. For the discovering device to be able to identify the network devices, those devices must contain information of the type the discovering device is searching for. Along with the discovery of the network, an NMS uses monitoring to be able to keep track of the network's statistics.

NMSs enable you to monitor your network 24 hours a day from a central location, and alert you in case of failure or other alarms configured by the administrator. An NMS enables you to gather information about a network, such as details about packets, errors, hosts, connectivity, and performance. NMSs use SNMP (Simple Network Management Protocol), discussed later in this chapter, to communicate with devices on the network. For your network to be managed by SNMP, you must have managed devices, such as routers and switches, running an SNMP software agent, and a central point that acts as the monitoring system.

How Network Monitors Work

When you think of a network monitor, you might think of it as a particular device or piece of equipment. However, a network monitor consists mainly of software that oversees the network monitoring. Network monitors continuously monitor the packets that are traversing the network, and track the information to provide a current snapshot of the network activity. Even though a network monitor looks at the packets, it only collects statistics; the packets are not analyzed for errors or problems.

A network monitor's main function is to keep track of all the statistical information about the network to provide a *baseline*, an average sample (using statistical data) of the activity on the network. After a baseline has been established, it can be configured to report any network activity that is considered abnormal. Network monitors alleviate the headache of trying to manually monitor the network all day, every day. Network monitors collect several pieces of information that enable you to see an accurate picture of the network. Some information a network monitoring system may gather includes the following:

➤ The number of packets being received or transmitted

➤ The size of the packets being sent and received

➤ Any errors in the packets

➤ Network utilization statistics

➤ Identities of hosts and their MAC addresses

➤ Connectivity with other devices

➤ Baseline statistics

➤ Average performance

A large network environment has hundreds and possibly thousands of devices promising a flawless network, especially in a large campus environment that is maintained 24 hours a day, 7 days a week. A network administrator or a group of network administrators can't possibly monitor all the devices without a monitoring system in place. An online system needs to be in place to control and report any network faults, as well as any performance, security, and accounting issues.

Simple Network Management Protocol (SNMP)

The most common protocol used in network monitoring is the Simple Network Management Protocol (SNMP). SNMP is a reporting and signaling protocol that enables network devices to exchange detailed device information about monitored devices. Online systems that use SNMP have proven to be dependable.

SNMP enables you to monitor network utilization, performance, uptime, and even traffic on ports for up to thousands of devices. Because most current network devices communicate with SNMP, an NMS can scan a network in about an hour, whereas it would take days for someone to physically walk around to all the devices and monitor each LAN or WAN segment. An SNMP online system enables system administrators to monitor the whole network from a central point, which can be anywhere from a network operations center to the desktop of the system administrator.

To have your network managed by SNMP, you have to implement the following types of devices:

➤ Managed devices—Any node (including routers, servers, switches, computers, or printers) on your network running an SNMP agent that is being monitored. The agent collects management information and sends it back to the NMSs using SNMP.

➤ Agent—The actual software module that runs on the managed devices and enables SNMP to communicate with the devices. The major requirement of the agent is to gather statistical information and store it in a management information base (MIB), a directory of the information and resources collected from the network that pertain to network management. SNMP uses MIBs to aid in monitoring the network. The device uses an MIB to store information about network management. The RMON MIB is one of the most widely used MIBs for remote access (you learn more about RMON MIB in an upcoming section of this chapter). The agent can also send traps or alarms, depending on the events happening on the network and how the agent is configured.

➤ Network management system—An application that provides control and management of the devices connected to it. The information is gathered by the managed devices, and is sent back to the NMSs to monitor the network.

SNMP Community Strings

For the SNMP manager and the agent to communicate, the SNMP *community string* must be set. The community string can be thought of as a string of passwords that need to be set to permit access to the agent on the router. Strings or community names can be created with the characteristics of access control lists, read-only rights, read-write rights, and MIB views. The string can be made up of characteristics that associate the access with the string name. For example, you can set a string name of Cisco that allows access to a specific MIB, or you can assign a string name of Router that associates read-only or read and write permissions for specified MIB objects. To configure a community string, use the following commands in Global Configuration Mode:

```
DCS2(config)#
DCS2(config)#snmp-server community router ?
  <1-99>  Std IP accesslist allowing access with this community string
  ro      Read-only access with this community string
  rw      Read-write access with this community string
  view    Restrict this community to a named MIB view
DCS2(config)#snmp-server community router ro
DCS2(config)#snmp-server community Cisco rw
DCS2(config)#snmp-server community Support view ?
  WORD  MIB view to which this community has access
DCS2#
```

Traps

A *trap* is an SNMP notification of an event that the router transmits to an NMS at the time of a severe network change. The event for which a trap should be sent can be defined by the network administrator. Configuring traps in your network will make life a lot easier for you as a network administrator, because you will be notified of any network problems when they happen. The trap is sent to the central location, thus triggering an alarm. Most systems are configured to alert a pager, for a faster response time, and usually enable you to be one step ahead of users' calls. Hopefully, with the few moments of advance notice from the network monitoring system, you can fix the problem before it has a large impact on users.

A trap is sent only once and is discarded as soon as it is sent so that it does not cause any congestion on the network, especially in cases in which the network may be suffering from congestion already. You can configure the router to send a trap to the central location when a network problem occurs, thereby sending an alarm. The following is an example of how to configure a router to send traps:

```
DCSRootRTR#
DCSRootRTR(config)#snmp-server enable traps ?
  appn         Enable SNMP appn traps
  bgp          Enable BGP state change traps
  config       Enable SNMP config traps
  dlsw         Enable SNMP dlsw traps
  entity       Enable SNMP entity traps
  frame-relay  Enable SNMP frame-relay traps
  isdn         Enable SNMP isdn traps
  rtr          Enable SNMP Response Time Reporter traps
  snmp         Enable SNMP traps
  syslog       Enable SNMP syslog traps
  <cr>
DCSRootRTR#
```

The above output shows the syntaxes available when enabling SNMP traps.

The next example shows how to designate a trap to be sent to a specific source for logging:

```
DCSRoot (config)#snmp-server trap-source ?
  BRI       ISDN Basic Rate Interface
  Ethernet  IEEE 802.3
  Null      Null interface
  Serial    Serial
DCSRoot(config)#snmp-server trap-source ethernet ?
  <0-0>   Ethernet interface number
DCSRoot(config)#snmp-server trap-source ethernet0
DCSRoot(config)#
```

The code above shows the process for designating an interface as an SNMP trap source.

The Remote Monitoring MIB (RMON MIB)

One of the most common MIBs is the Remote Monitoring, or RMON MIB. The RMON MIB is used in most devices to allow monitoring of different LAN segments in a network. RMON was defined by the user community (with the help of the Internet Engineering Task Force) to provide a mechanism for device communications; it became a standard as RFC 1757. RMON enables agents and network management systems to communicate with each other and exchange data. RMON also provides for comprehensive network-fault diagnosis, planning, and performance-tuning information using the MIB.

Several RMON groups apply to the standard, such as statistics for RMON (group 1) and history for RMON (group 2). Cisco devices are embedded with various RMON groups, depending on the device.

Cisco NMS Software

As stated previously, a monitoring system mainly consists of software. Cisco offers several software packages to maintain an NMS. The software is often referred to as Cisco Network Management Solutions. The software enables you to update the IOS, change configurations, provide baselines of your network, aid in troubleshooting, and instantly send an alarm in case of failure. This includes the following:

➤ CiscoWorks and CiscoView—The CiscoWorks software allows for monitoring, configuration, fault management, troubleshooting, and performance tuning using CiscoView to graphically display a physical view of the network. CiscoView software can be integrated with Sun Microsystems, HP Open View, and IBM NetView.

➤ Traffic Director—Analyzes network traffic patterns and reports the network trends in a switched internetwork. It can also be used for troubleshooting protocol problems and setting alarms to notify a system administrator in case of failure. Traffic Director utilizes the embedded RMON agents in catalyst switches to compile the data.

➤ CiscoWorks for Switched Internetworks (CWSI)—A software suite that includes Traffic Director, CiscoView, and VlanDirector. CWSI works with SNMP, Cisco Discovery Protocol (CDP), Virtual Trunk Protocol (VTP), automated VLAN arrangement, and RMON for traffic monitoring. CWSI auto-discovers and creates a topology to allow system administrators to view the relationships and display VLANs.

➤ Cisco Netsys—A simulation tool that enables the system administrator to see and test network performance of a new design before implementing it in the production network. Netsys uses object-oriented code that enables existing infrastructure code to be imported into Netsys, thereby allowing Netsys to simulate the performance of the new design before it is implemented.

The main function of a protocol analyzer is to capture, display, and analyze how a communications protocol is operating on the given network on a per-packet basis. The analyzer captures packets that are on the network at the given time, thus reporting in real time. To provide an accurate reading, the protocol analyzer must be physically attached to the specific network or broadcast domain you are trying to monitor. The protocol analyzer decodes the various layers and reports them in reference to each layer of the OSI model. A few examples of packet analyzers are NetBoy, LANWatch32, Wild Packets Etherpeek, Observer, Surveyor, Agilent Advisor, and Sniffer Pro.

When monitoring traffic, the protocol analyzer copies packets into its memory so that the packets can be analyzed without affecting the traffic. Using analyzers enables you to isolate a particular type of traffic or specify that you want to see only source and destination traffic. For example, if you are having an Ethernet problem, you don't need to look at all the routing traffic. This enables you to troubleshoot and analyze a particular area within a reasonably short period of time. Because many protocols are used in large campus environments, it is necessary to have a protocol analyzer that can discern different protocols.

Chapter Summary

In this chapter you learned the tools and commands you can use to make sure your Physical layer functions and performs properly. The router's interfaces and controllers are among your first troubleshooting targets. These router interfaces and controllers both continuously collect and store information on their performance and status.

Physical devices including TDRs, OTDRs, and cable testers can be used to test the physical cabling. This can help you determine whether connectivity issues are a result of faulty cabling or installations.

CDP can be use to see what devices the Cisco router or switch believes are directly connected. The show cdp command provides information as to the directly connected Cisco devices' platform, IOS version, connected ports, host names, and other important information.

NMS software and devices can be used to make monitoring the physical devices in your network easier. This can make diagnosing problems in your network quicker and easier. A number of software packages were discussed such as CiscoWorks, CWSI, Cisco Netsys, and Cisco View.

Also discussed in this chapter were protocol analyzers that are better known as network sniffers. These can be used to capture and take statistics of the data traffic traversing the physical network.

This chapter also discussed the Physical layer troubleshooting commands and their output. For the exam, it is important that you understand the Physical layer troubleshooting commands, when to use those commands, and how to interpret each command's output.

Exam Prep Practice Questions

Question 1

The most common protocol used in network monitoring is _____.

O A.   SNMP

O B.   TCP/IP

O C.   RIP

O D.   OSPF

O E.   Monitor

Answer: **A.** Simple Network Management Protocol (SNMP) is the most commonly used protocol.

Question 2

The NMS software suite that contains Traffic Director, CiscoView, and VlanDirector is _____.

O A.   Traffic Director

O B.   CiscoWorks

O C.   CiscoWorks for Switched Internetworks (CWSI)

O D.   Cisco Basics

O E.   Cisco Suite

Answer: **C.** CiscoWorks for Switched Internetworks (CWSI) contains all of the software mentioned.

Question 3

Network _____ continuously monitor(s) packets and provide(s) a current snapshot of the network activity.

- ○ A. Systems
- ○ B. Logging
- ○ C. Monitors
- ○ D. Statistics
- ○ E. Protocols

Answer: **C.** Network monitors monitor packets and provide a current snapshot.

Question 4

For the SNMP manager and agent to communicate, SNMP _____ _____ must be configured.

- ○ A. Community strings
- ○ B. Management names
- ○ C. Management properties
- ○ D. Community MIBs
- ○ E. Information bases

Answer: **A.** Community strings or community names must be configured for SNMP.

Question 5

The main function of a(n) _____ is to capture, display, and analyze (on a per-packet basis) how a communication protocol is operating on the network.

- ○ A. protocol packet
- ○ B. analyzer pro
- ○ C. analyzer protocol
- ○ D. protocol analyzer
- ○ E. packet collector

Answer: **D.** A protocol analyzer captures, displays, and analyzes how a communication protocol is operating on the network.

Question 6

> One of the most common MIBs used for remote monitoring is _____.
>
> O A. MIB 3
> O B. RMON
> O C. ROMN
> O D. ROMAN
> O E. MIB4

Answer: **B.** RMON is one of the most common MIBs used for remote monitoring.

Question 7

> Which **show** command enables you to look at all the collisions on a router's Fast Ethernet ports?
>
> O A. **show debug**
> O B. **show trace**
> O C. **show interfaces**
> O D. **show IPX**
> O E. **show arp**

Answer: **C.** The show interfaces command will show you all the interfaces on the router, including the interface error statistics.

Question 8

> A(n) _____ is a directory of information and resources collected from the network that pertains to network management.
>
> O A. Monitoring base
> O B. Base
> O C. Information base
> O D. Database
> O E. Management information base

Answer: **E.** A management information base (MIB) contains the information.

Question 9

> By default keepalives are sent on an Ethernet interface every _____.
>
> ○ A. 60 seconds
> ○ B. 3 minutes
> ○ C. 30 seconds
> ○ D. 10 seconds
> ○ E. 5 minutes

Answer: **D**. By default, keepalives are sent on an Ethernet interface every 10 seconds. Keepalives inform a router that an adjacent interface on the link is active and functioning correctly.

Question 10

> A cable tester that sends electric signals and waits for the signals to return is a
>
> _____.
>
> ○ A. Volt-ohm meter
> ○ B. Digital meter
> ○ C. Time domain reflector (TDR)
> ○ D. Circuit tester
> ○ E. Ping tester

Answer: **C**. A time domain reflector (TDR) will send an electronic signal and wait for a return.

Need to Know More?

 Wild Packets Etherpeek Sniffer Web site: `http://www.wildpackets.com/products/etherpeek`

 Agilent Advisor Sniffer Web site: `http://www.agilent.com`

 Sniffer Pro Web site: `http://www.sniffer.com/aboutus/default.asp`

 Shomiti's Surveyor Sniffer Web site: `ttp://www.finisar.com/product/product.php?product_id=104&product_category_id=96`

 Observer Sniffer information: `http://www.linklan.co.uk/products_next.html`

 LANWatch32 Sniffer information: `http://sandstorm.net/products/lanwatch/`

 CCO CiscoWorks Software information: `http://www.cisco.com/kobayashi/sw-center/cw2000/campus.shtml`

Troubleshooting the Data Link Layer

Terms you'll need to understand:

✓ Convergence Time
✓ Internetwork Operating System (IOS)
✓ Inter-Switch Link (ISL)
✓ POST (Power-on Self Test)
✓ Spanning Tree Protocol (STP)

Techniques you'll need to master:

✓ Troubleshoot switched connections
✓ Identify switch troubleshooting commands
✓ Troubleshoot switch hardware and software
✓ Troubleshoot VTP, ISL, and Spanning Tree Protocol configurations
✓ Identify switch troubleshooting and configuration software
✓ Recover a lost password
✓ Learn the diagnostic tools to apply to Catalyst 5000 problems
✓ Learn which diagnostic tools to apply to VLAN configuration problems
✓ Troubleshoot inter-VLAN routing configurations
✓ Troubleshoot trunk links and switches and routers

The Cisco Support Exam Layer 2 switch-troubleshooting objective focuses on your knowledge of the Set/Clear command set IOS, such as that used on the Cisco 5000 series switch and the Cisco Command Line Interface (CLI) IOS used in the Cisco 4500 series switch. The exam tests your knowledge on the LEDs found on the switch and its modules, the Set/Clear command set, and the show commands associated with the switch.

Cisco is introducing so many generations of switches and protocols that it seems natural that implementing different switches will cause problems. Switches have provided so many advantages over hubs and bridges that Cisco has implemented components, as well as software, to support data traffic not only at Layer 2, but also at Layers 3, 4, and even 5.

Hardware Troubleshooting

The operating system software that runs on a Cisco router or switch is called the *Internetwork Operating System* or *IOS*. Before we move on to troubleshooting problems using the Cisco Set/Clear IOS and the Cisco CLI IOS, we will first look at the hardware. Troubleshooting hardware requires a working knowledge of power failure issues, the information you can get from the Power-On Self Test (POST), switch cables, and what each light emitting diode (LED) light on the switch or its modules indicates.

Power Failure

A power failure is a very apparent sign of trouble. If there's no power to the switch, the fans fail to turn on, no indicator lights appear lit on the front or back of the switch, and no prompt appears on the console port.

Make sure you use proper grounding techniques before removing or touching any components, and make sure that the switch is unplugged from all power sources.

Follow these steps in troubleshooting a power failure:

1. Check the physical cable for breaks.

2. Check that all cables are securely installed.

3. Check the outlet with a multimeter for proper throughput.

4. Reseat the RAM in the chassis.

5. Check the connection and verify that all interfaces, cards, and modules are securely fastened in the chassis.

6. Make sure all gold-plated connections for the cards, modules, and RAM are not corroded and can make a good connection.

 To clean the gold-plated connections, use an eraser from a pencil.

7. Contact Cisco TAC or an authorized Cisco repair vendor for further troubleshooting and replacement parts.

Power-On Self Test (POST)

The *POST* can be a powerful tool in solving hardware issues. The POST is displayed on the screen when the switch powers up and performs a systematic check of the IOS running on the switch, the configuration files, and a comprehensive hardware test. Each LED on the switch becomes lit one at a time indicating that a different test is being performed.

The POST tests the following components:

➤ Ports (loopback)

➤ Ethernet address PROM

➤ CAM (MAC Address) Table

➤ RS-232 Console Port

➤ Realtime Clock

➤ CAM memory (SRAM)

➤ Timer interrupt

➤ Port control status

➤ Flag Memory (DRAM)

➤ Buffer Memory (DRAM)

➤ Forwarding Engine Memory (SRAM)

➤ Forwarding Engine CPU

➤ ECU memory (DRAM)

Switch Indicator Lights

Both the Catalyst 5000 and 4500 families of switches use quite a few LEDs that can indicate a problem or the current utilization of the switch. The Supervisor Engine has five different LEDs that indicate the system, fan, power supplies, load utilization, and whether or not the Supervisor Engine is active.

The Cisco 4500 Series uses Supervisor Engine IV. On this module, a series of round LEDs indicates loads from 1% to 100%, as shown in Figure 8.1.

The load bar indicates the current load on the switch. If the local bar is more than 80 percent, either a network problem exists, such as a broadcast storm, or an upgrade in the switching devices is needed.

Figure 8.1   The Cisco Supervisor Engine IV load bar.

The load bar on a Supervisor III, shown in Figure 8.2, uses a different set of LEDs to indicate system load and status. The System Status light indicates the following, depending on the color:

➤ Green—All diagnostics passed.

➤ Orange/Amber—The second power supply failed.

➤ Red—A diagnostic test on the switch failed.

The fan LED indicates the following:

➤ Red—The fan has failed to power up.

➤ Green—The fan is operating correctly.

The Supervisor III Power supply 1 (PS1) and Power Supply 2 (PS2) LEDs indicate the following:

➤ Red—Power supply failure.

➤ Green—Power supply operating normally.

➤ Off—The power supply bay is empty or off.

The Active LED indicates the following:

➤ Orange/Amber—The Supervisor Engine is in standby mode.

➤ Green—The Supervisor Engine is operating correctly.

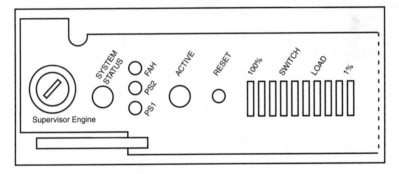

Figure 8.2 The Cisco Supervisor Engine III load bar.

LEDs also exist on each individual line module such as the Ethernet modules. Each module has a Status LED that displays green to indicate the module is functioning. On the newer modules, such as the 24- or 48-port 10/100 Ethernet modules, there is a single LED for each port. When the LED is green, the port is in use and there is an established link with the device connected to the port. A portion of a 48-port module on a Cisco 4506 is shown in Figure 8.3.

On older line modules, such as those used in the Cisco 5000 series, the green light indicates that a good established link exists. An orange or amber light indicates that a problem exists with the link. A red light indicates a nonport test has failed. On these modules there is sometimes a second LED called the

Speed (SP) LED. A green switch port (SP) LED indicates the port is operating at 100BaseT and functioning. When the SP light is off, it is operating in 10BaseT.

Figure 8.3 LEDs on a Cisco 10/100 Ethernet module on a Cisco 4506.

Troubleshooting Cables

Data can move around today's networks at greater speeds than ever. These high speeds add network complexities. Early implementations allowed cable lengths to have greater distances and flexibility. In today's high-speed networks, the distance limitations should be strictly adhered to. Many times, administrators will upgrade the network interface cards on both ends of a former 10Mbps link and find that the 100Mbps link begins to receive an excessive number of errors, forcing the link to become unusable. Going over on the 10BaseT cable distance limits didn't have the detrimental effects that it does with 100BaseT or 1000BaseT.

You may also have a noncompatible cable type. For instance, 10BaseT will work over Category 3, 4, 5, or 6 twisted-pair cable, whereas 100BaseT or 1000BaseT requires Category 5 or 6. Table 8.1 examines the common cable limits for cabling in today's networks.

Table 8.1 The Common Network Cabling Limitations		
Cable	**Distance Limit**	**Cable Speed (Mbps)**
Category 3	100 meters	10
Category 4	100 meters	16
Category 5	100 meters	10/100/1000
Category 6	100 meters	10/100/1000
Multimode fiber (half)	2,000 meters	10/100
Single/Multimode fiber (full)	400 meters	10/100
Single-mode fiber	10,000 meters	10/100

Cable problems can appear suddenly or as an intermittent problem. Intermittent errors are sometimes hard to troubleshoot and can appear as problems unrelated to cabling. As an administrator, you have to be aware that almost any connectivity issue can be cable-related, and to resolve connectivity issues, you must replace a cable with a cable that you know works.

As discussed in Chapter 7, "Troubleshooting the Physical Layer," you can also use multimeters, time domain reflectometers (TDRs), cable analyzers, or breakout boxes to test for cable connectivity errors.

 Never conclude that just because a cable is installed or tested by a certified cable installer that it can't be improperly made, have a break, or have a failure in its connectors. Cables are moving parts and, as with any moving parts, are subject to wear and tear.

Use the Correct Ethernet Cable

You need to use the correct cable for the equipment you are using. A connection to a network node from a switch or hub uses a *straight-through cable*. A *crossover cable* is used to connect two network devices, such as a hub to a hub, a switch to a switch, a switch to a router, and so on. When trying to configure switches or routers, you will fail to get a connection between the devices if you use a straight-through cable when you should be using a crossover cable.

Layer 2 Switching Troubleshooting Basics

To understand why a switch is instrumental in today's networks, you need to have an understanding of many aspects of basic switching. You need to have a clear understanding of network traffic types, how broadcasts take away from the network bandwidth, the different media types in a network, and how switches overcome the problems inherent in bridges and switches. This section defines the following switch basics:

➤ Broadcast and unicast forwarding

➤ Aggregate bandwidth

➤ Full-duplex and half-duplex

➤ Supported media types

➤ Differences between bridges and switches

Broadcast and Unicast Forwarding

Knowing how switches and hubs treat broadcasts and unicasts can be an asset when you are troubleshooting switches. A general rule to remember about unicasts is that on a switch, unicasts are sent only to the destination port if the switch has learned the port the destination resides on. If the switch hasn't learned which port the destination resides on, the switch forwards the unicast out of all the ports that are members of the same virtual LAN (VLAN) as the source, with the exception of the port of arrival. A hub forwards unicasts and all data traffic out of its ports.

Broadcasts are sent to all the ports with the same VLAN membership as the receiving port, because everyone is the destination. A hub could care less about VLANs, and will send broadcasts to all of its ports.

Aggregate Bandwidth

Sometimes bottlenecks can develop in your network because the total number of ports that can bring data in equals more than the speed the trunk links can handle. For instance, a switch with 24 ports at 10Mbps each is capable of providing a total *aggregate bandwidth* of 240Mbps. If you have a 100Mbps trunk link between switches, the total amount of data coming from the ports can overwhelm the trunk link and cause a bottleneck. On a hub, the speed of the entire network is always equal to the speed of the physical media. For example, if you have a 10BaseT hub, the hub provides a total of 10Mbps of throughput.

Full-Duplex Versus Half-Duplex

Switches support half-duplex or full-duplex communications. *Full-duplex* refers to two-way communication that can take place simultaneously. A telephone call is an example of two-way communications. Both parties can speak and hear each other simultaneously.

Hubs support only *half-duplex*, which is communication that takes place on a single line. This can be similar to communication that takes place with a CB radio. The person holding down the button gets to speak while the other must listen. If both try to communicate simultaneously, a "collision" occurs.

Supported Media Types

The Catalyst 5000 and 4500 families of switches can support multiple mixed physical media types, such as Token Ring, Ethernet, Gigabit Ethernet, and Fiber Distributed Data Interface (FDDI), depending on the switch and the modules you have installed. The different modules in the switch provide the translations necessary between the different physical media types.

Differences Between Bridges and Switches

Some differences exist between bridges and switches and the types of physical media they support. Bridges and switches can provide support for mixed physical media environments, depending on the configuration and components installed on them. Switches process frames using application-specific integrated circuits (ASICs), which are chips that provide one or two tasks faster than a processor can. Bridges use software or generic hardware to provide processor tasks.

Another difference between bridges and switches is the number of ports each can support. Switches can provide ports that number in the hundreds. Bridges are typically 2- to 16-port devices.

Catalyst Switch Troubleshooting Software

Cisco Catalyst switches have quite a few network designs, diagnostics, and administrative tools available to administer Cisco switches. These tools are located in several pieces of software that are available from Cisco or third parties.

CWSI (CiscoWorks for Switched Internetworks) is software that's available from Cisco to manage a switched internetwork. The next section discusses some of the components of CWSI and then looks at the troubleshooting commands that can be used on the Cisco IOS found on Cisco's >line of enterprise switches.

CWSI

CWSI, also known as Campus Manager, can run as a standalone application on Windows NT or Unix operating systems. These systems include Solaris, HP-Unix, and AIX. The CWSI application includes numerous components that aid not only in troubleshooting, but also in installing, designing, and monitoring switched networks. The following list describes these components, all of which are GUI applications:

➤ CiscoView—Provides a graphical view of the chassis, configuration, and performance monitoring. This component provides very little in the way of troubleshooting functionality.

➤ User Tracking—Used in the creation and management of dynamic VLANs. Cisco switches permit VLAN assignments based on dynamic VLAN assignments. This means that the MAC address is used to assign the port to a specific VLAN. User Tracking defines these dynamic VLANs and maintains the whereabouts of workstations throughout the network.

➤ VlanDirector—A very powerful tool to aid in the creation of multiple VLANs on a switch. This tool helps the administrator add users and assign ports, and makes managing VLANs easy.

➤ TrafficDirector—A great tool to create usage baselines and troubleshoot switched environments. This tool enables you to view both the switched network and trunked and switched ports. TrafficDirector requires a VTP server to be configured in the network.

➤ ATMDirector—In Asynchronous Transfer Mode (ATM) networks, this tool can be used to configure, administer, and troubleshoot ATM switched networks.

RMON (Remote Monitoring)

Remote Monitoring is an industry-standard method used to provide statistics on a network using Simple Network Management Protocol (SNMP) as the medium to report its findings. A switch configured for RMON enables a network administrator to obtain information about a switch's Layer 1 and Layer 2 environment.

RMON collects a lot of information regarding the switch's physical connections, performance, configuration, and other pertinent statistics. After RMON is configured on the switch, it runs continuously even when no clients are checking statistics. In fact, communication with an SNMP management station is not necessary. RMON can be configured to send Trap messages to notify a management station when an error condition occurs that exceeds a currently configured maximum threshold.

Nine different groups are available that can provide RMON information, four of which can be configured to provide information on a Cisco Catalyst switch without an external device, such as a Switched Port Analyzer (SPAN).

Cisco Catalyst switches support RMON information for Ethernet traffic for the following four groups:

➤ Statistics—This group's basic function is to maintain utilization and error statistics. It monitors collisions, oversized packets, undersized packets, network jabber, packet fragmentation, and multicast and unicast bandwidth utilization.

➤ History—This group provides periodical statistical information, such as bandwidth utilization, frame counts, and error counts, that can be stored for later use.

➤ Alarm—This group enables you to configure thresholds for alarms and the intervals to check statistics. Any monitored event can be set to alarm the management station with a Trap message regarding an absolute or relative value or threshold.

➤ Event—This group's responsibility is to monitor log events on the switches. It also sends Trap messages to the management station with the time and date of the logged event. This enables the management station to be able to create customized reports based on the Alarm group's thresholds. Reports can be printed or logged for future use.

On Token Ring switches, RMON provides support for the following groups of the Token Ring extensions:

➤ MAC-layer statistics—A collection of statistics from the MAC sublayer of the Data Link layer, kept for each Token Ring interface. This group collects information such as the total number of MAC layer packets received and the number of times the port entered an error state.

➤ Promiscuous statistics—A collection of promiscuous statistics kept for non-MAC packets on each Token Ring interface. This group collects information such as the total number of good non-MAC frames received that were directed to a Logical-Link Control (LLC) broadcast address.

➤ Ring station—A collection of statistics and status information associated with each Token Ring station on the local ring. This group also provides status information for each ring being monitored.

➤ Ring station order—A listing order of stations on the monitored Token Ring network's rings.

Lost Password

Sometimes an administrator will find that he has inherited the job of caring for a network's switch from someone else. That past employee had the passwords to the switch buried somewhere in his head and now he is nowhere to be found. This means that you need to recover the password to the switch. A lost password on the Cisco Catalyst 5000 switch can be recovered using the following steps:

1. Attach a workstation to the console port.

2. Recycle the power on the switch.

3. Press the Enter key at the prompt. There is a null password for the first 30 seconds. This means that you can press the Enter key from the console because the password is blank.

4. Use the `enable` command and press Enter again for the password. Again there is a null password, meaning no password is required for the first 30 seconds.

5. Use the `set password` and `set enablepass` commands to set the password.

If you are using a Supervisor III or IV Engine, the password recovery steps are as follows:

1. Turn the switch off, and then back on.

2. Within seconds of turning the switch back on, press **control+C** to prevent autobooting. You will now be at a ROM Monitor Prompt mode.

3. Enter the `confreg` command at the ROM Monitor Prompt.

4. Type `reset` to make the module reboot.

5. Type `enable` at the Switch prompt, and then use the `show version` command to check the configuration register value. Verify that the configuration register value is 0x2142, which will force the module to boot from the Flash and ignore any saved configuration. It should appear as "Configuration register is 0x2142."

6. Type the `copy startup-config running-config` command to save the configuration.

 Do not use the **configure terminal** command to save the configuration or there will be only a default configuration on the module.

7. Change the configuration register value back to `0x2102` at the config prompt.

Switch Troubleshooting Commands

Some command-line interface commands are available that can aid you in troubleshooting a switch. Likewise, a few GUI applications are available that you can use to simplify some of the functions of maintaining and configuring the Cisco IOS. These helpful applications are discussed later in this chapter.

This section looks at some of the commands that you can use to view the switch configuration and perform diagnostics to troubleshoot switch problems and configuration issues.

Throughout this section I will first show you the output of each command from a Cisco 5000 series switch. Whenever possible the similar command and output used on the Cisco 4500 series switch will follow. Let's look at the following troubleshooting commands that can be used on the Cisco 5000:

➤ show cam

➤ show cdp

➤ show config

➤ show flash

➤ show interface

➤ show log

➤ show mac

➤ show module

➤ show port

➤ show spantree

➤ show system

➤ show test

➤ show version

➤ show vtp domain

show cam Command

Problems occur when network devices are configured with identical MAC addresses on more than one interface of a switch. When this happens, particularly in the same broadcast domain, it can become a major problem in your network. Imagine ARP trying to resolve an IP address to a MAC address and getting more than one response.

Using the show cam command, you can view the list of known MAC addresses for interfaces attached to each switch port. Many dual-homed Unix workstations, such as those from Sun Microsystems, come with the same MAC address manually assigned on all the installed interfaces. This leaves the door wide open for a duplicate MAC address in the local network, preventing communication.

 If you are part of a network that divides the administration of network devices within the organization, it is recommended that a central process be created to review and document assigned MAC addresses. Such processes help avoid the problem of the same MAC address being assigned to more than one device in your network.

The following is an example of the output resulting from using the show cam command:

```
Catalyst5002> (enable) show cam ?
Usage: show cam [count] <dynamic|static|permanent|system>    [vlan]
       show cam <dynamic|static|permanent> <mod_num/port_num>
       show cam <mac_addr> [vlan]
       show cam agingtime
```

```
Catalyst5002> (enable) show cam dynamic 2
VLAN  Dest MAC/Route Des  Destination Ports or VCs
2     00-30-19-4C-80-A6   2/4
2     00-30-19-4C-80-A8   2/18
2     00-30-19-4C-80-A6   2/15
2     00-30-19-4C-80-A6   2/12
2     00-30-19-4C-80-BC   2/9
2     00-30-19-4C-80-3F   2/10
2     00-30-19-4C-80-D4   2/6
2     00-30-19-4C-80-B3   2/7
2     00-30-19-4C-80-A2   2/2
2     00-80-00-00-12-D0   2/22
2     00-30-19-4C-80-C4   2/1
2     00-30-19-4C-80-3B   2/23
Total Matching CAM Entries Displayed = 12
```

Let's view similar information using the show mac-address-table command on a Cisco 4506 that uses the Cisco CLI IOS as shown below:

```
4506#show mac-address-table
Unicast Entries
 vlan   mac address    type        protocols             port
-------+--------------+--------+---------------------+-------------------
   1    000c.3032.8f7f   static ip,ipx,assigned,other  Switch
   1    000c.30fb.7300  dynamic ip,other               FastEthernet6/48
   1    0030.f10e.504f  dynamic ip                     FastEthernet3/1

Multicast Entries
 vlan    mac address    type     ports
-------+--------------+--------+----------------------------------------
   1     ffff.ffff.ffff  static Switch,Fa3/1,Fa6/48
4506#
```

Both of the commands in the output above show the MAC address of the host attached to each port listed in the output. They also show the protocols that are being used by the hosts attached to the switch.

show cdp Command

Cisco Discovery Protocol is a Cisco proprietary protocol used to discover neighboring Cisco devices. The show cdp command displays the hardware, IOS version, active interfaces, and much more. This information is passed between Cisco devices through CDP packets sent between Cisco devices on physical media that supports SNAP.

CDP packets are multicast packets that are advertised by the Cisco router or switches but not forwarded. This protocol is available on Cisco IOS version IOS 10.3 and later. The show cdp command has two syntaxes. The following code shows the command and the output from the two available syntaxes:

```
DCSCatalyst5000>(enable) show cdp ?
  neighbors            Show CDP neighbors info
  port                 Show CDP port info
  <cr>
```

Now let's take a look at the `show cdp` command:

```
DCSCatalyst5000>(enable) show cdp
CDP                 : enabled
Message Interval    : 60
Hold Time           : 180
Version             : V2
DCSCatalyst5000>(enable)
DCSCatalyst5000>(enable) show cdp neighbors
* - indicates vlan mismatch.
# - indicates duplex mismatch.
Port       Device-ID                        Port-ID            Platform
----       ---------                        -------            --------
2/24       Router                           FastEthernet0#     cisco 1750
DCSCatalyst5000>(enable) show cdp port 2/24
CDP                 : enabled
Message Interval    : 60
Hold Time           : 180
Version             : V2
Port       CDP Status
----       ----------
2/24       enabled
DCSCatalyst5000>(enable)
```

Let's view the `show cdp neighbors` command from the Cisco 4506 switch using the Cisco CLI shown below:

```
4506#show cdp neighbors
Capability Codes: R - Router, T - Trans Bridge, B - Source Route Bridge
                  S - Switch, H - Host, I - IGMP, r - Repeater, P - Phone
Device ID        Local Intrfce    Holdtme    Capability  Platform  Port ID
DCSRTR           Fas 6/48         137        R S         3725      Fas 0/0
4506#
```

show config Command

The `show config` command displays the entire configuration of the switch and its modules except for the installed ATM modules. Of course, the internal route processors are separate entities and store their own configurations, so those modules are not included in the output. The accumulation of all the information from these components provides a large amount of troubleshooting information. The output from this includes the configured passwords, system information, protocol settings, interface configurations, and system log settings.

The following is an example of the `show config` command and its output:

```
Catalyst5002> (enable) show config
.....
begin
!
set password $22$hgjhru^jf#sdc
set enablepass $22$hgjhru$fhkn
set prompt Catlayst5002
set length 24 default
```

```
set logout 0
set banner motd 'Unauthorized Use Prohibited!'
!
#system
set system baud  9600
set system modem disable
set system name  Catalyst5002
set system location Sacramento, CA
set system contact Sean Odom
!
#snmp
set snmp community read-only       public
set snmp community read-write      private
set snmp community read-write-all all
set snmp rmon disable
set snmp trap enable   module
set snmp trap enable   chassis
set snmp trap enable   bridge
set snmp trap enable   repeater
set snmp trap enable   vtp
set snmp trap enable   auth
set snmp trap enable   ippermit
set snmp trap enable   vmps
!
#ip
set interface sc0 2 68.127.186.100 255.255.255.0 68.127.186.255
set interface sl0 0.0.0.0 0.0.0.0
set arp agingtime 1200
set ip redirect    enable
set ip unreachable    enable
set ip fragmentation enable
set ip route 0.0.0.0 68.127.186.254 0
set ip alias default 0.0.0.0
<OUTPUT CUT>
```

Just like on the Cisco CLI IOS based routers the show running-config command displays the configuration of the Cisco 4500 series switch. Let's take a look at the output from a Cisco 4506 switch:

```
4506#show running-config
Building configuration...
Current configuration : 6996 bytes
!
version 12.1
no service pad
service timestamps debug uptime
service timestamps log uptime
no service password-encryption
service compress-config
!
hostname 4506
!
boot system flash bootflash:cat4000-is-mz.121-13.EW.bin
enable password g0
!
ip subnet-zero
ip domain-name DigitalCrawlSpaces.com
!
spanning-tree extend system-id
!
```

```
interface GigabitEthernet1/1
!
interface GigabitEthernet1/2
!
interface GigabitEthernet2/1
!
interface GigabitEthernet2/2
!
interface GigabitEthernet2/3
!
interface GigabitEthernet2/4
!
interface GigabitEthernet2/5
!
interface GigabitEthernet2/6
!
interface GigabitEthernet2/7
!
interface GigabitEthernet2/8
!
interface GigabitEthernet2/9
!
interface GigabitEthernet2/10
!
interface GigabitEthernet2/11
!
interface GigabitEthernet2/12
!
interface GigabitEthernet2/13
!
interface GigabitEthernet2/14
!
interface GigabitEthernet2/15
!
interface GigabitEthernet2/16
!
interface GigabitEthernet2/17
!
interface GigabitEthernet2/18
!
interface GigabitEthernet2/19
!
interface GigabitEthernet2/20
!
interface GigabitEthernet2/21
!
interface GigabitEthernet2/22
!
interface GigabitEthernet2/23
!
interface GigabitEthernet2/24
!
interface Vlan1
 ip address 10.1.2.55 255.255.0.0
 ip rip send version 1
 ip rip receive version 1
!
ip default-gateway 10.1.1.1
ip classless
no ip http server
!
```

```
line con 0
 stopbits 1
line vty 0 5
 password g0
 login
!
end
4506#
```

The above shows the configuration of the Cisco 4506 switch we are using for this chapter.

show flash and show platform Commands

The Cisco 5000 IOS uses a Set/Clear–based command set that is different from the IOS found on Cisco routers. The IOS is stored in the flash memory stored on the Supervisor Engine module. The show flash command reports the space required for the installed software and the version of code. This includes the file names, date installed, time installed, and file sizes.

The following is an example of output from installing a brand-new Supervisor Engine 3 module and software in a switch:

```
DCSCatalyst5000>(enable) show flash
-#- ED --type-- --crc--- -seek- nlen -length- ------date/time----- name
  1 .. ffffffff d45a43c9  4eae44   22  4894147 Aug 09 2000 14:09:25
    cat5000-sup3.5-5-2.bin
2707900 bytes available (4894276 bytes used)
DCSCatalyst5000>(enable)
```

On the Cisco 4506 switch using the Supervisor Engine 4 module and software you use show platform nvramenv, which displays similar information:

```
4506#show platform nvramenv
PS1="rommon ! >"
ConfigReg="0x2102"
RET_2_RTS="10:08:11 UTC Sun Mar 24 2002"
BOOT="bootflash:cat4000-is-mz.121-13.EW.bin,1"
RommonVer="12.1(12r)EW"
BootedFileName="bootflash:cat4000-is-mz.121-13.EW.bin"
SkipDiags="0"
BootStatus="Success"
BSI="0"
RET_2_RUTC=""
```

The following lists other syntaxes of the show platform command that might be useful for troubleshooting:

```
4506#show platform ?
  chassis     show platform chassis debug state
  cpu         show CPU related information
  crashdump   show most recent crashdump
  hardware    show platform hardware debug state
  health      show platform statistics gauging health of the system
```

```
logfeatures    show enabled debugging log features
memory         show SDRAM or hardware registers
nvramenv       show nvram environment variables
portmap        show internal port mapping of an interface
software       show platform software debug state
```

The above output shows the many syntaxes available for the show platform command.

show interface Command

The show interface command can be used to get the IP configuration of the Supervisor Engine module. The VLAN information shown is for the management VLAN for the SC0 interface. This is the interface assigned to the default Supervisor Engine used for configuring the IP information for the switch, as well as the broadcast address. The following is the output:

```
Catalyst5002> (enable) show interface
sl0: flags=51<UP,POINTOPOINT,RUNNING>
        slip 0.0.0.0 dest 0.0.0.0
sc0: flags=63<UP,BROADCAST,RUNNING>
        vlan 1 inet 68.127.187.1 netmask 255.255.255.0 broadcast
    68.127.187.255
```

The command on the Cisco 4500 series is the same as the Cisco 5000; however, the output looks quite different, and similar to that on a Cisco CLI-based router. Here is the output of the VLAN 1 interface, a Gigabit Ethernet Interface, and then a Fast Ethernet Interface:

```
4506#show interface
Vlan1 is up, line protocol is up
  Hardware is Ethernet SVI, address is 000c.3032.8f7f (bia 000c.3032.8f7f)
  Internet address is 10.1.2.55/16
  MTU 1500 bytes, BW 1000000 Kbit, DLY 10 usec,
     reliability 255/255, txload 1/255, rxload 1/255
  Encapsulation ARPA, loopback not set
  ARP type: ARPA, ARP Timeout 04:00:00
  Last input 00:00:00, output never, output hang never
  Last clearing of "show interface" counters never
  Input queue: 0/75/0/0 (size/max/drops/flushes); Total output drops: 0
  Queueing strategy: fifo
  Output queue: 0/40 (size/max)
  5 minute input rate 0 bits/sec, 0 packets/sec
  5 minute output rate 0 bits/sec, 0 packets/sec
  L3 in Switched: ucast: 2842 pkt, 131721 bytes - mcast: 0 pkt, 0 bytes
  L3 out Switched: ucast: 0 pkt, 0 bytes - mcast: 0 pkt, 0 bytes
     2842 packets input, 131721 bytes, 0 no buffer
     Received 16614 broadcasts (0 IP multicast)
     0 runts, 0 giants, 0 throttles
     0 input errors, 0 CRC, 0 frame, 0 overrun, 0 ignored
     0 packets output, 0 bytes, 0 underruns
     0 output errors, 0 interface resets
     0 output buffer failures, 0 output buffers swapped out
```

```
GigabitEthernet1/1 is up, line protocol is down (notconnect)
  Hardware is Gigabit Ethernet Port, address is 000c.3032.8f40
                  (bia 000c.3032.8f40)

  MTU 1500 bytes, BW 1000000 Kbit, DLY 10 usec,
     reliability 255/255, txload 1/255, rxload 1/255
  Encapsulation ARPA, loopback not set
  Keepalive set (10 sec)
  Auto-duplex, Auto-speed
  input flow-control is off, output flow-control is off
  ARP type: ARPA, ARP Timeout 04:00:00
  Last input never, output never, output hang never
  Last clearing of "show interface" counters never
  Input queue: 0/2000/0/0 (size/max/drops/flushes); Total output drops: 0
  Queueing strategy: fifo
  Output queue: 0/40 (size/max)
  5 minute input rate 0 bits/sec, 0 packets/sec
  5 minute output rate 0 bits/sec, 0 packets/sec
     0 packets input, 0 bytes, 0 no buffer
     Received 0 broadcasts (0 multicast)
     0 runts, 0 giants, 0 throttles
     0 input errors, 0 CRC, 0 frame, 0 overrun, 0 ignored
     0 input packets with dribble condition detected
     0 packets output, 0 bytes, 0 underruns
     0 output errors, 0 collisions, 0 interface resets
     0 babbles, 0 late collision, 0 deferred
     0 lost carrier, 0 no carrier
     0 output buffer failures, 0 output buffers swapped out
FastEthernet3/1 is up, line protocol is up (connected)
  Hardware is Fast Ethernet Port, address is 000b.fd07.3030
                  (bia 000b.fd07.3030)
  MTU 1500 bytes, BW 100000 Kbit, DLY 100 usec,
     reliability 255/255, txload 1/255, rxload 1/255
  Encapsulation ARPA, loopback not set
  Keepalive set (10 sec)
  Full-duplex, 100Mb/s
  input flow-control is off, output flow-control is off
  ARP type: ARPA, ARP Timeout 04:00:00
  Last input never, output never, output hang never
  Last clearing of "show interface" counters never
  Input queue: 0/2000/0/0 (size/max/drops/flushes); Total output drops: 0
  Queueing strategy: fifo
  Output queue: 0/40 (size/max)
  5 minute input rate 1000 bits/sec, 2 packets/sec
  5 minute output rate 2000 bits/sec, 2 packets/sec
     27978 packets input, 2263913 bytes, 0 no buffer
     Received 4090 broadcasts (0 multicast)
     0 runts, 0 giants, 0 throttles
     29 input errors, 5 CRC, 0 frame, 0 overrun, 0 ignored
     0 input packets with dribble condition detected
     340648 packets output, 27974911 bytes, 0 underruns
     0 output errors, 0 collisions, 0 interface resets
     0 babbles, 0 late collision, 0 deferred
     1 lost carrier, 0 no carrier
     0 output buffer failures, 0 output buffers swapped out
```

The above output displays the current state of each of the interfaces on the switch. It displays the speed, duplex, the current line status, current protocol status, received packet statistics, and sent packet statistics.

show log Command

Using the show log command, you can look at the significant events. An example of the output for this command follows:

```
DCSCatalyst5000>(enable) show log
Network Management Processor (ACTIVE NMP) Log:
  Reset count:   30
  Re-boot History:   Aug 09 2000 14:26:18 0, Aug 09 2000 14:18:51 0
                     Aug 09 2000 13:44:30 0, Aug 09 2000 12:12: 8 0
                     Jul 07 2000 13: 5:32 0, Jul 07 2000 12:22:38 0
                     Jun 16 2000 16:53:25 0, Jun 16 2000 16: 7:48 0
                     Jun 16 2000 15:19:11 0, Jun 16 2000 12:17:32 0
    Bootrom Checksum Failures:     0   UART Failures:              0
    Flash Checksum Failures:       0   Flash Program Failures:     0
    Power Supply 1 Failures:      23   Power Supply 2 Failures:   17
    DRAM Failures:                 0
    Exceptions:                    0
    Loaded NMP version:         5.5(2)
    Reload same NMP version count: 1
    Last software reset by user: 8/9/2000,14:25:15
    MCP Exceptions/Hang:           0
Heap Memory Log:
Corrupted Block = none
NVRAM log:
01. 2/27/2000,15:28:39: updateRuntimeWithNVRAM:Redundancy switch over: 2
02. 1/14/1999,15:36:45: updateRuntimeWithNVRAM:Redundancy switch over: 2
03. 6/16/2000,12:18:16: updateRuntimeWithNVRAM:Redundancy switch over: 2
04. 6/16/2000,16:57:26: updateRuntimeWithNVRAM:Redundancy switch over: 2
05. 8/9/2000,14:21:41: convert_post_SAC_CiscoMIB:Block 0 converted
                       from version 6 to 11
06. 8/9/2000,14:22:17: supVersion:Nmp version 5.5(2.0)
Module 2 Log:
  Reset Count:   2
  Reset History: Wed Aug 9 2000, 14:26:58
                 Wed Aug 9 2000, 14:22:40
Module 3 Log:
  Reset Count:   2
  Reset History: Wed Aug 9 2000, 14:26:50
                 Wed Aug 9 2000, 14:22:32
02. 1/14/1999,15:36:45: updateRuntimeWithNVRAM:Redundancy switch over: 2
03. 6/16/2000,12:18:16: updateRuntimeWithNVRAM:Redundancy switch over: 2
04. 6/16/2000,16:57:26: updateRuntimeWithNVRAM:Redundancy switch over: 2
05. 8/9/2000,14:21:41: convert_post_SAC_CiscoMIB:Block 0 converted from
                       version 6 to 11
06. 8/9/2000,14:22:17: supVersion:Nmp version 5.5(2.0)
Module 2 Log:
  Reset Count:   2
  Reset History: Wed Aug 9 2000, 14:26:58
                 Wed Aug 9 2000, 14:22:40
Module 3 Log:
  Reset Count:   2
  Reset History: Wed Aug 9 2000, 14:26:50
                 Wed Aug 9 2000, 14:22:32
Module 5 Log:
  Reset Count:   2
  Reset History: Wed Aug 9 2000, 14:27:13
                 Wed Aug 9 2000, 14:23:17
DCSCatalyst5000>(enable)
```

Just like on a Cisco router's IOS, you can use the **clear counters** command to reset all the statistical counters on a Cisco switch.

In the preceding output you see some helpful troubleshooting information, including the number of reboots of all the modules, traps, logged events, and power-supply failures.

The command for the 4500 series switch is the same as the Cisco 5000 series switches. The following output shows the command used on the Cisco 4506. Notice that the output indicates that the device connected to Module 6 port 48 is experiencing a duplex misconfiguration problem where one end of the link is configured to half-duplex and the switch is configured for full-duplex:

```
4506#show log
Syslog logging: enabled (0 messages dropped, 0 messages rate-limited,
0 flushes, 0 overruns)

    Console logging: level debugging, 303 messages logged
    Monitor logging: level debugging, 0 messages logged
    Buffer logging: level debugging, 303 messages logged
    Exception Logging: size (8192 bytes)
    Trap logging: level informational, 308 message lines logged
Log Buffer (4096 bytes):
PADDR: Duplicate address 10.1.2.55 on Vlan1, sourced by 0006.2541.d799
04:33:26: %CDP-4-DUPLEX_MISMATCH: duplex mismatch discovered on
FastEthernet6/48,(not full duplex), with DCSRTR FastEthernet0/0(full
duplex).

05:01:04: %SYS-5-CONFIG_I: Configured from console by vty0 (10.1.2.25)
6d03h: %SYS-5-CONFIG_I: Configured from console by vty0 (10.1.5.0)
4506#
```

show mac Command

The output for this command is quite long, but it's very informative of the state of the switch ports. By using this command, you can display numerous counters that are maintained during normal operation on all the switch ports.

```
DCSCatalyst5000>(enable) show mac 2/24
Port    Rcv-Unicast         Rcv-Multicast         Rcv-Broadcast
----    -----------         -------------         -------------
2/24    71050               6221                  166
Port    Xmit-Unicast        Xmit-Multicast        Xmit-Broadcast
----    -----------         -------------         -------------
2/24    69874               213965                1
Port    Rcv-Octet           Xmit-Octet
----    -----------         ----------
2/24    7245197             20334845
MAC     Dely-Exced  MTU-Exced   In-Discard  Lrn-Discrd  In-Lost    Out-Lost
```

```
---        ----------  ----------   -----------  ----------  -------    --------
2/24    0          0            0            0           0          0
Last-Time-Cleared
Wed Jun 4 2003, 11:25:20
DCSCatalyst5000>(enable)
```

You will notice from the preceding output that the counter information includes information on the traffic for each port, the number of incoming frames, the number of frame discards, the total number of frames sent, and the maximum transmission unit (MTU) violations.

show module Command

This command displays the modules located inside the switch chassis, or each individual module, by identifying a module number. The following is an example of output from using the show module command on a Cisco Catalyst 5000 switch:

```
DCSCatalyst5000>(enable) show module
Mod Slot Ports Module-Type              Model           Sub Status
--- ---- ----- -----------              -----           --- ------
1   1    0     Supervisor III           WS-X5530        yes ok
2   2    24    10/100BaseTX Ethernet     WS-X5225R       no  ok
3   3    12    100BaseFX MM Ethernet     WS-X5111        no  ok
5   5    1     Network Analysis/RMON     WS-X5380        no  ok
Mod Module-Name         Serial-Num
--- -----------         ----------
1                       00011454261
2                       00013426578
3                       00003975931
5                       00012148595
Mod MAC-Address(es)                           Hw    Fw     Sw
--- ---------------                           --    --     --
1   00-50-bd-a0-b0-00 to 00-50-bd-a0-b3-ff 2.0   3.1.2  5.5(2)
2   00-d0-06-a1-de-a8 to 00-d0-06-a1-de-bf 3.3   4.3(1) 5.5(2)
3   00-60-5c-21-b5-24 to 00-60-5c-21-b5-2f 1.0   1.3    5.5(2)
5   00-60-09-ff-77-5c                       1.1   4.3.2  4.3(1a)
Mod Sub-Type Sub-Model Sub-Serial Sub-Hw
--- -------- --------- ---------- ------
Mod Slot Ports Module-Type              Model           Sub Status
--- ---- ----- -----------              -----           --- ------
1   1    0     Supervisor III           WS-X5530        yes ok
2   2    24    10/100BaseTX Ethernet     WS-X5225R       no  ok
3   3    12    100BaseFX MM Ethernet     WS-X5111        no  ok
5   5    1     Network Analysis/RMON     WS-X5380        no  ok
Mod Module-Name         Serial-Num
--- -----------         ----------
1                       00011454261
2                       00013426578
3                       00003975931
5                       00012148595
Mod MAC-Address(es)                           Hw    Fw     Sw
--- ---------------                           --    --     --
1   00-50-bd-a0-b0-00 to 00-50-bd-a0-b3-ff 2.0   3.1.2  5.5(2)
2   00-d0-06-a1-de-a8 to 00-d0-06-a1-de-bf 3.3   4.3(1) 5.5(2)
3   00-60-5c-21-b5-24 to 00-60-5c-21-b5-2f 1.0   1.3    5.5(2)
```

```
5   00-60-09-ff-77-5c                1.1    4.3.2     4.3(1a)
Mod Sub-Type Sub-Model Sub-Serial Sub-Hw
--- -------- --------- ---------- ------
1   NFFC     WS-F5521  0011455134 1.1
DCSCatalyst5000>(enable)
```

The command on the Cisco CLI IOS is the same and the outputs are similar as shown below:

```
4506#show module
Mod  Ports Card Type                            Model             Serial No.
----+-----+--------------------------------+--------------+----------
  1    2   1000BaseX (GBIC) Supervisor(active)  WS-X4515          JAB071105ME
  2   24   10/100/1000BaseTX (RJ45)             WS-X4424-GB-RJ45  JAB070905V4
  3   48   10/100BaseTX (RJ45)V                 WS-X4148-RJ45V    JAE0650023U
  4   48   10/100BaseTX (RJ45)                  WS-X4148-RJ       JAE065206JY
  5   48   10/100BaseTX (RJ45)                  WS-X4148-RJ       JAE0652061R
  6   48   10/100BaseTX (RJ45)                  WS-X4148-RJ       JAE065205J2
M MAC addresses                    Hw  Fw           Sw                Status
--+-----------------------------+---+---+-------------+-------------+--------
1 000c.3032.8f40 to 000c.3032.8f41 1.2 12.1(12r)EW  12.1(13)EW, EARL Ok
2 000a.f413.bb10 to 000a.f413.bb27 1.5                                Ok
3 000b.fd07.3030 to 000b.fd07.305f 2.6                                Ok
4 000b.5f25.f330 to 000b.5f25.f35f 3.1                                Ok
5 000b.5f45.e8a0 to 000b.5f45.e8cf 3.1                                Ok
6 000b.5f46.c7a0 to 000b.5f46.c7cf 3.1                                Ok
4506#
```

The preceding output is great for seeing the modules installed on the switch, their serial numbers, MAC addresses assigned, the hardware type, MAC address assigned, and the current status of all the modules installed in the switch.

Now, look at the module in slot 3 using the show module command followed by the slot number:

```
4506#show module 1
Mod  Ports Card Type                            Model          Serial No.
----+-----+--------------------------------+--------------+----------
  1    2   1000BaseX (GBIC) Supervisor(active)  WS-X4515       JAB071105ME
M MAC addresses                    Hw  Fw           Sw             Status
--+-----------------------------+---+---+-------------+-----------+--------
1 000c.3032.8f40 to 000c.3032.8f41 1.2 12.1(12r)EW  12.1(13)EW, EARL Ok
4506#
```

The preceding output narrows the information from the show modules command to a single module.

show port Command

With the show port command, you can obtain specific information about a single port or all the ports on a specified module. The show port command output for module 2, port 1 follows:

```
DCSCatalyst5000>(enable) show port 2/1
Port  Name      Status     Vlan Level  Duplex Speed  Type
....  ....      ......     .... .....  ...... .....  ....
2/1   Port1     normal     2    normal full   100    10/100BaseTX
Port Security Secure-Src-Addr Last-Src-Addr  Shutdown Trap
.... ........ ............... .............  ........ ....
2/1  enabled  0090.80a3.32a0  0090.80a3.32a0 No       disabled
Port      Broadcast-Limit Broadcast-Drop
....      ............... ..............
2/1              -               -
Port    Status      Channel   Channel    Neighbor      Neighbor
                    Mode      status     device        port
....    ......      .......   .......    ........      ........
2/1     connected   on        not channel
Port  Align-Err FCS-Err   Xmit-Err   Rcv-Err   UnderSize
....  ......... .......   ........   .......   .........
2/1   0         0         6          0         0
Port  Single-Col Multi-Coll Late-Coll Excess-Col Carri-Sen Runts  Giants
....  .......... .......... ......... .......... .......... .....  ......
2/1   3442       603        0         0          0         1      0
Last-Time-Cleared
Wed Aug 9 2000, 14:26:21
```

Other show port command syntaxes can be used to troubleshoot port and
port-related protocol issues. The following is output of the available syntaxes for the show port command:

```
DCSCatalyst5000>(enable) show port ?
  auxiliaryvlan          Show port auxiliary vlan information
  broadcast              Show port broadcast information
  cdp                    Show port CDP information
  capabilities           Show port capabilities
  channel                Show port channel information
  counters               Show port counters
  fddi                   Show port FDDI information
  flowcontrol            Show port traffic flowcontrol
  filter                 Show Token Ring port filtering information
  ifindex                Show port IfIndex information
  mac                    Show port MAC counters
  negotiation            Show port flowcontrol negotiation
  protocol               Show port protocol membership
  qos                    Show port QoS information
  security               Show port security information
  spantree               Show port spantree information
  status                 Show port status
  trap                   Show port trap information
  trunk                  Show port trunk information
  <mod>                  Module number
  <mod/port>             Module number and Port number(s)
  <cr>
```

The preceding output shows the syntaxes for the show port command on the
Catalyst 5000 switch.

show spantree Command

This command can be used to display the *Spanning Tree Protocol (STP)* configuration, which is a significant protocol in today's redundant-link networks. STP is used to calculate loop-free Layer 2 data paths through the network, and, at the same time, provide for redundant paths. The output from this command can provide information about whether STP is enabled or disabled, the bridge or port priorities, the root bridge priorities, the path cost to the root, the BPDU (Bridge Protocol Data Unit), the bridge MAC address, the timer, the port states, and the fast-start configuration of each port.

For the exam, be sure to remember that Spanning Tree Protocol is used to decide which port to disable based on three criteria: the port cost, the port priority, and the MAC address. Spanning Tree Protocol will decide which port to use by doing the following:

1. It will determine what the port cost is for each port connected to the bridge. If there is more than one port to the destination, the port or ports with the highest port cost will placed in blocking mode.

2. If the port cost is equal on the links, the port with the port with the lowest bridge priority will be used.

3. If both the port costs and the bridge priority are the same, the deciding factor is the MAC address. The port with the lowest MAC address will be used.

Having more than one path through the network can cause major problems. Data leaving on one port of the switch comes right back to the switch on another port. If this data is a broadcast, can you imagine how many times it would be rebroadcast? The numbers could become astronomical, including a worst case scenario of the broadcasts using all the bandwidth, in an event called a *broadcast storm*.

STP uses timers and a broadcast packet called a Bridge Protocol Data Unit (BPDU) to verify that there are no loops in the network. It transitions through several configured STP timers. First the FwdDelay timer, then the MaxAge timer and then the FwdDelay timer is used again.

Convergence is the time that STP members take to begin transmitting data on a redundant link after a link in forwarding mode has failed. It is also the initial period between the time when an STP port powers up and when the port is placed in forwarding mode, meaning the link is up and functioning. During the convergence time, no data is forwarded.

By default, the MaxAge timer is set to 20 seconds and the FwdDelay timer is 30 seconds. The FwdDelay is used by both the listening and learning states. You can adjust FwdDelay and MaxAge; however, doing so may cause a data loop temporarily in more complex networks. Using the following example, the downtime could be as high as 50 seconds using the following calculations:

$2 \times$ FwdDelay + MaxAge = Down Time

For example, using the defaults

$2 \times 15 + 20 = 50$ seconds

STP transitions each port through four port states in a designated order before the port can forward frames. These states are *blocking*, *listening*, *learning*, and *forwarding*. The *disabled* state is a fifth state that can be manually configured by the switch. The following are the different port states, along with a description of when each is used:

➤ Blocking—The port is not forwarding frames or learning new addresses. All ports start in blocking mode to prevent the bridge from creating a bridging loop. The port stays in a blocked state if STP determines that a lower-cost path to the root bridge exists.

➤ Listening—The port is not forwarding frames or learning new addresses. It is progressing to a forwarding state and listening to traffic coming in on the switch ports. Ports transition from a blocked state to the listening state. Ports use this time to attempt to learn whether any other paths exist to the root bridge. During the listening state, the port can listen to frames but cannot send or receive data. The port does not put any of the information it hears into the address table.

➤ Learning—The port is not forwarding frames but is learning addresses and putting them in the address table. The learning state is similar to the listening state, except the port can now add information it has learned to the address table. The port is still not allowed to send or receive frames.

➤ Forwarding—The port is forwarding frames, learning addresses, and adding addresses to the routing table. This state means that the port is capable of sending and receiving frames. A port is not placed in a forwarding state until no redundant links exist or the port determines the lowest-cost path to the root bridge or switch.

➤ Disabled—The port has been removed from all STP functions. Disabled is a special state indicating that the port has been manually shut down by the network administrator or by the system due to a hardware problem.

The show spantree command on the Cisco Set/Clear based IOS displays the timers and other STP information. Let's look at an example of the output:

```
DCSCatalyst5000>(enable) show spantree
VLAN 1
Spanning tree enabled
Spanning tree type         ieee
Designated Root            00-50-bd-a0-b0-00
Designated Root Priority   32768
Designated Root Cost       0
Designated Root Port       1/0
Root Max Age   12 sec    Hello Time 2  sec   Forward Delay 9  sec
Bridge ID MAC ADDR         00-50-bd-a0-b0-00
Bridge ID Priority         32768
Bridge Max Age 12 sec    Hello Time 2  sec   Forward Delay 9  sec
Port            Vlan Port-State   Cost  Priority Portfast   Channel_id
----            ---- ----------   ----  -------- --------   ----------
  2/1            1   not-connected  19        32 enabled    0
  2/2            1   not-connected  19        32 enabled    0
  2/3            1   not-connected  19        32 enabled    0
  2/4            1   not-connected  19        32 enabled    0
  2/5            1   not-connected  19        32 enabled    0
  2/6            1   not-connected  19        32 disabled   0
  2/7            1   not-connected  19        32 disabled   0
  2/7            1   not-connected  19        32 disabled   0
  2/8            1   not-connected  19        32 disabled   0
  2/9            1   not-connected 100        32 disabled   0
  2/10           1   not-connected 100        32 disabled   0
  2/11           1   not-connected 100        32 disabled   0
  2/12           1   not-connected 100        32 disabled   0
  2/13           1   not-connected 100        32 disabled   0
  2/14           1   not-connected 100        32 disabled   0
  2/15           1   not-connected 100        32 disabled   0
  2/16           1   not-connected 100        32 disabled   0
  2/17           1   not-connected 100        32 disabled   0
  2/18           1   not-connected 100        32 disabled   0
  2/19           1   not-connected 100        32 disabled   0
  2/20           1   not-connected 100        32 disabled   0
  2/21           1   not-connected 100        32 disabled   0
  2/22           1   not-connected 100        32 disabled   0
  2/23           1   not-connected 100        32 disabled   0
  2/24           1   forwarding     19        32 disabled   0
```

The preceding output shows each port on the switch, the current STP mode, port cost, port priority, whether Portfast is enabled, and the channel ID. This output also shows the currently configured MaxAge timer and Forward-Delay timer settings.

> The Disabled state is placed on a port by an administrator or the switch, not by STP, if a hardware problem exists.

The show spanning-tree command on the Cisco CLI switch displays the following:

```
4506#show spanning-tree
VLAN0001
```

```
Spanning tree enabled protocol ieee
Root ID     Priority    32769
            Address     000c.3032.8f40
            This bridge is the root
            Hello Time   2 sec  Max Age 20 sec  Forward Delay 15 sec
 Bridge ID  Priority    32769  (priority 32768 sys-id-ext 1)
            Address     000c.3032.8f40
            Hello Time   2 sec  Max Age 20 sec  Forward Delay 15 sec
            Aging Time 300
Interface        Role Sts Cost      Prio.Nbr Type
---------------- ---- --- --------- -------- ----------------------------

Fa3/1            Desg FWD 19        128.129  P2p
Fa6/48           Desg FWD 19        128.368  P2p
4506#
```

show system Command

The show system command enables you to obtain the component status of the switch components. These components include information on the status of the fans, power supplies, modem, uptime, and system identification configuration.

The output on a Cisco Catalyst 5002 follows:

```
DCSCatalyst5000>show system
PS1-Status PS2-Status
---------- ----------
ok         none
Fan-Status Temp-Alarm Sys-Status Uptime d,h:m:s Logout
---------- ---------- ---------- --------------- ------
ok         off        ok         5,05:45:19      20 min
PS1-Type    PS2-Type
--------    --------
WS-C5008A   none
Modem    Baud  Traffic Peak Peak-Time
-----    ----  ------- ---- ---------
disable  9600   0%      0% Wed Jun 4 2003, 14:46:27
System Name    System Location       System Contact
-----------    ---------------       --------------
               Sacramento, CA        Sean Odom
```

show test Command

The show test command is used to display the status of the switch chassis, interface cards, power supplies, Encoded Address and Recognition Logic (EARL) ASIC status tests, and whether an active loopback exists. It also displays the memory status of the read-only memory (ROM), flash EEPROM, serial EEPROM, and the nonvolatile RAM.

An example of the show test command output follows:

```
DCSCatalyst5000>(enable) show test
Diagnostic mode: complete    (mode at next reset: complete)
```

```
Environmental Status (. = Pass, F = Fail, U = Unknown, N = Not Present)
  PS (3.3V):   .   PS (12V): .   PS (24V):   .   PS1: .   PS2: N
  Temperature: .   Fan:       .
Module 1 : 0-port Supervisor III
Network Management Processor (NMP) Status: (. = Pass, F = Fail, U =
  Unknown)
  ROM:   .   Flash-EEPROM: .   Ser-EEPROM: .   NVRAM: .   MCP Comm: .
  EARL II Status :
        DisableIndexLearnTest:      U
        DontLearnTest:              U
        DisableNewLearnTest:        U
        ConditionalLearnTest:       U
        MonitorColorFloodTest:      U
        EarlTrapTest:               U
        StaticMacAndTypeTest:       U
        BadDvlanTest:               U
        BadBpduTest:                U
        IndexMatchTest:             U
        ProtocolTypeTest:           U
        ProtocolTypeTest:           U
        IgmpTest:                   U
        SourceMissTest:             U
        SourceModifiedTest:         U
        ArpaToArpaShortcutTest:     U
        ArpaToSnapShortcutTest:     U
        SnapToArpaShortcutTest:     U
        SnapToSnapShortcutTest:     U
        SoftwareShortcutTest:       U
        MulticastExpansionTest:     U
        DontShortcutTest:           U
        ShortcutTableFullTest:      U
Line Card Diag Status for Module 1  (. = Pass, F = Fail, N = N/A)
  CPU        : .   Sprom    : .   Bootcsum : .   Archsum  : .
  RAM        : .   LTL      : .   CBL      : N   DPRAM    : . SAMBA : N
  Saints     : .   Pkt Bufs : .   Repeater : N   FLASH    : .
  Phoenix    : . TrafficMeter: . UplinkSprom : . PhoenixSprom: .
  SAINT/SAGE Status :
  PHOENIX Port Status :
  SAINT/SAGE Status :
  PHOENIX Port Status :
    Ports 9   17   18   19   20   21   22
        INBAND A->B B->A B->C C->B A->C C->A
  Packet Buffer Status :

  PHOENIX Packet Buffer Status :
   Ports INBAND A<->B B<->C A<->C
  Loopback Status [Reported by Module 1] :
   Ports  1  2  9
          U  U  .
DCSCatalyst5000>(enable)
To display a test on a specific module, use the module number after the
command.  In this case I have a 24-port 10/100BaseTX module in slot 2:
DCSCatalyst5000>(enable) show test 2
Diagnostic mode: complete   (mode at next reset: complete)
Module 2 : 24-port 10/100BaseTX Ethernet
Line Card Diag Status for Module 2  (. = Pass, F = Fail, N = N/A)
  CPU        : .   Sprom    : .   Bootcsum : .   Archsum  : N
  RAM        : .   LTL      : .   CBL      : .   DPRAM    : N SAMBA : .
  Saints     : .   Pkt Bufs : .   Repeater : N   FLASH    : N
  SAINT/SAGE Status :
    Ports 1 2 3 4 5 6 7 8 9 10 11 12 13 14 15 16 17 18 19 20 21 22 23 24
```

```
-----------------------------------------------------------------------
             .  .  .  .  .  .  .  .  .  .     .   .   .   .   .   .   .   .
Packet Buffer Status :
  Ports 1 2 3 4 5 6 7 8 9 10 11 12 13 14 15 16 17 18 19 20 21 22 23 24
-----------------------------------------------------------------------
             .  .  .  .  .  .  .  .  .  .     .   .   .   .   .   .   .   .
Loopback Status [Reported by Module 1] :
  Ports 1 2 3 4 5 6 7 8 9 10 11 12 13 14 15 16 17 18 19 20 21 22 23 24
-----------------------------------------------------------------------
             .  .  .  .  .  .  .  .  .  .     .   .   .   .   .   .   .   .
Packet Buffer Status :
  Ports 1 2 3 4 5 6 7 8 9 10 11 12 13 14 15 16 17 18 19 20 21 22 23 24
-----------------------------------------------------------------------
             .  .  .  .  .  .  .  .  .  .     .   .   .   .   .   .   .   .
Loopback Status [Reported by Module 1] :
  Ports 1 2 3 4 5 6 7 8 9 10 11 12 13 14 15 16 17 18 19 20 21 22 23 24
-----------------------------------------------------------------------
             .  .  .  .  .  .  .  .  .  .     .   .   .   .   .   .   .   .
Channel Status :
  Ports 1 2 3 4 5 6 7 8 9 10 11 12 13 14 15 16 17 18 19 20 21 22 23 24
-----------------------------------------------------------------------
             .  .  .  .  .  .  .  .  .  .     .   .   .   .   .   .   .   .
InlineRewrite Status :
  Ports 1 2 3 4 5 6 7 8 9 10 11 12 13 14 15 16 17 18 19 20 21 22 23 24
-----------------------------------------------------------------------
             .  .  .  .  .  .  .  .  .  .     .   .   .   .   .   .   .   .
```

The output shows the results of the Supervisor module diagnostic tests. This command should be used if you suspect that there is a hardware problem with the switch.

show version Command

The show version command is used to provide hardware and software version numbers, in addition to the switch memory and the system uptime information. An example of this command follows:

```
DCSCatalyst5000>(enable) show version
WS-C5000 Software, Version McpSW: 5.5(2) NmpSW: 5.5(2)
Copyright (c) 1995-2000 by Cisco Systems
NMP S/W compiled on Jul 28 2000, 16:43:52
MCP S/W compiled on Jul 28 2000, 16:38:40
System Bootstrap Version: 3.1.2
Hardware Version: 2.0  Model: WS-C5000  Serial #: 011454261
Mod Port Model       Serial #  Versions
--- ---- -----       --------  --------
1   0    WS-X5530    011454261 Hw : 2.0
                               Fw : 3.1.2
                               Fw1: 4.2(1)
                               Sw : 5.5(2)
         WS-F5521    011455134 Hw : 1.1
2   24   WS-X5225R   013426578 Hw : 3.3
                               Fw : 4.3(1)
                               Sw : 5.5(2)
3   12   WS-X5111    003975931 Hw : 1.0
```

```
                                   Fw : 1.3
                                   Sw : 5.5(2)
5    1    WS-X5380    012148595 Hw : 1.1
Mod Port Model         Serial #  Versions
---  ---- -----        --------- --------
1    0    WS-X5530    011454261 Hw : 2.0
                                   Fw : 3.1.2
                                   Fw1: 4.2(1)
                                   Sw : 5.5(2)
         WS-F5521    011455134 Hw : 1.1
2    24   WS-X5225R   013426578 Hw : 3.3
                                   Fw : 4.3(1)
                                   Sw : 5.5(2)
3    12   WS-X5111    003975931 Hw : 1.0
                                   Fw : 1.3
                                   Sw : 5.5(2)
5    1    WS-X5380    012148595 Hw : 1.1
                                   Fw : 4.3.2
                                   Sw : 4.3(1a)
          DRAM                    FLASH                        NVRAM
Module Total   Used   Free    Total   Used   Free      Total Used  Free
------ -----   ----   ----    -----   ----   ----      ----- ----  ----
1      32640K  20434K 12206K  8192K   5548K  2644K     512K  185K  327K
Uptime is 4 days, 4 hours, 13 minutes
```

The preceding output is helpful in determining the software versions, hardware versions, and serial numbers being used on the switch.

show diagnostics

A command on the Cisco 4506 that is similar to the show version command is the show diagnostics power-on command. The output from this command being used on a Cisco 4506 switch is shown below:

```
4506#show diagnostics power-on
Power-On-Self-Test Results for ACTIVE Supervisor
Power-on-self-test for Module 1:  WS-X4515
 Port/Test Status: (. = Pass, F = Fail)
Port Traffic: L2 Serdes Loopback ...
 0: . 1: . 2: . 3: . 4: . 5: . 6: . 7: . 8: . 9: . 10: . 11: .
12: . 13: . 14: . 15: . 16: . 17: . 18: . 19: . 20: . 21: . 22: . 23: .
24: . 25: . 26: . 27: . 28: . 29: . 30: . 31: .
Port Traffic: L2 Asic Loopback ...
 0: . 1: . 2: . 3: . 4: . 5: . 6: . 7: . 8: . 9: . 10: . 11: .
12: . 13: . 14: . 15: . 16: . 17: . 18: . 19: . 20: . 21: . 22: . 23: .
24: . 25: . 26: . 27: . 28: . 29: . 30: . 31: .
Port Traffic: L3 Asic Loopback ...
 0: . 1: . 2: . 3: . 4: . 5: . 6: . 7: . 8: . 9: . 10: . 11: .
12: . 13: . 14: . 15: . 16: . 17: . 18: . 19: . 20: . 21: . 22: . 23: .
24: . 25: . 26: . 27: . 28: . 29: . 30: . 31: . audit: .
Switch Subsystem Memory ...
 1: . 2: . 3: . 4: . 5: . 6: . 7: . 8: . 9: . 10: . 11: . 12: .
13: . 14: . 15: . 16: . 17: . 18: . 19: . 20: . 21: . 22: . 23: . 24: .
25: . 26: . 27: . 28: . 29: . 30: . 31: . 32: . 33: . 34: . 35: . 36: .
37: . 38: . 39: . 40: . 41: . 42: . 43: . 44: . 45: . 46: . 47: . 48: .
49: . 50: . 51: . 52: . 53: . 54: . 55: .
Module 1 Passed
```

You can use `show diagnostics online module` followed by the module number to get real-time information regarding the module. The output below shows the last module on the 4506 switch:

```
4506#show diagnostics online module 6
Slot Ports Card Type                        Diag Status      Diag Details
---- ----- -------------------------------- ---------------- ------------
  6    48   10/100BaseTX (RJ45)              Passed           None
Detailed Status
---------------
. = Pass                 U = Unknown
L = Loopback failure     S = Stub failure
I = Ilc failure          P = Port failure
E = SEEPROM failure      G = GBIC integrity check failure
Ports  1   2   3   4   5   6   7   8   9  10  11  12  13  14  15  16
       .   .   .   .   .   .   .   .   .   .   .   .   .   .   .   .
Ports 17  18  19  20  21  22  23  24  25  26  27  28  29  30  31  32
       .   .   .   .   .   .   .   .   .   .   .   .   .   .   .   .
Ports 33  34  35  36  37  38  39  40  41  42  43  44  45  46  47  48
       .   .   .   .   .   .   .   .   .   .   .   .   .   .   .   .

4506#
```

Chapter Summary

This chapter detailed the basic troubleshooting commands for the Cisco Set/Clear and CLI IOSs used on Cisco's Catalyst switches. It also provided a basic explanation of Spanning Tree Protocol, possible cabling problems, and the switch module LEDs.

This chapter covered many aspects of switching, including parts of the switching architecture, the switch functions, and commands available to monitor those functions. It also covered Cisco Catalyst hardware and software problems.

Some of the problems areas covered in this chapter include

➤ Locating duplicate MAC addresses

➤ Checking cable requirements

➤ Looking at Spanning Tree Protocol statistics

In the next chapter "Troubleshooting VLANs," we will learn how to use, configure, and troubleshoot switches in a Layer 3 environment using VLAN, Etherchannel, and many other protocols.

Exam Prep Practice Questions

Question 1

> If you are receiving a duplicate MAC address error, which of the following com-
> mands will show the MAC address of all nodes attached to a Set/Clear based IOS
> switch or a Cisco CLI based switch? [Choose all that apply.]
>
> ❑ A. **show port all**
> ❑ B. **debug mac**
> ❑ C. **show mac cache**
> ❑ D. **show cam dynamic**
> ❑ E. **show mac-address-table**

Answer: **D, E.** The CAM table on a Set/Clear based switch is used to keep
all the MAC addresses of all the attached nodes on each port. The show cam
dynamic command is used to view those addresses. The show cam static command can be used if port security is in place on the switch. On a Cisco CLI
based switch, such as the 4500 series, the command to view the dynamically
collected MAC addresses is show mac-address-table.

Question 2

> To determine the amount of time the switch has been up since the power was
> last recycled, which of the following commands would be used?
>
> ○ A. **show all**
> ○ B. **show uptime**
> ○ C. **show config**
> ○ D. **show version**

Answer: **D.** You can use the show version command to determine the amount
of time the switch has been up since the switch was last rebooted.

Question 3

Which of the following Catalyst switch commands enable you to gather statistics regarding the Spanning Tree Protocol? [Choose the two best answers.]

☐ A. **show span**

☐ B. **show vlan**

☐ C. **show spantree**

☐ D. **show port spantree**

Answer: **C, D**. This question is somewhat tricky because of the similarities in the commands. The show span command is also a valid answer, but it gives statistics related to the switched port analyzer, so it is wrong.

Question 4

The Catalyst 5000 switch's utilization statistics can be viewed by which of the following commands? [Choose the two best answers.]

☐ A. Viewing LEDs on the Ethernet Module

☐ B. Using the **show test** command

☐ C. Using Cisco software such as CWSI

☐ D. Using the **show all** command

☐ E. Viewing the Load LED on the Supervisor Engine module

☐ F. All of the above

Answer: **C, E**. Some CLI-based commands can aid in getting utilization statistics, but the only two valid answers shown are C and E.

Question 5

Which of the following cable types cannot support Ethernet 100BaseTX traffic?

○ A. Category 5

○ B. Category 3

○ C. Category 6

○ D. All of the above

Answer: **B**. Category 3 cable can support 10BaseTX but not 100BaseTX. Both Category 5 and 6 can support 100 Mbps data traffic over Ethernet.

Question 6

Which of the following commands provides information such as the status and errors on an Cisco Catalyst 5000's Ethernet Module port?

- ○ A. **show all**
- ○ B. **show port**
- ○ C. **show port config**
- ○ D. **show port all**

Answer: **B**. The show port command, followed by the module number and port number, is used by the switch to display the port status and error counters on a Set/Clear based switch.

Question 7

Spanning Tree Protocol stops data loops by placing redundant ports in which of the following states?

- ○ A. Stopped
- ○ B. Disabled
- ○ C. Closed
- ○ D. Blocked

Answer: **D**. Spanning Tree Protocol places redundant ports in the Blocked state. The Disabled state is placed on a port by an administrator or the switch, not by STP, if a hardware problem exists.

Question 8

If two paths, such as a primary path and a secondary path, exist between two points in the network, the second path is referred to as which of the following?

- ○ A. A cheaper path
- ○ B. A redundant path
- ○ C. A forced path
- ○ D. A helper path

Answer: **B**. The second path between two destinations in a network is called the redundant path.

Question 9

> Which of the following is not a timer used to influence the convergence time of STP?
>
> ○ A. Hello Time
>
> ○ B. MaxAge Time
>
> ○ C. Link State Time
>
> ○ D. FwdDelay

Answer: **C.** The Link State Time is not a timer used to influence the convergence time of STP.

Question 10

> Without loop avoidance schemes in place, which of the following is a worst-case scenario?
>
> ○ A. Slow convergence times
>
> ○ B. A broadcast storm
>
> ○ C. Links won't be able to send a multicast
>
> ○ D. Serial link failure

Answer: **B.** A broadcast storm, which is a total halt to the network, is the worst-case scenario resulting from data loops in the network.

Need to Know More?

 Deal, Richard. *CCNP BCMSN Exam Cram 2*, Que, 2003. ISBN: 0-7897-2991-1.

 Cisco CCO: Troubleshooting STP, `http://www.cisco.com/en/US/customer/tech/tk389/tk621/technologies_tech_note09186a0080136673.shtml`

Troubleshooting Virtual LAN

Terms you'll need to understand:

✓ Frame Tagging
✓ VLAN
✓ VLAN Port
✓ VLAN Trunk

✓ IEEE 802.10
✓ IEEE 802.1Q
✓ Inter-Switch Link (ISL)

Techniques you'll need to master:

✓ Differentiating between trunk links and access links
✓ Using VTP and VTP pruning
✓ Differentiating between dynamic and static VLAN ports
✓ Differentiating between internal and external route processing
✓ Configuring VLANs, trunking, VTP, and VTP pruning on a Catalyst switches
✓ Troubleshooting switched connections
✓ Identifying switch troubleshooting commands

✓ Troubleshooting switch hardware and software
✓ Troubleshooting VTP, ISL, and Spanning Tree Protocol configurations
✓ Knowing the diagnostic tools which apply to VLAN configuration problems
✓ Troubleshooting inter-VLAN routing configurations
✓ Troubleshooting trunk links and switches and routers

This chapter focuses on Virtual LANs (VLANs), which were created by the different switch manufacturers to provide individual broadcast domains. By assigning each port to an individual VLAN, each VLAN becomes its own broadcast domain. In IP networks, each VLAN is considered its own subnet and must be addressed as such. Each VLAN is commonly referred to as a color.

When a VLAN is created and ports on a single or multiple switches are assigned to that VLAN, only those ports that are members of the same VLAN will receive broadcasts from any other member of their assigned VLAN; these are called VLAN Ports. VLAN trunks are used to provide a way for data frames belonging to more than one VLAN to travel a single physical link between network devices.

The coloring of data traffic across a backbone is done by inserting a header between the source MAC address and the Link Service Access Point (LSAP) of frames leaving a switch. The 4-byte header is called the **VLAN ID**, or **color**.

VLAN Trunks

Trunk links using trunking protocols enable multiple VLANs to travel from one switch port to another switch port, from one switch port to a router, from router to router, or, in some cases, a server using a NIC card that supports a trunking protocol. Trunk links are point-to-point high-speed links, from 100Mbps to 10Gbps, configured to carry multiple VLANs.

The trunk protocols, frame tagging, and additional headers must be stripped from the frames before they are sent out the Access layer switch to the end user (you learn more about frame tagging in "IEEE 802.1Q," later in this chapter). The process of adding and removing trunking information must remain transparent to the end users' interface, because they do not understand the trunking process.

Four different methods or protocols enable you to track VLAN frames as they traverse a trunk link:

➤ IEEE 802.10

➤ IEEE 802.1Q

➤ Inter-Switch Link (ISL)

➤ LAN Emulation (LANE)

The following sections discuss these methods.

IEEE 802.10

The IEEE 802.10 standard is used to send multiple VLAN sessions over a Fiber Distributed Data Interface (FDDI) physical link. This standard uses a clear header, which is added to VLAN frames traversing an FDDI trunk. A clear header contains three fields: a Security Association Identifier (SAID), a Link Service Access Point (LSAP), and the Management Defined Field (MDF).

The SAID field in the frame header is the field used to identify which VLAN the port is a member of. This protocol is proprietary to Cisco devices and is used primarily to transport VLAN information over FDDI backbones between Cisco routers and switches.

IEEE 802.1Q

The IEEE 802.1Q standard is referred to as the "Standard for Virtual Bridged Local Area Networks." This standard was agreed upon by members of the IEEE as a method of frame tagging, the process of inserting into a frame a field that is used to identify the frame's VLAN membership over a trunk link. This process works as follows:

1. As a frame enters the switch fabric through a VLAN port, the data is tagged with the VLAN information of the port the frame arrived on. Just as in ISL, the tag remains in the frame as it is forwarded from switch to switch, and is removed prior to exiting the access link to the destination interface. Unlike ISL, however, which uses an external tagging process, 802.1Q uses an internal tagging process, by modifying the existing Ethernet frame itself.

2. IEEE 802.1Q changes the frame header with a standard VLAN format, which allows multiple-vendor VLAN implementations. This enables a Bay Networks device or a 3Com device to pass VLAN traffic to a Cisco device and vice versa.

3. When the frame is passed to an Access layer device to be sent directly to the destination interface, the frame is stripped of the tagging information, making the whole process transparent to the destination and sending device.

Inter-Switch Link (ISL)

Cisco created the ISL protocol and chose to keep ISL proprietary in nature to Cisco devices. ISL is a way of explicitly tagging VLAN information onto an Ethernet frame that is traversing the network through trunk links. This tagging information enables VLANs to be multiplexed over a trunk link through an external encapsulation method. By running ISL, you can interconnect multiple switches and still maintain VLAN information as traffic travels between switches on trunk links. The ISL process works like this:

1. Each frame is tagged as it enters a trunk link on the switch. The original frame is not altered; it is encapsulated within a new 26-byte ISL header and a 4-byte frame check sequence (FCS) at the end of the frame.

2. After the frame is tagged with the appropriate VLAN information, the frame can go through all Cisco devices in the network without being reencapsulated.

3. The ISL encapsulation is removed from the frame if the frame is set to exit out of a nontrunked link. The ISL header, shown in Figure 9.1, is entered into the frame.

Figure 9.1   Here you see the placement of ISL header information in an ISL packet.

The ISL header contains the following:

➤ Destination address (DA)—A 40-bit multicast address set to 01-00-0c-00-00. This address signals to the receiver that this packet is in ISL format.

➤ Type—Indicates the media type that the frame is supporting. The possible options are 0000 for Ethernet, 0001 for token ring, 0010 for FDDI, and 0011 for Asynchronous Transfer Mode (ATM).

➤ User field—A 4-bit field used to identify one of four possible priorities of the frame: XX00 for normal, XX01 for priority 1, XX02 for priority 2, and XX11 for the highest priority.

➤ Source MAC address (SA)—Shows the sending switch port's IEEE 802.3 MAC address. Some receiving devices ignore the SA field.

➤ LEN field—This 16-bit field shows the length of the packet, in bytes, minus the excluded fields. The excluded fields are the CRC, DA, Type, User, and SA fields, as well as the LEN field itself. The total of the excluded fields is 18 bytes. Therefore, the LEN field contains the total packet size minus 18 bytes from the excluded fields.

➤ AAAA03—Indicates an 802.2 Logical Link Control (LLC) header.

➤ High bit of source address (HSA)—The 3-byte manufacturer's portion of the SA field or vendor field of the source port's MAC address.

➤ 15-bit descriptor—Used to distinguish the frame from other VLANs or colors; 10 bits are used to indicate the source port.

➤ Bridge Protocol Data Units (BPDU) bit—Used to indicate Spanning Tree Protocol (STP) or Cisco Discovery Protocol (CDP) topology information.

➤ Index—Used to indicate the port address as the frame exits the switch. This 16-bit index value can be set to any value and can be used for diagnostic purposes only.

➤ Reserve—Used by FDDI and token ring. In token ring, the Frame Control (FC) and token ring AC bits (AC) fields are placed in the header. For FDDI, the FC is placed in the field. For Ethernet, the field contains all zeros.

LANE

LAN Emulation (LANE) is an IEEE standard for transporting VLANs over ATM networks. This process uses no encapsulation or frame tagging. ATM and LANE are beyond the scope of this book and thus are not covered in great detail.

The VLAN Trunk Protocol (VTP)

The VLAN Trunking Protocol (VTP) is used to provide administrators an easy way of managing VLANs across a Cisco switched network. VTP enables you to configure a VLAN on one switch and have the information propagate to all of your switches in a VTP domain. This enables an administrator to fairly easily add, delete, and rename VLANs.

One of the best features of VTP is its ability to maintain consistent VLAN configurations throughout the network. VTP keeps an identical VLAN configuration by propagating the VLAN mapping scheme of the VTP domain across the network. VTP provides for a plug-and-play type of connection. When you add additional VLANs, VTP provides tracking, monitoring, and reporting of VLANs in the network.

A Cisco switch can be a member of only one VTP domain.

In IOS version 3.1(1) of the Catalyst software, a second version of VTP was introduced, thereby making two versions: version 1 and version 2. The primary differences between the two versions are significant enough to render them incompatible. They will not work together in the same network.

Only VTP version 2 will be tested on the exam. Your understanding of Version 1 or the differences between the two versions is not an exam objective.

Version 1 is the default on Cisco Catalyst switches. If all the switches in the network support VTP version 2, then only one switch needs to have version 2 enabled in order to enable version 2 on all the switches participating in a VTP domain.

Version 2 provides the following additional features beyond support for Ethernet:

➤ Consistency checks—Performed when new information is entered by an administrator through the command-line interface (CLI) or through the Simple Network Management Protocol (SNMP).

➤ Token ring support—Includes token ring LAN switching and VLANs.

➤ Transparent Mode change support—Allows switches to forward only messages and advertisements. A switch using this mode will not add any new information received to its own database.

In version 1, the switch checks the VTP domain name and version before forwarding. In version 2, the switch forwards the VTP messages and advertisements without checking the version number.

➤ Unrecognized type-length value support—If a VTP advertisement is received and has an unrecognized type-length value, the VTP server or client will continue to propagate its configuration changes to the configured trunk links, even for TLVs that it is unable to parse. The unrecognized Type Length Value (TLV) is then saved in non-volatile random access memory (NVRAM).

Switches in a VTP management domain share VLAN information through the use of VTP advertisement messages. Three types of advertisement messages exist:

➤ Advertisement (Client) request—Clients use this type of advertisement to request VLAN information for the current network. A VTP client sends this type of advertisement in response to requests that have the appropriate summary and subset advertisements. The advertisement frame includes a version field, code field, reserved field, management domain name field (up to 32 bytes), and start value field.

➤ Summary advertisement—This type of advertisement is sent automatically every five minutes (300 seconds) to all the switches on the network. A summary advertisement can also be sent when a topology change to the network occurs, such as a switch drop or addition. The summary advertisement frame contains the version field, the code field, a follower's field, a management domain name field, a configuration revision number field, the updater's identity, the updater's timestamp, and the MD5 digest field.

➤ Subset advertisement—This type of advertisement contains very detailed information about the network. It contains the version, code, sequence number, management domain name, configuration revision number, and VLAN information fields.

 VTP will work only if at least one trunk port is configured to carry at least one valid VLAN. A trunk link using ISL encapsulation can carry up to 1024 VLANs.

VTP Advertisements

VTP advertisement frames are sent to a multicast address so that all the VTP devices in the same management domain are able to receive the frames. All VTP management domain clients and servers update their databases regarding all deletions and additions to the network, based on information contained in the VTP advertisements and the revision number contained in the advertisements the switch receives.

Each advertisement contains a revision number, which is one of the most important parts of the VTP advertisement. When a new VTP revision number is sent throughout the VTP domain, the switches believe that the highest revision number has the most up-to-date information about all the VLANs. If a switch participating in a VTP domain receives an advertisement with different VLAN configuration information than it currently has, it updates its information only if the revision number in the received advertisement is higher than the one that allowed the last change.

As a VTP server's database is modified, the VTP server increments the revision number by 1. The VTP server then advertises this information from the database with the new configure revision number.

Inter-VLAN Routing

VTP aids in propagating VLAN information, and trunk links allow for the traffic from more than one VLAN to traverse a link. How do switches use these trunk links to allow VLANs to communicate with one another? Through a process called inter-VLAN routing, which is explained in this section of the chapter.

Trunking protocols are designed to allow VLANs to flow from one networking device to another. These trunking protocols either tag the VLAN frames or add a header that uniquely identifies the source and destinations of the data as well as the VLAN the data is a member of. If data from one VLAN needs to be forwarded to another VLAN, it requires some type of Layer 3 device to do the routing. This process is shown in Figure 9.2, in which switch A is sending data from VLANs 1 through 3 to VLAN 6, which is configured on switch B.

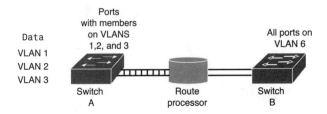

Figure 9.2 An inter-VLAN routing process.

To route VLAN frames between VLANs requires a Layer 3 device, which can be an external router or any number of modules known as internal route processors that are located inside a switch.

When a node needs to communicate with a member of another VLAN on the same network, the node sends a packet to the other node, assuming that it resides on the same network. The packet destined for another VLAN, which can even be another port on the same switch, must find a path on which to send the frame.

Because switches operate at Layer 2 and are designed to isolate traffic to broadcast domains or subnets, they cannot, by default, forward data from one VLAN to another VLAN without some other Layer 3 device, such as an internal or external route processor. The Layer 3 device is known as a "router on a stick." This device is used to route the data and create routing tables of other networks and devices. This also adds a layer of security, because now access lists can be added to permit and deny certain traffic.

Route processors can be used to route data between foreign VLANs and other logically segmented parts of the network, such as subnets. They also route data to remote WAN segments, networks, or the Internet.

An internal route processor uses internal modules or cards located inside the switch chassis that are similar to routers to route data between VLANs. The following are some of the available types of internal route processors for Catalyst switches:

➤ NetFlow Feature Card and NetFlow Feature Card II

➤ Route Switch Module

➤ Multilayer Switch Module

➤ Multilayer Switch Feature Card

➤ Route Switch Feature Card

➤ Cisco Route Processor (x)

➤ Cisco Route Processor PR

➤ Cisco Route Processor Module (PR, XF, RPM)

 The Catalyst 6000 series also uses a FlexWAN module, a description of which is beyond the scope of this book.

The following series of routers are external route processors with 100BaseT interfaces that support ISL:

➤ Cisco 1600 series routers

➤ Cisco 1700 Series routers

➤ Cisco 2600 series routers

➤ Cisco 3600 series routers

➤ Cisco 3700 series routers

➤ Cisco 4000 series routers

➤ Cisco 5400 series storage routers

➤ Cisco 7000 series routers

➤ Cisco 7100 series routers

➤ Cisco 7200 series routers

➤ Cisco 7500 series routers

➤ Cisco 7600 series routers

➤ Cisco 8500 series campus switch/routers

➤ Cisco 10000 series routers

➤ Cisco 12000 series routers

VLAN Configuration

By configuring VLANs, you control the size of your broadcast domains and keep local traffic local. A problem is created, however, when an end station in one VLAN needs to communicate with an end station in another VLAN. To fix the problem, inter-VLAN routing needs to take place to resolve the address, even if the ports belonging to different VLANs are side by side in the same switch. This type of communication is called inter-VLAN routing, where a Layer 3 device resolves the address just as it would if they were nodes residing on two different network segments. You configure one or more routers to route traffic to the appropriate destination VLAN.

All ports on the switch are configured as static access ports to VLAN 1 by default. VLAN 1 is also assigned as the default management VLAN. You can change the VLAN port information using the console, Cisco Visual Switch Manager (CVSM), or SNMP. This section covers the basics of VLAN configuration, as well as how to assign multi-VLAN memberships and how to view the configuration on each type of switch. It also covers configuring VLANs on a Set/Clear command–based switch, as well as on a CLI-based switch.

The following are the available options for the set vlan command:

```
set vlan <vlan_num> [name <name>] [type <type>] [state <state>][said <said>]
 [mtu <mtu>] [ring <hex_ring_number>][decring <decimal_ring_number>][bridge
<bridge_number>] [parent <vlan_num>][mode <bridge_mode>] [stp <stp_type>]
[translation <vlan_num>] [backupcrf<off¦on>][aremaxhop <hopcount>]
[stemaxhop <hopcount>]
```

To begin configuring the VLANs, you need to be in Privileged Mode on your switch and identify an interface on the switch. If you have a 12-port 10/100 module in slot 7 of a Catalyst 5500 series switch that has 13 available slots, the ports are referred to as "7/1–12." Most of the commands on this series of switches use this method to identify the interface. Cisco routers begin with slot and port numbers that start at 0. On the Cisco Catalyst 4000, 5000, and 6000 families of switches, the slot and port numbers start at 1. The first port on a Cisco router would be 0/0, but on a Catalyst 5500, it would be 1/1.

To configure the four ports on VLAN 3 for ports 3 through 6 on the module residing in slot 7, use these commands:

```
set vlan <vlan_num> <mod/ports>
set vlan 3 7/3
set vlan 3 7/4
set vlan 3 7/5
set vlan 3 7/6
```

You could also use a shortcut and configure all the ports at once by using this command:

```
set vlan 3 7/3-6
```

 Using a space between the numbers in the VLAN configuration command creates an error. The switch views the number following the space as a new command argument.

You can assign a VLAN a name that is up to 32 characters to help identify it when doing troubleshooting. To assign VLAN 3 and identify it as the VLAN that engineers use, use the following command:

```
set vlan <vlan_num> name <name>
set vlan 3 name Engineering
```

You can set the type of VLAN using one of the valid types, which are `ethernet`, `fddi`, `fddinet`, `trcrf`, and `trbrf`. The default is Ethernet if a type is not specified. Use the following command to map VLAN 3 to Ethernet:

```
set vlan <vlan_num> type <type>
set vlan 3 type ethernet
```

`Active` is the default state for a configured VLAN, but you can configure it for `active` or `suspend`. Use the following command to suspend VLAN 3:

```
set vlan <vlan_num> state <state>
set vlan 3 state suspend
```

SAIDs are used as a VLAN identifier when trunking across 802.10 FDDI or CDDI networks. The default SAID value is 100000 plus the VLAN number. For example, VLAN 3's SAID would be a value of 100003. You should be able to leave the SAID at the configured default. However, if a conflicting SAID exists in the network, you can use the following command to change the SAID to 100103:

```
set vlan <vlan_num> said <said>
set vlan 3 said 100103
```

Different media types have different maximum transmission unit (MTU) sizes. Ethernet, for example, is 1,500 bytes. If you need to change the MTU, use the following command:

```
set vlan <vlan_num> mtu <mtu>
set vlan 3 mtu 1500
```

If a node on the network is attached to a port on the switch and does not have the ability to negotiate the port speed, you can set the speed. To set the port speed manually, use the following command:

```
set port speed <mod_num/port_num> <4¦10¦16¦100¦auto>
set port speed 7/1 100
```

To set the port duplex on an Ethernet module, use the following command:

```
set port duplex <mod_num/port_num> <full¦half>
set port duplex 7/1 full
```

 You cannot set the duplex if the duplex is manually configured to auto, or the port speed has been set manually.

Enabling security on a Catalyst switch means that the switch will accept frames only from a particular MAC address on Ethernet modules. You can identify a specific MAC address. If the MAC address is not identified, the first interface to use the port will be the only interface allowed to use that port. If an unauthorized MAC address attempts to use the port, the port will become disabled and the light on the switch corresponding with that port will change from the color green to orange. To configure port security, use the following command:

```
set port security  <mod_num/port_num> <enable¦disable> [mac_addr]
set port security 3/1 enable
```

To verify the configured VLAN information, at the Privilege EXEC Mode prompt, you can use the `show vlan` command, which is used for all Catalyst switches:

```
show vlan
```

To remove a VLAN configured on a port, at the Privilege EXEC Mode prompt, you can use the following command (the VLAN being removed is VLAN 3, affecting all ports that have VLAN 3 configured):

```
clear vlan 3
```

 When you clear a VLAN that has ports assigned to it, by default, those ports revert to VLAN 1. Every port must be assigned to a VLAN.

Configuring VLAN Trunks

VLAN trunks can be configured between two switches, between two routers, or between a switch and a router. In some special circumstances, a file server has an ISL- or 802.1Q-aware NIC card that understands VLAN tagging.

One thing to be aware of when configuring a trunk is that your device needs to be able to handle the load so that the introduction of latency doesn't affect your network devices. This latency will not be noticeable on small data files, but it will be very noticeable when you're using voice or video if your equipment cannot handle the load placed upon it.

Before you create a trunk, you must understand some of the main pieces of the trunk sub variables. You must know whether the trunking method to be used is 802.1Q, 802.10, ISL, LANE, or negotiate.

 VLANs can be configured as local VLANs, which means that they are local to one specific geographical area. Trunk links allow VLANs to be created end to end, meaning they can span more than one geographical area.

For Fast Ethernet or Gigabit Ethernet, you set the trunking mode for each port as well as the protocol to use. To configure the domain name and set the password on the switch, use the following command in Privileged Mode (the name DCS refers to the switch domain name, and the password is set to 1234):

```
set vtp domain dcs passwd 1234
```

The domain can be 1 to 32 characters long, and the password can be 8 to 64 characters long.

To see the VTP domain information, use the following show command from the Privileged Mode prompt:

```
show vtp domain
```

The output will look similar to this:

```
Domain Name Domain Index VTP Version Local Mode  Password
DCS    1              2            server        -
Vlan-count Max-vlan-storage  Config Revision  Notifications
12          1023                 8             disabled
Last Updater    V2 Mode   Pruning    PruneEligible on Vlans
172.1.1.1       disabled  disabled   2-1000
```

To set the VTP mode to Server, Client, or Transparent Mode, use the following Privileged Mode command (DCS refers to the domain that the switch will join):

```
set vtp domain <domain name> mode [client¦server¦transparent]
set vtp domain DCS mode server
```

Managing Revision Numbers

What happens when a new switch is configured as a server and the revision number is higher than the current revision number used in the domain? Oops! If the rest of the domain gets that information, it will reconfigure every single member with the configuration on that new switch. This event could become a disaster on your network. Unfortunately, any time a switch sees a higher revision number, it takes the information it just received, considers it more current, and overwrites the existing database with the new configuration information.

Many network administrators make the bad mistake of using the **clear config all** command, believing that it will erase the current revision number. This command doesn't do what it says it does—it doesn't really "clear all." VTP has its own non-volatile random access memory (NVRAM), so the VTP information, as well as the revision number, will still be present if you execute the clear config all command. You can overcome the problem of not clearing the VTP configration in either of two ways, the easiest of which is to cycle the power on the switch after placing the switch in client mode. The switch must be in client mode because the switch will store VTP information in the special NVRAM when the server is in server mode. As a result, merely powering down the switch will not reset the revision number or cause the switch to lose its VTP database.

The other way to address this problem is to make the switch a client. Connect it to the network to get new revisions and then configure the switch as a VTP server. You can also reset the revision number with the **set vtp domain** name command.

Use the following command to configure a trunk port. The port being configured is on module 3, port 1, and the VLAN range is VLANs 2 through 12:

```
set trunk <mod_num/port_num> [on¦off¦desirable¦auto¦nonegotiate]
<vlan_range> [isl¦dot1q¦dot10¦lane¦negotiate]
set trunk 3/1 desirable 2-12 isl
```

To remove a VLAN from a trunk, use the following Privileged Mode command (in this demonstration, the module number is 3 and the port number is 1; the VLAN being removed is 13):

```
Clear trunk <mod_num/port_num> <vlan_range>
Clear trunk 3/1 13
```

For more than one VLAN, such as VLANs 13 through 200, issue the following Privileged Mode command:

```
Clear trunk 3/1 13-200
```

To display all the trunks configured on the switch, use the following command in Privileged Mode:

```
Switch> (enable) show trunk
```

The output should look similar to this:

```
Port   Mode             Encapsulation  Status          Native vlan
----   ----             -------------  ------          -----------
1/1    desirable        isl            trunking        1
2/1    desirable        isl            trunking        1
2/2    desirable        isl            trunking        1
2/3    desirable        isl            trunking        1
3/1    desirable        isl            trunking        1
Port            Vlans allowed on trunk
----            ----------------------
1/1             1-100,1003-1005
2/1             1-100,1003-1005
2/2             1-100,1003-1005
2/3             1-100,1003-1005
3/1             1-100,1003-1005
Port            Vlans allowed and active in management domain
----            ---------------------------------------------
1/1             1,6-9,1003-1005
2/1             1,6-9,1003-1005
2/2             1,6-9,1003-1005
2/3             1,6-9,1003-1005
3/1             1,6-9,1003-1005
Port            Vlans in spanning tree forwarding state and not pruned
----            ------------------------------------------------------
1/1             1,1003-1005
2/1             1,1003-1005
2/2             1,1003-1005
2/3             1,1003-1005
3/1             1,1003-1005
```

To get a statistical view of the VTP traffic, use the following command:

```
show vtp statistics
```

VTP Pruning

VTP pruning enhances the network's bandwidth by reducing unnecessary network traffic. VTP restricts flooded data traffic to those trunk links that the traffic must use to access the appropriate network devices. By default, VTP pruning is disabled.

VTP pruning requires all switches to be set to Server Mode, and also requires the establishment of the same common VTP domain between all the switches. To enable pruning on a Set/Clear-based switch, use this command in Privileged Mode:

```
set vtp pruning <enable¦disable>
set vtp pruning enable
```

When you enable VTP pruning, it affects all the VLANs on the switch. If you want to enable VTP pruning only on certain VLANs, first clear the VLAN prune-eligible list using the following command for all VLANs:

```
clear vtp pruneeligible <vlan_range>
clear vtp pruneeligible 2-1000
```

Next, set the VLANs for which you wish to enable pruning:

```
set vtp pruneeligible <vlan_range>
set vtp pruneeligible 2-30
```

 NOTE   VTP pruning cannot be enabled on VLAN 1, and every switch participating in VTP pruning must be configured as a VTP server. Enabling VTP pruning on one server enables VTP pruning on all the servers in the management domain. By default, VLANs 2 through 1,000 are eligible for pruning. VTP pruning will not take place on VLANs that are pruning-ineligible.

Assigning a VLAN Membership to a 1900 Series Switch

On the 1900 series switch, you must choose "k" from the initial user interface menu to get into command-line interface for the switch IOS, as shown here:

```
1 user(s) now active on Management Console.
      User Interface Menu
   [M] Menus
   [K] Command Line
   [I] IP Configuration
```

```
Enter Selection:  k
     CLI session with the switch is open.
     To end the CLI session, enter [Exit].
```

To configure the 1900 series switch ports with VLANs, you must enter global configuration mode, as shown next; to help identify the switch, we will give it the hostname 1912EN:

```
>enable
#config terminal
Enter configuration commands, one per line.  End with CNTL/Z
(config)#hostname 1912EN
```

To configure VLANs on an IOS-based switch, use the following command:

```
vlan <vlan> name <vlan name>
1912E(config)#vlan 3 name engineering
```

You can configure each interface (port) on a switch to be in a VLAN by using the vlan-membership command. Unfortunately you must configure VLANs one by one for each port, because no command exists to assign more than one port to a VLAN. The following is the vlan-membership command and its options:

```
1912EN(config-if)#vlan-membership ?
  dynamic  Set VLAN membership type as dynamic
  static   Set VLAN membership type as static
1912EN(config-if)#vlan-membership static ?
  <1-1005>  ISL VLAN index
```

Static and Dynamic VLANs

A static VLAN is the most common type of VLAN and the easiest to administer. The switch port always remains in the VLAN that is assigned by an administrator until an administrator changes the port assignment. Static VLAN configurations allow for VLAN configurations that are easy to configure and monitor, and that work well in a network in which the movement of users within the network remains controlled. You can also use network management software, such as CiscoWorks for Switched Internetworks (CWSI), to configure the ports on the switch. This software is available from any Cisco Value Added Reseller (VAR). If you work for a VAR, you can get this software online from the Cisco CCO Web site.

A dynamic VLAN determines a node's VLAN assignment automatically using a server called a VLAN Management Policy Server (VMPS) to set up a database of MAC addresses that can be used for dynamic addressing of VLANs. VMPS is a MAC-address-to-VLAN mapping database that contains a database of allowable MAC or physical addresses that are mapped to a particular

VLAN. When the user boots up, the switch learns the MAC address and checks the database for the appropriate VLAN assigned to that MAC address. This enables a user to remain in the same VLAN throughout the network regardless of the location in which the user resides.

A lot of network management is required to maintain the databases of MAC addresses. Therefore, dynamic VLANs are not very effective in larger networks. Using intelligent network management software enables you to match a VLAN number to a hardware (MAC) address, protocol, or even an application address to create static VLANs.

In the following code, you see that the interface configuration mode has been entered for ports 1 and 2, and then the VLAN is assigned two ports:

```
1912EN(config-if)#interface e0/1
1912EN(config-if)#vlan-membership static 3
1912EN(config-if)#interface e0/2
1912EN(config-if)#vlan-membership static 3
```

The Catalyst 1900 switch has the same options as the 5000 and 6000 series do for ISL. The 1900 switch does, however, run the Dynamic Inter-Switch Link (DISL) encapsulation method to create trunks. The Cisco Catalyst 1912EN switch has two trunkable ports that are Fast Ethernet ports: Interface 26 (Port A) and Interface 27 (Port B). The following lists the available options of the trunk command and sets the trunk to on for Port B:

```
1912EN(config)#interface f0/27
1912EN(config-if)#trunk ?
  auto        Set DISL state to AUTO
  desirable   Set DISL state to DESIRABLE
  nonegotiate Set DISL state to NONEGOTIATE
  off         Set DISL state to OFF
  on          Set DISL state to ON
1912EN(config-if)#trunk on
```

Configuring VLAN and Enabling VTP on the 1900EN Series Switch

To remove a VLAN from a trunk port on a 1900EN series switch, use the interface configuration mode command no trunk-vlan command. The following takes a look at the syntaxes available and then removes VLAN 3 from its ability to send VLAN traffic across the trunk:

```
1912EN(config-if)#no trunk-vlan ?
  <1-1005>  ISL VLAN index
1912EN(config-if)#no trunk-vlan 3
```

No command exists to clear more than one VLAN simultaneously.

To view the trunks on a Cisco Catalyst 1900EN, use the show trunk command just as you would on a 5000 series switch. A difference does exist, however: this command can be used only on Fast Ethernet ports 26 (Port A) and 27 (Port B). The following are the show trunk command options:

```
1912EN#show trunk ?
  A   Trunk A
  B   Trunk B
1912EN#show trunk a ?
  allowed-vlans   Display allowed vlans
  joined-vlans    Display joined vlans
  joining-vlans   Display joining vlans
  prune-eligible  Display pruning eligible vlans
```

As an example of the show trunk command, look at the allowed VLANs on Port B:

```
1900EN#show trunk b allowed-vlans
1-3, 6-8
```

The following lists the options when enabling VTP in global configuration mode on the 1900 series switch:

```
1912EN(config)#vtp ?
  client       VTP client
  domain       Set VTP domain name
  password     Set VTP password
  pruning      VTP pruning
  server       VTP server
  transparent  VTP transparent
  trap         VTP trap
```

Let's go ahead and configure this switch as a VTP server for the DCS domain, and set the password using the commands in the preceding list:

```
1912EN(config)#vtp server
1912EN(config)#vtp domain dcs
1912EN(config)#vtp password 1234
```

Configuring Inter-VLAN Routing on an External Router

When a switch receives a packet from a port on one VLAN destined for the port of another VLAN, the switch must find a path on which to send the frame. Switches work at Layer 2 and are designed to isolate traffic to collision domains or subnets; they cannot, by default, forward data from one VLAN to another VLAN or network without some other Layer 3 devices. The Layer 3 device known as a `router on a stick` is used to route the data and create routing tables of other networks and devices.

As discussed earlier in the chapter, route processors can be used to route data between foreign VLANs and other logically segmented parts of the network, such as subnets. They also route data to remote WAN segments, networks, or the Internet.

Layer 3 routing takes place between VLANs. This can become a challenging problem for an administrator to overcome. Two types of route processors exist: external and internal. As you learned in the previous section, an external route processor uses an external router (such as the Cisco devices you are familiar with) to route data from one VLAN to another VLAN. An internal route processor uses internal modules and cards located inside the switch route data between VLANs.

Each type of Layer 3 routable protocol that does not have to be IP can have its own mapping for a VLAN. In an IP network, each subnetwork is mapped to an individual VLAN. In an IPX network, each VLAN is mapped to the IPX network number. With AppleTalk, a cable range and AppleTalk zone name are associated with each VLAN.

By configuring VLANs, you control the size of your broadcast domains and keep local traffic local. However, when an end station in one VLAN needs to communicate with an end station in another VLAN, this communication is supported by inter-VLAN routing. You configure one or more routers to route traffic to the appropriate destination VLAN.

To understand this section, you need to become familiar with Cisco IOS software running on Cisco routers. This demonstration is going to configure a Cisco 7505, with the goal of making the process as clear as possible:

1. To enable IP routing on the router, enter the global configuration mode and use the `ip routing` command:

```
7505#configure terminal
Enter configuration commands, one per line.  End with CNTL/Z.
7505 (config)#ip routing
```

2. Specify an IP routing protocol, such as OSPF, RIP, IGRP, or EIGRP, and identify the network:

```
Cisco7505(config)#router rip
Cisco7505(config-router)#network 192.1.0.0
```

3. Create a subinterface on a physical interface in interface configuration mode for the port connected to the switch:

```
7505(config-router)#interface fastethernet2/0.100
```

4. Specify the encapsulation type and VLAN number to use on the subinterface:

```
7505 (config-subif)#encapsulation isl 100
```

5. Assign an IP address and subnet mask to the subinterface:

```
7505 (config-subif)#ip address 192.1.1.1 255.255.255.0
```

6. To configure any other interfaces, repeat Steps 3 through 5 for each VLAN you need to become a member of the trunk link or would like to route traffic between:

```
7505 (config-router)#interface fastethernet2/0.200
7505 (config-subif)#encapsulation isl 200
7505 (config-subif)#ip address 192.1.2.3 255.255.255.0
```

To configure inter-VLAN routing for IPX, perform this task beginning in global configuration mode:

1. To enable IP routing on the router, enter the global configuration mode and use the ipx routing command:

```
7505#configure terminal
```

Enter configuration commands, one per line. End with CTRL/Z.

```
7505 (config)#ipx routing
```

2. Specify an IPX routing protocol, such as IPX RIP, and identify all the networks:

```
Cisco7505(config)#ipx router rip
Cisco7505(config-router)#network all
```

3. Create a subinterface on a physical interface in interface configuration mode for the port connected to the switch:

```
7505(config-router)#interface fastethernet2/0.1
```

4. Specify the encapsulation type and VLAN number to use on the subinterface:

```
7505 (config-subif)#ipx encapsulation isl 1
```

5. Assign a network number to the subinterface and identify an encapsulation type for IPX, such as `snap`, `novell-ether`, `arpa`, or `sap`:

```
7505 (config-subif)# ipx network 1 encapsulation sap
```

6. To configure any other interfaces, repeat Steps 3 through 5 for each VLAN you need to become a member of the trunk link or would like to route traffic between.

```
7505(config-subif)#interface fastethernet2/0.2
7505(config-subif)#encapsulation isl 2
7505(config-subif)#ipx network 2 encapsulation sap
```

> You need to know what the IP configuration is for each component, and ensure that the switch is configured with the correct default gateway for each VLAN. The **show port** command is used to find and resolve these types of issues.

Inter-Switch Link (ISL)

Because switches operate at Layer 2, a switch cannot forward data from one VLAN to another VLAN without a Layer 3 device, such as a router or internal route processor, to perform a Layer 3 resolution function. An Access layer port can carry the traffic of only one VLAN; a port that is trunked using ISL can carry more than one or all of the VLANs configured on the switches.

`Inter-Switch Link (ISL)` is a Cisco proprietary protocol used to interconnect two devices with a trunk link to carry multiple VLANs. ISL must be configured on a 10/100BaseTX port between two Cisco devices that support ISL. ISL operates in a point-to-point VLAN environment supporting up to 1000 VLANs. You can define VLANs as you would logical networks.

ISL is available on Cisco routers beginning with the 2600 series. Gigabit Ethernet trunk links default to using the IEEE 802.1Q encapsulation for creating a trunk port. Ethernet has the ability to negotiate whether ISL or 802.1Q encapsulation methods are being used. Fast Ethernet, however, defaults to using ISL as the trunking encapsulation method.

When you configure ISL between two devices, some specific rules must be followed:

➤ Use ISL only on 100Mbps or higher speed links. (A 10Mbps link can be used, but this choice is not recommended.)

➤ Verify that you have sufficient memory on the switch or router, because ISL encapsulates and de-encapsulates the frame needing higher processing overhead.

➤ Use ISL+ to encapsulate Token Ring.

➤ Configure ISL links as point-to-point links.

IEEE 802.1Q Standard

The IEEE 802.1Q standard is an industry standard for trunking and can be used when a Cisco device needs to have a trunked link to a non-Cisco device. On the Cisco router, you can use the `encapsulation dot1q` command on Cisco IOS version 12.0.1(t) or higher.

You can configure the trunk link to use the IEEE 802.1q protocol on the Catalyst 5000 series software version 4.1 or later, using the `set trunk` command as shown below:

```
DCSCatalyst5000>(enable) set trunk 2/1 ?
  <mode>                    Trunk mode
                              (on,off,desirable,auto,nonegotiate)
  <type>                    Trunk type
                              (isl,dot1q,dot10,lane,negotiate)
  <vlan>                    VLAN number

DCSCatalyst5000>(enable) set trunk 2/1 on dot1q
Port(s)  2/1 trunk mode set to on.
Port(s)  2/1 trunk type set to dot1q.
DCSCatalyst5000>(enable)
```

The output above shows the module 2 port 1 set to use the IEEE 802.1q trunking protocol. The 802.1Q header is somewhat different than that of the ISL header. Only 4 bytes are added to the frame. ISL adds 30 bytes to an ISL header and trailer. Instead of encapsulating the frame, as ISL does, 802.1Q adds the VLAN number inside the frame.

Most trunking issues result from a misconfiguration of the VLANs or the interfaces on each side of a trunk link. ISL and 802.1Q cannot be used on the same trunk link.

Inter-VLAN Routing Troubleshooting

The Route Switch Module (RSM) is one of many external modules and cards called `internal route processors` that are available for the 5000 and 6000 families of switches. These cards and modules give the switch a local resource to resolve Layer 3 addresses and perform inter-VLAN routing.

Although you need to know about the RSM role in troubleshooting and that it uses an IOS similar to that used on a router, you need to learn about other cards as well. These cards include the Multilayer Switch Module (MSM), Multilayer Switch Feature Card (MSFC), Route Switch Feature Card (RSFC), FlexWAN module, NetFlow Feature Card (NFFC), and NetFlow Feature Card II (NFFCII).

The internal route processor can be used to provide routing between VLANs. Using an external router to route between VLANs adds additional overhead and complexity that an internal route processor can relieve. An internal route processor on the switch uses an internal connection to the switch and does not need to use up an interface on the switch to create a trunk port from the switch to the internal route processor.

An external router should be used when you need a higher performance level, such as that provided by the 7000 series routers or the 12000 Gigabit Switch Router (GSR). You can also combine the RSM with a NetFlow Feature Card (NFFC or NFFC II), which is a daughter card that can provide multilayer switching (MLS).

The internal route processor uses an IOS that is similar to that used on a router. To access an internal route processor on the Cisco Catalyst 5000 family of switches, use the session command followed by the slot number:

```
catalyst5000>(enable) session 3
Building configuration...
Current configuration:
!
version 11.3
service timestamps debug uptime
service timestamps log uptime
no service password-encryption
!
hostname RSM1
!
interface Vlan1
 description VLAN1
 ip address 38.187.128.10 255.255.255.0
 no ip redirects
 standby 1 timers 5 15
 standby 1 priority 10
 standby 1 preempt
 standby 1 ip 38.187.128.11
```

To configure an external router for each type of connection, each VLAN must be defined on a subinterface, and the main interface must be left without a configuration. To keep track of the VLANs on an interface, it's good practice to make the subinterface number the same as the VLAN number. The following code displays the commands involved in configuring FastEthernet port 2, subinterface 1 for VLAN 1, and setting the encapsulation method on the link for ISL trunking:

```
interface fastethernet 0/2
no ip address
no shutdown
full-duplex
interface fastethernet 0/2.1
description vlan1
ip address 10.1.1.1 255.255.255.0
encapsulation isl 1
```

show vtp domain Command

The VLAN Trunk Protocol (VTP) is used to maintain a consistent VLAN configuration throughout the switches in the network. In a VTP management domain, a configuration change is done only once on a VTP server–configured switch. The new configuration is propagated throughout the network. The show vtp domain command provides the status and configuration information for VTP.

An example of using the show vtp domain command follows:

```
DCSCatalyst5000>(enable) show vtp ?
  domain                      Show VTP domain information
  statistics                  Show VTP statistic information
DCSCatalyst5000>(enable) show vtp domain
Domain Name  Domain Index  VTP Version  Local Mode  Password
----------   ------------  -----------  ----------  --------
DCS      1                2              server      sean1
Vlan-count Max-vlan-storage Config Revision Notifications
---------- ---------------- --------------- -------------
5          1023             355             enabled
Last Updater   V2 Mode  Pruning  PruneEligible on Vlans
-----------    -------  -------  ----------------------
68.38.127.5    enabled  enabled  2-1000
```

The show vtp command is used to gather similar information on the Cisco CLI-based switches. There are three syntaxes. We will look at the output from the counters and status syntaxes below:

```
4506#show vtp ?
  counters  VTP statistics
  password  VTP password
  status    VTP domain status
4506#show vtp status
VTP Version                     : 2
Configuration Revision          : 17
Maximum VLANs supported locally : 1005
Number of existing VLANs        : 5
VTP Operating Mode              : Server
VTP Domain Name                 : DCS
VTP Pruning Mode                : Disabled
VTP V2 Mode                     : Disabled
VTP Traps Generation            : Disabled
MD5 digest                      : 0xC6 0x5B 0x77 0xDD 0xA1 0x84 0x14 0xC3
Configuration last modified by 0.0.0.0 at 3-24-02 10:08:05
Local updater ID is 10.1.2.55 on interface Vl1
```

```
         (lowest numbered VLAN interface found)
4506#show vtp counters
VTP statistics:
Summary advertisements received    : 0
Subset advertisements received     : 0
Request advertisements received    : 0
Summary advertisements transmitted : 0
Subset advertisements transmitted  : 0
Request advertisements transmitted : 0
Number of config revision errors   : 0
Number of config digest errors     : 0
Number of V1 summary errors        : 0
VTP pruning statistics:
Trunk         Join Transmitted Join Received   Summary advts received from
                                               non-pruning-capable device
------------- ---------------- ---------------- ---------------------------
4506#
```

The above output shows the different items displayed by the show vtp counters command. The VTP counters are shown as zeros since the interface counters have just been reset.

Chapter Summary

When thinking of VLANs, most administrators who merely support an already configured network think of switches, because the switch is both the access point for the workstations and the location where the VLANs are created.

After a VLAN is created, inter-VLAN routing enables nodes in one VLAN to talk to a node in another VLAN. An access port leading to the end user can be assigned only to one VLAN, sometimes referred to as a color. In this chapter, you learned that trunking using certain protocols enables you to send the traffic of more than one VLAN down a single pipe between wiring closet devices such as switches or routers. Here are those protocols:

➤ IEEE 802.10—A Cisco proprietary protocol used primarily to transport VLAN information over FDDI.

➤ IEEE 802.1Q—The standard protocol used for inserting a frame tag VLAN identifier in the frame header. As a frame enters the switch fabric, it is tagged with additional information regarding the VLAN properties. The tag remains in the frame as it is forwarded between switches, and is removed prior to exiting the access link to the destination interface. This process is completely transparent to the end user.

➤ Inter-Switch Link (ISL)—A special Cisco proprietary Ethernet protocol that assigns a 26-byte header and a 4-byte checksum, sometimes referred to as the FCS or the CRC, to an encapsulated frame header.

➤ LAN Emulation (LANE)—An IEEE standard for transporting VLANs over ATM networks. This process uses no encapsulation or frame tagging. ATM and LANE are beyond the scope of this book and thus were not covered in great detail.

This chapter also covered the VLAN Trunking Protocol (VTP), which is used to enable a single server operating in a VTP domain to configure all the switches in the domain with VLAN information to keep them consistent in the network. VTP enables you to configure one device and have the same configuration propagated to all the devices in the switch block. The different VTP modes—Server, Client, and Transparent—were also discussed.

Review Questions

Question 1

Which of the following port types allows more than one VLAN to traverse its links?

O A. Any switched port

O B. Any port that uses 10BaseT

O C. An EtherChannel port

O D. A switched port with ISL encapsulation configured

Answer: **D.** A switched port with ISL encapsulation configured would be a trunked port. Both ISL and IEEE 802.1Q allow more than one VLAN to traverse the link.

Question 2

Which command will enable you to display the following output?

```
Domain Name Domain Index VTP   Version  Local Mode Password
----------- ------ --------- -------  ---------- --------
DCS                    1              2          server     sean1
Vlan-count Max-vlan-storage Config Revision Notifications
---------- ---------------- ---------------- -------------
5          1023                  355              enabled

Last Updater   V2 Mode  Pruning  PruneEligible on Vlans
-----------    -------  -------  ----------------------
68.38.127.5    enabled  enabled  2-1000
```

O A. **show vtp**

O B. **show vlan**

O C. **show vtp all**

O D. **show vtp domain**

Answer: **D.** The show vtp domain command will enable you to display the output.

Question 3

Which of the following commands can be used on a router's subinterface to assign an encapsulation type?

- ○ A. **set encapsulation isl 1**
- ○ B. **encapsulation isl 1**
- ○ C. **interface encasulation isl 1**
- ○ D. **isl encapsulation 1**

Answer: **B.** The ISL encapsulation type on a router's interface can be assigned using the `encapsulation isl 1` command.

Question 4

Which of the following trunking types would be used on a switch port if the port were connecting to a non-Cisco router or switch?

- ○ A. IEEE 802.5
- ○ B. IEEE 802.3
- ○ C. ISL
- ○ D. IEEE 802.1Q

Answer: **D.** IEEE 802.1Q is an industry-standard protocol supported on Cisco switches and routers to connect a trunked link to a non-Cisco router or switch.

Question 5

Although the management VLAN can be changed, what VLAN is the management VLAN by default?

- ○ A. VLAN 1
- ○ B. The VLAN assigned to an ISL trunked port
- ○ C. VLAN 1005
- ○ D. VLAN 64

Answer: **A.** All ports begin in VLAN 1 by default, which is also the VLAN management VLAN by default.

Question 6

Which of the following are VLAN encapsulation types supported on Cisco switches? [Choose the two best answers.]

- ❏ A. Inter-Switch Link (ISL)
- ❏ B. IEEE 802.5
- ❏ C. STP
- ❏ D. IEEE 802.1Q

Answer: **A, D**. A Cisco switch and router support both the IEEE 802.1Q protocol, which allows trunking to a non-Cisco device, and the Inter-Switch Link, which is a Cisco proprietary protocol for trunking.

Question 7

Which of the following devices enables you to route between VLANs?

- ○ A. An external route processor
- ○ B. A Route Switch Module (RSM)
- ○ C. A Route Switch Feature Card (RSFC)
- ○ D. All of the above

Answer: **D**. An internal or external route processor must be used to route between VLANs at Layer 3. An external route processor is a router. The RSM and RSFC are both internal route processors. All of which can route Layer 3 VLANs.

Question 8

Which of the following are benefits of implementing switches and virtual LANs?

- ○ A. Efficient bandwidth utilization
- ○ B. Load balancing among multiple paths
- ○ C. Isolation between problem components
- ○ D. All of the above

Answer: **D**. Efficient bandwidth utilization, load balancing among multiple paths, and isolation between problem components are all benefits of implementing switches and VLANs.

Question 9

Which of the following best describes a trunk link?

○ A. A link that enables access to the Internet

○ B. A link that enables FTP and HTTP to flow together

○ C. A link that can carry traffic for multiple VLANs

○ D. A link that is used only in token ring environments

Answer: **C.** A link that can carry traffic for multiple VLANs best describes a trunk link.

Need to Know More?

 CCNP BCMSN Exam Cram 2, Que, 2003, Richard Deal, ISBN: 0-7897-2991-1

 Cisco CCO: Troubleshooting STP, http://www.cisco.com/en/US/customer/tech/tk389/tk621/technologies_tech_note09186a0080136673.shtml

Troubleshooting Serial Links

Terms you'll need to understand:

✓ CSU/DSU Channel Service Unit/Digital Service Unit
✓ Frame Relay
✓ Encapsulation
✓ HDLC High-level Data Link Control
✓ Loopback
✓ PVC Permanent Virtual Connection
✓ SVC Switched Virtual Connection
✓ X.25

Techniques you'll need to master:

✓ Troubleshoot Frame Relay problems
✓ Troubleshoot X.25 problems
✓ Troubleshoot serial link problems
✓ Determine whether serial link problems are hardware or software issues
✓ Perform a local or remote loopback test
✓ Troubleshoot IOS serial link configuration issues
✓ Use IOS commands that will aid in isolating problems

Many different protocols can use a serial link. Serial links send data bit by bit over their links or circuits. Frame Relay and X.25 are all protocols used on serial links. These protocols have many common troubleshooting commands, as well as techniques to help you, the administrator, locate configuration and hardware problems.

Frame relay is a telecommunication service designed for cost-efficient data transmission for intermittent traffic between local area networks (LANs) and between end-points in a wide area network (WAN). Frame relay puts data in a variable-size unit called a frame and leaves any necessary error correction (retransmission of data) up to the end-points, which speeds up overall data transmission.

Before Frame Relay was adopted as a standard, the X.25 protocol was adopted as a standard by the Consultative Committee for International Telegraph and Telephone (CCITT). The X.25 protocol allows computers on different public networks to communicate through an intermediary computer at the network layer level.

This chapter will focus on what you need to know to troubleshoot serial links and the protocols used on serial links. You learn techniques for troubleshooting serial links, including CSU/DSU Loopback Testing and common serial link troubleshooting commands. The chapter also discusses frame relay troubleshooting and techniques for troubleshooting X.25. The information you learn here will help in your preparation for the CIT Exam.

 An in-depth discussion of configuring Frame Relay and X.25 is quite lengthy and beyond the scope of this book. If you would like to learn more about configuring Frame Relay and X.25, I recommend reading *CCNP BCRAN Exam Cram 2* by Eric Quinn and Fred Glauser, ISBN: 0-7897-3020-0.

Diagnosing Serial Link Symptoms with the **show interface** Command

There are many different types of encapsulations and protocols that can run over serial links. This can create many possible configuration problems. Most serial link problems unrelated to hardware are caused by a mismatched configuration on either side of the serial link. Both ends of a serial link must use the same encapsulation types, speed, and protocol types.

You can use the show interface command to reveal information that will help you in troubleshooting serial links. The output of the show interface command gives you a variety of information about each interface's status.

For the exam, you should know that *encapsulation* is a technique used by layered protocols to add header information to a protocol data unit (PDU). This process sometimes adds a footer that includes a Cyclic Redundancy Check (CRC).

Each of the following sub-sections discusses a problem that can be revealed in the output of the show interface command, and discusses some potential causes for those problems. Here are the serial interface symptoms diagnosed from the show interface command in these sections:

➤ Interface is administratively down; line protocol is down

➤ Interface is down; line protocol is down

➤ Keepalive sequencing not incrementing

➤ Interface is up; line protocol is down

➤ Interface is up; line protocol is up (looped)

➤ Incrementing carrier transition counter

➤ Incrementing interface resets

➤ Input drops, CRC, and framing errors

Interface Is Administratively Down; Line Protocol Is Down

The Interface Is Administratively Down; Line Protocol Is Down error shown by the router indicates that a manual change to the router's configuration has been made.

Here are some potential causes:

1. The interface has not been placed in shutdown state by an administrator.

2. Check to see that a duplicate IP address has not been used.

Interface Is Down; Line Protocol Is Down

The Interface Is Down; Line Protocol Is Down error shown by the router indicates that the line is not making a connection and the protocols configured are not sending valid keepalive messages. This can be an indicator of many types of problems.

To troubleshoot this problem, use the following steps:

1. Check the cabling to make sure there is not a break or other problem affecting connectivity.

2. Check that a carrier signal from a local provider exists.

3. Consider a hardware failure on the interface or CSU/DSU.

Interface Is Up; Line Protocol Is Down

To troubleshoot this problem, use the following steps:

1. Check the interface for a problem with addressing, protocol, or interface configurations.

2. Check with the local provider to verify that it is not having line issues.

Keepalive Sequencing Not Incrementing

The Keepalive Sequencing Not Incrementing error is usually an indicator of a line problem, meaning that the configured protocols and the router are not receiving keepalive messages.

To troubleshoot this problem, use the following steps:

1. Check for a local hardware failure.

2. Check the remote hardware for configuration or hardware failures.

3. Check whether the line is noisy or has other connection problems. You may have to contact your service provider to test this.

4. Check for a timing mismatch.

Interface Is Up; Line Protocol Is Up (Looped)

To troubleshoot this problem, use the following step:

1. Verify whether the circuit is in loopback. In serial lines and telephone systems, a *loopback* is a test signal sent to a network destination that is returned as received to the originator. The returned signal may help diagnose a problem. Sending a loopback test to each telephone system piece of equipment in succession, one at a time, is a technique for isolating a problem.

Incrementing Carrier Transition Counter

An increasing Carrier Transition Counter on a serial interface shown by the `show interface` command output indicates that the interface is not staying active.

To troubleshoot this problem, use the following steps:

1. Check for cable faults.

2. Check for line issues with the local provider.

3. Consider a hardware failure on the interface or Channel Service Unit/Digital Service Unit (CSU/DSU).

Incrementing Interface Resets

When the Interface Resets counter is incrementing, this means the interface is performing the equivalent of reboot.

To troubleshoot this problem, use the following steps:

1. Check for physical cabling problems or faults causing the loss of the Carrier Detect.

2. Consider a hardware failure on the interface, router, or the CSU/DSU.

3. Check for congestion or overuse of the bandwidth on the line.

Input Drops, CRC, and Framing Errors

Increasing line drops, CRC, and framing errors can be an indication of a serious problem. When these errors occur, sent data is not making it to its destination.

To troubleshoot this problem, use the following steps:

1. Check for mismatched line speeds.

2. Check with the local provider for issues.

3. Check whether the line is noisy.

4. Check for faulty cabling.

5. Consider a hardware failure on the interface or CSU/DSU.

6. Check that the line speed does not overload the router's capacity.

Troubleshooting Techniques for Serial Link Problems

Now that you have reviewed the list of symptoms and the checklist of potential problems associated with each symptom, walk step by step through the directions for how to handle each item on the checklist. The following sections offer step-by-step instructions for troubleshooting these serial link problems:

➤ Cable faults causing the loss of the Carrier Detect (CD)

➤ Faulty cabling

➤ Incorrect Interface configurations

➤ Keepalive problems

➤ Circuit is in loopback mode

➤ Interface has not been placed in shutdown state

➤ Line speed overloads the router's capacity

➤ Interface speed is higher than the line speed can support

Cable Faults Causing Loss of the Carrier Detect

To troubleshoot this problem, use the following steps:

1. Check the CD, RX, and TX on the CSU/DSU to verify the circuit is transmitting and receiving data.

2. Contact the local service provider to check for problems and for help in troubleshooting the problem.

Faulty Cabling

To troubleshoot this problem, use the following steps:

1. Make sure that you are using the proper cable for the equipment being used.

2. Use a breakout box or other cable tester to verify the throughput on the cables.

3. Replace the faulty cables.

Incorrect Interface Configurations

To troubleshoot this problem, use the following steps:

1. Use the `show running-config` command to verify the proper configuration.

2. Verify the proper configuration for the interfaces, both on the problem device and on the device at the opposite end of the link.

3. Use the `show interface` command (discussed previously in this chapter) to verify the proper configuration of the interface, including the encapsulation type being used.

Keepalive Problems

To troubleshoot this problem, use the following steps:

1. Use the `show interface` command to verify that keepalives are being sent.

2. Use the `debug serial interface` command to view the keepalive sending process. The output for this command is shown in the next section, "Serial Link Troubleshooting Commands."

3. Verify that sequence numbers are incrementing properly.

4. If the sequence numbers are not incrementing, you can run loopback tests at the local or the remote ends of the circuit.

 NOTE   If you still cannot get the sequence numbers to increment, even when the CSU/DSU is in loopback, you most likely have a hardware or cabling problem where the faulty hardware resides on either the router or the CSU/DSU.

Circuit Is in Loopback Mode

To troubleshoot this problem, use the following steps:

1. Use the `show interface` command to check the interface configuration.

2. Use the `no` command to disable any loopback entries in the interface configuration. An example would be to the `no interface loopback 0` command used in global configuration mode.

3. Check the CSU/DSU to make sure that it is not in loopback mode.

4. Check with the local service provider for possible problems and to make sure that the circuit is not in loopback mode.

Interface Hasn't Been Placed in Shutdown State

To troubleshoot this problem, use the following steps:

1. Use the `show interface` command to verify the interface has not been manually shutdown.

2. Check to make sure that the IP address is not being used on another interface.

3. In interface configuration mode for the interface having problems, use the `no shut` command.

Line Speed Overloads the Router's Capacity

To troubleshoot this problem, use the following steps:

1. Use the `hold-queue` command to reduce input queue size. This command allows you to buffer data before it is sent on the link.

2. Increase the output queue's size on the other interfaces.

Interface Speed Is Higher Than the Line Speed

To troubleshoot this problem, use the following steps:

1. Implement Quality of Service (queuing) to control traffic. More on queuing can be found in Appendix C, "Policy Networking."

2. Increase the output queue size.

3. Reduce the broadcast traffic that utilizes the link, if possible.

CSU/DSU Loopback Testing

By using loopback testing, you can isolate serial line problems. Four different loopback tests can be performed on a circuit to aid in troubleshooting it, including

➤ Local CSU/DSU loopback to the local router

➤ Remote CSU/DSU loopback to the local router

➤ Loopback from the local CO (Central Office) switch to the remote CSU/DSU

➤ Loopback from the remote CO switch to the local CSU/DSU

The administrator of the local equipment can perform the first two tests, and the local service provider can perform the other two tests. In Figure 10.1, you see the device locations for the loopback tests to be performed.

The Local Management Interface (LMI) is the signaling standard between the local router connecting to the CSU/DSU and the Central Office (CO) switch, and provides support for keepalive devices to verify data flow. The CO is the place where telephone companies terminate customer lines and locate switching equipment to interconnect those lines with other networks.

Keepalives are packets that each device in the virtual circuit generates and sends to notify the other devices of connectivity. Just as their name suggests, keepalives "keep alive" a connection.

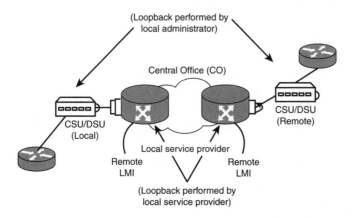

Figure 10.1 The four types of loopback tests used in troubleshooting serial links.

When using loopback tests for troubleshooting, you should follow these steps:

1. Perform the local loopback test from the local router to the CSU/DSU, by placing the CSU/DSU in loopback mode.

2. Check the LMI status when using Frame Relay on the interface to see if it increments using the `show interface` command

3. Perform a local loopback test on the remote CSU/DSU at the destination location, if the local router passes its loopback.

If the LMIs are showing 1023 for the Cisco type's LMI, and you cannot get the remote side of the circuit to successfully loop back, you need to contact your service provider to help with additional testing.

If the local router's interface connecting to the CSU/DSU is working properly during a loopback test, then the local protocol and link should be functioning properly. When this is the case, however, it only confirms that the local equipment is functioning properly. This condition doesn't guarantee that the remote equipment is functioning properly, either.

When putting the CSU/DSU into loopback mode, the signal is sent from the local router interface to the CSU/DSU and is immediately sent back by the CSU/DSU as though it were a remote signal coming back. When using the show interface command, the line protocol will show up in the output and it will appear that the connection is functioning normally.

When configuring end-to-end connectivity to a remote site, both side's LMI (routers) status should say that the interface and protocol are up, and the LMI DLCI should state 1023, as shown in the following output using the show interfaces serial command:

```
Sean2514#show interface serial 0
Serial0 is up, line protocol is up
  Hardware is HD64570
  Internet address is 207.212.78.107/24
  MTU 1500 bytes, BW 64 Kbit, DLY 20000 usec, rely 255/255, load 1/255
  Encapsulation FRAME-RELAY IETF, loopback not set, keepalive set (10 sec)
  LMI enq sent   7107, LMI stat recvd 7164, LMI upd recvd 0, DTE LMI up
  LMI enq recvd 219, LMI stat sent  0, LMI upd sent  0
  LMI DLCI 1023   LMI type is CISCO   frame relay DTE
  Broadcast queue 0/64, broadcasts sent/dropped 1195/0,
                  interface broadcasts 0
  Last input 00:00:01, output 00:00:01, output hang never
  Last clearing of "show interface" counters 22:23:54
  Input queue: 0/75/0 (size/max/drops); Total output drops: 0
  Queueing strategy: weighted fair
  Output queue: 0/1000/64/0 (size/max total/threshold/drops)
     Conversations  0/1/256 (active/max active/max total)
     Reserved Conversations 0/0 (allocated/max allocated)
  5 minute input rate 0 bits/sec, 0 packets/sec
  5 minute output rate 0 bits/sec, 0 packets/sec
     11501 packets input, 586321 bytes, 0 no buffer
     Received 888 broadcasts, 0 runts, 0 giants, 0 throttles
     0 input errors, 0 CRC, 0 frame, 0 overrun, 0 ignored, 0 abort
     9455 packets output, 184195 bytes, 0 underruns
     0 output errors, 0 collisions, 51 interface resets
     0 output buffer failures, 0 output buffers swapped out
     124 carrier transitions
     DCD=up  DSR=up  DTR=up  RTS=up  CTS=up
Sean2514#
```

All the carrier operation switches (also known as the central office, or CO, switches) that participate in the *permanent virtual circuit (PVC)* or *switched virtual circuit (SVC)* provided by the local service provider must be working properly as well. An SVC is a virtual circuit that is established dynamically on demand to form a dedicated link and is then shut down when a transmission is complete. A PVC is a virtual circuit that, once connected, is active regardless of whether or not there is data to transmit. The local service provider can perform loopback tests on its equipment to confirm the functionality of the circuit.

Serial Link Troubleshooting Commands

Several `clear`, `show`, and `debug` commands can be used to troubleshoot serial links. This section covers the following commands:

➤ `clear counters serial`

➤ `debug serial interface`

➤ `show buffers`

➤ `show controllers serial`

➤ `show interface serial`

The `clear counters serial` Command

The `clear counters serial` command clears the counters on the serial links that are displayed using the `show interfaces serial` command. By placing the `serial` syntax after the `show interfaces` command, you are only displaying the serial interfaces on the router. The following is the output from using this command:

```
Sean2514#clear counters serial 0
Clear "show interface" counters on this interface [confirm]
03:54:37: %CLEAR-5-COUNTERS: Clear counter on interface Serial0 by console
Sean2514#
```

You will see the counters reset after using the command. Let's take a look:

```
Sean2514#show interfaces serial 0
1d03h: %CLEAR-5-COUNTERS: Clear counter on interface Serial0 by console
Serial0 is up, line protocol is up
  Hardware is HD64570
  Internet address is 63.78.39.174/24
  MTU 1500 bytes, BW 64 Kbit, DLY 20000 usec, rely 255/255, load 1/255
  Encapsulation FRAME-RELAY IETF, loopback not set, keepalive set (10 sec)
  LMI enq sent  1, LMI stat recvd 1, LMI upd recvd 0, DTE LMI up
  LMI enq recvd 0, LMI stat sent  0, LMI upd sent  0
  LMI DLCI 1023  LMI type is CISCO  frame relay DTE
  Broadcast queue 0/64, broadcasts sent/dropped 0/0, interface broadcasts 0
  Last input 00:00:01, output 00:00:02, output hang never
  Last clearing of "show interface" counters 00:00:02
  Input queue: 0/75/0 (size/max/drops); Total output drops: 0
  Queueing strategy: weighted fair
```

```
Output queue: 0/1000/64/0 (size/max total/threshold/drops)
   Conversations  0/1/256 (active/max active/max total)
   Reserved Conversations 0/0 (allocated/max allocated)
5 minute input rate 0 bits/sec, 0 packets/sec
5 minute output rate 0 bits/sec, 0 packets/sec
   0 packets input, 0 bytes, 0 no buffer
   Received 0 broadcasts, 0 runts, 0 giants, 0 throttles
   0 input errors, 0 CRC, 0 frame, 0 overrun, 0 ignored, 0 abort
   0 packets output, 0 bytes, 0 underruns
   0 output errors, 0 collisions, 0 interface resets
   0 output buffer failures, 0 output buffers swapped out
   0 carrier transitions
   DCD=up  DSR=up  DTR=up  RTS=up  CTS=up
Sean2514#
```

The **debug serial interface** Command

This debug command is used to provide real-time information on the line status, DTE status, and Serial interface sequencing information. Debugging of the serial interface also displays information on the HDLC and Frame Relay communication messages. Here is an example of output for HDLC messages:

You need to remember that the **debug** commands can be used to help the Cisco Technical Assistance Center decipher problems with the router or serial interfaces. If you cannot resolve a problem displayed in the **debug** output, the Cisco TAC most likely has the resources to resolve it.

```
Sean2514#debug serial interface
Serial network interface debugging is on
1d03h: Serial0(out): StEnq, myseq 80, yourseen 79, DTE up
1d03h: Serial0(in):  Status, myseq 80
1d03h: Serial0(out): StEnq, myseq 81, yourseen 80, DTE up
1d03h: Serial0(in):  Status, myseq 81
1d03h: Serial0(out): StEnq, myseq 82, yourseen 81, DTE up
1d03h: Serial0(in):  Status, myseq 82
1d03h: Serial0(out): StEnq, myseq 83, yourseen 82, DTE up
```

Table 10.1 defines the acronyms from the preceding output.

Table 10.1	Acronyms Displayed in the debug serial interface Command
Field	**Description**
StEnq	The LMI status inquiry sent from the LMI (router) to the local service provider's Frame Relay switch.
Status	The reply sent to the LMI from the Frame Relay switch.
mysec	The local keepalive number, also known as the sequence identifier.

(continued)

Table 10.1	Acronyms Displayed in the debug serial interface Command *(continued)*
yourseen	The keepalive sent by the opposite side of the serial connection.
DTE	The data-termination equipment status.
in/out	Specifies the direction the packets were sent through the interface. Outbound packets are keepalives sent by the local interface. Inbound packets are the keepalives sent from the opposite side of the serial link.

When the sequence numbers for an interface don't increment, the cause may be a timing or line issue. If two out of six consecutive keepalive packets fail to increment their sequence numbers, the line resets. Using the debug serial interface command, look at the debugging output for the HDLC protocol on a Cisco 2514 router:

```
Sean2514#debug serial interface
Serial network interface debugging is on
03:52:22: Serial0: HDLC myseq 1390, mineseen 1390*, yourseen 1404, line up
03:52:32: Serial0: HDLC myseq 1391, mineseen 1391*, yourseen 1405, line up
03:52:42: Serial0: HDLC myseq 1392, mineseen 1392*, yourseen 1406, line up
03:52:52: Serial0: HDLC myseq 1393, mineseen 1393*, yourseen 1407, line up
```

In this situation shown above, the Layer 3 protocol considers the line protocol to be down, but the protocol operating at Layer 2 continues to send keepalive messages. As soon as the Layer 2 protocol receives three consecutive sequenced keepalive packets, the line protocol will be brought back up.

The show buffers Command

The show buffers command is used to show the router buffer pool statistics. Buffer pools are areas where the router stores received and sent data before it is processed, returned, or forwarded out an interface. The output is shown below:

```
Sean2514#show buffers
Buffer elements:
     500 in free list (500 max allowed)
     3621 hits, 0 misses, 0 created
Public buffer pools:
Small buffers, 134 bytes (total 50, permanent 50):
     44 in free list (20 min, 150 max allowed)
     1226 hits, 0 misses, 0 trims, 0 created
     0 failures (0 no memory)
Middle buffers, 600 bytes (total 25, permanent 25):
     25 in free list (10 min, 150 max allowed)
     22 hits, 0 misses, 0 trims, 0 created
     0 failures (0 no memory)
Big buffers, 1524 bytes (total 50, permanent 50):
     50 in free list (5 min, 150 max allowed)
     222 hits, 0 misses, 0 trims, 0 created
```

```
    0 failures (0 no memory)
VeryBig buffers, 4520 bytes (total 10, permanent 10):
    10 in free list (0 min, 100 max allowed)
    0 hits, 0 misses, 0 trims, 0 created
    0 failures (0 no memory)
Large buffers, 5024 bytes (total 0, permanent 0):
    0 in free list (0 min, 10 max allowed)
    0 hits, 0 misses, 0 trims, 0 created
    0 failures (0 no memory)
Huge buffers, 18024 bytes (total 0, permanent 0):
    0 in free list (0 min, 4 max allowed)
    0 hits, 0 misses, 0 trims, 0 created
    0 failures (0 no memory)
Interface buffer pools:
Ethernet0 buffers, 1524 bytes (total 32, permanent 32):
    8 in free list (0 min, 32 max allowed)
    24 hits, 0 fallbacks
    8 max cache size, 8 in cache
Ethernet1 buffers, 1524 bytes (total 32, permanent 32):
    8 in free list (0 min, 32 max allowed)
    24 hits, 0 fallbacks
    8 max cache size, 8 in cache
Serial0 buffers, 1524 bytes (total 32, permanent 32):
    7 in free list (0 min, 32 max allowed)
    25 hits, 0 fallbacks
    8 max cache size, 8 in cache
Serial1 buffers, 1524 bytes (total 32, permanent 32):
    7 in free list (0 min, 32 max allowed)
    25 hits, 0 fallbacks
    8 max cache size, 8 in cache
Sean2514#
```

The small buffers shown above in bold show all the frames received that are under 104 bytes. The failures indicate the number of frames that were discarded due to unavailable memory in the buffers.

 When analyzing the output of the **show buffers** command, remember that buffer hits are good; when the number of misses increases, you should concern yourself with the number of buffer misses.

The show controllers serial Command

Using the show controllers serial command, you can display the interface status, and whether a data terminal equipment (DTE) cable or a data communication equipment (DCE) cable is connected to an interface or is reversed. Rising hardware and data link errors may indicate a problem with the cable or a misconfigured interface.

This is a particularly good command if you have a router in a rack and can't physically see that the serial cables are connected properly to the interface.

The following is the output you should see from the show controllers serial command (this output is the DCE end of the cable; the DTE end is connected to the serial port on a Cisco 1005):

```
Sean2514#show controller serial 0
HD unit 0, idb = 0xF7A98, driver structure at 0xFCF18
buffer size 1524   HD unit 0, V.35 DCE cable, clockrate 64000
cpb = 0x62, eda = 0x2918, cda = 0x292C
RX ring with 16 entries at 0x622800
00 bd_ptr=0x2800 pak=0x0FE350 ds=0x6267C4 status=80 pak_size=22
01 bd_ptr=0x2814 pak=0x0FE150 ds=0x626108 status=80 pak_size=22
02 bd_ptr=0x2828 pak=0x0FDF50 ds=0x625A4C status=80 pak_size=22
03 bd_ptr=0x283C pak=0x0FFF50 ds=0x62C60C status=80 pak_size=22
04 bd_ptr=0x2850 pak=0x100150 ds=0x62CCC8 status=80 pak_size=22
05 bd_ptr=0x2864 pak=0x0FFD50 ds=0x62BF50 status=80 pak_size=22
06 bd_ptr=0x2878 pak=0x0FFB50 ds=0x62B894 status=80 pak_size=278
07 bd_ptr=0x288C pak=0x0FF950 ds=0x62B1D8 status=80 pak_size=22
08 bd_ptr=0x28A0 pak=0x0FF750 ds=0x62AB1C status=80 pak_size=22
09 bd_ptr=0x28B4 pak=0x0FF550 ds=0x62A460 status=80 pak_size=22
10 bd_ptr=0x28C8 pak=0x0FF350 ds=0x629DA4 status=80 pak_size=22
11 bd_ptr=0x28DC pak=0x0FF150 ds=0x6296E8 status=80 pak_size=22
12 bd_ptr=0x28F0 pak=0x0FEF50 ds=0x62902C status=80 pak_size=22
13 bd_ptr=0x2904 pak=0x0FED50 ds=0x628970 status=80 pak_size=278
14 bd_ptr=0x2918 pak=0x0FEB50 ds=0x6282B4 status=80 pak_size=22
15 bd_ptr=0x292C pak=0x0FE750 ds=0x62753C status=80 pak_size=22
16 bd_ptr=0x2940 pak=0x0FE550 ds=0x626E80 status=80 pak_size=278
cpb = 0x62, eda = 0x3014, cda = 0x3014
TX ring with 1 entries at 0x623000
00 bd_ptr=0x3000 pak=0x000000 ds=0x653E04 status=80 pak_size=284
01 bd_ptr=0x3014 pak=0x000000 ds=0x622EA4 status=80 pak_size=22
0 missed datagrams, 0 overruns
0 bad datagram encapsulations, 0 memory errors
0 transmitter underruns
0 residual bit errors
Sean2514#
```

The next code block is the output from the DTE end of the interface, connected to a Cisco 1005 router:

```
Seans1005#show controllers serial 0
QUICC Serial unit 0, idb at 0x22C2C20, driver data structure at 0x22C495C
SCC Registers:
General [GSMR]=0x2:0x00000030, Protocol-specific [PSMR]=0x0
Events [SCCE]=0x0000, Mask [SCCM]=0x001F, Status [SCCS]=0x0006
Transmit on Demand [TODR]=0x0, Data Sync [DSR]=0x7E7E
Interrupt Registers:
Config [CICR]=0x00368460, Pending [CIPR]=0x04004804
Mask   [CIMR]=0x48000012, In-srv  [CISR]=0x00000000
Command register [CR]=0x6C0
Port A [PADIR]=0x0008, [PAPAR]=0x5AC3
       [PAODR]=0x0000, [PADAT]=0xD06A
```

```
Port B [PBDIR]=0x020F1F, [PBPAR]=0x0000C0
       [PBODR]=0x000000, [PBDAT]=0x000EC0
Port C [PCDIR]=0x038C, [PCPAR]=0x0001
       [PCSO]=0x0C30,  [PCDAT]=0x0300, [PCINT]=0x0000
DTE V.35 serial cable attached. TX and RX clocks detected.
SCC GENERAL PARAMETER RAM (at 0xFF00F00)
Rx BD Base [RBASE]=0x560, Fn Code [RFCR]=0x18
Tx BD Base [TBASE]=0x5E0, Fn Code [TFCR]=0x18
Max Rx Buff Len [MRBLR]=1524
Rx State [RSTATE]=0x18008240, BD Ptr [RBPTR]=0x598
Tx State [TSTATE]=0x18000348, BD Ptr [TBPTR]=0x5E8
SCC HDLC PARAMETER RAM (at 0xFF00F38)
CRC Preset [C_PRES]=0xFFFF, Mask [C_MASK]=0xF0B8
Errors: CRC [CRCEC]=0, Aborts [ABTSC]=0, Discards [DISFC]=0
Nonmatch Addr Cntr [NMARC]=0
Retry Count [RETRC]=0
Max Frame Length [MFLR]=1524
Rx Int Threshold [RFTHR]=0, Frame Cnt [RFCNT]=55929
User-defined Address 0000/0000/0000/0000
User-defined Address Mask 0x0000
buffer size 1524
RX ring with 16 entries at 0xFF00560, Buffer size 1524
Rxhead = 0xFF00598 (7), Rxp = 0x22C4994 (7)
00 pak=0x22C7B3C buf=0x2395FE0 status=9000 pak_size=0
01 pak=0x22C798C buf=0x2395928 status=9000 pak_size=0
02 pak=0x22C77DC buf=0x2395270 status=9000 pak_size=0
03 pak=0x22C762C buf=0x23A1548 status=9000 pak_size=0
04 pak=0x22C747C buf=0x23A0E90 status=9000 pak_size=0
05 pak=0x2309D88 buf=0x23B942C status=9000 pak_size=0
06 pak=0x230A7A8 buf=0x23BBC7C status=9000 pak_size=0
07 pak=0x230A0E8 buf=0x23BA19C status=9000 pak_size=0
08 pak=0x230A958 buf=0x23BC334 status=9000 pak_size=0
09 pak=0x230A448 buf=0x23BAF0C status=9000 pak_size=0
10 pak=0x230A5F8 buf=0x23BB5C4 status=9000 pak_size=0
11 pak=0x2309BD8 buf=0x23B8D74 status=9000 pak_size=0
12 pak=0x2309A28 buf=0x23B86BC status=9000 pak_size=0
13 pak=0x2309F38 buf=0x23B9AE4 status=9000 pak_size=0
14 pak=0x22C7E9C buf=0x2396D50 status=9000 pak_size=0
15 pak=0x22C7CEC buf=0x2396698 status=B000 pak_size=0
TX ring with 2 entries at 0xFF005E0, tx_count = 0
tx_head = 0xFF005E8 (1), head_txp = 0x22C49D8 (1)
tx_tail = 0xFF005E8 (1), tail_txp = 0x22C49D8 (1)
00 pak=0x0000000 buf=0x0000000 status=0000 pak_size=0
01 pak=0x0000000 buf=0x0000000 status=2000 pak_size=0
QUICC SCC specific errors:
0 input aborts on receiving flag sequence
0 throttles, 0 enables
0 overruns
0 transmitter underruns
0 transmitter CTS losts
Seans1005#
```

The show controllers serial command output above provides information on the interface status, cable types, missed datagrams, overruns, bad encapsulated frames, memory errors, underruns, clock rate, and bit errors. In addition, it indicates the interface clock rate, as well as the cable type that is connected to the interface.

The **show interface serial** Command

The `show interface serial` command provides a wealth of information to help you troubleshoot serial line and serial interface related problems. The output from this command is shown here:

```
Sean2514#show interface serial 0
Serial0 is up, line protocol is up
  Hardware is HD64570
  Internet address is 207.212.78.107/24
  MTU 1500 bytes, BW 64 Kbit, DLY 20000 usec, rely 255/255, load 1/255
  Encapsulation HDLC, loopback not set, keepalive set (10 sec)
  Last input 00:00:08, output 00:00:06, output hang never
  Last clearing of "show interface" counters never
  Input queue: 0/75/0 (size/max/drops); Total output drops: 0
  Queueing strategy: weighted fair
  Output queue: 0/1000/64/0 (size/max total/threshold/drops)
    Conversations  0/1/256 (active/max active/max total)
    Reserved Conversations 0/0 (allocated/max allocated)
  5 minute input rate 0 bits/sec, 0 packets/sec
  5 minute output rate 0 bits/sec, 0 packets/sec
    1609 packets input, 94022 bytes, 0 no buffer
    Received 1609 broadcasts, 0 runts, 0 giants, 0 throttles
    0 input errors, 0 CRC, 0 frame, 0 overrun, 0 ignored, 0 abort
    1600 packets output, 97280 bytes, 0 underruns
    0 output errors, 0 collisions, 1 interface resets
    0 output buffer failures, 0 output buffers swapped out
    2 carrier transitions
    DCD=up  DSR=up  DTR=up  RTS=up  CTS=up
```

 For the exam you should know that the **clear counters serial** command can be used to clear the counters on only the serial interfaces.

Table 10.2 shows the description of the variables found in the preceding output.

Table 10.2	The Description of Variables from the **show interface serial** Command
Variable	**Description**
Serial0	Shows the port or VLAN number of the displayed interface, and the status indicates whether the interface is active or disabled. A status of "disabled" indicates that the router has received more than 5,000 errors in 10 seconds, which is the default keepalive interval.
Line protocol	An indicator of whether the line protocol believes the interface is usable, based on the keepalives it has received, or whether the interface has been manually shut down.

(continued)

Table 10.2 The Description of Variables from the show interface serial Command (continued)	
Internet address	The IP address of the interface.
MTU	Displays the maximum transmission unit (MTU) size for the interface.
BW	Displays the bandwidth the interface is configured to use. You can modify this parameter by using the **bandwidth** command in Interface Configuration mode.
DLY	Displays the interface delay in microseconds.
Rely	Displays the interface in a fraction of 255. This means that if the interface is running at 100 percent, the displayed value would be 255 out of 255.
Load	Displays the interface load in a fraction of 255. This means that if the interface is running a 100 percent load, the displayed value would be 255 out of 255.
Encapsulation	Displays the encapsulation method used by the interface.
ARP Type	Displays the frames encapsulation type, such as ARPA, SNAP, Novell-Ether, or SAP.
Loopback	Indicates whether the interface is in loopback mode.
Keepalives	Indicates whether keepalives are being sent.
Last Input/Output	Indicates how much time has occurred since the last packet was received by the interface.
Last Clearing	Indicates the amount of time since the counters have been reset.
Input/Output Queues	Displays the maximum size of the queue, as well as the number of packets dropped due to a full queue.
Input/Output Rates	Displays the average number of bits and packets transmitted in the last 300 seconds (5 minutes).
Packets Input	Displays the number of successfully received packets to the interface since the last interface counter reset.
No Buffer	Displays the number of received packets discarded by a full buffer.
Broadcasts	Displays the number of multicast and broadcast packets received.
Runts	Displays the number of packets discarded because they were smaller than the MTU size allowed on the physical media.
Giants	Displays the number of packets discarded because they exceeded the maximum MTU size of the physical media.
CRC	Displays the number of CRC errors received on an interface.

(continued)

Table 10.2 The Description of Variables from the show interface serial Command (continued)	
Frame	Displays the number of packets received with CRC errors.
Overrun	Displays the number of times the receiver was unable to receive data into its buffers because the data input rate exceeded the rate which the receiving buffers and interface could handle.
Underruns	Displays the number of instances in which the transmitter has run faster than the router.
Output Errors	Displays the total number of transmitted errors on the interface.
Collisions	Displays the number of collisions that took place with transmitted media on an Ethernet interface.
Interface Resets	Displays a count of the number of times an interface has been recycled.
Ignored	Displays the number of packets ignored by the interface due to exceeded buffer demands.
Packets Output	Displays the total number of packets transmitted on the interface.
Input Errors	Displays the total number of errors, which includes the runts, giants, CRCs, discarded frames, overruns, and ignored errors.

For the exam, you can expect that several questions will involve a knowledge of the output from the **show interfaces serial** command. The variables and their descriptions are located in Table 10.2.

Troubleshooting Frame Relay

Using Frame Relay is a common solution for connecting one or more LANs through a WAN. Frame Relay uses PVCs to establish a data link from one location to another (Point-to-Point) or from one location to multiple locations (Multi-point). These virtual circuits are built by using a Data-Link Connection Identifier (DLCI), which is used to identify the virtual circuits in a Frame Relay cloud.

DLCI numbers are only significant locally. The packets sent through the Frame Relay cloud are actually encapsulated with an identifier to enable each packet to traverse the local service provider's switched network. This encapsulation is added by the CSU/DSU and is stripped off by the remote end's CSU/DSU when the packet reaches its destination.

The frame does not make a straight connection to its destination. In fact, many other companies will use the same link that your packet is traveling on.

The local service provider shares the bandwidth with multiple customers and each connection is identified by the DLCI number. Each customer is given a guarantee of bandwidth called the committed information rate (CIR).

Frame Relay Troubleshooting Steps

The following sections list a number of Frame Relay troubleshooting problems. Each section also offers a series of steps you can take to troubleshoot the associated Frame Relay problem.

Frame Relay Link Is Down

To troubleshoot this problem, use the following steps:

1. Check the cabling.

2. Check for faulty hardware.

3. Check with the local service provider for problems.

4. Check for an LMI type mismatch.

5. Check whether keepalives are being sent.

6. Check the encapsulation type to see if it matches the external device's configuration.

7. Check for a DLCI mismatch.

Can't Ping a Remote Host Across a Frame Relay Network

To troubleshoot this problem, use the following steps:

1. Check that the DLCI is not assigned to the wrong subinterface.

2. Check the encapsulation types on both ends.

3. Check access list entries to make sure the proper data traffic is permitted. For more information see the "Access List Issues" section later in this chapter.

4. Check the Serial interface configuration for configuration problems.

Faulty Cabling

To troubleshoot this problem, use the following steps:

1. Check the cabling for physical breaks and to make sure they are secure.

2. Use a breakout box or other cable tester to test the cabling leads.

3. Replace faulty cables.

Faulty Hardware

To troubleshoot this problem, use the following steps:

1. Use loopback tests to isolate the faulty hardware components.

2. Move the cable to a different interface on the router and configure that interface to see whether the link comes up; if it does, you know that you have a configuration or hardware issue on the other interface. If it doesn't come up there is most likely another hardware or software issue you need to look for.

3. Replace the hardware component that has failed.

Local Service Provider Issue

One of the best indications that a local service provider issue exists is if you perform a loopback test and the LMI state changes to "up." To troubleshoot this problem, use the following steps:

1. Check for a DLCI mismatch or an encapsulation mismatch. If this is not the issue, go to Step 2.

2. Contact the local service provider to help resolve the issue.

LMI Type Mismatch

To troubleshoot this problem, use the following steps:

1. Check that the LMI type on the router matches the LMI used by the CO switches on the DCE end of the circuit.

2. If you do not know the LMI type the local service provider uses, you need to contact them, or set the LMI type to dynamically detect the LMI type (if you are using IOS version 11.2 or later).

Keepalive Issues

To troubleshoot a keepalive issue, follow these steps:

1. Use the `show interface` command to verify that keepalives are not disabled or misconfigured.

2. Verify that the keepalive interval is correct on the interface.

Encapsulation Type Issues

To troubleshoot this issue, follow these steps:

1. Check that the same encapsulation types are used on both sides of the router.

2. Use the `show frame-relay map` command if you are using non-Cisco equipment. Also verify that the encapsulation types on both interface in the PVC are set to IETF. Use the `encapsulation frame-relay ietf` command to change the encapsulation type from Cisco to IETF.

DLCI Mismatch

To troubleshoot this issue, follow these steps:

1. Use the `show running-config` command to display the DLCI number, to verify the DLCI number is assigned to the proper interface. The `show frame-relay pvc` command can also display the DLCI assigned to the interface.

2. If the correct DLCI number is configured on the proper interface, contact the local carrier to verify that it has the same DLCI configured on the Frame Relay switch.

Access List Issues

Access lists are very complex and if you don't have a handle on how they work, you may be in trouble. You need to have a good understanding of how protocols and their addressing work with the router because many problems can occur as a result of misconfiguring an access list. Problems can be caused by a blocked IP address, port, or any number of protocols. Not only that, many administrators forget that there is an invisible "deny all" at the end of every access list. So if you don't permit the traffic you want in the access list, it will be blocked.

To troubleshoot this issue, follow these steps:

1. Use the `show ip interface` command to display all the access lists applied to the routers interfaces.

2. Check each access list, keeping in mind that an invisible, implied "deny all" is at the end of the list.

3. Remove the access list to see whether the problem is resolved.

4. Make modifications to the access list and then reapply the access list. For more information on access lists see Appendix C.

Frame Relay Troubleshooting Commands

You can use the following show and debug commands, discussed in the following sections, to troubleshoot Frame Relay:

➤ debug frame-relay events

➤ debug frame-relay lmi

➤ show frame-relay lmi

➤ show frame-relay map

➤ show frame-relay pvc

➤ show interfaces

The following sections discuss the use of these commands in troubleshooting frame relay problems.

The **debug frame-relay events** Command

The debug frame-relay events command enables you to analyze packets and events occurring on a Frame Relay network. Data provided by this command is useful because it gives details about protocols and applications using the DLCI. This includes the interface of arrival, the datagram size, and the type of frame received.

```
Sean2514#debug frame-relay events
Frame Relay events debugging is on
Sean2514#
07:05:20: Serial0: FR ARP input
07:05:20: datagramstart = 0x628970, datagramsize = 30
07:05:20: FR encap = 0x18E10300
07:05:20: 80 00 00 00 08 06 00 0F 08 00 02 04 00 09 00 00
07:05:20: 3F 4E 26 AE 18 E1 3F 4E 27 AE
07:05:20:
Sean2514#
```

The preceding output shows that the Serial0 interface received an ARP reply, and also displays the datagram size. The numbers 08 06 mean 0x0806, which indicates an Ethernet type code. The packet type also indicates the types of applications on the circuit. Use this command to troubleshoot connectivity problems during the installation of a new Frame Relay network.

The **debug frame-relay lmi** Command

The debug frame-relay lmi command enables you to obtain information with the router and the local service provider's switched network. The following is sample output:

```
Sean2514#debug frame-relay lmi
Frame Relay LMI debugging is on
Displaying all Frame Relay LMI data
06:53:30: Serial0(out): StEnq, myseq 174, yourseen 173, DTE up
06:53:30: datagramstart = 0x622EA4, datagramsize = 13
06:53:30: FR encap = 0xFCF10309
06:53:30: 00 75 01 01 01 03 02 AE AD
06:53:30:
06:53:30: Serial0(in): Status, myseq 174
06:53:30: RT IE 1, length 1, type 1
06:53:30: KA IE 3, length 2, yourseq 174, myseq 174
```

Notice above that the Frame Relay process is displayed step by step in the output above. For the exam you might want to brush up on your CCNA knowledge of Frame Relay connection steps.

The **show frame-relay lmi** Command

Using the show frame-relay lmi command, you can obtain LMI statistical information. The LMI provides communication and synchronization between the network and the local demarcation point devices. The following is an example of the output produced by using the show frame-relay lmi command:

```
Sean2514#show frame-relay lmi
LMI Statistics for interface Serial0 (Frame Relay DTE) LMI TYPE = CISCO
  Invalid Unnumbered info 0         Invalid Prot Disc 0
  Invalid dummy Call Ref 0          Invalid Msg Type 0
  Invalid Status Message 0          Invalid Lock Shift 0
  Invalid Information ID 0          Invalid Report IE Len 0
  Invalid Report Request 0          Invalid Keep IE Len 0
  Num Status Enq. Sent 288          Num Status msgs Rcvd 288
  Num Update Status Rcvd 17         Num Status Timeouts 0
Sean2514#
```

The highlighted line indicates the interface and its role in the network. In this case, it acts as the DTE side of the interface. If the number of sent messages does not match the number received, a problem may exist with the sending and receiving keepalive messages. This type of problem can indicate a potential problem with the network equipment.

The **show frame-relay map** Command

Using the show frame-relay map command, you can obtain information about the DLCI numbers, encapsulation type, and status of all the Frame Relay interfaces. The following is an example of the output produced by using the `show frame-relay map` command:

```
Serial0 (up): ip 207.212.78.174 dlci 120(0x78,0x1C80), static,
              broadcast,
              IETF, status deleted
Serial0 (up): ip 207.212.78.175 dlci 102(0x66,0x1860), dynamic,
              broadcast,
              IETF, status defined, active
Serial0 (up): ip 207.212.78.174 dlci 120(0x78,0x1C80), static,
              broadcast,
              IETF, status deleted
Serial0.2 (down): point-to-point dlci, dlci 202(0xCA,0x30A0), broadcast
                  status deleted
```

Notice in the output above that whether the interface is active or not is indicated with the up or down state. This command also indicates whether this is a static or dynamic interface and whether the interface type is point-to-point or multipoint.

The **show frame-relay pvc** Command

The `show frame-relay pvc` command provides statistics about the PVCs and the LMI status of every DLCI on the router.

You should know for the exam that two types of DLCI numbers exist: those used on the local DTE and those used on the CO switched network.

An example of the output produced by this command follows:

```
Sean2514#show frame-relay pvc
PVC Statistics for interface Serial0 (Frame Relay DTE)
DLCI = 120, DLCI USAGE = LOCAL, PVC STATUS = DELETED, INTERFACE = Serial0
  input pkts 0           output pkts 0          in bytes 0
  out bytes 0            dropped pkts 0         in FECN pkts 0
  in BECN pkts 0         out FECN pkts 0        out BECN pkts 0
  in DE pkts 0           out DE pkts 0
  out bcast pkts 0       out bcast bytes 0
  pvc create time 00:33:13, last time pvc status changed 00:24:49
DLCI = 202, DLCI USAGE = LOCAL, PVC STATUS = DELETED, INTERFACE = Serial0.2
  input pkts 0           output pkts 0          in bytes 0
  out bytes 0            dropped pkts 0         in FECN pkts 0
  in BECN pkts 0         out FECN pkts 0        out BECN pkts 0
  in DE pkts 0           out DE pkts 0
  out bcast pkts 0       out bcast bytes 0
  pvc create time 00:37:35, last time pvc status changed 00:24:20
Sean2514#
```

You should monitor the number of Forward Explicit Congestion Notifications (FECNs) and Backward Explicit Congestion Notifications (BECNs), which are packets created when the transmitted rate is above the

CIR. Each packet sent is given a discard eligible bit, which means that if the CO switches get congested, they will drop those packets with the discard eligible bit. When the packets are discarded, the FECN packets are sent to the receiving DTE participating devices to notify them to implement flow control. BECN messages notify the sending station that congestion was experienced and to reduce the transmission rate.

The show interfaces Command

The show interfaces command, previously discussed with regard to troubleshooting serial links, can also be used to troubleshoot Frame Relay problems. Line-by-line detail has already been given for a normal serial interface earlier in the chapter. The following is an example of the command's output:

```
Sean2514#show interface serial 0
Serial0 is up, line protocol is up
  Hardware is HD64570
  Internet address is 207.212.77.174/24
  MTU 1500 bytes, BW 64 Kbit, DLY 20000 usec, rely 255/255, load 1/255
  Encapsulation FRAME-RELAY IETF, loopback not set, keepalive set (10 sec)
  LMI enq sent   270, LMI stat recvd 127, LMI upd recvd 0, DTE LMI up
  LMI enq recvd 119, LMI stat sent   0, LMI upd sent   0
  LMI DCLI 1023  LMI type is CISCO  frame relay DTE
  Broadcast queue 0/64, broadcasts sent/dropped 22/0, interface broadcasts 0
  Last input 00:00:06, output 00:00:06, output hang never
  Last clearing of "show interface" counters 02:51:08
  Input queue: 0/75/0 (size/max/drops); Total output drops: 0
  Queueing strategy: weighted fair
  Output queue: 0/1000/64/0 (size/max total/threshold/drops)
     Conversations  0/1/256 (active/max active/max total)
     Reserved Conversations 0/0 (allocated/max allocated)
  5 minute input rate 0 bits/sec, 0 packets/sec
  5 minute output rate 0 bits/sec, 0 packets/sec
     1238 packets input, 66402 bytes, 0 no buffer
     Received 888 broadcasts, 0 runts, 0 giants, 0 throttles
     0 input errors, 0 CRC, 0 frame, 0 overrun, 0 ignored, 0 abort
     1245 packets output, 57524 bytes, 0 underruns
     0 output errors, 0 collisions, 51 interface resets
     0 output buffer failures, 0 output buffers swapped out
     124 carrier transitions
     DCD=up  DSR=up  DTR=up  RTS=up  CTS=up
```

Table 10.3 below lists and describes the troubleshooting fields that are presented in bold text in the preceding output.

Table 10.3 Troubleshooting Fields Found in the show interface Command	
Field	**Description**
Encapsulation	One of two encapsulation methods supported by Cisco switches for Frame Relay, which are Cisco and IETF
LMI enq sent	The number of LMI enquiries sent

(continued)

Table 10.3 Troubleshooting Fields Found in the show interface Command (continued)	
LMI stat recvd	The number of LMI status packets received
LMI upd recvd	The number of LMI updates received
DTE LMI	The DTE LMI status
LMI enq recvd	The number of LMI enquiries received
LMI stat sent	The number of LMI status updates sent
LMI upd sent	The number of LMI updates sent
LMI DLCI	The DLCI number used for LMI
LMI type	The LMI type used by the interface

NOTE   When the router is working properly, the Cisco LMI type should state 1023 for the LMI DLCI, and the ANSI type should state 0. The three types are Cisco, ANSI, and ITU-T. The default is Cisco. The LMI type configured on the router must be the same LMI type used by the CO switches.

Troubleshooting X.25

X.25 has been around for quite some time and is actually a suite of protocols. The first of these protocols originated sometime in the 1970s, shortly after the successful introduction of Telnet and TYMNET packet-switching networks (PSNs). The creators of the X.25 protocol suite had a goal of enabling data to be transmitted and received between two alphanumeric terminals through analog, plain old telephone system (POTS) phone lines. Early versions of X.25 enabled alphanumeric terminals to communicate remotely and access applications on servers and mainframes located on both ends of the analog telephone line.

One drawback existed, however—modern desktop applications needed to connect two, sometimes dissimilar, LANs with a WAN. This meant that LAN-to-WAN-to-LAN data communications were necessary. Again, the designers went back and created newer forms of wide-area networking technology, such as Integrated Services Digital Network (ISDN) and Frame Relay. These newer WAN protocols complement or extend the features of the X.25 protocol suite in the network without replacing the need for the protocol.

Troubleshooting X.25 is similar to troubleshooting a serial line or a Frame Relay line. This section first looks at some of the steps you can use to resolve X.25 circuit issues, and then looks at some of the show and debug commands that can be useful to resolving and identifying the issues.

For the exam, you should have a good knowledge of X.25 and Frame-Relay configuration and hardware troubleshooting procedures. Particularly, you should know which problems are a result of a configuration problem and which problems are a result of a cabling or Physical Layer problem.

X.25 and Packet-Layer Protocol (PLP)

Many different Layer 3 protocols can be transmitted across X.25 VCs. The X.25 protocol is only the tunnel that enables Layer 3 protocol packets within the X.25 Layer 3 packets to find their way from one end of a VC to the other. X.25 is the protocol that keeps the addressing valid for each Layer 3 protocol, while the X.25 VC transports the packet through a circuit.

The Packet-Layer Protocol (PLP) is used by X.25 to manage packet exchanges within a VC. PLP can be used over Logical-Link Control 2 (LLC2) or Integrated Services Digital Network (ISDN) operating on interfaces running Link Access Procedure on D channel (LAPD). PLP operates in five different modes:

➤ Call Setup Mode—Used to create an SVC between two DTE devices, using the X.121 addressing scheme (discussed in the following section) to create a VC.

➤ Data-transfer Mode—Used to transfer the physical data between two DTE devices through an already established VC. This mode assists PLP with packet segmentation, packet reassembly, and error and flow control.

➤ Idle Mode—Used when a VC is established and data transfer is not occurring. This mode is executed on a per-VC basis on SVCs.

➤ Call-clearing Mode—Used by an SVC to end communication sessions between two DTE devices.

➤ Restarting Mode—Used to restart a transmission between a DTE device and a DCE device located within the PSN.

Call setup and Call-clearing are used on SVCs only. PVCs are constant connections.

X.25 PLP packet headers are made up of three fields, as shown in Figure 10.2:

➤ GFI—A 4-bit field used to indicate the general formatting of the packet header

➤ LCI—A 12-bit field used to identify the VC information, and whether the packet is for a DTE or DCE interface

➤ PTI—An 8-bit field used to identify individual packet types

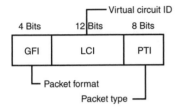

Figure 10.2 The X.25 PLP packet header fields.

X.121 Address Format

The standard format defined for an X.25 VC is called X.121 and is an ITU-T standard. In a private X.25 network, each network is assigned a base address in decimal digits. These decimal digits, which are 1 to 15 digits, are defined for X.121 addresses to enable network protocols to connect across an X.25 link. The X.121 address enables the DTE end router to map the next-hop Layer 3 address to an X.121 address. These statements are logically equivalent to the Media Access Control (MAC) address. Maps are required for each protocol, because ARP is not supported in an X.25 network.

The first four digits of the X.121 address define the Data Network Identification Code (DNIC). The first three digits specify the country code. The fourth digit is the provider number assigned by the ITU-T. Countries that require more than 10 provider numbers are assigned multiple country codes. For example, the United States is assigned country codes 310 through 316. To view the complete listing of ITU-T country code assignments, visit ITU-T's Web site (www.itu.org) and refer to the ITU-T Recommendation X.121.

The remaining 8 to 11 digits specify the network terminal number (NTN) assigned by the PSN provider. You must contact your local service provider to get your individual DNIC code. Figure 10.3 shows an example of the X.121 used across a PVC.

Now that you have a basic overview, you are ready to look at some troubleshooting techniques.

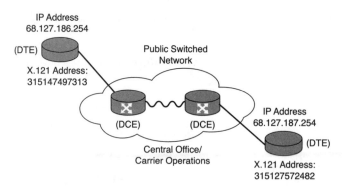

Figure 10.3   The X.121 protocol used across a PVC.

X.25 Troubleshooting Problems

X.25 can experience a range of symptoms and potential problems. The sections that follow outline typical problems and some of their potential causes, including

➤ Faulty hardware or cabling

➤ LABP connect state failure

➤ Misconfigured interfaces or protocol

➤ X.25 connection failures

X.25 Connection Failure

When you have X.25 protocol connection failures, your link will show the protocol as down.

To troubleshoot this issue, follow these steps:

1. Check whether the link is down.

2. Check for faulty-hardware issues.

3. Check whether the cables are seated correctly.

4. Check to see whether a cable may be faulty by checking connections and the cables throughput.

5. Check whether the interface is configured properly.

Unwarranted Errors

Many times your error counters will increase for no apparent reason, even though the configuration and routers appear to be functioning correctly.

To troubleshoot this issue, follow these steps:

1. Check for faulty hardware. Refer to Chapter 7, " Troubleshooting the Physical Layer," for more information on troubleshooting the physical hardware.

2. Check for incorrect cabling.

3. Consider faulty cabling.

LABP CONNECT State Failure

When LABP will not go into the CONNECT state, the problem can be difficult to troubleshoot. There can be many possible causes for LABP CONNECT state failures. The troubleshooting steps below only help to identify the problem. If the problem results from a configuration issue, you may need to do some more research to correct the problem. To troubleshoot this issue, follow these steps:

1. Check the interface to verify that the LAPB is in a CONNECT state.

2. Use the `debug lapb` command to determine why the interface is failing to go into the CONNECT state.

3. Replace the faulty equipment.

Misconfigured Interfaces or Protocol

This is typically the problem with new, reconfigured, moved, or replaced equipment. Unless there is a hardware change, a good configuration on a router typically will not change on its own. To troubleshoot this issue, follow these steps:

1. Use the `show running-config` command to verify the configuration.

2. Use the `debug lapb` command to see whether Set Asynchronous Balance Mode (SABMs) requests are being sent.

3. If no SABMs are being sent, use the `debug x25 events` command to learn more about why they are not being sent.

4. Observe the output of the debugging commands for RESTART messages.

5. Check the LAPB configuration on the interface.

X.25 Troubleshooting Commands

As discussed earlier in the chapter with respect to troubleshooting Frame Relay and serial links, certain debug and show commands can be used to obtain more information about the troubleshooting issues you are facing. This section looks at the following X.25 troubleshooting commands:

➤ debug x25 events

➤ debug lapb

➤ show interface serial

The debug x25 events Command

The debug x25 events command can be used to detect events and obtain diagnostic information on X.25-configured interfaces. Note that when using this command, due to the large amount of output generated by calls and other data such as Receive Ready (RR) flow control packets, these events are not displayed by the router.

The debug lapb Command

The debug lapb command debugs the events at Layer 2 of the X.25 circuits. This command should be used when an X.25 interface experiences frequent restarts. Because X.25 relies on LAPB to maintain stability, if problems arise with the LAPB configuration, it affects the X.25 protocol and the participating X.25 interfaces.

The show interface serial Command

When a serial interface is configured to use X.25, the show interface serial command provides information specific to the X.25 protocol. Here is a sample of the show interface serial command's output when X.25 is configured on the interface:

```
Sean2514#show interfaces serial 0
1d03h: %CLEAR-5-COUNTERS: Clear counter on interface Serial0 by console
Serial0 is up, line protocol is up
  Hardware is HD64570
  Internet address is 207.212.77.174/24
    Hardware is HD64570
  Internet address is 172.16.30.5/30
  MTU 1500 bytes, BW 1544 Kbit, DLY 20000 usec, rely 255/  255, load 51/255
  Encapsulation X25, loopback not set
LAPB DTE, state CONNECT, modulo 8, k 7, N1 12043, N2 10
T1 3000, interface outage (partial T3) 0, T4 0
VS 1, VR 1, Remote VR 1, Retransmissions 0
   IFRAMEs 1/1 RNRs 0/0 REJs 0/0 SABM/Es 1/0 FRMRs 0/0 DISCs 0/0
X25 DTE, address 190118, state R1, modulo 8, timer 0
Defaults: cisco encapsulation, idle 0, nvc 1
Input/output window sizes 2/2, packet sizes 128/128
```

```
Timers: T20 180, T21 200, T22 180, T23 180, TH 0
Channels: Incoming-only none, Two-way 5-1024, Outgoing-only none
RESTARTs 1/1 CALLs 0+0/0+0/0+0 DIAGs 0/0
  Last input 00:00:00, output 00:00:00, output hang never
  Last clearing of "show interface" counters 00:48:96
  Input queue: 1/75/0 (size/max/drops); Total output drops: 0
  Queueing strategy: weighted fair
  Output queue: 0/1000/64/0 (size/max total/threshold/drops)
    Conversations  0/2/256 (active/max active/max total)
    Reserved Conversations 0/0 (allocated/max allocated)
  5 minute input rate 0 bits/sec, 0 packets/sec
  5 minute output rate 0 bits/sec, 0 packets/sec
    0 packets input, 0 bytes, 0 no buffer
    Received 0 broadcasts, 0 runts, 0 giants, 0 throttles
    0 input errors, 0 CRC, 0 frame, 0 overrun, 0 ignored, 0 abort
    0 packets output, 0 bytes, 0 underruns
    0 output errors, 0 collisions, 0 interface resets
    0 output buffer failures, 0 output buffers swapped out
    0 carrier transitions
    DCD=up  DSR=up  DTR=up  RTS=up  CTS=up
Sean2514#
```

The preceding output shows an X.25 serial interface that has just come up operating properly.

Chapter Summary

This chapter focused on troubleshooting techniques for overcoming problems with serial links. This included troubleshooting protocols such as HDLC, serial link LMI types, X.25, and Frame Relay. Step-by-step checklists can be used to troubleshoot each issue, whether it is related to hardware, cabling, IOS configuration, or connectivity.

You need to remember the many tools at your disposal, such as debug commands, show commands, loopback tests, and as a last resort, the Cisco Technical Assistance Center to help decipher the output.

Exam Prep Practice Questions

Question 1

Which of the following should you do if a router's interface is administratively down? [Choose the two best answers.]

- ❑ A. Check the cabling.
- ❑ B. Check whether the interface is manually shut down.
- ❑ C. Check for duplicate IP addresses.
- ❑ D. Check with the local service provider.

Answer: **B, C.** If the interface is administratively down, you should check that the interface is not manually shut down or that a duplicate IP address is not configured on another interface.

Question 2

Which of the following are displayed when using the show interface serial command? [Choose the two best answers.]

- ❑ A. Error information
- ❑ B. Encapsulation type
- ❑ C. AUI interface configuration
- ❑ D. Switch model information

Answer: **A, B.** The show interface serial command displays error information as well as the *encapsulation* type configured on the interface. The AUI interface is not a serial interface and the command does not display the switch model information.

Question 3

Using the **debug serial interface** command displays which of the following information fields?

- ○ A. **mineseen**
- ○ B. **myseq**
- ○ C. **yourseen**
- ○ D. All of the above
- ○ E. None of the above

Answer: **D**. The `debug serial interface` command displays the mineseen, myseq, and yourseen fields.

Question 4

Which of the following elements are displayed by using the **show controller serial** command? [Choose the two best answers.]

- ❑ A. Clock rate
- ❑ B. Cable type
- ❑ C. LMI type
- ❑ D. Error information

Answer: **A, B**. The `show controller serial` command displays the clock rate and cable type. It does not display the LMI type or the error information.

Question 5

Which of the following commands displays the FECN and BECN statistics?

- ○ A. **show x25 events**
- ○ B. **show frame-relay pvc**
- ○ C. **show interface serial**
- ○ D. **show running-config**

Answer: **B**. The `show frame-relay pvc` command displays the FECN and BECN statistics.

Question 6

Which encapsulation is used by default on Cisco serial interfaces?

- ○ A. HDLC
- ○ B. Frame Relay
- ○ C. SDLC
- ○ D. X.25

Answer: **A.** The default encapsulation type used on Cisco serial interfaces is HDLC.

Question 7

If the keepalives are not sequencing on a serial interface, which of the following is not a troubleshooting step?

- ○ A. Check the local hardware.
- ○ B. Check for noise on the line.
- ○ C. Check for a timing mismatch.
- ○ D. Check the local router's hostname.

Answer: **D.** If the keepalives are not sequencing on a serial interface, you should check the local hardware, check for noise on the line, and check for a timing mismatch. Regardless of whether a hostname is configured, it will not affect any functioning component of the router.

Question 8

To test end-to-end connectivity on a serial link, which of the following would be used?

- ○ A. Route trace test
- ○ B. SNMP test
- ○ C. Loopback test
- ○ D. Connectivity test
- ○ E. Ping 127.0.0.1

Answer: **C.** To test end-to-end connectivity on a serial link, you would use one of the different loopback tests.

Question 9

The following output is displayed using which of the following commands?

```
Serial0 is up, line protocol is up
  Hardware is HD64570
  Internet address is 63.78.39.174/24
  MTU 1500 bytes, BW 64 Kbit, DLY 20000 usec,
                rely 255/255, load 1/255
  Encapsulation FRAME-RELAY IETF, loopback not set,
                keepalive set (10 sec)
  LMI enq sent  270, LMI stat recvd 127, LMI upd recvd 0,
                DTE LMI up
  LMI enq recvd 119, LMI stat sent  0, LMI upd sent  0
  LMI DLCI 1023  LMI type is CISCO  frame relay DTE
  Broadcast queue 0/64, broadcasts sent/dropped 22/0,
                interface  broadcasts 0

  Last input 00:00:06, output 00:00:06, output hang never
  Last clearing of "show interface" counters 02:51:08
  Input queue:0/75/0(size/max/drops); Total output drops: 0
  Queueing strategy: weighted fair
  Output queue: 0/1000/64/0 (size/max total/threshold/drops)
```

○ A. **show frame-relay map**

○ B. **show interface**

○ C. **show frame-relay pvc**

○ D. **show frame relay lmi**

Answer: **B**. The output displayed is from the show interface command.

Question 10

If you need to connect a Cisco router to a non-Cisco device, which encapsulation type would you use?

○ A. DLCI

○ B. X.25

○ C. ANSI

○ D. Cisco

○ E. IETF

Answer: **E**. To connect a Cisco router to a non-Cisco device, you need to use the IETF encapsulation type.

Need to Know More?

 Glauser, Fred, and Eric Quinn. *CCNP BCRAN Exam Cram 2*, 2003, Que, ISBN: 0-7897-3020-0.

 Cisco CCO Web site, Troubleshooting Frame Relay, http://www.cisco.com/en/US/customer/tech/tk713/tk237/technologies_tech_note09186a0080093bd4.shtml

 Cisco CCO Web site, Troubleshooting Layer 1/Serial Links Flow Chart: http://www.cisco.com/en/US/customer/tech/tk713/tk584/technologies_tech_note09186a00800a70f3.shtml

Troubleshooting Routing Protocols

. . . .

Terms you'll need to understand:

✓ Static Route

✓ Dynamic Route

✓ Routing Information Protocol (RIP)

✓ Interior Gateway Routing Protocol (IGRP)

✓ Enhanced Interior Gateway Routing Protocol (EIGRP)

✓ Autonomous System (AS)

✓ Open Shortest Path First (OSPF)

✓ Border Gateway Protocol (BGP)

✓ Intermediate System-to-Intermediate System (IS-IS)

Techniques you'll need to master:

✓ Know the differences between static and dynamic routing

✓ Know the differences between distance-vector versus link-state routing protocols

✓ Know the different types of routing protocols

✓ How to use IOS commands to troubleshoot routing protocol problems

Routers need to be able to learn about attached networks and routes through the network. In smaller networks it is easy to use manually entered routes to let the router know where to route data it receives. Entering routes manually can be as simple as setting the network information on the inside and outside interfaces. Manually entered routes are called *static routes*.

Alternatively, routers can learn about networks and routes through the network from other network routers; in these situations, the learned routes are called *dynamic routes*. This chapter discusses the different dynamic routing protocols used in Cisco networks and explains how they work. This chapter also describes the commands related to troubleshooting routing protocols that you need to know to pass the exam successfully.

Routing Protocols

Routing protocols are a necessity in the networking world. Learning how routers use routing protocols to make a routing decision and how each routing protocol works is necessary to overcome this part of the exam. Interior routing is implemented at the Internet layer of the TCP/IP suite of protocols. Interior routing protocols use IP as a routing protocol and use a specific algorithm for different protocols. Each type of interior routing protocol uses different algorithms and mechanisms to accomplish routing. The following are a few examples of interior routing protocols:

➤ *Routing Information Protocol (RIP)*—RIP is one of the most commonly used routing protocols for the Internet. RIP uses a maximum hop count of 15 to calculate a routing path. RIP is a distance-vector routing protocol, and has a default distance of 120.

➤ *Interior Gateway Routing Protocol (IGRP)*—IGRP is a protocol proprietary to Cisco equipment. It was designed to overcome some of RIP's limitations. IGRP uses a hop count of a maximum of 255 to calculate a routing path. IGRP is a distance-vector routing protocol, and has a default distance of 100 (you learn more about distance-vector and link-state routing protocols in upcoming sections of this chapter).

➤ *Open Shortest Path First (OSPF)*—OSPF is a link-state routing protocol that uses an autonomous system to accomplish routing. It is used for large networks, because its maximum metric limit is 65,535. OSPF has a default distance of 110.

An *autonomous system* is defined as a set of routers under a single technical administration, using an interior gateway protocol and common metric to route packets within the autonomous system (AS), and using an exterior gateway protocol to route packets to other autonomous systems (ASs).

➤ *Enhanced Interior Gateway Routing Protocol (EIGRP)*—EIGRP is a proprietary routing protocol for Cisco. EIGRP combines link-state routing and distance-vector routing to achieve a balanced hybrid routing protocol. EIGRP has a default distance of 90.

Different routing protocols use different techniques, algorithms, and type of protocols to dynamically learn routes, share routes with other routers, and make sure that the information the router keeps is as current as possible. The following sections discuss these routing protocol features:

➤ Link-state protocols

➤ Convergence time

➤ Distance-vector routing protocols

➤ Split horizon

➤ Split horizon-poison reverse

➤ Hold-down timers

➤ Triggered updates

Link-State Routing Protocols

Protocols using the link-state routing algorithm possess a complex table of network topology information for routing. The *link-state routing* process uses link-state packets (LSPs) to inform other routers of distant links. The routers all use these "hello packets" to inform the other routers on the network where they are and their proximity to each other. After the routers have all updated their fellow routers, each router will possess a routing table to refer to when it needs to make routing decisions that incorporate the best path.

One of the benefits of using a link-state routing algorithm is how it reports the best path. The best path may not be the shortest distance, but instead is the fastest way. Link-state uses many factors when declaring the best path, such as hop count, bandwidth, congestion, and link speed.

Convergence Time

Convergence is the time required for all the routers to update their routing tables after a change to the network. When one router is informed of a change on the network, it reports the change to its neighbors, and its neighbors report to their neighbors, and so on. Convergence time is not a set period of time, but depends on the number of routers and the size of the network.

For a router to converge with its neighbors, it must remember its name and the *cost* (distance) of the path to the neighboring router. Then it must send an LSP with the information to a neighboring router. Routers must also receive LSPs so that they can update their own routing tables. After they have exchanged the information, the routers will have a topology of the existing network and the best paths.

Distance-Vector Routing Protocols

Distance-vector routing protocols are designed to send a copy of a router's entire routing table to all of its neighbors. This enables all the routers to know the routing paths and determine the lowest cost (shortest distance) for the traffic before forwarding the packets. This information comprises the local routing table and is re-advertised to the router's neighbors for an optimal route on the network. When operating a large campus environment, finding the best path for traffic will make better use of the network.

Using distance-vector routing does have a drawback: It does not update the routers at the same time. Distance-vector routing protocols update the routers on the network every 30 to 90 seconds, so when a router fails, the other routers on the network may not receive the information that it has failed. Because of the time difference in route updates, there may be a router or routers that don't realize a path isn't working.

It is very important for your network to learn and update its neighboring routers on the best path for traffic in order to prevent problems of a routing loop. A routing loop is data that makes a virtual circle through the network and passes through an interface repeatedly until something occurs to stop the looping data.

Routing loops can destroy an internetwork and can multiply for a long time trying to find the packet destination. Distance-vector protocols use a few different methods to prevent routing loops. These include split horizon, poison reverse, triggered updates, and hold-down timers.

Split Horizon

The split horizon method can reduce incorrect routing information and excessive routing with a simple rule. The split-horizon rule uses the premise of not sending information back the same way that it came. With the split-horizon rule, if a router receives an update from network A through interface B, the router will not update that route to network A through interface B.

Split Horizon-Poison Reverse

The split horizon method is designed to stop routing loops between routers that have formed nearby relationships with other routers. The poison-reverse technique allows networks to be advertised with a hop count set to infinity, thus causing all routes to be flushed from the routing tables. In this type of environment, the split-horizon-poison-reverse method will stop a two-node routing loop and reduce the possibility of large routing loops.

Hold-Down Timers

Hold-down timers are used to prevent routers from sending inaccurate routing updates. It is common in networking for a router or interface to go down for various reasons, including loss of power, a loose cable, or an accidental hit of the power switch. When a router or interface goes down, the down router will trigger the other routers to update their routing tables.

If the down router or interface suddenly comes back online, the rest of the routers on the network will still be trying to update their tables. Hold-down timers help eliminate this problem. You can set the routers' hold-down timers for a period of time to prevent routers from trying to update as a result of brief network glitches. With the hold-down timer, if a router or interface goes down, the router's hold-down timer will wait a specified amount of time before it tries to update the routing table. In most cases, if the down router is caused by a minor glitch, the router will come back online and the network will not be affected.

Triggered Updates

Triggered updates are used to allow routers to inform their neighbors immediately of routing changes, so they don't have to wait for the regular timed updates. Some protocols, such as EIGRP, use only triggered updates to let the network know of a change.

Routing Information Protocol (RIP)

Routing Information Protocol, or *RIP*, is a distance-vector protocol that uses hop-count metrics to get from one router to the next. RIP is limited to 15 hop counts. RIP is mostly used in the routing of global Internet and is an *Interior Gateway Protocol (IGP)*. What this means is that RIP performs routing in a single autonomous system. On the other side is the *Exterior Gateway Protocol (EGP)*, which is used to perform routing updates on different autonomous systems.

RIPv2 is another version of RIP. The main difference between the two is that RIP is used only for classful routing and RIPv2 is used for classless routing. RIP sends routing updates at regular intervals and when a routing table has changed. Routers running the RIP protocol maintain the best route because it is the shortest or the one with fewest hops. After the router updates its routing table, the router sends information about the routes it knows out to all its interfaces, informing all of its neighboring routers. This process is done independently of the other updates.

RIP uses a single routing metric. RIP measures the distance between the source and destination network. When a router receives an update that has new or changed information in it, the router will add a metric to that source address, which is the IP address of the sender. In the path from source to destination, each interface to the destination would be defined as one additional hop in the hop count, with a maximum hop count of 15. The next hop would be 16, and then it would be sent back as an unreachable network or destination address.

By implementing a hop count limit, the RIP protocol prevents routing loops from an infinite cycle. In order for RIP to adjust for rapid changes in the network, it implements the split horizon and hold-down timers to prevent incorrect routing information from being propagated. The RIP hop count also helps prevent routing loops in an infinite circle. RIP also uses timers to help regulate its performance. These timers include

➤ The *routing-update timer*, usually set to 30 seconds, clocks the periodic update intervals. To prevent collisions, the router puts in a random number of seconds each time the timer is reset.

➤ The *route-timeout*; when this timeout expires, the route is determined to be unreachable.

➤ The *route-flush timer*; an unreachable route is maintained in the routing table until this timeout expires. The update timer is 30 seconds, the invalid timer is 90 seconds, the hold-down timer is 100 seconds, and the flush timer is 270 seconds.

Troubleshooting RIP

Two versions of RIP exist, the distinction between them is that RIP1 had limited use and scalability. RIP2 is almost the same, but the new version is able to support Classless Interdomain Routing (CIDR), route summarization, and variable-length subnet masks (VLSMs). The following example shows a few commands used in troubleshooting RIP, as well as the output. The show ip route command displays the routing table of the networks and how they are reaching other networks.

```
DCSRTR#
DCSRTR#show ip route
Codes: C - connected, S - static, I - IGRP, R - RIP, M - mobile,
 B - BGPD - EIGRP, EX - EIGRP external, O - OSPF,
IA - OSPF inter area
N1 - OSPF NSSA external type 1,
N2 - OSPF NSSA external type 2
E1 - OSPF external type 1, E2 - OSPF external type 2,
E - EGP
i - IS-IS, L1 - IS-IS level-1, L2 - IS-IS level-2,
* - candidate default
U - per-user static route, o - ODR
Gateway of last resort is not set
     172.16.0.0/24 is subnetted, 6 subnets
R       currentip  [120/2] via 172.16.20.2, 00:00:12, Serial0
R       10.10.20.0 [120/2] via 172.16.20.2, 00:00:12, Serial0
R       10.10.20.0 [120/2] via 172.16.20.2, 00:00:12, Serial0
R       172.16.30.0 [120/2] via 172.16.20.2, 00:00:12, Serial0
C       172.16.30.0 is directly connected, Serial0
C       10.10.20.0 is directly connected, Ethernet0
DCSRTR#
```

This is one of the best commands for learning the routes the router knows about and discovering how the router learned the routes. In the highlighted commands above, notice the letter preceding the route information. This letter indicates how the route was learned (the letters and their meaning are listed in the first lines of the example). The item Serial0 is the interface through which the data exits to get to the network specified.

When using the show ip protocol command, you will be able to identify the protocol or protocols running on the router, as the following example demonstrates:

```
DCSRTR#show ip protocol
Routing Protocol is "rip"
  Sending updates every 30 seconds, next due in 13 seconds
  Invalid after 180 seconds, hold down 180, flushed after 240
  Outgoing update filter list for all interfaces is not set
  Incoming update filter list for all interfaces is not set
  Redistributing: rip
  Default version control: send version 1, receive version 1
    Interface           Send  Recv  Triggered RIP  Key-chain
    FastEthernet0/0      1     1
    Serial0/0.1         1     1
```

```
   FastEthernet0/1        1      1
Automatic network summarization is in effect
Maximum path: 4
Routing for Networks:
   10.0.0.0
   64.0.0.0
   66.0.0.0
Routing Information Sources:
   Gateway         Distance      Last Update
   10.1.1.1             120      00:00:14
   10.1.2.55            120      00:00:19
Distance: (default is 120)

DCSRTR#
```

The above shows the status and protocols running on each interface. Notice that the beginning of the output shows how often updates are sent to RIP enabled routers in the network.

Internet Gateway Routing Protocol (IGRP)

IGRP is a Cisco proprietary routing protocol that was designed as a new version or upgrade from RIP, the only existing protocol at the time. IGRP does not use RIP's hop count of 15; the IGRP routing protocol uses up to 255 hops. IGRP is a classful routing protocol, meaning it does not include any subnet information about the network.

Three types of routes are recognized by IGRP:

➤ *Interior*—A network directly connected to a router interface.

➤ *System*—Advertised routes by other IGRP neighbors within the same AS (autonomous system) number. The *AS* is the number that identifies the IGRP individual session.

➤ *Exterior*—Routes learned from other IGRP sessions with different AS numbers. This information is used by the router to set the *gateway of last resort*—the route a packet takes if it is not specified to a certain route.

IGRP also uses more than just hop counts to determine the best path from or to a network. It uses a combination of internetwork delay, bandwidth, link reliability, and load to determine the best path on the network. IGRP also uses split horizon, poison reverse, hold-down timers, and triggered updates, as described earlier in this chapter. When using IGRP, if routing metrics have increased by 1.1 or more, the poison-reverse update is started. The reason for this is if there is an increase in the routing metrics, than there might be a routing loop. Not unlike RIP, the IGRP routing protocol also implements a number of timers.

Troubleshooting IGRP

IGRP uses distance-vector routing and, because of this, uses a one-dimensional array of information to calculate the best path. The vector consists of four elements: bandwidth, delay, load, and reliability. The MTU, or maximum transfer unit, is not part of the vector of metrics but is used in the final route information. IGRP is intended to replace RIP in order to create a more stable, quick-converging protocol that can scale up to a growing network.

 If you implement a large-scale network, you may want to use the link-state protocol, because the distance-vector protocols come with overhead and delay time.

The IGRP protocol has a few items that provide a quick convergence time:

➤ *Configurable metrics*—Metrics involved in the algorithm responsible for calculating route information may be configured by the user.

➤ *Flash updates*—Updates are sent out immediately when the metrics route changes, there is no waiting for routine updates.

➤ *Poison reverse*—Used to prevent routing loops.

➤ *Unequal-cost load balancing*—Allows packets to be changed/distributed across multiple paths.

Open Shortest Path First (OSPF)

OSPF uses the link-state technology, as does RIP. The Internet Engineering Task Force (IETF) developed OSPF in 1988. The most recent version is OSPFv2 (more information is available in RFC 1583). OSPF is an interior gateway protocol that was developed to address large, scalable internetworks that RIP was not able to address. OSPF sends its link-state information every 30 minutes (unlike RIP, which sends updates every 30 seconds). OSPF addresses a few issues that were of concern in earlier protocols. These issues include speed convergence, support for variable subnet mask, network reachability, use of bandwidth, and path selection.

Implementing the OSPF protocol requires proper planning and design in a large-scale network environment. OSPF is different from IGRP and EIGRP because it uses pure-link routing. It is also an *open standard* routing protocol, which means that it was not designed specifically to run on Cisco routers; it was designed to run quickly, to be scalable, and to run efficiently on any routing equipment. Complete details of the OSPF protocol can be found in RFC1131.

Troubleshooting OSPF

Compared to RIP, OSPF fares better in a large network. OSPF does not update every 30 seconds, has a lower cost, and thus preserves the bandwidth. When changes occur on the network, the CPU has to deal with processing and calculating all the routes on the network. In general, if at all possible, do not add more than 100 routers per area and not more than 700 routers throughout the network. This is not the minimum or the maximum router capacity for OSPF, but a guideline. The more links that exist in a network, the greater the number of routing updates and CPU cycles.

A few commands are very helpful in troubleshooting OSPF. Knowing when and where to use these commands will help you isolate the problem and fix the problem sooner. The show commands are used to provide information on the configuration and function of OSPF on the router.

Using the show ip route command displays the IP route information:

```
DCSRTR#show ip route
Codes: C - connected, S - static, I - IGRP, R - RIP, M - mobile, B - BGP
       D - EIGRP, EX - EIGRP external, O - OSPF, IA - OSPF inter area
       N1 - OSPF NSSA external type 1, N2 - OSPF NSSA external type 2
       E1 - OSPF external type 1, E2 - OSPF external type 2, E - EGP
       i - IS-IS, L1 - IS-IS level-1, L2 - IS-IS level-2, * - candidate
         default
       U - per-user static route, o - ODR
Gateway of last resort is not set

     10.0.0.0/8 is variably subnetted, 4 subnets, 3 masks
O       10.10.0.0/16 [110/74] via 172.68.16.3, 00:03:30, Serial1
                     [110/74] via 172.68.16.1, 00:03:30, Serial0
C       10.0.0.2/32 is directly connected, Loopback0
O       10.0.0.1/32 [110/65] via 172.68.16.3, 00:03:30, Serial1
                    [110/65] via 172.68.16.1, 00:03:30, Serial0
C       10.10.20.0/24 is directly connected, Ethernet0
DCSRTR#
```

The above output shows the networks the router knows about, as well as the interface on the router to those networks. Using the show ip route ospf command shows the OSPF routes only:

```
DCSRTR#show ip route ospf
     10.0.0.0/8 is variably subnetted, 4 subnets, 3 masks
O       10.10.0.0/16 [110/74] via 172.68.16.3, 00:02:57, Serial1
                     [110/74] via 172.68.16.1, 00:02:57, Serial0
O       10.0.0.1/32 [110/65] via 172.68.16.3, 00:02:57, Serial1
                    [110/65] via 172.68.16.1, 00:02:57, Serial0
DCSRTR#
```

Notice in the above output that only the OSPF protocol learned routes are shown. Using the `show ip ospf <process id>` command shows information related to the process ID:

```
DCSRTR#
DCSRTR#show ip ospf
 Routing Process "ospf 100" with ID 172.68.16.4
 Supports only single TOS(TOS0) routes
 SPF schedule delay 5 secs, Hold time between two SPFs 10 secs
 Minimum LSA interval 5 secs. Minimum LSA arrival 1 secs
 Number of external LSA 0. Checksum Sum 0x0
 Number of DCbitless external LSA 0
 Number of DoNotAge external LSA 0
 Number of areas in this router is 1. 1 normal 0 stub 0 nssa
    Area BACKBONE(0)
        Number of interfaces in this area is 4
        Area has no authentication
        SPF algorithm executed 4 times
        Area ranges are
        Number of LSA 2. Checksum Sum 0x839B
        Number of DCbitless LSA 0
        Number of indication LSA 0
        Number of DoNotAge LSA 0
DCSRTR#
```

The above output shows the OSPF configuration statistics for the OSPF 100 process running on the router. Using the `show ip ospf border-routers` command shows the routes that join the network from different paths:

```
DCSRTR#
DCSRTR#show ip ospf border-routers
OSPF Process 100 internal Routing Table
Codes: i - Intra-area route, I - Inter-area route
DCSRTR#
```

Using the `show ip ospf database` command shows the database of the OSPF summaries:

```
DCSRTR#
DCSRTR#show ip ospf database
        OSPF Router with ID (172.68.16.4) (Process ID 100)
                Router Link States (Area 0)
Link ID         ADV Router      Age       Seq#          Checksum Link count
172.68.16.3     172.68.16.3     379       0x80000008 0xB8F    6
172.68.16.4     172.68.16.4     362       0x80000007 0x780C   6
DCSRTR#
```

Using the `show ip ospf interface` command shows the OSPF information on the specified interface:

```
DCSRTR#
DCSRTR#show ip ospf interface
Ethernet0 is up, line protocol is up
  Internet Address 10.10.20.2/24, Area 0
  Process ID 100, Router ID 172.68.16.4, Network Type BROADCAST, Cost: 10
  Transmit Delay is 1 sec, State DR, Priority 1
  Designated Router (ID) 172.68.16.4, Interface address 10.10.20.2
```

```
    No backup designated router on this network
    Timer intervals configured, Hello 10, Dead 40, Wait 40, Retransmit 5
      Hello due in 00:00:00
    Neighbor Count is 0, Adjacent neighbor count is 0
    Suppress hello for 0 neighbor(s)
Loopback0 is up, line protocol is up
    Internet Address 10.0.0.2/32, Area 0
    Process ID 100, Router ID 172.68.16.4, Network Type LOOPBACK, Cost: 1
    Loopback interface is treated as a stub Host
Serial0 is up, line protocol is up
    Internet Address 172.68.16.2/24, Area 0
    Process ID 100, Router ID 172.68.16.4,
              Network Type POINT_TO_POINT, Cost: 64
    Transmit Delay is 1 sec, State POINT_TO_POINT,
    Timer intervals configured, Hello 10, Dead 40, Wait 40, Retransmit 5
      Hello due in 00:00:04
    Neighbor Count is 1, Adjacent neighbor count is 1
      Adjacent with neighbor 172.68.16.3
    Suppress hello for 0 neighbor(s)
Serial1 is up, line protocol is up
    Internet Address 172.68.16.4/24, Area 0
    Process ID 100, Router ID 172.68.16.4,
              Network Type POINT_TO_POINT, Cost: 64
    Transmit Delay is 1 sec, State POINT_TO_POINT,
    Timer intervals configured, Hello 10, Dead 40, Wait 40, Retransmit 5
      Hello due in 00:00:03
    Neighbor Count is 1, Adjacent neighbor count is 1
      Adjacent with neighbor 172.68.16.3
    Suppress hello for 0 neighbor(s)
DCSRTR#
```

The above output shows the complete OSPF statistics for all the interfaces on the router. Using the show ip ospf neighbor command shows related neighbor information:

```
DCSRTR#
DCSRTR#show ip ospf neighbor
Neighbor ID     Pri   State       Dead Time   Address       Interface
172.68.16.3      1    FULL/   -    00:00:34    172.68.16.1    Serial0
172.68.16.3      1    FULL/   -    00:00:34    172.68.16.3    Serial1
DCSRTR#
```

Using the show ip ospf summary-address command shows the summary addresses of the redistribution list:

```
DCSRTR#
DCSRTR#show ip ospf summary-address
OSPF Process 100, Summary-address
Summary#
```

When properly used, the debug commands in the IOS can show you answers to the most difficult problems. When issuing a debug command, you may find that an invalid host assignment exists on the subnetwork or that some incorrect routing information is coming from an upstream router. In looking at the following code, you are able to see many options that are available with OSPF debugging.

```
DCSRTR#
DCSRTR#debug ip ospf ?
  adj              OSPF adjacency events
  database-timer   OSPF database timer
  events           OSPF events
  flood            OSPF flooding
  lsa-generation   OSPF lsa generation
  packet           OSPF packets
  retransmission   OSPF retransmission events
  spf              OSPF spf
  tree             OSPF database tree
DCSRTR#
```

Using the debug ip ospf events command shows all the OSPF events:

```
DCSRTR#
DCSRTR# debug ip ospf events
OSPF:hello with invalid timers on interface Ethernet0
hello interval received 10 configured 10
net mask received 255.255.255.0 configured 255.255.255.0
dead interval received 40 configured 30
DCSRTR#
```

 Another good command for troubleshooting OSPF configurations is the **show running-config** command, which displays the running configuration on the router.

Using the debug ip ospf packet command enables you to see the OSPF packet:

```
DCSRTR#
DCSRTR# debug ip ospf packet
OSPF: rcv. v:2 t:1 l:48 rid:200.0.0.117
      aid:0.0.0.0 chk:6AB2 aut:0 auk
DCSRTR#
```

IGRP Versus EIGRP

IGRP was developed in the mid 1980s as an improvement for RIP. Although RIP is still a good routing protocol for smaller networks (up to 15 hops), EIGRP may be a more efficient protocol in a large network. IGRP has some improvements, such as hop counts of 1 to 255, and uses an autonomous system (AS). IGRP is a distance-vector protocol that was designed to be more stable than RIP and to be used on larger network environments. IGRP is a classful routing protocol, meaning it does not include subnets in the route field information. Only three types of routes are recognized by IGRP: interior, system, and exterior. IGRP also uses routing stability, which includes hold-down timers, split horizon, and poison-reverse updates. After IGRP was used for a while, Cisco released another proprietary protocol, the Enhanced Interior Gateway Routing Protocol (EIGRP).

Benefits of EIGRP

One of the problems resolved by EIGRP was that IGRP, when running, would send its whole route table if some change occurred in the network. EIGRP is a hybrid, because it uses both distance-vector and link-state routing algorithms. Enabling EIGRP to support both routing algorithms means less opportunity exists for route failure. EIGRP is much better than IGRP because it uses equal-cost load balancing, formal relationships, and incremental routing updates. EIGRP, like IGRP, is very scalable and stable. EIGRP also uses an autonomous system to distinguish a route. You can even have multiple sessions with EIGRP in order for EIGRP to calculate the best route and load sharing. It uses the route database, the topology database, and a neighbor table. EIGRP converges more quickly than IGRP because it calculates only when a change in the network directly affects the routing table.

EIGRP Features

EIGRP was created by Cisco to help make up for IGRP's inherent problems. Being a hybrid protocol enables EIGRP to be a much more efficient routing protocol. EIGRP is also very easy to configure. One of the nicest features about using this protocol is that you are not limited by hop counts, and you also have the use of timing, clocking, and load balancing. The following are some of the prominent features of EIGRP:

➤ *Route tagging*—Makes a distinction between routes learned via a different EIGRP session.

➤ *Neighbor relationships*—Uses hello packets to establish peering.

➤ *Incremental routing updates*—Only changes are advertised, not the whole routing table.

➤ *Classless routing*—Supports VLSM and subnets.

➤ *Configurable networks*—Information can be set through configuration commands.

➤ *Equal-cost load balancing*—Traffic is sent equally across multiple connections to be able to calculate the best path for load sharing. EIGRP uses a database structure to store information for the routed information. All the databases are the same for IP-EIGRP, IPX-EIGRP, AT-EIGRP, and Apple-Talk-EIGRP. EIGRP uses hello packets to update its routing table, and then allows the exchange of route information. EIGRP sends hello packets every 5 seconds on a high-bandwidth level, and every 60 seconds on a low-bandwidth level.

When EIGRP sends a hello packet continuously at a configured time on the router, the configured time is called a *hello interval*. The hello interval can be adjusted using the `ip eigrp hello-interval` command. EIGRP also uses a *hold time*, which is the amount of time used before the router will consider the neighbor alive and start to accept hello packets. The hold time is usually set at three times the hold-time value, normally 15 seconds to 180 seconds, but you can change this range by issuing the command `ip eigrp hold-down interface`. If you are going to adjust the hold-time values, you must be careful calculating the values. If the interval is too long, the updates to the routing tables may not be made soon enough to add downed routes or additions. If the rate is too quick, you may use a lot of unnecessary bandwidth for updates.

For the exam you should know that the default timers for EIGRP are as follows:

➤ Update timer used to set the frequency of routing updates is 90 seconds.

➤ Invalid timer used before declaring a route invalid is 270 seconds.

➤ Hold-down timer used before announcing route updates is 280 seconds.

➤ Flush timer used before a route is flushed from the routing table is set to 630 seconds.

EIGRP Troubleshooting Commands

The `show` commands are helpful in troubleshooting any type of protocol problem. Knowing the commands that will return the information you are looking for is very helpful. The following are a few commonly used commands to aid in troubleshooting EIGRP.

Using `show ip route eigrp` displays only EIGRP routes:

```
DCSRTR#
DCSRTR#show ip route eigrp
     172.68.0.0/16 is variably subnetted, 2 subnets, 2 masks
D       172.68.0.0/16 is a summary, 00:07:33, Null0
     10.0.0.0/8 is variably subnetted, 2 subnets, 2 masks
D       10.0.0.0/8 is a summary, 00:07:34, Null0
DCSRTR#
```

Using `show ip eigrp neighbors` displays the connected neighbor and the route summary for the neighbor:

```
DCSRTR#
DCSRTR#show ip eigrp neighbors
IP-EIGRP neighbors for process 100
H   Address                  Interface   Hold Uptime   SRTT   RTO  Q   Seq
                                         (sec)         (ms)        Cnt Num
```

```
1    10.10.20.1              Et0          11 00:08:10 1576  5000  0  11
3    172.68.16.3            Se1          12 00:08:15     0  4500  0  10
2    172.68.16.1            Se0          12 00:08:15     0  4500  0  9
0    10.10.20.3             Et0          13 00:09:07    13   200  0  8
DCSRTR#
```

Using `show ip eigrp topology` displays the topology table for EIGRP:

```
DCSRTR#
DCSRTR#show ip eigrp topology
IP-EIGRP Topology Table for process 100
Codes: P - Passive, A - Active, U - Update, Q - Query, R - Reply,
       r - Reply status
P 10.0.0.0/8, 1 successors, FD is 281600
        via Summary (281600/0), Null0
P 10.10.20.0/24, 1 successors, FD is 281600
        via Connected, Ethernet0
P 172.68.0.0/16, 1 successors, FD is 2169856
        via Summary (2169856/0), Null0
P 172.68.16.0/24, 1 successors, FD is 2169856
        via Connected, Serial0
        via Connected, Serial1
DCSRTR#
```

The above output shows the members for the entire EIGRP 100 network, and the interfaces on the router to reach each network. Using `show ip eigrp traffic` displays the hello and routing updates:

```
DCSRTR#
DCSRTR#show ip eigrp traffic
IP-EIGRP Traffic Statistics for process 100
  Hellos sent/received: 434/544
  Updates sent/received: 14/19
  Queries sent/received: 0/2
  Replies sent/received: 2/0
  Acks sent/received: 11/5
  Input queue high water mark 3, 0 drops
DCSRTR#
```

Using `show ip eigrp events` displays a log of the most recent EIGRP information pertaining to what is happening on the network:

```
DCSRTR#
DCSRTR#show ip eigrp events
Event information for AS 100:
1    00:52:19.879 Poison squashed: 172.68.0.0/16 reverse
2    00:52:18.807 Metric set: 172.68.0.0/16 2169856
3    00:52:18.807 Route install: 172.68.0.0/16 0.0.0.0
4    00:52:18.807 FC sat rdbmet/succmet: 2169856 0
5    00:52:18.807 FC sat nh/ndbmet: 0.0.0.0 2169856
6    00:52:18.807 Find FS: 172.68.0.0/16 2169856
7    00:52:18.807 Rcv update met/succmet: 2707456 2195456
8    00:52:18.807 Rcv update dest/nh: 172.68.0.0/16 172.68.16.3
9    00:52:18.799 Metric set: 172.68.0.0/16 2169856
10   00:52:18.799 Route install: 172.68.0.0/16 0.0.0.0
11   00:52:18.799 FC sat rdbmet/succmet: 2169856 0
12   00:52:18.799 FC sat nh/ndbmet: 0.0.0.0 2169856
13   00:52:18.799 Find FS: 172.68.0.0/16 2169856
```

```
14   00:52:18.799 Rcv update met/succmet: 2707456 2195456
15   00:52:18.799 Rcv update dest/nh: 172.68.0.0/16 172.68.16.1
16   00:52:18.279 Peer up: 10.10.20.1 Ethernet0
17   00:52:18.079 Metric set: 172.68.16.0/24 2169856
18   00:52:18.079 FC sat rdbmet/succmet: 2169856 0
19   00:52:18.079 FC sat nh/ndbmet: 0.0.0.0 2169856
20   00:52:18.079 Find FS: 172.68.16.0/24 2169856
21   00:52:18.079 Rcv update met/succmet: 2681856 2169856
22   00:52:18.079 Rcv update dest/nh: 172.68.16.0/24 172.68.16.3
DCSRTR#
```

In the above output, you see each event that takes place on the router running the EIGRP process. You see the metric set, a routing installed, updates received, and the router finding a network.

Border Gateway Protocol (BGP)

Border Gateway Protocol (BGP) version 4 is the latest version of BGP and is defined in RFC 1771. BGP is an exterior routing protocol used to connect between autonomous systems.

Exterior Routing Protocols

The best way to categorize routing protocols is to decide if they are interior or exterior. An interior routing protocol, such as RIP or IGRP, is used to exchange routing information *within* an autonomous system. An exterior routing protocol, such as BGP, is used to connect *between* autonomous systems. BGP is the most widely used exterior routing protocol; it is used by almost anyone who wants to communicate on the Internet.

The main goal of BGP is to provide an interdomain routing system that will guarantee a loop-free exchange or routing information between autonomous systems. BGP was designed to allow ISPs to communicate and exchange packets.

BGP is not always the best protocol to use in all networks. If any of the following describes your network, you might want to use another protocol:

➤ If your network only has a single connection to the internet or another AS

➤ Limited memory or processor power on BGP routers to handle constant updates

➤ Very limited understanding of route filtering and BGP path selection process

➤ Very little bandwidth between autonomous systems

If your network is limited to the above list, you may want to use static routes to connect to another autonomous system.

Intermediate System-to-Intermediate System (IS-IS)

The International Organization for Standardization (ISO) came up with a routing protocol to use with the Open System Interconnection (OSI) protocol suite. The ISO protocol suite includes the Intermediate System-to-Intermediate System (IS-IS) protocol, End System-to-Intermediate System (ES-IS) protocol, and Interdomain Routing Protocol (IDRP).

The IS-IS protocol was originally used in ISO Connectionless Network Protocol (CLNP) networks. A version of IS-IS has been created to work on both the CLNP and IP networks. This version is referred to as *integrated IS-IS* (also referred to as *dual IS-IS*). You can find more information on the OSI protocol suite in the ISO document that defines IS-IS, which is ISO 10589.

The ISO networking model uses some specific terminology. These terms are the basis for the ES-IS and IS-IS OSI products. The ES-IS protocol enables ES and IS to discover each other. The IS-IS protocol provides routing between ISs. The following are some important terms relating to IS-IS:

➤ *Area*—A group of contiguous networks and an attached host specified to be an area by the network administrator

➤ *Domain*—A collection of connected areas; for example, a routing domain provides full connectivity to all end systems within the domain

➤ *End system (ES)*—Any non-routing network nodes

➤ *Intermediate system (IS)*—A router

➤ *Level 1 routing*—Routing within a level 1 area

➤ *Level 2 routing*—Routing between two level 1 areas

IS-IS is an OSI link-state hierarchical routing protocol that floods the network with link-state information in order to build a complete picture of the network topology. To simplify the router design and operation, IS-IS distinguishes between two levels of IS. Level 1 IS communicates within a level 1 area, and level 2 IS routes between level 1 areas and creates an interdomain routing backbone. IS-IS uses a default metric with a maximum path value of 1,024. The use of the metric is arbitrary and usually assigned by the network administrator. Any single link can have a maximum value of 64, and path links are calculated by summing the link values.

IS-IS also defines three optional metrics (cost):

> *Delay*—Deals with the delay on the link

> *Expense*—Deals with the communication cost associated with the link

> *Error*—Deals with the error rate on the link

IS-IS maintains a mapping of these metrics to the Quality of Service (QoS) option in the CLNP packet header. IS-IS uses the mapping to compute routes through the internetwork.

IS-IS uses three basic packet formats: hello packets, link-state packets, and sequence-numbers packets (SNPs). Each of the packet formats has a complex format with three different logical parts. The first is an 8-byte fixed header shared by all three packet formats. The second is packet type specific (either hello, link state, or sequence-numbers packets) with a fixed format. The third is also packet-type specific (either hello, link state, or sequence-numbers packets), but it is a variable length.

Chapter Summary

This chapter discussed interior routing protocols, such as RIP, OSPF, IGRP, and EIGRP. Interior routing protocols use IP routing protocols and routing algorithms to route data from one point in the network to another.

RIP is a distance-vector routing protocol that uses hop counts for a measurement. OSPF is a link-state routing protocol that uses an autonomous system to achieve its routing. IGRP is a distance-vector protocol that is proprietary to Cisco. EIGRP combines link-state and distance-vector routing to achieve its routing and is also a Cisco proprietary protocol.

Distance-vector routing protocols are designed to send a copy of their entire routing table to all of their neighbors, allowing all the routers to know the routing paths and determine the lowest cost (shortest distance). The link-state routing process uses link-state packets to inform other routers of distant links and proximity. After the routers have all updated their fellow routers, each router will possess a routing table to refer to when it needs to make routing decisions and choose the best path.

The chapter also discussed an exterior gateway protocol, Border Gateway Protocol (BGP). The main goal of BGP is to provide an interdomain routing system that will guarantee a loop-free exchange of routing information between autonomous systems. BGP was designed to allow ISPs to communicate and exchange packets.

You should develop a good understanding of how routing protocols operate and determine paths through the network. By doing this, it will make troubleshooting routing problems in your network much easier. Using the `show` and `debug` commands found in this chapter will also help you isolate routing problems in your network.

Exam Prep Practice Questions

Question 1

Which of the following is a process by which a router immediately informs its neighbors about routing updates?

○ A. Split horizon

○ B. Poison reverse

○ C. Hold-down timers

○ D. Triggered updates

Answer: **D.** Routers use triggered updates to inform neighbors about routing updates immediately, so they don't have to wait for regular timed updates.

Question 2

Which command enables you to see the routing table?

○ A. **show ip route rip**

○ B. **show ip route**

○ C. **show ip interface**

○ D. **show running-configuration**

Answer: **B.** Using the show ip route command enables you to see the routing table.

Question 3

RIP2, following RIP1, is able to support which of the following? [Choose the three best answers.]

❑ A. Subnetting

❑ B. Classless Interdomain Routing (CIDR)

❑ C. Route summarization

❑ D. Variable length subnet mask (VLSM)

Answer: **B, C, D.** RIP2 is able to support Classless Interdomain Routing (CIDR), route summarization, and variable-length subnet masks (VLSMs).

Question 4

Suppose you are running OSPF in your core backbone routers and running RIP on the edge networks. You notice that a few of the networks are not receiving IP packets. After logging in to the router, what command should you use to see who is running OSPF?

- ○ A. **show ip protocols**
- ○ B. **show ip ospf neighbors**
- ○ C. **show ip interface**
- ○ D. **sh ip arp**

Answer: **B.** Using the show ip ospf neighbors command enables you to see who is running OSPF, and will list all routing information on all of the enabled OSPF interfaces.

Question 5

Which routing methods might cause a routing loop? [Choose the two best answers.]

- ❑ A. Split horizon has been disabled on an interface
- ❑ B. IP multicast routing is not enabled
- ❑ C. Hold-down timers are not consistent across the network
- ❑ D. Invalid IP addresses exist on the network

Answer: **A, C.** If split horizon has been disabled on the interface or the hold-down timers are not consistent across the network, a routing loop may be caused.

Question 6

Of the following, which protocol is considered a hybrid (meaning it uses both distance-vector and link-state routing algorithm)?

- ○ A. RIP
- ○ B. EIGRP
- ○ C. IGRP
- ○ D. IS-IS

Answer: **B.** EIGRP is an enhanced version of IGRP. EIGRP supports both routing algorithms and provides less opportunity for routing failures.

EIGRP also converges very fast because it only calculates when a change in the network directly affects the routing table.

Question 7

Classless subnet masks can be used by which of the following routing protocols? [Choose the two best answers.]

❑ A. IGRP

❑ B. EIGRP

❑ C. OSPF

❑ D. RIP v1

Answer: **B, C.** EIGRP and OSPF support variable-length subnet masks (VLSMs) and classless address spaces. Answers A and D are incorrect because neither RIP v1 nor IGRP supports VLSM or classless addressing.

Question 8

Pick three valid IP **show** commands from the following:

❑ A. **show ip route**

❑ B. **show ip interface**

❑ C. **show ip protocols**

❑ D. **show ip-route**

❑ E. **show protocols**

❑ F. **show ip-interface**

Answer: **A, B, C.** The other commands are invalid.

Question 9

Which commands would you use to see the contents of a route map? [Choose the two best answers.]

❑ A. **show running-config**

❑ B. **show ip route-map**

❑ C. **show route-map**

❑ D. **show ip interface**

Answer: **A, C.** Using the `show running-config` and `show route-map` commands enables you to see the contents of a route map.

Question 10

Which of the following protocols is considered an exterior routing protocol?

○ A. RIP

○ B. EIGRP

○ C. BGP

○ D. OSPF

Answer: **C.** BGP is considered an exterior routing protocol that connects autonomous systems together. The latest version is BGP v4 and is mainly used by the ISP's.

Need to Know More?

 Shannon, Michael. *CCNP Routing Exam Cram 2*, 2003, Que Publishing, ISBN: 0-7897-3017-0.

 Cisco CCO Web site, Troubleshooting EIGRP, http://www.
cisco.com/en/US/customer/tech/tk365/tk207/technologies_tech
_note09186a0080094613.shtml

 Cisco CCO Web site, Troubleshooting OSPF, http://www.cisco.
com/en/US/customer/tech/tk365/tk480/technologies_tech_note0
9186a00800949f7.shtml

Troubleshooting ISDN

Terms you'll need to understand:

✓ Challenge Handshake Authentication Protocol (CHAP)
✓ Demarcation point
✓ Dial-on-demand routing (DDR)
✓ Integrated Services Digital Network (ISDN)
✓ Local Loop
✓ Point-to-Point Protocol (PPP)

Techniques you'll need to master:

✓ How to configure dial-on-demand routing
✓ Identify frequent ISDN problems
✓ Understand and know how to troubleshoot CHAP
✓ Troubleshoot dialer mappings
✓ Troubleshoot PPP
✓ Configure and troubleshoot dialer and access lists
✓ Understand Layer 1 through Layer 3 and the connection process
✓ Understand q.921 and q.931 signaling
✓ Use ISDN troubleshooting **show** and **debug** commands

ISDN is one of the more difficult wide area network (WAN) protocols to understand and to configure. Most companies are using this technology less and less with the introduction of DSL technologies. ISDN is still popular in rural areas because of the distance limitations of DSL. ISDN is still an option for administrators to consider when connecting LANs together through a WAN, and communicating through multimedia technologies, such as video conferencing. The Support exam will test your knowledge of troubleshooting ISDN protocols. This chapter begins with an overview of ISDN, then discusses techniques for troubleshooting an ISDN configuration. You also learn the ISDN troubleshooting commands you will need to know—both in your work and in preparation for the exam.

This chapter was written based on use of a Cisco 804 router. This router includes a four-port hub, as well as an ISDN/U (ISDN BRI) interface. Although this book focuses on troubleshooting, this chapter provides only a brief overview of ISDN. For a more in-depth discussion on ISDN, you should read *CCNP BCRAN Exam Cram 2*, by Eric Quinn and Fred Glauser, 2003, also published by Que.

ISDN Overview

In the late 1960s, telephone companies began the long process of upgrading their analog trunks and switches to digital networks that allow for clearer signals, compressible data, better trunk utilization, features such as caller ID and three-way calling, higher bandwidth using a single connection to a service provider, and the elimination of amplifiers in the network.

ISDN was originally used as a means to move the digital network into the household, to enable a single line to provide two standard phone lines, as well as digital services for data. The great thing about this is that ISDN can use the existing copper wire, enabling telephone providers to add an immediate service that translated into more revenue and improved their existing service.

Later, ISDN became popular for businesses to handle video conferencing, point-of-sale transactions, data transfers, and to connect small to medium-sized businesses, as well as households, to the Internet.

Most ISDN problems occur in certain areas and can be isolated and resolved easily with a good fundamental knowledge of ISDN. The next sections look at the following common issues:

➤ Dial-on-demand routing

➤ Configuring static routes

➤ ISDN misconfiguration problems

➤ Connecting at the Physical layer

➤ Troubleshooting the Data Link layer

Dial-On-Demand Routing

Dial-on-demand routing (DDR) is used to allow more than one Cisco ISDN router to dial an ISDN dial-up connection on an as-needed basis. DDR is designed to be used in low-volume and periodic network connections, using either a Public Switched Telephone Network (PSTN) or ISDN line.

If an access list is configured and a packet that meets the requirements of interesting (sendable) traffic is received on an interface on the inside network, the following steps take place:

1. The route to the destination network is determined.

2. A call is initiated to the destination network based on dialer information to that network.

3. The data is transmitted to the destination network.

4. The call is terminated if there is no more data to be transmitted over the link to that network and the configured idle-timeout period has been reached.

To configure Dial-on-Demand Routing (DDR) to dial a connection when there is interesting traffic to send, you use the following steps:

1. Create at least one static route entry that defines the route to the destination network.

2. Use access lists to specify the traffic that is considered interesting or allowed to be sent by the router.

3. Use a route map to configure the dialer information to get to the destination network.

The following section explains this configuration process in more detail.

Configuring Static Routes

To forward traffic across an ISDN link, you should configure static routes on each of the ISDN routers. If you are using a dynamic routing protocol, there will always be data to send and the ISDN link will never drop. A dynamic routing protocol sort of defeats the purpose of dialing the destination network only when data exists to send. Therefore, all participating ISDN routers should have a static route that defines all the known routes to other networks.

You first need to define the destination network, which is 207.212.78.0 (as shown in Figure 12.1), with the following command:

```
Seans804 (config)#ip route 207.212.78.0 255.255.255.0 172.16.1.1
```

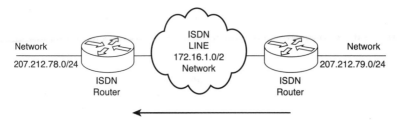

Figure 12.1 The two network subnets of the network. In between is the ISDN link with its own network and subnet.

You can also define which interface can be used to get to 207.212.78.0, which is the BRI0 interface, using the following command:

```
Seans804 (config)#ip route 207.212.78.0 255.255.255.0 bri0
```

Using Dialer Lists to Specify Interesting Traffic

After setting the route tables in each router, you need to configure the router to determine what brings up the ISDN line. An administrator using the dialer-list global configuration command defines interesting packets. The following are the commands to turn on all IP traffic:

```
Sean804(config)# dialer-list 1 protocol ip permit
Sean804(config)# int bri0
Sean804(config-if)# dialer-group 1
```

The `dialer-group` command sets the access list on the BRI interface. Extended access lists can be used with the `dialer-list` command to define interesting traffic to include only certain applications.

There are three other commands that you should use when configuring your BRI interface:

➤ dialer load-threshold

➤ dialer idle-timeout

➤ ppp multilink

The `dialer load-threshold` command instructs the BRI interface when to bring up the second B channel. You must specify how much of a load must exist on the first B channel before the second is used. This option ranges from 1 to 255, where 255 indicates that the second BRI channel should be brought up when the first is at 100 percent. You must also indicate whether this number is based on the load coming in, going out, or both (either) on this interface.

The `dialer idle-timeout` command is used to specify the number of seconds to wait before disconnecting a call if no data is sent. The default is 120 seconds. The following is an example of using the `dialer load-threshold`, `dialer idle-timeout`, and `ppp multilink` commands:

```
Seans804(config-if)# dialer load-threshold 200 either
Seans804(config-if)# dialer idle-timeout 200
Seans804(config-if)# ppp multilink
```

The `multilink ppp` (Multilink Point-to-Point Protocol, or MP) command allows load balancing between the two B channels in a BRI. Multilink PPP is not vendor-specific and it provides packet fragmentation and reassembly, sequencing, and load calculating. Cisco's MP is based on RFC 1990.

To verify the PPP multilink configuration, use the `show ppp multilink` command.

Troubleshooting ISDN Misconfigurations

Configuring ISDN is fairly simple and there are only a few commands needed for the basic configuration. This process does require that you have some knowledge, though, on how ISDN works, the different line protocols, and the proper placement of the equipment. To explain configuring the ISDN router interfaces correctly, this section of the chapter takes a look at the following issues:

➤ The Service Profile Identifier (SPID)

➤ Challenge Handshake Authentication Protocol (CHAP)

➤ Dialer mapping command

➤ Access lists

➤ Point-to-Point Protocol (PPP)

Service Profile Identifier

The phone-line identifier that is used in an analog phone environment is called a SPID (Service Profile ID). The SPID includes the actual seven-digit telephone number, including the area code and sometimes an extra few digits used by the service provider's switch. A SPID looks similar to this example:

80055515500100

The preceding example corresponds to the phone number 800-555-1550. The additional parameters, 0100, serve as an identifier for the local service provider's switch. If you don't have these numbers and you know the service has been connected, you may need to contact the local service provider to receive these numbers. The SPID can also contain a two digit prefix prior to the number, such as 0180055575500100.

 The SPID occasionally causes confusion because it isn't always necessary. When you configure the switch type, if you use Nortel DMS100 or Nation ISDN (basic-ni) switches, the SPID is required. If you are using Basic-5ess switches, the SPID may be optional. Your local service provider is the authority on this matter.

The ISDN SPID is a unique number that the local ISDN router must learn in order to successfully identify itself, but only in North America; the integration of the phone number into the SPID is usually only applicable in public telephone company ISDN installations. In a private ISDN network, the SPID can usually be any 10-digit or longer number.

 You must verify that the IP addresses and subnets assigned to the interfaces connecting the two sides of an ISDN link are in their own network and subnet, just as any other point-to-point WAN connection must be.

Challenge Handshake Authentication Protocol

CHAP (Challenge Handshake Authentication Protocol) provides ISDN with the capability to control access to each router by forcing the ISDN routers to use an authentication technique. This safeguard enables a business to be confident that implementing ISDN is a low security risk.

CHAP is used to require a username and encrypted password on all inbound connections. One of the most important items in troubleshooting CHAP is to verify that the CHAP-configured username and passwords match on both interfaces connecting the ISDN routers. One advantage Cisco has over other ISDN routers is the ability to support Microsoft CHAP (MS-CHAP), which was implemented in version 12 of the Cisco IOS, and the Password Authentication Protocol (PAP), which is an earlier version of CHAP.

 Your knowledge of PPP and CHAP are tested extensively when taking this certification exam.

To use CHAP authentication, you must enable PPP by using the `encapsulation ppp` command and assigning an authentication method, as follows:

```
Seans804(config-if)#ppp auth ?
chap     Challenge Handshake Authentication Protocol(CHAP)
ms-chap Microsoft Challenge Handshake Authentication Protocol(MS-CHAP)
pap      Password Authentication Protocol (PAP)
```

If you suspect a password might be the problem in authenticating, the best way to confirm this is by using the `debug ppp authentication` command. The following output shows the error you will receive when the authentication fails due to an incorrect password configuration:

```
Seans804#debug ppp authentication
PPP authentication debugging is on
Seans804#ping 207.212.78.107
Type escape sequence to abort.
04:02:36: BR0:1 PPP: Phase is AUTHENTICATING, by both
04:02:36: BR0:1 CHAP: O CHALLENGE id 7 len 27 from "Seans804"
04:02:36: BR0:1 CHAP: I CHALLENGE id 7 len 24 from "Seans804"
04:02:36: BR0:1 CHAP: O RESPONSE id 7 len 27 from "Seans804"
04:02:36: BR0:1 CHAP: I FAILURE id 7 len 25 msg is "MD/DES compare failed"
04:02:36: %ISDN-6-DISCONNECT: Interface BRI0:1 disconnected from
                    18005551559, call lasted 1 seconds
04:02:38: %LINK-3-UPDOWN: Interface BRI0:1, changed state to down.
04:02:38: %LINK-3-UPDOWN: Interface BRI0:1, changed state to up.
04:02:38: BR0:1 PPP: Treating connection as a callout
04:02:38: BR0:1 PPP: Phase is AUTHENTICATING, by both
04:02:38: BR0:1 CHAP: O CHALLENGE id 8 len 27 from "Seans804"
04:02:38: BR0:1 CHAP: I CHALLENGE id 8 len 24 from "Seans804"
04:02:38: BR0:1 CHAP: O RESPONSE id 8 len 27 from "Seans804"
04:02:38: BR0:1 CHAP: I FAILURE id 8 len 25 msg is "MD/DES compare failed"
```

As this output demonstrates, CHAP performs authentication by sending authentication packets that consist of an 8-bit Code field, an 8-bit Identifier field, a 16-bit Length field, and a Data field, which can vary in length. The Code field identifies the type of CHAP packet, which varies based on the type of packet being sent, and which may be any of the following four types:

➤ Challenge (Type 1)

➤ Response (Type 2)

➤ Success (Type 3)

➤ Failure (Type 4)

The following is the CHAP authentication process between the DCS1804 router and the DCS2804 router:

1. DCS1804 (Challenge) sends a Challenge packet to the DCS2804 (remote ISDN router).

2. The DCS2804 copies the identifier information into a new packet. It then sends a Response packet along with the hashed value, a value calculated from the encrypted password.

3. The DCS1804 receives the Response packet and checks the hashed value against its own hashed value. If both hashed values match, DCS1804 sends a Success packet back. Otherwise, it sends a Failure packet back to DCS1804.

Configuring CHAP authentication is a straightforward process. Here is an example of configuring an ISDN router with a username, password, and PPP CHAP authentication:

```
Seans804# config t
Seans804(config)# username Sean password cisco
Seans804(config)# interface bri0
Seans804(config-if)# encapsualtion ppp
Seans804(config-if)# ppp authentication chap
```

The dialer map Command

The `dialer map` command permits the ISDN router to dial an associated number when data that is destined for the next-hop interface is received. When data is received for the identified protocol on the other side of the ISDN line, this command instructs the ISDN router which number to call.

When using this command, you must make sure that the dialer map entries contain valid IP addresses and phone numbers, and that a dialer map statement exists for each protocol in the network. The following output walks you through using the `dialer map` command for the IP protocol:

```
Seans804(config)#int bri0
Seans804(config-if)#dialer map ?
  bridge    Bridging
  clns      ISO CLNS
  ip        IP
```

```
ip         IP
ipx        Novell IPX
llc2       LLC2
netbios    NETBIOS
snapshot   Snapshot routing support
Seans804(config-if)#dialer map ip ?
A.B.C.D  Protocol specific address
Seans804(config-if)#dialer map ip 172.16.1.1 ?
WORD             Dialer string
broadcast        Broadcasts should be forwarded to this address
class            dialer map class
modem-script     Specify regular expression to select modem dialing script
name             Map to a host
spc              Semi Permanent Connections
speed            Set dialer speed
system-script    Specify regular expression to select system dialing script
Sean804(config-if)#dialer map ip 207.212.78.107 18005551001
Sean804(config-if)#
```

The following example demonstrates the BRI0 interface using the show running-config command:

```
interface BRI0
 ip address 207.212.78.107 255.255.255.0
 no ip directed-broadcast
 no ip route-cache
 no ip mroute-cache
 dialer idle-timeout 100000
 dialer wait-for-carrier-time 120
 dialer map ip 172.16.1.1 18005551001
 dialer load-threshold 128 either
 dialer-group 1
 isdn switch-type basic-ni
 isdn spid1 5551001401
!
```

The above shows the BRI0 interface configuration. It shows all the dialer settings, as well as the SPID used to dial the ISDN router on the other side of the link.

Access Lists

Access lists are used with ISDN connections to keep certain types of traffic from being sent across the ISDN link and causing the ISDN router to make an unnecessary connection. Using the rule that the more calls you make, the more you pay, access lists save money. Some services offer Centrix ISDN and other options that circumvent higher costs. Cetrix ISDN is typically billed by the megabyte sent instead of by the minute or hour that the ISDN connection is used. Still, if you need a constant connection (more than 40 hours per month), Frame Relay, DSL, and many other permanent virtual connection (PVC) technologies are available with the same or greater bandwidth at a much lower cost.

The following example demonstrates a configured access list, using the `dialer-group` command to apply it to an interface. This access list, shown here in the `show running-config` command, is configured to allow only IP protocols, allowing all IP protocols with the exception of HTTP, which uses port 80.

```
interface BRI0
 ip address 172.16.1.2 255.255.255.0
 no ip directed-broadcast
 no ip route-cache
 no ip mroute-cache
 dialer idle-timeout 100000
 dialer wait-for-carrier-time 120
 dialer map ip 172.16.1.1 18008358664
 dialer map ip 172.16.1.1 18005551002
 dialer load-threshold 128 either
 dialer-group 1
 isdn switch-type basic-ni
 isdn switch-type basic-ni
!
router rip
 redistribute static
 network 63.0.0.0
 network 172.16.0.0
!
ip classless
ip route 0.0.0.0 0.0.0.0 172.16.1.1
ip route 63.78.39.0 255.255.255.0 172.16.1.1
!
access-list 155 deny tcp any any eq 80
access-list 155 permit ip any any
dialer-list 1 protocol ip list 155
!
line con 0
 transport input none
 stopbits 1
line vty 0 4
 password sean
login
!
```

The bolded lines in the preceding code sample show the access list that is used to decide what is interesting traffic. The access list shows that every IP packet is considered interesting traffic except for Web-based traffic on port 80.

Point-To-Point Protocol (PPP)

The recommended choice for a secure connection with ISDN routers is PPP. Several other options are available that include a simulated serial connection using HDLC. When you are troubleshooting, PPP provides additional information regarding the connection, including the protocol type. This rarely presents itself in a manner that is usable to administrators, however. Rather, an understanding of the protocol and its capability to provide useful functions, including CHAP, is more often helpful to administrators. Note that the PPP protocol is the same for analog or ISDN connections, so the configuration of PPP on a workstation using an analog modem requires PPP encapsulation on the ISDN host router. PPP also supports compression.

When using the `debug ppp` command, the output provides information about PPP. PPP contains a Protocol field in the output, which can be used to identify the upper-layer information included in the datagram. Table 12.1 lists the protocol values.

Table 12.1	PPP Protocol Field Values
Hex Value	Protocol
0021	IP
0029	AppleTalk
002B	IPX
003D	MultiLink
0201	802.1d Hello Packets
0203	Source Route Bridge Protocol Data Units
8021	IPCP
8029	ATCP
802B	IPXCP
C223	CHAP
C023	PAP

Troubleshooting Connections at the Physical Layer

One of the first areas to consider when troubleshooting ISDN is the Physical layer, particularly with new installations. The wiring is one of the most important aspects to consider when no connection can be made. When using ISDN for videoconferencing equipment or connecting to PBX equipment in the local network, you can use Category 3, 4, 5, or even 6 cabling.

An RJ-45, RJ-11, or RJ-14 can be used for ISDN terminations, however, it is recommended that you use an RJ-45.

This chapter, however, will focus on asynchronous Basic Rate Interface (BRI) connections, which use standard copper-pair wiring and which are the standard connection type in the United States.

ISDN BRI was originally designed to provide digital services over existing pairs of copper telephone wire so that the already existing analog phone lines wouldn't need to be replaced. A BRI can be used for videoconferencing, voice services, or data. An additional control channel, called the D channel, is used by BRI as a replacement for legacy X.25 networks.

BRI interface connections are different from primary rate interface (PRI) connections. PRI uses a T-1 or DS-1, which is the equivalent of 24 individual 64K channels. A voice connection basic rate is referred to as a DS-0, or a single 64Kbps B channel of the T-1 connection.

Each ISDN BRI is a 192Kbps circuit that is divided into three individual channels in a connection. The B channels are used as the primary data channels, providing 64Kbps of bandwidth in each direction. The D channel provides 16Kbps of bandwidth for control signaling. The remaining bandwidth of 48Kbps is used for overhead.

A frame that traverses the BRI interfaces is 48 bits, and each BRI circuit can send 4,000 frames per second. A service called Always On can use the D channel to send data, which reflects a nondemand mode for the channel. The Always On service is usually used to replace X.25 in point-of-sale (POS) circuits that use 9.6Kbps of bandwidth for the application.

For the exam you should remember the total circuit bandwidth for a BRI, the bandwidth of the B and D channels, as well as the size of frames that can traverse the link.

The Local Loop and Its Connections

It is good to keep in mind that a local loop exists on the remote side that must be functioning properly. The *local loop* is the circuit between your side of the demarcation point and the central office (CO), also known as the carrier operations. The *demarcation point* is the point at which your ISDN connection connects to the wall in your facility. This is also the point at which the telephone company begins and ends its responsibility for the connection. The local service provider's responsibility is to verify that a connection exists at the wall, and from there it is the local administrator's responsibility to get the connection functioning. Of course, it is also the responsibility of the local service provider to provide you with the proper SPIDs and connection type information.

The local loop at this point in the network is referred to as the RT. The RT allows the connection to overcome distance limitations so that a clear signal can reach the CO. The local loop connects your local ISDN router and the ISDN switch belonging to the local service provider. The local loop is necessary because all digital signals have distance limitations between two devices.

Now that you know about the local loop and the connections, you are ready to learn how to troubleshoot beyond the Physical Layer connectivity. The next section discusses that troubleshooting process.

Terminology for Troubleshooting After the Physical Layer

This section focuses on the other aspects of troubleshooting ISDN, when the problems aren't found at the Physical layer. To better understand this (and the rest of this chapter), a quick terminology lesson is necessary to familiarize you with the terms used to describe the ISDN components shown in Figure 12.2. After that, we will discuss the techniques and commands for troubleshooting ISDN configurations.

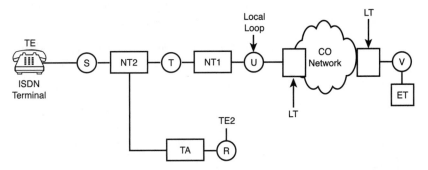

Figure 12.2   The ISDN Physical layer components.

The following lists the terms you need to know:

➤ Line termination (LT) point—Handles line termination of the local loop and switching functions. An NT1 device is located at the local service provider's site.

➤ Exchange termination (ET) point—Handles line termination of the local loop and switching functions.

➤ Network termination (NT1)—The network termination point. This is often the demarcation point.

➤ Terminal equipment type 1 (TE1)—This is a device that uses a four-wire, twisted-pair digital interface. Most ISDN devices found in today's networks are this type.

➤ Terminal equipment type 2 (TE2)—This is a device that does not contain an ISDN interface and that requires a terminal adapter (TA).

➤ R reference point (R)—Identifies the reference point between non-ISDN equipment and a TA. This point in the network allows a non-ISDN device to appear to the network as an ISDN device.

➤ S reference point (S)—The connection point between the user-end equipment and an NT1 or an NT2. The user-end equipment can be the ISDN router, a TE1, or a TA.

➤ T reference point (T)—Defines the reference point between an NT1 device and an NT2 device.

➤ S/T interface—A combination of both the S and T interfaces. This interface is governed by the ITU I.430 standard, which defines the connection as a four-wire connection and the ISO 8877 physical connector. The S/T interface is an RJ 45, 8-pin cable using pins 3 and 6 to receive data and pins 4 and 5 to transmit data. A straight-through pin configuration connects the terminal end point (TE) to the NT.

➤ U reference point (U)—The connection point between an NT1 and the LE. It is normally serviced on a single twisted-pair cable to reduce data delivery costs and simplify installations.

➤ V reference point (V)—The termination point within the local loop.

NOTE Both the LT and the ET typically are just referred to as the local exchange (LE).

Troubleshooting Misconfigured Provider Switches

Unfortunately, when a problem exists with ISDN, your own site and the remote site are not the only areas you have to consider. Because this is a WAN-type issue, an administrator must consider the possibility that the service provider failed to configure the ISDN switch properly, particularly when this is a new installation.

To know when the local service provider's equipment may be the reason for a problem in the network, you should have a clear understanding of all the layers in which ISDN may be a problem. Those are Layers 1 through 3 of the OSI Reference model.

Troubleshooting the Data Link Layer: q.921 and PPP

Layer 2 of the OSI Reference model has two protocols that need to be working properly, if they are configured: q.921 and PPP. There is also a service access point identifier associated with q.921.

The q.921 Protocol

The q.921 protocol defines the signaling method used by ISDN at Layer 2 of the OSI Reference model. The q.921 protocol uses the D channel by using the Link Access Procedure on D channel (LAPD) protocol, which is used by X.25. If the q.921 connection between the CO switch and the local ISDN router does not occur and complete, there can be no network (Layer 3) connectivity.

If you use the show isdn status command and find that a Layer 2 problem exists, the best way to troubleshoot q.921 protocol problems is to use the debug isdn q921 command. Usually, a problem with q.921 relates to the terminal end point identifier (TEI). The TEI value uniquely identifies every terminal in the network. A value of 127 represents the broadcast address to all the terminals. TEIs 64 through 126 are reserved for use after the completion of a Layer 2 ISDN connection. You cannot assign this value, because it is a dynamic assignment.

The following output is from the show isdn status command on an incorrectly configured interface:

```
Seans804# show isdn status
Global ISDN Switchtype = basic-ni
ISDN BRI0 interface
dsl 0, interface ISDN Switchtype = basic-ni
    Layer 1 Status:
ACTIVE
    Layer 2 Status:
TEI = 79, Ces = 1, SAPI = 0, State = MULTIPLE_FRAME_    ESTABLISHED
```

```
      Spid Status:
TEI 79, ces = 1, state = 8(established)
      spid1 configured, no LDN, spid1 NOT sent, spid1 NOT valid
TEI Not Assigned, ces = 2, state = 1(terminal down)
      spid2 configured, no LDN, spid2 NOT sent, spid2 NOT valid
      Layer 3 Status:
0 Active Layer 3 Call(s)
      Activated dsl 0 CCBs = 1
CCB:callid=0x0, sapi=0x0, ces=0x1, B-chan=0 calltype = INTERNAL
Total Allocated ISDN CCBs = 1
```

The output above shows that the ISDN connection was established, but the
SPIDs configured are invalid, as shown in the bolded lines.

The following output is correctly configured and shows that all the layers are
active and configured correctly:

```
Seans804#show isdn status
Global ISDN Switchtype = basic-ni
ISDN BRI0 interface
      dsl 0, interface ISDN Switchtype = basic-ni
    Layer 1 Status:
        ACTIVE
    Layer 2 Status:
        TEI = 105, Ces = 1, SAPI = 0, State = MULTIPLE_FRAME_ESTABLISHED
    Spid Status:
        TEI 105, ces = 1, state = 5(init)
            spid1 configured, no LDN, spid1 sent, spid1 valid
            Endpoint ID Info: epsf = 0, usid = 3, tid = 1
    Layer 3 Status:
        2 Active Layer 3 Call(s)
    Activated dsl 0 CCBs = 0
```

Watch for Layer 3 Signaling and SABME Messages

You can use the **debug isdn q921** command to identify the process that is running when a failure occurs. One thing to watch for in the output of the **debug isdn q921** command is the SAPI, or service access point identifier, field. If this field lists a SAPI of 0, then Layer 3 signaling is present. This signaling is provided by q.931, which is covered later in this chapter, under the section "Troubleshooting the Network Layer." The value of 63 indicates a management SAPI for the assignment of the TEI values. A value of 64 indicates that q921 is using call control.

Another field to look at is the set asynchronous balanced mode extended (SABME) messages. SABME messages are exchanged with TEI message type 7. Should the SABME fail, a disconnect response message is sent and the link establishment is terminated. In this situation, you must determine the reason for the SABME failure.

When the SABME succeeds, an acknowledgment is sent that a Layer 2 connection is established. When this occurs, you should see the TE begin to send INFO-type frames.

PPP (Point-to-Point Protocol)

To troubleshoot the PPP protocol and isolate CHAP problems, you should first check both sides of the ISDN link to verify that the usernames and passwords are configured correctly. Knowing the steps that PPP and CHAP use in negotiating a connection can also aid in determining the problem. The following are the steps taken by PPP and CHAP to establish a link. These steps are sometimes referred to as targets.

1. The TE sends a CONFREQ, which is a configuration request specifying certain router options.

2. If the request is accepted, a CONFACK is sent back to the TE, which is an acknowledgment. If the request is denied, a CONFREJ is sent to the requesting TE.

3. If CHAP is used for authentication, it continues to steps 4 through 6, which are the three-way handshake process.

4. A challenge message is sent to the remote TE.

5. The remote TE sends a response message.

6. If the response values match, authentication is given.

The following is an example of using the debug ppp negotiation command, which is extremely helpful in researching PPP problems and resolving them:

```
Seans804#debug ppp negotiation
PPP protocol negotiation debugging is on
Seans804# ping 172.16.1.1
Type escape sequence to abort.
Sending 5, 100-byte ICMP Echos to 172.16.1.1, timeout is 2    seconds:
02:26:33: %LINK-3-UPDOWN: Interface BRI0:1, changed state to    up
02:26:33: BR0:1 PPP: Treating connection as a callout
02:26:33: BR0:1 PPP: Phase is ESTABLISHING, Active Open
02:26:33: BR0:1 LCP: O CONFREQ [Closed] id 3 len 10
02:26:33: BR0:1 LCP:    MagicNumber 0x50239604    (0x050650239604)
02:26:33: BR0:1 LCP: I CONFREQ [REQsent] id 13 len 10
02:26:33: BR0:1 LCP:    MagicNumber 0x5023961F    (0x05065023961F)
02:26:33: BR0:1 LCP: O CONFACK [REQsent] id 13 len 10
02:26:33: BR0:1 LCP:    MagicNumber 0x5.023961F    (0x05065023961F)
02:26:33: BR0:1 LCP: I CONFACK [ACKsent] id 3 len 10
02:26:33: BR0:1 LCP:    MagicNumber 0x50239604    (0x050650239604)
02:26:33: BR0:1 LCP: State is Open
02:26:33: BR0:1 PPP: Phase is UP
02:26:33: BR0:1 CDPCP: O CONFREQ [Closed] id 3 len 4
02:26:33: BR0:1 IPCP: O CONFREQ [Closed] id 3 len 10
02:26:33: BR0:1 IPCP:    Address 10.1.1.2 (0x03060A010102)
02:26:33: BR0:1 CDPCP: I CONFREQ [REQsent] id 3 len 4
02:26:33: BR0:1 CDPCP: O CONFACK [REQsent] id 3 len 4
02:26:33: BR0:1 IPCP: I CONFREQ [REQsent] id 3 len 10
02:26:33: BR0:1 IPCP:    Address 172.16.1.1 (0x03060A010101)
```

```
02:26:33: BR0:1 IPCP: O CONFACK [REQsent] id 3 len 10
02:26:33: BR0:1 IPCP:    Address 10.1.1.1 (0x03060A010101)
02:26:33: BR0:1 CDPCP: I CONFACK [ACKsent] id 3 len 4
02:26:33: BR0:1 CDPCP: State is Open
02:26:33: BR0:1 IPCP: I CONFACK [ACKsent] id 3 len 10
02:26:33: BR0:1 IPCP:    Address 172.16.1.2 (0x03060A010102)
02:26:33: BR0:1 IPCP: State is Open
02:26:33: BR0 IPCP: Install route to 172.16.1.1
!!!!!
Success rate is 100 percent (5/5), round-trip min/avg/max = 32/38/48 ms
```

The above output shows the entire PPP negotiation process for authenticating an ISDN connection. You will notice that the interesting traffic that activated the ISDN connection was an ICMP ping.

The `debug ppp packet` command reports the real-time PPP packet flow, including the type of packet and the B channel that is being used. As with other debug packet commands, the `debug ppp packet` command records each packet and can be used to monitor traffic flows. The following is the output generated from a successful ping:

```
Sean804# debug ppp packet
PPP packet display debugging is on
Seans804#ping 172.16.1.1
Type escape sequence to abort.
Sending 5, 100-byte ICMP Echos to 172.16.1.1, timeout is 2 seconds:
01:11:19: %LINK-3-UPDOWN: Interface BRI0:1, changed state to up.
01:11:19: BR0:1 LCP: O CONFREQ [Closed] id 4 len 10
01:11:19: BR0:1 LCP:    MagicNumber 0x5025BF23 (0x05065025BF23)
01:11:19: BR0:1 PPP: I pkt type 0xC021, datagramsize 14
01:11:19: BR0:1 PPP: I pkt type 0xC021, datagramsize 14
01:11:19: BR0:1 LCP: I CONFREQ [REQsent] id 14 len 10
01:11:19: BR0:1 LCP:    MagicNumber 0x5025BF46   (0x05065025BF46)
01:11:19: BR0:1 LCP: O CONFACK [REQsent] id 14 len 10
01:11:19: BR0:1 LCP:    MagicNumber 0x5025BF46   (0x05065025BF46)
01:11:19: BR0:1 LCP: I CONFACK [ACKsent] id 4 len 10
01:11:19: BR0:1 LCP:    MagicNumber 0x5025BF23   (0x05065025BF23)
01:11:20: BR0:1 PPP: I pkt type 0x8207, datagramsize 8
01:11:20: BR0:1 PPP: I pkt type 0x8021, datagramsize 14
01:11:20: BR0:1 CDPCP: O CONFREQ [Closed] id 4 len 4
01:11:20: BR0:1 PPP: I pkt type 0x8207, datagramsize 8
01:11:20: BR0:1 IPCP: O CONFREQ [Closed] id 4 len 10
01:11:20: BR0:1 IPCP:    Address 10.1.1.2 (0x03060A010102)
01:11:20: BR0:1 CDPCP: I CONFREQ [REQsent] id 4 len 4
```

Troubleshooting the Network Layer

ISDN uses the q.931 signaling that is defined in the ITU-T I.451 to connect at Layer 3 of the OSI model. This signaling is responsible for a call's setup and disconnection using the D channel of an ISDN connection. Quite a few message commands exist, which can be viewed by using the `debug isdn q931` command. These messages include the following:

➤ Call setup

➤ Connect

➤ Release

➤ Cancel

➤ Status

➤ Disconnect

➤ User information

The q.931 signaling operates on the D channel, and the `debug isdn q931` command includes information on the reference flag, message types, and information elements.

Call Reference Flag Definitions and Message Types

The two reference flag values are 0 and 1. The reference flag value 0 indicates that this is a call from another oriSeantor. Reference flag value 1 indicates that this is a call to an originator.

The following are the three different message type values associated with the q.931 protocol:

➤ 0x05—Setup message type

➤ 0x45—Disconnect message type

➤ 0x7d—Status message type

Information Elements

When troubleshooting q.931 signaling at Layer 3, information elements are included in the output that can help identify problems. The following are some information elements and what they mean:

➤ 0x04—Bearer capability

➤ 0x2c—Keypad facility

➤ 0x6c—Calling party number

➤ 0x70—Called party number

➤ 0x3a—SPID

Call Setup Steps for q.931 Signaling

ISDN establishes a Layer 3 connection between the local ISDN router and the local service provider's switch over the D channel. The local service provider's switch establishes another connection to the remote switch, which in turn is responsible for setting up a call to the remote ISDN router.

Before you look at the output from `debug isdn q931` command, review the following to get an understanding of some of the pieces of the output and what they mean:

➤ ALERT—An alert from the remote TE to the local TE with a ring-back signal.

➤ SETUP—The SETUP process sends information for the connection between the local TE and the remote TE.

➤ Call Proceeding (CALL_PROC)—A call-proceeding signal between the ET and the TE.

➤ CONNECT—The remote TE acknowledges a call and stops the local ring-back process.

➤ Connect Acknowledgment (CONNECT_ACK)—An acknowledgment of the remote exchange termination point to the remote Terminal Equipment indicating the setup is complete.

The following is the output of the `debug isdn q931` command:

```
Seans804# debug isdn q931
ISDN Q931 packets debugging is on
12:13:324523: ISDN BR0: RX <- STATUS_ENQ pd = 8 callref = 0x82
12:13:47: ISDN BR0: TX -> STATUS pd = 8  callref = 0x02
12:13:47: Cause i = 0x809E - Response to STATUS
 ENQUIRY or number unassigned
12:13:47: Call State i = 0x0A
12:13:3246744: ISDN BR0: RX <- STATUS_ENQ pd = 8 callref = 0x06
12:13:47: ISDN BR0: TX ->  STATUS pd = 8  callref = 0x86
12:13:47: Cause i = 0x809E - Response to STATUS
 ENQUIRY or number unassigned
12:13:47: Call State i = 0x0A
12:13:3246951: ISDN BR0: RX <- STATUS_ENQ pd = 8 callref = 0x82
12:13:47: ISDN BR0: TX ->  STATUS pd = 8  callref = 0x02
12:13:47: Cause i = 0x809E - Response to STATUS
 ENQUIRY or number unassigned
12:13:49: Call State i = 0x0A
12:13:3247341: ISDN BR0: RX <- STATUS_ENQ pd = 8 callref = 0x06
12:13:49: ISDN BR0: TX ->  STATUS pd = 8  callref = 0x86
12:13:49: Cause i = 0x809E - Response to STATUS
ENQUIRY or number unassigned
12:13:49: Call State i = 0x0A
12:13:3248465: ISDN BR0: RX <- DISCONNECT pd = 8 callref = 0x82
12:13:3248465: Cause i = 0x8290 - Normal call    clearing
```

```
12:13:3248465: Signal i = 0x3F - Tones off
12:13:49: %ISDN-6-DISCONNECT:
Interface BRI0:1 disconnected from 18005551001
To p, call lasted 120 seconds
12:13:49: %LINK-3-UPDOWN: Interface BRI0:1, changed state to down
12:13:49: ISDN BR0: TX -> RELEASE pd = 8  callref = 0x02
12:13:3248465: ISDN BR0: RX <- RELEASE_COMP pd = 8 callref = 0x82
12:13:3248465: %ISDN-6-DISCONNECT:
Interface BRI0:2 disconnected from 8358 663, call lasted 120 seconds
12:13:49: ISDN BR0: TX -> DISCONNECT pd = 8  callref = 0x86
12:13:49: Cause i = 0x8090 - Normal call clearing
12:13:3248465: ISDN BR0: RX <- RELEASE pd = 8 callref = 0x06
12:13:49: %LINK-3-UPDOWN: Interface BRI0:2, changed state to down
12:13:49: ISDN BR0: TX ->
RELEASE_COMP pd = 8  callref =   0x86
12:13:50: %LINEPROTO-5-UPDOWN: Line protocol on Interface
BRI0:1, changed state to down
12:13:50: %LINEPROTO-5-UPDOWN: Line protocol on Interface
BRI0:2, changed state to down
```

The above debug output shows the complete q.931 process, from activating the interface, sending the data, and then disconnecting.

Correct Switch Types

ISDN uses a connection between the ISDN router and the phone company's central office switch. Both sides of the connection must be configured with the same switch type. If the switch types are different, it is like putting two people in the same room who speak different languages. The isdn switch-type command can be used in both the global and interface configuration modes. The following output from the help command lists the different switch types that are supported on the Cisco 804 ISDN router:

```
Seans804(config)# isdn switch-type ?
  basic-1tr6    1TR6 switch type for Germany
  basic-5ess    AT&T 5ESS switch type for the U.S.
  basic-dms100  Northern DMS-100 switch type
  basic-net3    NET3 switch type for UK and Europe
  basic-ni      National ISDN switch type
  basic-ts013   TS013 switch type for Australia
  ntt           NTT switch type for Japan
  vn3           VN3 and VN4 switch types for France
```

You can use the isdn autodetect command to automatically detect the switch type if you do not know the correct switching type.

Many routers don't support the auto-detect feature, but it is supported on the Cisco 804 router, most ISDN routers, and most routers with BRI modules so long as the IOS version you install supports it. The switch type is only specific to the local loop switch, and not on the remote side of the connection, which can use a completely different switch type.

ISDN Troubleshooting Commands to Know

For the exam there are a few other commands that you need to know and understand. Here are some commands you'll need to know that haven't been covered elsewhere in the chapter:

➤ clear interface bri

➤ debug bri

➤ debug dialer

➤ show controller bri

➤ show dialer

The following sections discuss these commands in detail.

The **clear interface bri** Command

The clear interface bri command followed by the BRI interface number resets the ISDN counters that are available on an ISDN interface. This will also terminate any active connection on an ISDN interface. As the following example indicates, the command has no output:

```
Seans804# clear int bri0
Seans804#
```

The **debug bri** Command

The debug bri command provides information, such as bandwidth, about the B channels used in a BRI interface.

A router can still connect if only one B channel fails. If this occurs, check for a mis-configured SPID or other interface configuration issue.

The following output demonstrates the command in action:

```
Seans804# debug bri
Basic Rate network interface debugging is on
Seans804# ping 172.16.1.2
Type escape sequence to abort.
```

```
Sending 5, 100-byte ICMP Echos to 172.16.1.2, timeout is 2 seconds:
00:29:48: BRI: enable channel B1
00:29:48: BRI0:MC145572 state handler current state 3 actions 1 next state 3
00:29:48: BRI0:Starting activation
00:29:48: %LINK-3-UPDOWN: Interface BRI0:1, changed state to up.
00:29:49: BRI 0 B1: Set bandwidth to 64Kb
00:29:50: %LINEPROTO-5-UPDOWN: Line protocol on Interface
BRI0:1, changed state to up
00:29:50: BRI 0 B2: Set bandwidth to 64Kb
00:29:50: BRI: enable channel B2
00:29:50: BRI0:MC145572 state handler current state 3 actions 1 next state 3
00:29:50: BRI0:Starting activation
00:29:50: %LINK-3-UPDOWN: Interface BRI0:2, changed state to up.!!!
Success rate is 60 percent (3/5), round-trip min/avg/max = 36/41/52 ms
00:29:50: BRI: enable channel B2
00:29:50: BRI0:MC145572 state handler current state 3 actions 1 next state 3
00:29:50: BRI0:Starting activation
00:29:50: BRI 0 B2: Set bandwidth to 64Kb
00:29:51: %LINEPROTO-5-UPDOWN: Line protocol on Interface
BRI0:2, changed state to up
```

The A and B channels are used to carry the data across the active link. Any error on an activates B channel will prevent the flow of data. The above output shows a successful ISDN data transfer.

The **debug dialer** Command

The debug dialer command can be used to show information regarding the cause of a dialing connection problem. The following is an example of using the command:

```
Seans804# debug dialer
Dial on demand events debugging is on
Seans804#ping 172.16.1.1
Type escape sequence to abort.
Sending 5, 100-byte ICMP Echos to 172.16.1.1, timeout is 2 seconds:
00:36:15: BRI0: Dialing cause ip (s=172.16.1.2, d=172.16.1.1)
00:36:15: BRI0: Attempting to dial 18005551001
00:36:15: %LINK-3-UPDOWN: Interface BRI0:1, changed state to up.
00:36:15: dialer Protocol up for BR0:1
00:36:15: %LINEPROTO-5-UPDOWN: Line protocol on Interface
BRI0:1, changed state to up
00:36:15: %LINK-3-UPDOWN: Interface BRI0:2, changed state to up.
!!!!!
Success rate is 100 percent(5/5),
            round-trip min/avg/max=32/37/48/23/33 ms
00:36:15: dialer Protocol up for BR0:2
00:36:15: %LINEPROTO-5-UPDOWN: Line protocol on Interface
BRI0:2, changed state to up
```

The debug dialer command output above shows the complete process the dialer takes when an ICMP ping is the interesting traffic activating the ISDN BRI interface.

The **show controller bri** Command

The show controller bri command displays the interface hardware controller information. This command is most useful when troubleshooting with Cisco's TAC, obtaining the status of an interface, and obtaining the superframe error counter information. The following is the output from this command:

```
Sean804# show controller bri
BRI unit 0:BRI unit 0 with U interface and POTS:
Layer 1 internal state is ACTIVATED
Layer 1 U interface is ACTIVATED.
ISDN Line Information:
    Current EOC commands:
        RTN - Return to normal
    Received overhead bits:
        AIB=1, UOA=1, SCO=1, DEA=1, ACT=1, M50=1, M51=1, M60=1, FEBE=1
    Errors:  [FEBE]=0, [NEBE]=0
    Errors:  [Superframe Sync Loss]=0, [IDL2 Data    Transparency Loss]=0
             [M4 ACT 1 -> 0]=0
BRI U MLT Timers:  [TPULSE]=0, [T75S]=0
BRI U MLT Timers:  [TPULSE]=0, [T75S]=0
Motorola MC145572 registers:
NR0  = 0      NR1  = 4      NR2  = 0      NR3  = 0      NR4  = E      NR5  = 6
BR0  = F7     BR1  = 7F     BR2  = F0     BR3  = 40     BR4  = 0      BR5  = 0
BR6  = 0      BR7  = 1      BR8  = 1      BR9  = C      BR10 = 0      BR11 = C
BR12 = 0      BR13 = 0      BR14 = 0      BR15 = 46
OR0  = 0      OR1  = 4      OR2  = 8      OR3  = 0      OR4  = 4      OR5  = 8
OR6  = E0     OR7  = 11     OR8  = 0      OR9  = 0
D Channel Information:
Using SCC3, Microcode ver 101
idb at 0x272BF38, driver data structure at 0x273FB90
SCC Registers:
General [GSMR]=0x780:0x0000003A, Protocol-specific [PSMR]=0x0
Events [SCCE]=0x0000, Mask [SCCM]=0x001F, Status [SCCS]=0x0002
Transmit on Demand [TODR]=0x0, Data Sync [DSR]=0x7E7E
Interrupt Registers:
Config [CICR]=0x00368481, Pending [CIPR]=0x00000640
Mask   [CIMR]=0x30061090, In-srv  [CISR]=0x00000000
Command register [CR]=0xE84
Port A [PADIR]=0x08C3, [PAPAR]=0x07CC
       [PAODR]=0x0040, [PADAT]=0x0FCF
Port B [PBDIR]=0x00E02E, [PBPAR]=0x0020DE
       [PBODR]=0x000000, [PBDAT]=0x0053CF
Port C [PCDIR]=0x000C, [PCPAR]=0x0800
       [PCSO]=0x00C0,  [PCDAT]=0x0433, [PCINT]=0x0000
Port D [PDDIR]=0x001FFF, [PDPAR]=0x000000
       [PDDAT]=0x001FFB
SI     [SIMODE]=0x00001141,  [SIGMR]=0x04, [SISTR]=0x00
       [SICR]=0x00403500
BRGC   [BRGC2]=0x000101A8,  [BRGC3]=0x00000000
SPI Mode [SPMODE]=0x3771, Events [SPIE]=0x0
    Mask [SPIM]=0x0, Command [SPCOM]=0x0
SI Mode [SIMODE]=0x1141, Global [SIGMR]=0x4
    Cmnd [SICMR]=0x0, Stat [SISTR]=0x0
SI Clock Route [SICR]=0x00403500
<Some Output Cut>
```

```
0 missed datagrams, 0 overruns
0 bad datagram encapsulations, 0 memory errors
0 transmitter underruns
```

The **show dialer** Command

The `show dialer` command displays information about DDR connections. The output from this command follows:

```
Seans804# show dialer
BRI0 - dialer type = ISDN
Dial String      Successes    Failures    Last called    Last status
18005551001             2           6       00:03:36       successful
8 incoming call(s) have been screened.
0 incoming call(s) rejected for callback.
BRI0:1 - dialer type = ISDN
Idle timer (120 secs), Fast idle timer (20 secs)
Wait for carrier (30 secs), Re-enable (15 secs)
Dialer state is idle
BRI0:2 - dialer type = ISDN
Idle timer (120 secs), Fast idle timer (20 secs)
Wait for carrier (30 secs), Re-enable (15 secs)
Dialer state is idle
```

The output above shows the phone number dialed, connection successes, idle timers, and the number of calls that were accepted or rejected due to an administrative policy configuration.

Chapter Summary

This chapter focused on configuration and troubleshooting issues related to ISDN, its physical cabling, and its related protocols. After reading this chapter, you should understand the common issues confronting administrators in ISDN networks, ISDN encapsulation, and how to use SPIDs. You also have learned about the ISDN connection process, including how to identify interesting data traffic and the protocols used in ISDN.

This chapter covered much of what you need to know to answer exam questions on the topic of troubleshooting ISDN connections. Pay particular attention to the router configurations that were discussed. And remember that when trying to diagnose an ISDN problem, you should consider faulty physical cabling, incorrect telephone company switch configurations, and protocol issues such as q.921 and q.931 signaling.

Exam Prep Practice Questions

Question 1

CHAP requires which of the following to be configured? [Choose the two best answers.]

☐ A. Telnet

☐ B. Virtual Private Networking

☐ C. Username

☐ D. The secret password on the router

☐ E. PPP

Answer: **C, E.** CHAP requires PPP and the username to be configured to allow for authentication.

Question 2

Which ISDN command will bring up the second B channel when the first has reached a load of approximately 50 percent?

○ A. **isdn load-balance 50**

○ B. **isdn dialer load-threshold 50**

○ C. **dialer load-threshold 125**

○ D. **load 50 start**

Answer: **C.** The `dialer load-threshold 125` command will bring up the second B channel when the first reaches approximately 50 percent load. The command will accept a value of 1 to 255, with 1 being the lowest load and 255 being 100 percent load.

Question 3

To verify all three layers of an ISDN circuit prior to dialing, an administrator should use which of the following commands?

- ○ A. **show ppp multilink**
- ○ B. **debug ppp**
- ○ C. **debug bri**
- ○ D. **show run**
- ○ E. **show isdn status**

Answer: **E**. The show isdn status command provides the connection status of all three layers, as well as calls in progress.

Question 4

Which of the following is a valid North American SPID?

- ○ A. 172.16.1.1
- ○ B. 800.555.1.002
- ○ C. 300.106
- ○ D. 5551002
- ○ E. 91655510020100

Answer: **E**. The SPID is the complete phone number, including the area code, plus a 4-digit value added to the 7-digit dialer number, without punctuation. Some service providers add an additional two digit prefix to the number. However, the only valid answer above would be E.

Question 5

If you have a newly configured router and an ISDN call succeeds, but pings and other packets fail, which of the following can be the cause? [Choose all that apply.]

- ❑ A. CHAP misconfiguration
- ❑ B. PPP is not enabled
- ❑ C. Incorrect line speeds are configured
- ❑ D. Static routes are incorrectly configured
- ❑ E. A faulty cable

Answer: **A, B, C,** and **D.** All of these causes are possibilities and should be checked. **E** is incorrect, because if the cable were faulty, the call would not succeed.

Question 6

If an ISDN router will not dial, which of the following is the likely problem? [Choose all that apply.]

- ❏ A. Misconfigured SPID
- ❏ B. A dialer list filter
- ❏ C. Incorrect switch type
- ❏ D. Power problem
- ❏ E. Misconfigured dialer map
- ❏ F. All of the above

Answer: **F.** All of these are possible causes of why the router will not dial.

Question 7

Which of the following are advantages of using CHAP authentication? [Choose the two best answers.]

- ❏ A. Password authentication
- ❏ B. Password encryption
- ❏ C. Compression and encryption of data packets
- ❏ D. Virtual LANs are attached to ISDN switched connections

Answer: **A, B.** CHAP is used for password authentication, and encrypts the password for more secure connections.

Question 8

Which of the following two command prompts can execute the **isdn switch-type** command?

- ❏ A. User mode command prompt
- ❏ B. Privilege EXEC Mode command prompt
- ❏ C. Global configuration mode command prompt
- ❏ D. Interface configuration mode command prompt

Answer: **C, D**. You can use the `isdn switch-type` command in the global or interface configuration modes.

Question 9

ISDN Basic Rate Interface (BRI) provides which of the following?

○ A. Two 64Kbps B channels and one 16Kbps D channel

○ B. Total bit rate of up to 768Kbps

○ C. Two 56Kbps B channels for data

○ D. 10Mbps on two channels and a third for control using 192Kbps

Answer: **A**. ISDN BRI provides B channels for data (64Kbps each) and one D channel (16Kbps) for clocking and control.

Question 10

Which one of the following ISDN-specific protocols is used to establish a Layer 2 connection?

○ A. q.921

○ B. PPP

○ C. CHAP

○ D. q.931

○ E. Ethernet

Answer: **A**. The q.921 protocol is used for Layer 2 connections. CHAP and PPP are not specific to ISDN. Ethernet is a Layer 1 topology, and q.931 is used for call connection establishment at Layer 3.

Question 11

On certain routers, if the switch type is unknown, which one of the following commands should you use?

○ A. **isdn switch-type 0**

○ B. **isdn auto switch-type**

○ C. **config switch-type auto**

○ D. **isdn switch-type all**

○ E. **isdn autodetect**

Answer: **E.** The `isdn autodetect` command instructs the router to detect the switch type. The other commands are all invalid commands.

Need to Know More?

 Glauser, Fred, and Eric Quinn. *CCNP BCRAN Exam Cram 2*, 2003, Que, ISBN: 0-7897-3020-0.

 Flanagan, William A. *ISDN: A Practical Guide To Getting Up And Running*, 2000, CMP Books, ISBN: 1578200482.

 ISDN Tutorial: `http://www.ralphb.net/ISDN/`

Practice Exam 1

In this chapter and Chapter 15, you have an opportunity to practice the skills you've gained while working through the preceding chapters of this book. The practice exam in this chapter offers 60 questions that draw upon the same body of knowledge you'll be tested on when you take the Internet Troubleshooting Support Exam (CIT 642-831). In Chapter 14, you'll find the answer key to this test; the answer explanations for the second practice exam appear in chapter 16.

Questions, Questions, Questions

There should be no doubt in your mind that you are facing a test full of specific and pointed questions. As mentioned in Chapter 1, "Overview of Cisco Certification," if you take a fixed-length version of the actual exam, it will include 55–65 questions, and you will be allotted 75 minutes to complete the exam.

On the actual examination, questions will belong to one of five basic types:

➤ Multiple choice with a single answer

➤ Multiple choice with multiple answers

➤ Multipart with a single answer

➤ Multipart with multiple answers

➤ Simulations where you click on a GUI screen capture to simulate using the Cisco Troubleshooting interface

The exams in this book can include any of the first four question types listed. In this practice exam, as in the actual exam, you should always take the time to read a question at least twice before selecting an answer. Not every question has only one answer; some require multiple answers. Therefore, you should read each question carefully, determine how many answers are necessary or possible, and look for additional hints or instructions when selecting answers. Questions which may have multiple correct answers will instruct you to "Choose all that apply," and answer choices will be preceded by squares rather than circles.

Choosing the Correct Answers

Obviously, the only way to pass any exam is to select enough of the right answers to obtain a passing score. However, Cisco's exams are not standardized like the SAT and GRE exams; they are far more convoluted. In some cases, questions are strangely worded, and deciphering them can be a real challenge. In those cases, you may need to rely on answer-elimination skills. Almost always, at least one answer out of the possible choices for a question can be eliminated immediately because it matches one of these conditions:

➤ The answer does not apply to the situation.

➤ The answer describes a nonexistent issue, an invalid option, or an imaginary state.

➤ The answer may be eliminated because of information in the question itself.

After you eliminate all answers that are obviously wrong, you can apply your retained knowledge to eliminate further answers. Look for items that sound correct but refer to actions, commands, or features that are not present or not available in the situation that the question describes.

If you're still faced with a blind guess between two or more potentially correct answers, reread the question. Try to picture how each of the possible remaining answers would alter the situation. *Be especially sensitive to terminology*; sometimes the choice of words ("remove" instead of "disable") can make the difference between a right answer and a wrong one.

Only when you've exhausted your ability to eliminate answers but remain unclear about which of the remaining possibilities is correct should you guess at an answer. An unanswered question offers you no points, but guessing gives you at least some chance of getting a question right; just don't be too hasty when making a blind guess.

Tips for Success

Chapter 1 includes a wealth of information to help you prepare for the exam. You may want to reread that chapter before proceeding with this practice exam. But for now, keep these tips in mind:

➤ Questions often give away their answers, but you have to be Sherlock Holmes to see the clues. Often, subtle hints appear in the question text in such a way that they seem almost irrelevant to the situation. You must realize that each question is a test unto itself and that you need to inspect and successfully navigate each question to pass the exam. Look for small clues, such as the mention of times, group permissions and names, and configuration settings.

➤ The test questions appear in random order, and many elements or issues that are mentioned in one question may also crop up in other questions. It's not uncommon to find that an incorrect answer to one question is the correct answer to another question, or vice versa. Take the time to read every answer to each question, even if you recognize the correct answer to a question immediately. That extra reading may spark a memory, or remind you about a Cisco troubleshooting feature or function, that helps you on another question elsewhere in the exam.

➤ If you see something in a question or in one of the answers that jogs your memory on a topic, or that you feel you should record if the topic appears in another question, write it down on your piece of paper. Just because you can't go back to a question in an adaptive test doesn't mean you can't take notes on what you see early in the test, in hopes that it might help you later in the test.

Don't be afraid to take notes on what you see in various questions. Sometimes, what you record from one question can help you on other questions later on, especially if it's not as familiar as it should be or it reminds you of the name or use of some utility or interface details.

➤ Give yourself 75 minutes to take the exam, and keep yourself on the honor system--don't look at earlier text in the book or jump ahead to the answer key. When your time is up or you've finished the questions, you can check your work in Chapter 14. Pay special attention to the explanations for the incorrect answers; these can also help to reinforce your knowledge of the material. Knowing how to recognize correct answers is good, but understanding why incorrect answers are wrong can be equally valuable.

➤ Set a maximum time limit for questions, and watch your time on long or complex questions. If you hit your limit, it's time to guess and move on. Don't deprive yourself of the opportunity to see more questions by taking too long to puzzle over questions, unless you think you can figure out the answer. Otherwise, you're limiting your opportunities to pass.

That's it for pointers. Now, it's time to take the practice exam. Good luck!

Question 1

You are interested in creating excellent and detailed network configuration documentation in order to quickly learn specific information about network devices during troubleshooting sessions. Which of the following are valid guidelines defined by Cisco for creating effective network documentation? Choose all that apply.

❑ A. Determine the scope

❑ B. Maintain the documentation

❑ C. Be consistent

❑ D. Know your objective

❑ E. Document all obtainable parameters

❑ F. Keep the documents accessible

❑ G. Only document physical interfaces

Question 2

Which of the following elements would you expect to see in a network configuration table for a Layer 2 switch? Choose all that apply.

❑ A. Management IP address

❑ B. Address

❑ C. Speed

❑ D. Duplex

❑ E. Interface Name

❑ F. VLAN

❑ G. Routing protocol

Question 3

Which of the following elements would you expect to see in a network configuration table for an end-system (workstation)? Choose all that apply.

❑ A. Device Name (Purpose)

❑ B. DNS Server Address

❑ C. Network Applications

❑ D. VLAN

❑ E. Interface Name

❑ F. IP Address/Subnet Mask

❑ G. Trunk mode

Question 4

You are attempting to gather network information from your Windows-based end-system. Which command should you use to display IP information?

○ A. **route print**

○ B. **tracert –d**

○ C. **ipconfig /all**

○ D. **arp –a**

○ E. **ping**

○ F. **ifconfig -a**

Question 5

You are attempting to gather network information from your Unix-based end-system. Which command should you use to display IP information?

○ A. **ifconfig –a**

○ B. **traceroute**

○ C. **route –n**

○ D. **arp -1**

○ E. **ping**

○ F. **ipconfig /all**

Question 6

You are troubleshooting a standard switch in your enterprise network. Which layers of the logical network model pertain to this device? Choose all that apply.

❑ A. Physical

❑ B. Application

❑ C. Network

❏ D. Data Link

❏ E. Transport

❏ F. Session

❏ G. Presentation

Question 7

You are following the general troubleshooting process recommended by Cisco Systems. What step should you perform following the gathering of symptoms?

○ A. Isolate the problem

○ B. Correct the problem

○ C. Document the solution

○ D. Reverse any changes that did not correct the problem

Question 8

You are engaged in the process of gathering symptoms from a network in order to troubleshoot a problem. You have determined that the problem is within your boundary of control. What should you do next?

○ A. Document the symptoms

○ B. Document the solution

○ C. Determine the symptoms

○ D. Narrow the scope

Question 9

You are troubleshooting a complex problem in your network. You begin troubleshooting by immediately using ICMP-related commands in order to begin your troubleshooting steps. What troubleshooting approach are you using?

○ A. Divide and Conquer

○ B. Top-Down

○ C. Bottom-Up

○ D. Logical Hierarchy

Question 10

You are troubleshooting a complex problem in your network and you begin by executing a **show ip route** command. Next you engage in a **show cdp neighbors** command followed by several application layer tests. What troubleshooting approach are you using?

○ A. Divide and Conquer

○ B. Top-Down

○ C. Bottom-Up

○ D. Logical Hierarchy

Question 11

Which of the following are valid guidelines for selecting an effective troubleshooting approach according to Cisco Systems? Choose all that apply.

❑ A. Analyze the symptoms

❑ B. Determine the scope of the problem

❑ C. Apply your experience

❑ D. Document the problem

Question 12

Which of the following is not a common symptom of a Physical layer problem?

○ A. Framing errors

○ B. Line coding errors

○ C. Synchronization errors

○ D. Address resolution errors

Question 13

Which of the following is not a common symptom of a Data Link layer problem?

○ A. The link is functional, but is operating either consistently or intermittently less than the baseline level

○ B. No connectivity on the link as seen from the network layer

○ C. Address resolution errors

○ D. Increased number of interface errors

Question 14

You are interested in using the **ping** command in order to troubleshoot your Cisco internetwork. From what modes is the **ping** command available? Choose all that apply.

❑ A. User

❑ B. Global configuration

❑ C. Privileged

❑ D. Line configuration mode

Question 15

You have issued the **show interfaces** command on your Cisco router and you have received the following indication:

```
Ethernet0/0 is up, line protocol is down
```

What is the most common reason for this output?

○ A. There is a problem at the Physical layer for the interface

○ B. There is a problem at the Data Link layer for the interface

○ C. The interface has been administratively disabled

○ D. The interface is not CDP enabled and this is required in the current configuration

Question 16

Which of the following Cisco commands, used to isolate Physical layer problems in the network, allows you to verify the cable type in use on a serial interface?

○ A. **show version**

○ B. **show ip interfaces**

○ C. **show ip interface brief**

○ D. **show controllers**

Question 17

You need to access the IP address of a neighboring device so that you can tel-net to the device and make some configuration changes. Which of the following commands helps you obtain the IP address?

- ○ A. **show cdp neighbors**
- ○ B. **show cdp neighbor detail**
- ○ C. **show controllers**
- ○ D. **show cdp ip interface brief**

Question 18

You are working on a Sun Solaris end system and you would like to see the rout-ing table information on this system. You do not want DNS lookups to be per-formed in order to prepare the output. What command should you use?

- ○ A. **ping –rt**
- ○ B. **arp –a**
- ○ C. **show ip arp –n**
- ○ D. **netstat –rn**

Question 19

You are working with a Windows Millennium Edition end system. You are trou-bleshooting network connectivity and you need to verify the IP configuration in place on the device. You need the most detailed information possible. What command should you use?

- ○ A. **ipconfig**
- ○ B. **ipconfig /all**
- ○ C. **tracert –d**
- ○ D. **winipcfg**

Question 20

You are using the **debug frame-relay lmi** command in order to troubleshoot your Frame Relay network. You are analyzing the full status message output from this command. You notice that the status indication is 0x02. What does this indicate?

○ A. Added/inactive

○ B. Added/active

○ C. Deleted

○ D. New/inactive

○ E. New/active

Question 21

You initiate a **show interfaces** command on your router to view information about your Fast Ethernet interfaces. One of the interfaces features a rapidly incrementing late collisions counter. What is the most likely cause of this error?

○ A. A poorly seated cable

○ B. A duplex mismatch

○ C. An encapsulation mismatch

○ D. An administratively downed interface

Question 22

Which of the following is not a Cisco guideline for isolating problems at the Physical and Data Link layers?

○ A. Check for correct cable pin-out

○ B. Verify proper interface configurations

○ C. Check operational status and data error rates

○ D. Test connectivity at each hop of a path

○ E. Check for bad cables or connections

Question 23

You are troubleshooting Network layer problems in your enterprise network. You need to stop the transmission of routing updates out a particular interface due to WAN issues. You still need to receive updates on the interface, however. What command would you use in this situation?

○ A. **no ip split-horizon**

○ B. **ip split-horizon**

○ C. **passive-interface**

○ D. **no ip route**

Question 24

You are troubleshooting Layer 3 issues in your enterprise network. You are at an end system in the engineering department and you need to release the DHCP information that the client currently possesses. The client operating system in use is Windows XP Professional. What commands/steps should you use?

○ A. Start, Control Panel, Network Settings, Properties, Release

○ B. **winipcfg**

○ C. **ipconfig /release**

○ D. **nslookup**

Question 25

You are troubleshooting Layer 3 issues in your enterprise network. You would like to view the routing update information as it is received on your local router. What command should you use in order to accomplish this?

○ A. **show ip routing**

○ B. **debug ip events**

○ C. **debug ip packets**

○ D. **debug ip routing**

○ E. **debug routing**

Question 26

You are troubleshooting your enterprise network at Layer 3 and you are follow-ing the procedures outlined by Cisco for correcting problems at this layer. What should you do after you make your initial configuration changes?

○ A. Verify that you have a saved configuration for any device that is to be modified

○ B. Evaluate and document the results of each change that you make

○ C. Verify that the changes you made actually fixed the problem without introducing new problems

○ D. Continue making changes until the problem appears solved

○ E. Fully document the symptoms that led to the configuration changes

Question 27

You are troubleshooting problems at the Transport and Application layers in your enterprise network. You would like to check if a particular access list is applied to an interface. What command should you use?

○ A. **show running-config | begin ip access-list extended ListName**

○ B. **show ip route**

○ C. **show access-lists**

○ D. **show logging**

○ E. **show ip interface**

○ F. **show running-config | begin interfaces**

Question 28

You are troubleshooting your enterprise network at the Application layer. You are following the guidelines as prescribed by Cisco. What is your first step?

○ A. Establish whether IP connectivity exists between the source and desti-nation

○ B. Test the sending and receiving email functions separately

○ C. Check the RFCs to find out detailed information about a malfunctioning transport layer protocol

○ D. Document the symptoms discovered

○ E. Check the patch levels of the malfunctioning application

Question 29

You are troubleshooting Transport and Application layer problems in your Cisco network. What command do you enter at a Unix end-system in order to quickly find the address of the name server?

- ○ A. **tcptrace**
- ○ B. **nslookup**
- ○ C. **winipcfg**
- ○ D. **ipconfig**
- ○ E. **ttcp**
- ○ F. **ifconfig**

Question 30

You are attempting to isolate problems that your organization is currently experiencing with email transmissions. What command should you use in order to troubleshoot problems with SMTP?

- ○ A. **telnet {ip address} 25**
- ○ B. **telnet {ip address} 110**
- ○ C. **copy flash tftp**
- ○ D. **debug smtp events**
- ○ E. **ping**

Question 31

You are troubleshooting your Cisco network and you discover that an access list is created correctly but the access list is not applied properly to an interface. What command do you use to apply an access list to an interface?

- ○ A. **access-list**
- ○ B. **access-list apply**
- ○ C. **ip access-group**
- ○ D. **access-group**
- ○ E. **access-list group**

Question 32

You need to apply a read-write community string to your Cisco router. What is the correct command to make this configuration change?

○ A. **snmp-server community rw {string}**

○ B. **snmp-server password rw {string}**

○ C. **snmp-server {string} rw**

○ D. **snmp-community {string} rw**

○ E. **snmp-community rw {string}**

Question 33

You are troubleshooting your Cisco network and you need to place a call to TAC for assistance. You have determined that the problem is restricted to just three routers in your environment. What command should you use on these three routers?

○ A. **copy flash tftp**

○ B. **copy startup-config tftp**

○ C. **show tech**

○ D. **show ip int brief**

○ E. **show version**

Question 34

You would like to configure your Cisco gear so that unsolicited network management alarms are sent when a particular threshold is reached. What configuration command should you use?

○ A. **ip http accounting**

○ B. **snmp-server enable traps**

○ C. **ip helper-address**

○ D. **service dhcp**

○ E. **enable snmp traps**

Question 35

You are troubleshooting Transport and Application layer problems in your Cisco network. You have backed up your configurations and you have made initial configuration changes. You have evaluated the results and documented each change. What should you do next if you are following the Cisco procedure?

○ A. Get input from outside resources

○ B. Document the solution

○ C. Verify that the changes you made fixed the problem without introducing new problems

○ D. Restore the original configurations on all devices

○ E. Explore possible causes of symptoms

Question 36

You are using Cisco's recommendations for the creation of network configuration documentation. Which stage of this process most likely involves the use of the **show cdp neighbor** command?

○ A. Log In

○ B. Document

○ C. Transfer

○ D. Device Discovery

○ E. Device Topology Documentation

Question 37

You are troubleshooting ISDN in your Cisco network. Which Cisco IOS command provides the quickest summary indication of the three ISDN layers?

○ A. **show isdn summary**

○ B. **show isdn layers**

○ C. **show isdn status**

○ D. **show interface | begin isdn**

○ E. **show isdn network summary**

Question 38

You suspect the problem in your Cisco network resides with name resolution issues between Layers 2 and 3. What Cisco IOS command should you use to verify proper name resolution?

- ○ A. **show ip hosts**
- ○ B. **show ip route**
- ○ C. **show ip interface**
- ○ D. **show ip arp**
- ○ E. **show dns entries**

Question 39

You are troubleshooting the Frame Relay network in your organization. You need to verify the association between the DLCI and IP address. Which command displays information about this association?

- ○ A. **show frame-relay**
- ○ B. **show frame-relay map**
- ○ C. **show frame relay dlci**
- ○ D. **show frame-relay counters**
- ○ E. **show arp**

Question 40

You would like to set the datagram size as well as the repeat count for a ping test that you are performing in your Cisco network. Which statements below are true about this test? Choose all that apply.

- ❏ A. The test must be performed in privileged mode
- ❏ B. The test may be performed in user mode or privileged mode
- ❏ C. Type **ping** to initiate the test
- ❏ D. espond with Yes at the Extended Command prompt
- ❏ E. This particular ping test is not possible

Question 41

You are troubleshooting your Cisco network. You want to verify that problems in your network are not due to DNS. How can you do this in the quickest manner possible?

○ A. By examining the routing table entries

○ B. By examining the router's configuration

○ C. By using IP addresses rather than names

○ D. By checking for obsolete address resolution entries

○ E. By using **ping** or **trace** to verify the communication path

○ F. By pinging the fully qualified domain name of the DNS server

Question 42

Which command displays the flow of IP packets transmitted between local and remote hosts?

○ A. **show ip access**

○ B. **debug ip packet**

○ C. **show ip buffers**

○ D. **debug ip traffic**

○ E. **show ip transmitted**

○ F. **show ip protocols**

Question 43

You are considering the **debug arp** command while you are troubleshooting Layer 2 issues in your Cisco network. What can you use this command for?

○ A. To display the ARP cache contents

○ B. To show the flow of active routing packets

○ C. To send an ARP request to all attached routing neighbors

○ D. To determine whether the router is sending and receiving ARP requests/relies

○ E. To enable ARP on the Cisco router

Question 44

You are troubleshooting Frame Relay in your Cisco network. What is the default configuration for the LMI type in 12.0 Cisco IOS versions?

○ A. Q933a

○ B. ANSI

○ C. Cisco

○ D. Auto-detect

○ E. IETF

Question 45

You are investigating the system error messaging capabilities of your Cisco equipment. Where is the output of debug and system error messages sent by default?

○ A. Output is written to a Syslog server

○ B. Output is sent to the console terminal

○ C. Output is sent to a TFTP server

○ D. Output is sent to a buffer

○ E. Output is sent to a remote terminal

Question 46

You are investigating the system error messaging capabilities of your Cisco equipment. Which error logging method produces the least overhead?

○ A. Log on alert only

○ B. Logging to the console

○ C. Logging to a Syslog server

○ D. Logging to an internal buffer

○ E. Logging to a remote terminal

Question 47

You need to access network protocol addresses in order to ping and telnet to Cisco devices. Which command should you use to obtain this information from Cisco devices across a data link?

○ A. **show interfaces detail**

○ B. **debug ip packet detail**

○ C. **show controller detail**

○ D. **show ip protocol details**

○ E. **show cdp neighbors detail**

○ F. **show cdp ip**

Question 48

You are using the following Cisco IOS command to assist in troubleshooting your network:

```
show interface serial 0/0
```

One status field in the output from this command is the number of interface resets. Which situation is not a cause for a complete interface reset?

○ A. A problem with the synchronous clocking signal

○ B. A problem with the Frame Relay switch or DSU/CSU

○ C. A hardware problem with the router interface or cable

○ D. Interface counters cleared

Question 49

Which of the following are Cisco guidelines for creating useful network configuration documentation? Choose all that apply.

❑ A. Use consistent symbols, terminology, and styles

❑ B. Know the scope of the documentation

❑ C. Update the documentation once every year

❑ D. Store the documents in a logical location

❑ E. Include all practical Layer 2 information available for the network in the documentation

Question 50

You are currently preparing network baseline information for your Cisco network. You are planning to create end-system network documentation in addition to network component documents. Which of the following lists components of a topology diagram related to end-systems only?

○ A. Trunk Status, PortFast, Subnet Mask

○ B. IP Address, Subnet Mask, STP State

○ C. MAC Address, Network Applications, IP Address

○ D. Duplex, Speed, State

○ E. Trunk Mode, IP Address, MAC Address, Default Gateway

Question 51

You are engaged in troubleshooting within your Cisco network and you are currently logged in to a Windows 2000 Professional end-system. Which command provides a list of all the active routes for a host?

○ A. **ipconfig /all**

○ B. **tracert**

○ C. **route print**

○ D. **telnet**

○ E. **traceroute**

○ F. **show ip route**

○ G. **show route**

Question 52

A user within your organization sends an email. Your Cisco network encapsulates the transmission beginning with Layer 7 of the OSI model. The transmission is now at a stage where the source system knows the port number of the destination computer, but the logical address remains unknown. At what layer of the OSI model does the data presently reside?

○ A. Layer 7

○ B. Layer 5

○ C. Layer 4

○ D. Layer 3

○ E. Layer 6

○ F. Layer 2

○ G. Layer 1

Question 53

Which phase of sending encapsulated data between two end systems involves an interface receiving data from a physical medium, removing the data control information, and converting the data as needed for use within a target application?

○ A. Origination

○ B. Transport

○ C. Forwarding

○ D. Terminating

○ E. Converting

○ F. Presenting

Question 54

Which of the following are valid steps in the general troubleshooting process as described by Cisco? Choose all that apply.

❏ A. Gather symptoms

❏ B. Clear all logs

❏ C. Isolate the problem

❏ D. Correct the problem

❏ E. Identify the scope

Question 55

While there are many possible approaches to troubleshooting, Cisco identifies several very popular and successful approaches. Which approach is encouraged by the Cisco IOS command set?

○ A. Bottom-up

○ B. Top-down

○ C. Divide and conquer

○ D. Scatter

Question 56

Which key network management area is not one of the ISO-defined functional areas of network management?

- O A. Fault management
- O B. Security management
- O C. Accounting management
- O D. Quality of service management
- O E. Configuration and name management

Question 57

Which type of device is commonly used to check STP, UTP, 10BaseT, and coax for near-end crosstalk and noise?

- O A. Cable tester
- O B. Breakout box
- O C. Volt-ohm meter
- O D. Protocol analyzer
- O E. Digital Multimeter

Question 58

You are studying protocol types as you prepare for a career in network troubleshooting. Which type of protocol requires an application to request retransmission of missing or corrupt packets?

- O A. Host-to-host
- O B. Connection-oriented
- O C. Client/server
- O D. Connectionless
- O E. Quality-of-service oriented

Question 59

You are studying protocol types as you prepare for a career in network troubleshooting. Which of the following is a valid advantage of a connectionless protocol?

○ A. Speed

○ B. Security

○ C. Enhanced auditing capabilities

○ D. No need for upper layer connections

Question 60

Which statement about the embedded RMON agent in Cisco Catalyst software is true?

○ A. Currently Cisco only supports RMON, not RMON2 groups

○ B. RMON is enabled by default

○ C. The embedded RMON agent allows the switch to monitor network traffic from all ports simultaneously at the Data Link layer of the OSI model without requiring a dedicated monitoring probe or network analyzer

○ D. The functions can monitor segments as long they use 10BaseT or 100BaseT

Answer Key 1

1. A, B, C, D, F	**21.** B	**41.** C
2. A, C, D, F	**22.** D	**42.** B
3. A, B, C, F	**23.** C	**43.** D
4. C	**24.** C	**44.** D
5. A	**25.** D	**45.** B
6. A, D	**26.** B	**46.** D
7. A	**27.** E	**47.** E
8. D	**28.** A	**48.** D
9. C	**29.** B	**49.** A, B, D
10. A	**30.** A	**50.** C
11. A, B, C	**31.** C	**51.** C
12. D	**32.** A	**52.** C
13. D	**33.** C	**53.** D
14. A, C	**34.** B	**54.** A, C, D, E
15. B	**35.** C	**55.** C
16. D	**36.** D	**56.** D
17. B	**37.** C	**57.** A
18. D	**38.** D	**58.** B
19. D	**39.** B	**59.** A
20. B	**40.** A, C	**60.** C

1. Answers A, B, C, D, and F are all correct. When creating documentation, you should determine the scope, maintain the documentation, be
consistent, know your objective, and keep the documents accessible.

Answer E is incorrect. You should only collect data that is relevant to
your objective—you should not attempt to document all obtainable
parameters. Answer G is also incorrect. Cisco does not recommend
documenting only physical interfaces.

2. Answers A, C, D, and F are all correct. Management IP address, speed,
duplex, and VLAN information is all expected for a Layer 2 switch
network configuration table.

Answers B and E are incorrect. IP Address and Interface Name are elements that you would expect to see in a network configuration table
for a router—not a switch. Answer G—routing protocol—is also
appropriate for a router network configuration table.

3. Answers A, B, C, and F are all correct. The Device name and purpose,
DNS server address, network applications, and IP address/subnet mask
information are all perfectly appropriate for a network configuration
table for an end system.

Answer D and E are incorrect. VLAN and Interface Name are more
appropriate for the network configuration table of a switch. Answer G
is incorrect. Trunk mode is appropriate for a switch network configuration table as well.

4. Answer C is correct. `ipconfig /all` displays IP information for hosts
running Windows NT/2000/XP.

Answer A allows you to view the routing table on Windows-based system. Answer B allows you to trace a path that packets take in the network. Answer D allows you to view the arp table, and answer E allows
you to test connectivity between two systems.

5. Answer A is correct. `ifconfig -a` displays IP information for Unix and
Mac OS hosts.

Answer B is incorrect. The `traceroute` command allows you to trace the
path packets take through an internetwork. Answer C is incorrect. The
`route` command displays routing table information. Answer D is incorrect. The `arp` command allows the viewing of Layer 2 to Layer 3
address information. Answer E is incorrect. Ping allows you to test
connectivity, not view all IP information. Answer F is incorrect.
`Ipconfig` allows you to view IP information, but on a Windows-based
machine.

6. Answers A and D are correct. Switches function at Layers 1 and 2 of the OSI reference model. Multilayer switches have the ability to also function at higher layers.

   Answers B, C, E, F, and G are all incorrect. Only multilayer switches function at the higher layers of the OSI model. These layers include the Network, Transport, Session, Presentation, and Application layers.

7. Answer A is correct. You should gather symptoms and then attempt to isolate the problem.

   Answers B, C, and D are all incorrect. You do not start correcting the problem after gathering symptoms—you first attempt to isolate the problem. You also cannot document your solution at this time. Finally, you do not reverse any changes that did not correct the problem—this might be performed later in the process.

8. Answer D is correct. Following the determination that a problem is within your boundary of control, you should narrow the scope, then determine and document symptoms.

   Answers A, B, and C are all incorrect. You do not document the symptoms, nor document the solution until you have narrowed the scope of the problem.

9. Answer C is correct. A Bottom-Up troubleshooting approach starts with the physical layer and works up the OSI model. Traceroute and ping are often used initially in this approach to test the first few layers.

   Answer A is incorrect. The divide and conquer approach does not involve starting at the bottom of the OSI model—using this approach, any layer of the model might be appropriate for a start. Answer B is incorrect. The top down approach is not used here—since ping and traceroute commands test lower layers. Answer D is also incorrect. Finally, there is no such troubleshooting approach as the logical hierarchy.

10. Answer A is correct. When you apply the divide and conquer approach toward troubleshooting, you select a layer and test in both directions from the starting layer.

    Answer B is incorrect. The top down approach would have you starting at the upper layers and working your way down. Answer C is incorrect. The bottom up approach would have you starting from the first couple of layers and moving up. Finally, answer D is incorrect. There is no such troubleshooting approach as the logical hierarchy.

11. Answers A, B, and C are correct. You should always determine the scope of the problem, apply your experience, and analyze the symptoms when you are selecting a troubleshooting approach.

   Answer D is incorrect. Documenting the problem is not considered a valid guideline according to Cisco Systems approach.

12. Answer D is correct. Address resolution errors are common symptoms of Data Link layer problems.

   Answers A, B, and C are all incorrect. Framing, line coding, and synchronization errors are all possible and common symptoms of Physical layer problems.

13. Answer D is correct. An increased number of interface errors is a possible symptom of Physical layer problems.

   Answers A, B, and C are all common symptoms of Data Link layer problems.

14. Answer A and C are correct. Ping is available from both user and privileged modes on Cisco equipment.

   Answers B and D are incorrect. Ping is not available from global configuration mode, nor line configuration mode.

15. Answer B is correct. If a network problem is at the Data Link layer and not the Physical layer, then the show interface command will indicate that the interface is up, but the line protocol is down.

   Answer A is incorrect. A Physical layer problem would show a "down, down" indication. Answer C is incorrect. If the interface has been administratively disabled, the results of the command will state that. Answer D is incorrect. Finally, the CDP configuration has no bearing on the output of this command.

16. Answer D is correct. The show controllers command displays the current internal status information for the interface controller cards. This command is often used to learn information about the cable type used with serial interfaces.

   Answer A is incorrect. The show version command provides information about the hardware in use. Answer B is incorrect. The show ip interfaces provides information regarding the TCP/IP configuration on interfaces. Answer C is incorrect. The show ip interfaces brief command provides a summary of IP information for interfaces.

17. Answer B is correct. The `show cdp neighbor detail` command displays device type, IP address, and the Cisco IOS version of the neighboring device.

Answer A is incorrect. The `show cdp neighbors` command is excellent—yet it does not display Layer 3 address information. Answer C is incorrect. The `show controllers` command displays the current internal status information for the interface controller cards. This command is often used to learn information about the cable type used with serial interfaces. Answer D is incorrect. There is no such command as `show cdp ip interface brief`.

18. Answer D is correct. `netstat -rn` displays the routing table in numeric form without querying a Domain Name System (DNS) server.

Answer A is incorrect. The `ping` command allows you to test connectivity between two systems. Answer B is incorrect. The `arp` command displays the Layer 2 to Layer 3 address resolution information. Answer C is incorrect. There is no such command as `show ip arp` on such an end system.

19. Answer D is correct. `winipcfg` displays IP information for hosts running Windows 9x and Me.

Answers A and B are incorrect. `Ipconfig` does not function on an Me-based system, nor does `ipconfig /all`. Answer C is incorrect. `Tracert` does not provide extensive IP configuration information.

20. Answer B is correct. A status indication of 0x02 means the Frame Relay switch has the DLCI and everything is operational.

Answer A, C, D, and E are all incorrect. Possible values for the status field are as follows:

➤ 0x00—Added/inactive

➤ 0x02—Added/active

➤ 0x04—Deleted

➤ 0x08—New/inactive

➤ 0x0a—New/active

21. Answer B is correct. Late collisions are an indication that there may be a mismatch in the duplex configurations of the interfaces on a connection.

Answers A, C, and D are incorrect. Neither a poorly seated cable, nor an encapsulation mismatch produce late collisions. If the interface is administratively downed, late collisions are not possible.

22. Answer D is correct. Testing connectivity at each hop of a path is an excellent troubleshooting guideline, but at the Network layer.

    Answer A, B, C, and E are all incorrect. Checking pin outs, verifying interface configurations, checking operational status, and checking for bad cables are all excellent Physical and Data Link layer guidelines.

23. Answer C is correct. The `passive interface` command disables the sending of routing update information from a particular interface.

    Answers A and B are incorrect. Enabling or disabling split horizon controls whether an interface sends update information out an interface from which it was received. Answer D is incorrect. The `no ip route` command is used to remove a static route.

24. Answer C is correct. The `ipconfig` command when used with the `/release` switch releases DHCP information for the client.

    Answer A, B, and D are incorrect. There is no release option in the Network Settings applet of Control Panel. The `winipcfg` utility is not available. Finally, `nslookup` cannot release DHCP information.

25. Answer D is correct. You use the `debug ip routing` command to watch for routing updates.

    Answer A is incorrect. There is no command `show ip routing`. Answer B is incorrect. `Debug ip events` is not a valid command. Answer C is incorrect. `Debug ip packets` is not a valid command. Finally, there is no `debug routing` command so answer E is incorrect.

26. Answer B is correct. Following the initial configuration changes, you should evaluate the results and document the results of the changes. You should then verify that the problem is solved.

    Answers A, C, D, and E are incorrect. All other options here are valid guidelines; however, they should not be performed after making the initial configuration change.

27. Answer E is correct. The `show ip interface` command provides a wealth of information about the interface, including Layer 3 address information and outgoing and inbound access lists applied.

    The command in answer A is not a valid command. Answer B is incorrect. The `show ip route` command displays the IP routing table on the device. Answer C is incorrect. The `show access-lists` command displays the content of all access-lists. Answer D is incorrect. The `show logging` command allows you to view the contents of the logging buffer. The command used in answer F also is not a valid command.

28. Answer A is correct. You should first establish whether IP connectivity exists between the source and the destination according to Cisco's guidelines.

    All of the other options listed here are valid guidelines except answer E. None of these options should be the first step in the troubleshooting process.

29. Answer B is correct. You may use the `nslookup` command in order to quickly display the identity of the name server being used.

    There is no such command as answer A. Answers C and D is incorrect. `Winipcfg` is not a command available on a Unix system, nor is `ipconfig`. Answer E is incorrect. `ttcp` is not a valid command. Answer F is incorrect. `Ifconfig` is a valid command on a Unix system, but it would not be as efficient as `nslookup` in this case.

30. Answer A is correct. You can use the `telnet {ip address} 25` command in order to quickly verify and test SMTP protocol functionality.

    Answer B is incorrect. The port of 110 is inappropriate for testing SMTP. Answer C does not properly test SMTP, nor does the `debug smtp events` command (answer D), which is not a valid command. Answer E is incorrect. The `ping` command can be used to test connectivity, but it does not test SMTP specifically.

31. Answer C is correct. You use the `ip access-group` command in order to apply an IP access list to an interface. This is an interface configuration command.

    Answers A and B are not valid commands, nor are answers D and E.

32. Answer A is correct. A read-write community string helps to protect read/write access to Cisco devices using Cisco SNMP. The correct command to apply a read-write string to your router is

    `snmp-server community rw {string}`

    Answers B, C, D, and E are incorrect. All other commands presented here are invalid commands.

33. Answer C is correct. If you are calling TAC for assistance and the problem appears to be with only a few routers, you should capture the output from the show tech command on these routers.

Answer A is incorrect. The `copy flash tftp` command allows you to back up your IOS. Answer B allows you to back up your backup configuration. Answer D allows you to see a summary of interface information. Finally, answer E allows you to obtain specific information about the hardware in use.

34. Answer B is correct. Use the `snmp-server enable traps` command to configure unsolicited network management alarms. Typically, you configure the router to send these alarms to a trap receiver, such as a CiscoWorks 2000 system.

   Answer A is incorrect. The `ip http accounting` command allows you to audit HTTP usage. Answer C is incorrect. The `ip helper-address` command allows you to forward broadcast messages. Answer D is incorrect. The `service dhcp` command allows the configuration of a DHCP server. Answer E is incorrect. The `enable snmp traps` command produces an error, as it is not a valid command.

35. Answer C is correct. Once you have made initial configuration changes and documented these changes, you should verify that the problem is solved and ensure that your solution did not introduce other problems.

   All of the answers listed here are valid guidelines except answer E. Only one of these guidelines should follow the step described, however.

36. Answer D is correct. You can rely on the `show cdp neighbor` command in order to complete the Device Discovery stage of the network documentation process.

   All of the other options listed here are valid stages except answer E. None of these would involve the show `cdp neighbor` command with the exception of the Device Discovery stage.

37. Answer C is correct. You should use the `show isdn status` command to display information about memory, Layer 2 and Layer 3 timers, and the status of ISDN channels.

   Answer A is incorrect. `show isdn summary` is not a valid command. Answer B is incorrect. The `show isdn layers` command is not valid. Answer D is not a valid command, nor is answer E.

38. Answer D is correct. You should use the `show ip arp` command to display the Address Resolution Protocol (ARP) cache.

   Answer A is incorrect. The `show ip hosts` command allows you to see the name to IP mappings created on the device. Answer B is incorrect.

The `show ip route` command displays the routing table. Answer C is incorrect. The `show ip interface` command displays IP-specific information regarding interfaces. Answer E is not a valid command.

39. Answer B is correct. You should use the `show frame-relay map` command to display the current map entries and information about the connections.

Answer A is incorrect. `Show frame-relay` is used with additional keywords. Answer C is not a valid command. Nor is answer D. Answer E is incorrect. The `show arp` command provides information about Ethernet ARP, not frame-relay.

40. Answer A and C are correct. In order to perform this test, you must use `ping` in Privileged mode. You initiate the test by typing the `ping` command and responding to the prompts. Both of these options mentioned are available without accessing the extended commands.

Answer B is incorrect. Extended pings cannot be performed in user mode. Answer D is incorrect. You do not need the extended commands in order to configure the test described here. Answer E is incorrect. This ping test described is indeed possible.

41. Answer C is correct. A quick method of verifying DNS is to use IP addresses in place of host names when testing for connectivity. If tests pass with IP addresses and not with names, DNS is a potential problem.

Answer A is incorrect. Routing table entries do not typically troubleshoot DNS issues. Answer B is incorrect. Examining the router configuration is also not a typical DNS troubleshooting step. Answer D is incorrect. There is no such thing as obsolete address resolution entries. Answer E is incorrect. Ping or trace can be used, but this is not the simplest testing method available. Answer F is also incorrect. Pinging the fully qualified domain name of the DNS server is not a help.

42. Answer B is correct. You use the `debug ip packet` EXEC command to display general IP debugging information and IP security option (IPSO) security transactions.

Answer A is incorrect. There is no such command as `show ip access`. Answer C is incorrect. The `show ip buffers` command is not valid. Answer D is incorrect. `debug ip traffic` is not a valid command. Answer E is incorrect. `Show ip transmitted` is not a valid command. Answer F is incorrect. `Show ip protocols` is used to verify the dynamic routing protocols running on a router.

43. Answer D is correct. You can use the `debug arp` privileged EXEC command to display information on Address Resolution Protocol (ARP) transactions.

Answers A, B, C, and E are incorrect. None of the other options in this question are completed through the use of the `debug arp` command.

44. Answer D is correct. Modern versions of the Cisco IOS cause the LMI type to be auto detected.

While answers A, B, and C are all valid LMI types, the default configuration is auto-detection. Answer E is not an LMI type.

45. Answer B is correct. By default, logging of messages is sent to the console terminal.

Answers A, C, D, and E are all incorrect. All other options here are not the default configuration.

46. Answer D is correct. Logging to the console is the default configuration on Cisco equipment. Logging to an internal buffer produces the least overhead, however.

Answers A, B, C, and E are all incorrect. All other answers listed here produce more overhead than logging to the internal buffer.

47. Answer E is correct. You can use the `show cdp neighbors detail` command in order to view network protocol information about neighboring Cisco devices.

Answers A, B, C, D, and F are invalid commands.

48. Answer D is correct. Clearing the counters will not produce an interface reset.

Answers A, B, and C are incorrect because they all produce such behavior.

49. Answers A, B, and D are correct. You should be consistent with documentation. It should all use the same symbols, terminology, and styles. You should know the scope of your network documentation. You should also store the documentation where it is accessible on the job.

Answers C and E are incorrect. You should maintain the documentation at all times, not just once per year. It is not recommended to include all Layer 2 information.

50. Answer C is correct. Topology diagram components that are related to end systems include physical location, access VLAN, ip address, subnet mask, device name, device purpose, operating system, version, network applications, and MAC address.

Answers A, B, and D are incorrect. All other answers listed here include components that would be appropriate for switching topology diagrams.

51. Answer C is correct. The `route print` command allows you to view the routing table on an ip host.

Answer A is incorrect. `ipconfig` allows you to view IP configuration information. Answer B is incorrect. `tracert` allows you to trace the path data takes as it moves through the network. Answer D is incorrect. `Telnet` allows you to log in to a remote system. Answer E is incorrect. `Traceroute` allows you to trace paths. Answer F is incorrect. Answers F and G are incorrect. `show ip route` and `show route` are not valid end system commands.

52. Answer C is correct. The data is at Layer 4, the Transport layer.

Answers A, B, D, E, F, and G are all incorrect. The data exists at the Transport layer – and can be at no other simultaneously.

53. Answer D is correct. The terminating phase involves removing the data control information and passing the data to an upper-layer application.

Answers A, B, C, E, and F are incorrect. No other option involves converting the data as needed for the target application.

54. Answers A, C, D, E are all correct. All of the steps listed are valid with the exception of clear all logs.

Answer B is incorrect. Clear all logs is not a valid step in the general troubleshooting process.

55. Answer C is correct. The Cisco IOS command set excels at allowing you to choose an intermediate level at which to begin troubleshooting. This is thanks to the many show and debug commands that are available in the Cisco IOS.

Answer A and B are incorrect. The bottom-up and top-down approaches do not exploit the Cisco IOS command set like the divide and conquer approach does. Answer D is incorrect. There is no such approach as scatter.

56. Answer D is correct. There is no such functional area as Quality of Service management.

Answers A, B, C, and E are incorrect. You can remember the five functional areas with the acronym FCAPS (Fault Management, Configuration Management, Accounting Management, Performance Management, and Security Management).

57. Answer A is correct. A cable tester is commonly used to check STP, UTP, 10BaseT, and coax for near-end crosstalk and noise.

Answers B, C, D, and E are all incorrect. All other devices listed here server other purposes for network troubleshooting.

58. Answer B is correct. Connection-oriented protocols will request retransmission of data should the data prove to be missing or corrupt.

Answer A is incorrect. There is no host-to-host protocol type in this course of study. Answer C is incorrect. Client/server is also not a valid protocol type for this discussion. Answer D is incorrect. Connectionless protocols are considered very fast, but they do not feature reliability, therefore there is not a request for retransmission of information. Answer E is incorrect. This is not a valid protocol type.

59. Answer A is correct. Connectionless protocols have the advantage of being fast. This is because they do not have to deal with the overhead incurred by connection-oriented protocols.

Answers B, C, and D are incorrect. Connectionless protocols do not feature enhanced security or enhanced auditing, nor do they eliminate the need for upper-layer connections.

60. Answer C is correct. The embedded RMON agent allows monitoring of network traffic and does not require the use of a dedicated hardware probe of any kind.

Answer A is incorrect. Cisco supports RMON1 and RMON2. Answer B is incorrect. RMON is disabled by default. Answer D is incorrect. RMON can monitor many types of segments, not just 10BaseT or 100BaseT.

Practice Exam 2

Question 1

You are creating a network configuration table. According to Cisco, which of the following should you document? Choose all that apply.

- ❑ A. The device name
- ❑ B. The applications running on the device
- ❑ C. Data Link layer addresses and implemented features
- ❑ D. Network layer addresses and implemented features
- ❑ E. Any important information about physical aspects of the device
- ❑ F. All features of the IOS in place

Question 2

Which of the following components would you expect to find in a network configuration table related to troubleshooting? Choose all that apply.

- ❑ A. Flash memory
- ❑ B. Interface names
- ❑ C. Network applications
- ❑ D. Service pack levels
- ❑ E. Access lists

Question 3

Which of the following components are appropriate for a Cisco topology diagram? Choose all that apply.

- ❑ A. Device Name
- ❑ B. Interface Name
- ❑ C. MAC Address
- ❑ D. IP Address
- ❑ E. Routing Protocol

Question 4

You would like to receive information about the physical RAM installed in your Cisco router. You would also like to learn IOS version information and uptime information, as well as information about physical interfaces in use. What command should you use?

- ○ A. **show ip interfaces**
- ○ B. **show version**
- ○ C. **show ip interfaces brief**
- ○ D. **show controllers**

Question 5

You are interested in discovering the MAC address used on your Fast Ethernet interface on your Cisco router. What command allows you to document this information?

- ❑ A. **show ip interfaces brief**
- ❑ B. **show version**
- ❑ C. **show mac-address-table**
- ❑ D. **show interfaces**

Question 6

You would like to determine which routes in your Cisco router will be advertised
to neighboring routers running an appropriate dynamic routing protocol. Which
commands should you use to learn this information? Choose two.

❑ A. **show ip route**

❑ B. **show ip interfaces brief**

❑ C. **show route advertise**

❑ D. **show ip protocols**

Question 7

You need to obtain the IP addresses of devices that are connected to your Cisco
switch. What commands should you use? Choose all that apply.

❑ A. **show ip protocols**

❑ B. **show cdp entry ***

❑ C. **show spanning-tree summary**

❑ D. **show cdp neighbors**

❑ E. **show cdp neighbors detail**

Question 8

You are examining the following output on your Catalyst 6500 series switch:

```
UplinkFast is disabled
BackboneFast is disabled
PortFast BPDU Guard is enabled
Name Blocking Listening Learning Forwarding STP Active
-------------------- -------- --------- -------- ----------
34 VLANs 0 0 0 36 36
```

What command produced this output?

◯ A. **show spanning-tree summary totals**

◯ B. **show spanning-tree**

◯ C. **show ip spanning-tree**

◯ D. **show spanning-tree vlan 34**

Question 9

You are working with TAC to troubleshoot a problem that has developed on your Cisco router. The TAC employee asks you to use the following command:

```
show tech-support password
```

What is the purpose of the **password** keyword in the command?

- ○ A. The password keyword hides password information from being displayed in the output
- ○ B. The password keyword encrypts the password information that displays in the output
- ○ C. The password keyword is an invalid parameter when used with the show tech-support command
- ○ D. The password keyword leaves passwords and other security information in the output

Question 10

You are following Cisco's recommended process for creating network documentation. What is the step that should be performed following a login?

- ○ A. Interface Discovery
- ○ B. Document
- ○ C. Diagram
- ○ D. Device Discovery

Question 11

You are attempting to gather network information from your Windows 2000-based end-system. Which command should you use to display IP information?

- ○ A. **winipcfg**
- ○ B. **tracert −d**
- ○ C. **arp −a**
- ○ D. **ipconfig /all**

Question 12

You are troubleshooting a standard router in your enterprise network. Which layer of the logical network model directly pertains to this device?

- ○ A. Physical
- ○ B. Application
- ○ C. Data Link
- ○ D. Network

Question 13

You are troubleshooting a standard hub in your enterprise network. Which layer of the logical network model directly pertains to this device?

- ○ A. Physical
- ○ B. Network
- ○ C. Data Link
- ○ D. Transport

Question 14

Which of the following are valid guidelines from Cisco regarding the creation of network documentation? Choose all that apply.

- ❑ A. Know your objective
- ❑ B. Document all possible parameters
- ❑ C. Be consistent
- ❑ D. Maintain the documentation
- ❑ E. Keep the documentation accessible

Question 15

Which of the following lists contain information appropriate for an end system network configuration table?

- ○ A. PortFast, Trunk Status, Network Applications, IP Address
- ○ B. IP Address, Subnet Mask, Duplex

○ C. IOS Type/Version, STP State, Default Gateway Address, IP Address

○ D. Manufacturer/Model, Access VLAN, IP Address, Network Applications

Question 16

Which of the following lists contains information appropriate for an end system topology diagram?

○ A. IP Address, Subnet Mask, STP State

○ B. Trunk Status, MAC Address, IP Address

○ C. Duplex, Interface Name, Routing Protocol

○ D. MAC Address, Network Applications, IP Address

Question 17

You need to view the WINS server addresses that a Windows 2000 end system is receiving from a DHCP server in your network. How can you view this information?

○ A. **route print**

○ B. **ipconfig /all**

○ C. **ping**

○ D. **show ip wins**

Question 18

You are following the general troubleshooting process recommended by Cisco Systems. What step should you perform following the gathering of symptoms?

○ A. Correct the problem

○ B. Document the solution

○ C. Reverse any changes that did not correct the problem

○ D. Isolate the problem

○ E. Use the **show tech** command

Question 19

Which phase of the encapsulation process involves converting data into segments?

- ○ A. Transport
- ○ B. Terminating
- ○ C. Forwarding
- ○ D. Origination
- ○ E. Transmission

Question 20

To which layers of the logical network model does a firewall directly relate? Choose all that apply.

- ❏ A. Physical
- ❏ B. Transport
- ❏ C. Application
- ❏ D. Data Link
- ❏ E. Network

Question 21

What is the second step of the process for gathering symptoms from a network, according to Cisco?

- ○ A. Narrow Scope
- ○ B. Determine Symptoms
- ○ C. Document Symptoms
- ○ D. Determine Ownership

Question 22

You are troubleshooting a complex problem in your network and you immediately begin using ICMP-related commands in order to begin your troubleshooting steps. What approach are you using?

- ○ A. Divide and Conquer
- ○ B. Top-Down
- ○ C. Logical Hierarchy
- ○ D. Bottom-Up

Question 23

You are troubleshooting a complex problem in your network and you begin by executing a **show ip route** command. Next you engage in a **show cdp neighbors** command, followed by several application layer tests. What approach are you using?

- ○ A. Top-Down
- ○ B. Bottom-Up
- ○ C. Logical Hierarchy
- ○ D. Divide and Conquer

Question 24

Which of the following is not a valid guideline for selecting an effective troubleshooting approach, according to Cisco?

- ○ A. Analyze the symptoms
- ○ B. Consult with external experts
- ○ C. Determine the scope of the problem
- ○ D. Apply your experience

Question 25

You have isolated a problem as involving an access list configuration. You are using the divide and conquer approach to troubleshooting. Which layer should you begin at?

○ A. Network

○ B. Physical

○ C. Data Link

○ D. Application

Question 26

You are following the general troubleshooting process as described by Cisco Systems. Which step in the process involves interviewing a user?

○ A. Isolating the Problem

○ B. Correcting the Problem

○ C. Gathering Symptoms

○ D. Discovering Systems

Question 27

Which of the following are valid guidelines for selecting an effective troubleshooting approach? Choose all that apply.

❏ A. Analyze the symptoms

❏ B. Determine the scope of the problem

❏ C. Apply your experience

❏ D. Document the problem

Question 28

You have made a console connection with your Cisco router and you are at the privileged mode prompt. You want to view the current configuration register setting. What command should you use?

○ A. **show boot**

○ B. **show version**

○ C. **show configuration**

○ D. **show confreg**

Question 29

You are experiencing intermittent connectivity issues on one of your WAN interfaces. Which of the following are possible causes? Choose all that apply.

❏ A. Faulty router interface

❏ B. Faulty CSU/DSU

❏ C. Congested link

❏ D. Timing issue

Question 30

You are troubleshooting one of your Catalyst 5000 series switches. The LK LED for one of your key ports appears orange. What does this indicate?

○ A. Hardware failure

○ B. Diagnostics running

○ C. Port disabled

○ D. System boot

○ E. Port is operational

Question 31

You need to inspect the number of interface resets. Which valid commands show you this statistic? Choose all that apply.

❏ A. **show ip interface**

❏ B. **show interface serial 3/1**

❏ C. **show async**

❏ D. **show environment**

❏ E. **show interface ethernet 0/1**

Question 32

You have issued a telnet to a router and you are at the privileged mode prompt. You issue the **debug ip packet** command. What command step must also be used to view the debug output?

- ○ A. **logging monitor**
- ○ B. **monitor terminal**
- ○ C. **logging on**
- ○ D. **terminal telnet**
- ○ E. **terminal monitor**

Question 33

Your Frame Relay provider has failed to inform you of the correct LMI type. What should you do?

- ○ A. Allow the router to auto-sense LMI
- ○ B. Set ANSI
- ○ C. Set Cisco
- ○ D. Set q933a

Question 34

End users of your network are complaining of connection difficulties. These clients are being forced to wait to obtain DHCP information upon initial login. The clients eventually receive the correct information, but there is a considerable delay. What should you try?

- ○ A. Enabling BackboneFast on all switches
- ○ B. Enabling UplinkFast on access layer switches
- ○ C. Disabling the Spanning Tree Protocol on all workstation ports
- ○ D. Enabling PortFast on workstation connected ports

Question 35

You would like to view the number of DE packets for DLCI 100. What command should you use?

- ○ A.   **show frame-relay dlci 100**
- ○ B.   **show frame-relay pvc 100**
- ○ C.   **show frame-relay 100**
- ○ D.   **show frame-relay lapf 100**

Question 36

You are troubleshooting a switch in your Cisco network and you want to determine which ports are the designated ports. What show command should be used?

- ○ A.   **show designated port**
- ○ B.   **show spantree**
- ○ C.   **show uplink-fast**
- ○ D.   **show vtp**

Question 37

A remote router is having a problem when it tries to connect to the central router. The encapsulation is PPP with CHAP authentication. What command should be used to verify the exchange of credentials?

- ○ A.   **show ppp chap**
- ○ B.   **debug ppp authentication chap**
- ○ C.   **debug ppp chap**
- ○ D.   **debug ppp password**
- ○ E.   **debug ppp authentication**

Question 38

When using the extended ping command, you can specify a source address in addition to the destination address. What source address can you specify?

- ○ A.   Any IP address within your organization
- ○ B.   Only the ping exit interface

○ C. Any active router interface

○ D. Any private IP address

Question 39

You want to set the counters on the Ethernet interface 0/0 back to zero. However, you do not want to reset the counters for your other interfaces. What command should you use?

○ A. **reset counters ethernet 0/0**

○ B. **counters reset ethernet 0/0**

○ C. **clear counters ethernet 0/0**

○ D. **counters clear ethernet 0/0**

Question 40

You are analyzing one of your serial interfaces through the use of the **interface serial** command. The number of times that your carrier detect signal was lost is indicated by which of the following?

○ A. Carrier transitions

○ B. Interface resets

○ C. Restarts

○ D. Line protocol down

Question 41

You want to view the router's uptime. What command will you use?

○ A. **show uptime**

○ B. **show system**

○ C. **show version**

○ D. **show reload**

Question 42

You have configured the Serial interface 0/0 on RouterA as DCE. What is the correct command to set the clock rate to 56Kbps?

○ A. **clock rate 56**

○ B. **clockrate 56**

○ C. **clockrate 56000**

○ D. **clock rate 56000**

Question 43

Cisco Discovery Protocol (CDP) packets are sent via which of the following methods?

○ A. Layer 2 broadcast

○ B. Layer 2 multicast

○ C. Layer 3 broadcast

○ D. Layer 3 multicast

Question 44

What troubleshooting command should you use if you want to check your ISDN end-to-end connectivity status?

○ A. **show isdn status**

○ B. **show dialer**

○ C. **show isdn**

○ D. **debug dialer**

○ E. **debug isdn**

Question 45

You need your router to be able to forward client DHCP requests to a DHCP server residing in another segment of your network. What command can you use to do this?

○ A. **service dhcp**

○ B. **snmp-server**

○ C. **ip helper-address**

○ D. **ip forward dhcp**

Question 46

You are having problems issuing the telnet command to access a particular remote device. Which command displays events during the negotiation process of a Telnet connection?

○ A. **telnet {address} log**

○ B. **debug telnet**

○ C. **debug telnet events**

○ D. **telnet {address} details**

Question 47

What is the default destination of syslog messages on a Cisco router?

○ A. Buffer

○ B. Console

○ C. No logging

○ D. Terminal

Question 48

You need to clear a BGP session because you have just made modifications to the inbound policy. Which command can you use to do this?

○ A. **reset bgp {as number}**

○ B. **clear bgp {as number}**

○ C. **reload bgp {as number}**

○ D. **clear ip bgp {as number}**

Question 49

You would like to prevent your Cisco router from querying a DNS system for host name to address translations. What command permits you to do this?

○ A. **no dns lookups**

○ B. **no ip domain lookup**

○ C. **no translate**

○ D. **no ip dns lookup**

Question 50

You suspect that you are having a problem with an access list configured in your Cisco network. What command allows you to view the contents of all access lists configured on a device?

○ A. **show ip access-lists**

○ B. **show lists**

○ C. **show filters**

○ D. **show access-groups**

Question 51

You are troubleshooting Transport and Application layer problems in your Cisco network. You have backed up your configurations and you have made initial configuration changes. You have evaluated the results and documented each change. What should you do next if you are following the Cisco procedure?

○ A. Get input from outside resources

○ B. Document the solution

○ C. Verify that the changes you made fixed the problem without introducing new problems

○ D. Restore the original configurations on all devices

Question 52

You are unable to reach a device using the device name, but you can reach it using the IP address. Which Cisco IOS command would help you determine whether you have a name resolution problem?

○ A. **show ip hosts**

○ B. **show ip route**

○ C. **show ip interface**

○ D. **show ip arp**

Question 53

You think you may have a problem with DNS name resolution. Which process would be the fastest way to see whether you do have a DNS issue?

○ A. By examining the routing table entries

○ B. By examining the router's configuration

○ C. By using IP addresses rather than names

○ D. By checking for obsolete address resolution entries

○ E. By using ping or trace to verify the communication path

Question 54

Which of the following is a possible symptom of a Data Link layer problem?

○ A. Excessive CRC error and frame check sequence errors

○ B. Excessive utilization

○ C. Increased number of interface errors

○ D. LEDs are off

Question 55

Which of the following is a possible symptom of a Physical layer problem?

○ A. Excessive utilization

○ B. Encapsulation errors

○ C. Address resolution errors

○ D. Large quantities of broadcast errors

Question 56

You are engaged in the Cisco recommended process for gathering symptoms from a network. What step should you complete after you narrow the scope?

○ A. Document symptoms

○ B. Determine symptoms

○ C. Solve the problem and document the solution

○ D. Begin isolating

Question 57

IP devices often use a table that shows the correspondence between network and LAN hardware addresses. When troubleshooting, which Cisco IOS command should you use to access this information?

○ A. **show ip arp**

○ B. **show ip hosts**

○ C. **show ip routes**

○ D. **show ip interface**

○ E. **show ip addresses**

Question 58

In contrast to half-duplex Ethernet, full-duplex Ethernet on a Catalyst switch does which of the following? Choose all that apply.

❏ A. Provides greater access to bandwidth

❏ B. Connects directly to end users or other switches

❏ C. Is usually limited to a maximum of 16 ports and 8 spanning trees

❏ D. Eliminates the possibility of collisions

Question 59

In Frame Relay, there is a configured association between a DLCI and another protocol address. Which command displays information about this association?

- ○ A. **show frame-relay**
- ○ B. **show frame-relay map**
- ○ C. **show frame relay dlci**
- ○ D. **show frame-relay counters**
- ○ E. **show interface [number] dlci**

Question 60

The **privileged ping** command in Cisco IOS software for TCP/IP allows you to check for MTU, set data patterns, set a source address, and record the route used. Which subcommand of **privileged ping** allows you to select these features?

- ○ A. **Verbose**
- ○ B. **Protocol options**
- ○ C. **Extended commands**
- ○ D. **IP header commands**

Answer Key 2

1. A, C, D, E
2. A, B, E
3. A, B, C, D, E
4. B
5. D
6. A, D
7. B, E
8. A
9. D
10. A
11. D
12. D
13. A
14. A, C, D, E
15. D
16. D
17. B
18. D
19. D
20. A, D, E

21. D
22. D
23. D
24. B
25. A
26. C
27. A, B, C
28. B
29. A, B, C, D
30. C
31. B, E
32. E
33. A
34. D
35. B
36. B
37. E
38. C
39. C
40. A

41. C
42. D
43. B
44. A
45. C
46. B
47. B
48. D
49. B
50. A
51. C
52. D
53. C
54. A
55. A
56. B
57. A
58. A, D
59. B
60. C

1. The correct answers are A, C, D, and E. Cisco recommends Physical, Data Link, and Network layer information in the network configuration table.

   B is incorrect because listing applications running on the device in the configuration table is not a recommendation from Cisco. Answer F is incorrect. Cisco also does not recommend documenting all features of the IOS in use.

2. The correct answers are A, B, and E. Flash memory, access lists, and interface names are all excellent ideas for a network configuration table related to troubleshooting.

   Answers C and D are incorrect. Network applications in use and service pack levels are appropriate for end system configuration tables.

3. The correct answers are A, B, C, D, and E. All of the listed components are appropriate for a Cisco network topology diagram.

4. The correct answer is B. The `show version` command allows you to view the name and model of the device, as well as the operating system that the device is running.

   Answer A is incorrect. `Show ip interfaces` displays information about IP configurations for each interface running IP on the router. Answer C is incorrect. `Show ip interfaces brief` provides an excellent summary table of information for each interface, including Layer 3 addresses and status information, but does not provide the information needed here.

   Answer D is incorrect. `Show controllers` shows hardware information for each interface but does not show router uptime and IOS information.

5. The correct answer is D. The `show interfaces` command allows you to view MAC address information for each of your Ethernet-based interfaces.

   Answer A is incorrect. `Show ip interfaces brief` does not show MAC address information; only Layer 3 address information is displayed. Answer B is incorrect. `Show version` displays IOS information and router uptime information as well as information regarding the interface hardware in place. Answer C is incorrect. `Show mac-address-table` is used on a switch in order to show the MAC addresses learned by a switch.

6. The correct answers are A, D. In order to view routes that are on the router, you can use the `show ip route` command. In order to view the

routing protocol in use, and the networks that will be advertised, use the `show ip protocols` command.

Answer B is incorrect. The `show ip interfaces brief` command does provide summary information regarding the interfaces on the device, but it does not indicate what routes are advertised to neighboring devices. Answer C is incorrect. There is no such command as the `show route advertise` command.

7. The correct answers are B, E. In order to view IP address information, you must use the `detail` keyword with the `show cdp neighbors` command. You can also use the `show cdp entry *` command in order to obtain Layer 3 address information.

Answer A is incorrect. `Show ip protocols` provides information about the dynamic routing protocols in use on the device, but it does not provide neighboring Layer 3 address information. Answer C is incorrect. `Show spanning-tree summary` provides spanning tree configuration information, but again, cannot be used to explore neighboring Layer 3 address information. Finally, `show cdp neighbors` without the `detail` switch does not provide Layer 3 address information about the neighboring devices, therefore answer D is incorrect.

8. The correct answer is A. The `show spanning-tree summary totals` command allows you to quickly verify the spanning tree configuration, including enabled features.

Answer B is incorrect. The `show spanning-tree` command does provide excellent information about spanning-tree, but it does not provide the information in a summary fashion as depicted here. Answer C is incorrect. There is no such command as `show ip spanning-tree`. Answer D is incorrect. `show spanning-tree vlan 34` is a valid command, but the command displays detailed spanning-tree information about VLAN 34 only.

9. The correct answer is D. The `password` keyword leaves passwords and other security information in the output. If not used, passwords and other security-sensitive information in the output are replaced with the label "`<removed>`" (this is the default).

Answer A is incorrect. The `password` keyword does not hide password information from being displayed in the output—in fact, it causes it to be left in the output. Answer B is incorrect. This keyword also does not encrypt the password information that displays in the output. Answer C is incorrect. The `password` keyword is a valid parameter.

10. The correct answer is A. After logging in to the device, you should discover relevant information about the device—this includes interface discovery.

Answer B is incorrect. You document your findings later in the process, not immediately after login. Answer C is incorrect. Creating the network diagram also takes place later in the process. Finally, the device discovery stage takes place after the current device is completely documented, therefore answer D is incorrect.

11. The correct answer is D. `ipconfig /all` displays IP information for hosts running Windows NT/2000/XP.

Answer A is incorrect. `winipcfg` does provide IP information for Windows-based end systems, but only systems running 9x or Me editions of Windows. Answers B and C are incorrect. The `tracert` and `arp` commands display limited IP information for end systems, and are not the best choices in this case.

12. The correct answer is D. Routers map directly to the Network layer of the OSI model.

Answers A and C are incorrect. Hubs map to the Physical layer, while switches map the Data Link layer. Answer B is incorrect. End systems typically run applications that encompass all layers of the OSI model.

13. The correct answer is A. Hubs map directly to the Physical layer of the OSI model.

Answer B is incorrect. Routers map directly to the Network layer of the OSI model. Answer C is incorrect. Switches map to the Data Link layer. Answer D is incorrect. Multilayer switches and routers do interact with the Transport layer, but they are not typically considered Transport layer devices.

14. The correct answers are A, C, D, and E. Valid guidelines from Cisco include knowing your objective, maintaining the documentation, keeping it accessible, and using consistent terms and symbols.

Answer B is incorrect. You should not document all possible parameters. You should only collect data that is relevant to your objective.

15. The correct answer is D. While an end system configuration table will contain different information depending on its usage, you should consider the parameters listed here.

"PortFast, Trunk Status, Network Applications, IP Address" contains switch parameters. "IP Address, Subnet Mask, Duplex" describes a router. "IOS Type/Version, STP State, Default Gateway Address, IP Address" also contains parameters that describe a switch.

16. The correct answer is D. While a topology diagram for an end system can contain many different components, you should consider MAC Address, Network Applications, and IP addresses when creating the diagram.

    Answer A is incorrect. "IP Address, Subnet Mask, STP State" is a list that is most appropriate for a multilayer switch. Answer B is incorrect. "Trunk Status, MAC Address, IP Address" is also multilayer switch relevant. Answer C is incorrect. "Duplex, Interface Name, Routing Protocol" are components that apply to routers.

17. The answer is B. The `ipconfig` command, when used with the `/all` switch, allows you to view all details of the IP configuration on the end system. This includes DHCP-assigned WINS information.

    Answer A is incorrect. `Route print` allows you to see all of the routes on a Windows-based end system. Answer C is incorrect. `Ping` is a diagnostic utility that allows you to test IP connectivity. Answer D is incorrect. There is no `show ip wins` command available.

18. The correct answer is D. You should gather symptoms and then attempt to isolate the problem.

    Answers A, B, and C are incorrect. Correcting the problem, documenting the solution, and reversing any changes that did not correct the problem are all valid steps, but they do not follow the gathering of symptoms. Answer E is incorrect. Using the `show tech` command is not part of the guidelines from Cisco.

19. The correct answer is D. The Origination phase involves taking data from applications and converting as needed for transmission on the network.

    Answers A, B, and C are all incorrect. Transport, Terminating, and Forwarding are the other phases. Answer E is incorrect. Transmission is not a valid phase.

20. The correct answers are A, D, and E. Firewalls directly relate to the Physical, Data Link, and Network layers, similar to a router.

    Answer B is incorrect. While they can impact the Transport later, there is not a direct correlation. Answer C is incorrect. They also do not directly correlate to the Application layer.

21. The correct answer is D. According to Cisco, you should determine ownership immediately after analyzing the existing symptoms. You always want to ensure that the network issues are in your realm of responsibility.

Answers A, B, and D are all incorrect. Narrowing scope, determining symptoms, and documenting symptoms are all valid steps, but they do not immediately follow analyzing existing systems.

22. The correct answer is D. A Bottom-Up troubleshooting approach starts with the Physical layer and works up the OSI model. Traceroute and ping are often used initially in this approach to test the first few layers.

Answers A and B are incorrect. The other valid approaches Cisco recommends are the Top Down approach and the Divide and Conquer approach. Answer C is incorrect because the Logical Hierarchy model is not valid.

23. The correct answer is D. When you apply the Divide and Conquer approach toward troubleshooting, you select a layer and test in both directions from the starting layer. This often enables you to more quickly isolate and repair the problem, especially when compared to other approaches.

Answers A and B are incorrect. The other valid approaches Cisco recommends are the Top Down and Bottom Up approaches. Answer C is incorrect as the Logical Hierarchy model is not valid.

24. The correct answer is B. Consulting with external experts is not part of three guidelines put forth by Cisco.

Answers A, C and D are all incorrect, as the guidelines recommend that you analyze the symptoms, determine the scope of the problem, and apply your experience.

25. The correct answer is A. Using the Divide and Conquer approach, you begin your troubleshooting at a suspected layer and move up and down from that layer in the OSI model. Using the Divide and Conquer approach to troubleshooting access list configuration problems, therefore, involves beginning your troubleshooting at the Network layer. Access lists are Network layer components.

Answers B, C, and D are incorrect. Access list problems are not considered Physical, Data Link, or Application layer problems.

26. The correct answer is C. Interviews with end users are typical in the symptom-gathering step of the process.

Answer A is incorrect. Isolating the problem involves gathering and documenting more symptoms. Answer B is incorrect. Correcting the problem involves implementing, testing, and documenting a solution. Answer D is incorrect. Discovering systems is not part of the process.

27. The correct answers are A, B, and C. You should always determine the scope of the problem, apply your experience, and analyze the symptoms when you are selecting a troubleshooting approach.

Answer D is incorrect. Documenting the problem is not a valid recommendation from Cisco.

28. The correct answer is B. Use the `show version` command to view the router's current configuration register setting.

Answers A, C, and D are incorrect. `show confreg` is not a valid command, nor are `show boot` and `show configuration`.

29. The correct answers are A, B, C, and D. All of these symptoms are possible when a WAN link is showing intermittent connectivity.

30. The correct answer is C. An orange light on a port module indicates that the port has been disabled by the system software.

Answer A is incorrect. A hardware failure does not cause this LED to turn orange. Answer B is incorrect as well, since this does not indicate that the diagnostics are running. Finally, answers D and E are also incorrect. An operation port is indicated by a steady green LED and a system boot causes the LEDs to flash.

31. The correct answers are B, E. Interface resets appear in the output of the `show interface` commands and are the result of missed keepalive packets.

Answer A is incorrect. The `show ip interface` command provides parameters particular to IP settings on the interface(s). Answer C is incorrect. There is no `show async` command. To display the status of activity on all lines configured for asynchronous support, use the `show async status` privileged EXEC command. Answer D is incorrect as well. There is no such command as the `show environment` command.

32. The correct answer is E. The EXEC command `terminal monitor` accomplishes the task of displaying the system error messages to a non-console terminal.

Answer A is incorrect. `logging monitor` sets the logging level. Answer B is incorrect. `monitor terminal` is an invalid command. Answer C is incorrect. Logging on enables logging to all supported destinations. Answer D is incorrect. `terminal telnet` is for telnet protocol specific configuration.

33. The correct answer is A. Beginning with IOS version 11.2, LMI can be auto-sensed by Cisco equipment.

    Answers B, C, and D are incorrect. Due to the default auto-sensing behavior of Cisco routers running the latest IOSs, the LMI does not have to be set to ansi, q933a, or cisco.

34. The correct answer is D. PortFast allows client workstation ports to enter the forwarding state almost immediately.

    Answer A is incorrect. BackboneFast is a valid spanning-tree enhancement, but it does not directly effect client logins. Answer B is incorrect. UplinkFast is also a valid enhancement, but it does not directly effect client logins. Answer C is incorrect. Cisco never recommends disabling spanning-tree.

35. The correct answer is B. The `show frame-relay pvc 100` command will display DLCI specific traffic statistics. Use the command without the DLCI number to view statistics for all DLCIs that have been configured.

    Answers A and C are incorrect. The command `show frame-relay dlci 100` is not valid, nor is `show frame-relay 100`. Answer D is incorrect. To display information about the status of the internals of Frame Relay Layer 2 (LAPF) if switched virtual circuits (SVCs) are configured, use the `show frame-relay lapf` EXEC command.

36. The correct answer is B. To view which ports are the designated ports use the `show spantree` command.

    Answers A, C, and D are incorrect. The only other valid command here is `show vtp`, yet this command is followed by the `status` keyword. `show vtp status` reports on the VTP configuration of a switch.

37. The correct answer is E. To verify PPP authentication using either PAP or CHAP, use the `debug ppp authentication` command.

    Answer A is incorrect. `Show ppp chap` is an invalid command. Answer B is incorrect. `debug ppp authentication chap` is also invalid. Answer C is incorrect. `debug ppp chap` is a valid command but it does not display authentication specific information. Answer D is incorrect. `debug ppp password` is an invalid command.

38. The correct answer is C. The source address specified in the `extended` `ping` command can be any active interface IP address of the local router.

Answers A and D are incorrect. The IP address cannot be any IP address from the organization, nor can it be any private address—the address must be from an active interface on the router. Answer B is also incorrect, as the IP address is not restricted to the ping exit interface.

39. The correct answer is C. The `clear` `counters` command will clear the counters on all of the interfaces. Adding `Ethernet` `0/0` at the end of the `clear` `counters` command will clear counters for that particular interface only.

Answers A, B, and D are incorrect. All other syntax examples listed here will produce an error.

40. The correct answer is A. Carrier transitions appear in the output of the `show` `interfaces` `serial` EXEC command whenever there is an interruption in the carrier signal (such as an interface reset at the remote end of a link).

Answers B, C, and D are all incorrect. Interface resets, restarts, and line protocol down do not provide an exact indication of an interruption in the carrier signal. Only carrier transitions indicate this.

41. The correct answer is C. Use the `show` `version` command to view the total uptime for the router.

Answer A is incorrect. `show` `uptime` is not a valid command. Answer B is incorrect. `show` `system` is not a valid command. Answer D is incorrect. To display the reload status on the router, use the `show` `reload` EXEC command.

42. The correct answer is D. The `clock` `rate` command accepts a parameter in bps, and 56000 is the correct way to express 56Kbps in bps.

Answers A, B, and C are all incorrect. All other syntax examples here produce an error.

43. The correct answer is B. CDP sends and receives packets on Layer 2 multicast address 01-00-0C-CC-CC.

Answers A, C, and D are incorrect. Because CDP packets are a Layer 2 multicast, no other option here is correct.

44. The correct answer is A. This command will show ISDN end-to-end connectivity status and all three layers of the ISDN connection.

Answer B is incorrect. To display general diagnostic information for interfaces configured for DDR (dial-on-demand routing), use the `show dialer` command in EXEC mode. Answer C is incorrect. To display the information about calls, history, memory, status, and Layer 2 and Layer 3 timers, use the `show isdn` EXEC command. Answer D is incorrect. Use the `debug dialer events` privileged EXEC command to display debugging information about the packets received on a dialer interface. Answer E is incorrect. `debug isdn` is used with additional keywords in order to capture ISDN-specific events.

45. The correct answer is C. `ip helper-address` forwards UDP broadcasts, including BOOTP, received on an interface.

Answer A is incorrect. To enable the Cisco IOS Dynamic Host Configuration Protocol (DHCP) server and relay agent features on your router, use the `service dhcp` global configuration command. Answer B is incorrect. To enable SNMP functionality,– you may use the `snmp-server` command with additional keywords. Answer D is incorrect. The command `ip forward dhcp` is invalid.

46. The correct answer is B. The `debug telnet` command allows you to display events during the negotiation process of a Telnet connection.

Answer A is incorrect. The `Telnet {ip address} log` command is not valid. Answer C is incorrect. The `debug telnet events` command is not valid. Answer D is incorrect. `Telnet {address} details` is not valid either.

47. The correct answer is B. By default, syslog messages are sent to the console.

Answers A, C, and D are all incorrect. Syslog messages are enabled by default and are sent to the console, not to a terminal or a buffer.

48. The correct answer is D. The `clear ip bgp {as number}` command allows you to clear the BGP session.

Answers A, B, and C are all incorrect. All other syntax examples listed here produce an error.

49. The correct answer is B. The `no ip domain lookup` command disables DNS-based host name to address translations.

Answers A, C, and D are all incorrect. All other syntax examples presented here produce an error.

50. The correct answer is A. The `show ip access-lists` command displays the contents of all access lists configured on the router.

Answers B, C, and D are all incorrect. All other syntax examples presented here produce an error.

51. The correct answer is C. Once you have made initial configuration changes and documented these changes, you should verify that the problem is solved and ensure that your solution did not introduce other problems.

Answer A is incorrect. You should get input from outside resources if you continue to make changes and cannot resolve the problem. Answer B is incorrect. You should document the solution, but this is the last step in the process. Answer D is incorrect. Restoring the original configurations on all devices is not a step in the procedure as defined by Cisco.

52. The correct answer is D. You should use the `show ip arp` command to display the Address Resolution Protocol (ARP) cache to see whether name resolution is working.

Answer A is incorrect. `show ip hosts` allows you to view the static host name to IP address mappings on the device. Answer B is incorrect. `show ip route` allows you to view the IP forwarding table. Answer C is incorrect. `show ip interface` allows you to view all parameters surrounding the interface, including error counter information.

53. The correct answer is C. A quick method of verifying DNS is to use IP addresses in place of host names when testing for connectivity. If tests pass with IP addresses and not with names, DNS is a potential problem.

Answer A is incorrect. Examining the routing table entries is not as efficient as testing connectivity using an IP address. Answer B is incorrect. Examining the router's configuration also is not efficient, and limits your investigation to the local router. Answer D is incorrect. Checking for obsolete address resolution entries is not valid. Answer E is incorrect. Using a ping is a correct method, but the IP address should be specified.

54. The correct answer is A. Symptoms that may be present during suboptimal performance of Data Link layer components includes excessive CRC and FCS errors.

Answers B, C, and D are all incorrect. Excessive utilization, an increased number of interface errors, and LEDs in an off indication are symptoms of a Physical layer problem.

55. The correct answer is A. Excessive utilization is a possible symptom of a Physical layer problem.

Answers B, C, and D are all incorrect. All other symptoms listed are Data Link layer related.

56. The correct answer is B. After narrowing the scope, you should use a layered troubleshooting approach to determine symptoms.

Answer A is incorrect. You document symptoms after you determine them. Answer C is incorrect. You solve the problem and document the solution as the last step. Answer D is incorrect. Finally, you begin isolating if you cannot solve the problem using the documented symptoms.

57. The correct answer is A. The show ip arp command allows you to see mappings between Layer 2 and Layer 3 network addresses.

Answer B is incorrect. show ip hosts allows you to view host name to ip address mappings. Answer C is incorrect. show ip routes allows you to view the IP forwarding table. Answer D is incorrect. show ip interface allows you to view IP parameters assigned to interfaces. Answer E is incorrect. show ip addresses is not a valid command.

58. The correct answers are A, D. Full-duplex permits greater bandwidth due to the elimination of collisions.

Answers B and C are incorrect. Full duplex connections cannot connect to other switches. Full duplex configurations are not limited to a maximum of 16 ports and 8 spanning trees.

59. The correct answer is B. You use the show frame-relay map command to view the mapping between the DLCI and a remote Layer 3 address.

Answer A is incorrect. show frame-relay is used with additional keywords. Answer C is incorrect. show frame relay dlci is not a valid command. Answer D is incorrect. show frame-relay counters is not a valid command. Answer E is incorrect. show interface [number] dlci is not a valid command.

60. The correct answer is C. You use the extended commands option to access these privileged mode ping features.

Answers A, B, and D are incorrect. Verbose, protocol options, and IP header commands are all valid privileged mode ping commands, yet none allow access to these features.

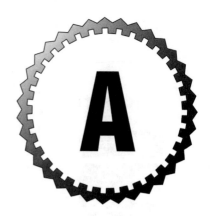

Top-Down and Bottom-Up Troubleshooting

Top-down and bottom-up troubleshooting are new terms that Cisco has added to this exam. Most of the time, when a user notices there is a problem, he or she notices a problem with the top layers of the OSI Reference model. This is because this is the point—somewhere between the Application layer and the Session layer—where the users interact with the applications they run.

Sometimes your user's problem may manifest itself as a problem connecting to the network. Immediately you might go check the cabling, check the switch LEDs, check the back of the NIC on the user's PC to see if there is a good connection and lit LEDs, then check the switch to see if there are any errors such as CRC errors or auto sensing errors. This type of troubleshooting involves checking items from the bottom layers of the OSI Reference model, which are somewhere between the Physical layers and Data Link layer.

If the problem is still not resolved, you will probably work your way up to the Network layer and check the IP addressing or other Network layer addressing to see if there is a problem there. Troubleshooting in this order within the OSI Reference model is an example of *bottom-up troubleshooting*.

To get a better picture in your mind of how the OSI Reference model looks, take a look at Figure A.1.

Let's add another scenario to our fictitious troubleshooting problem. Suppose that the first thing we do is open a Command Prompt on our problem user's PC, and the IP address we ping (to another device in the network) replies with successful Pings. This is a good indication that all of the system's bottom layers are working just fine.

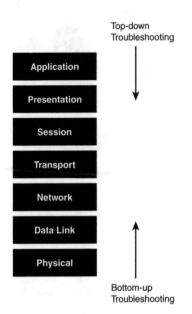

Top-down
Troubleshooting

Bottom-up
Troubleshooting

Figure A.1 The top-down and the bottom-up approaches to troubleshooting using the OSI Reference Model.

In this situation we will probably reverse our troubleshooting method and work from the top down. We would then start checking for upper-layer service issues, such as authentication, database service issues, compression problems, encryption problems, and so on. By starting our troubleshooting at the upper layers and working our way down, we are performing *top-down troubleshooting*.

The Cisco Campus Model

For the exam, you need to be able to take the same techniques that we applied to the OSI Reference Model and apply them to the Cisco Campus Model as well. Although the layers and functions are different, you can take a divide-and-conquer approach to the three layers of the Cisco Campus model and apply the same techniques learned previously. Your bottom-up troubleshooting would start by checking connectivity problems with your users accessing the campus from the Access layer. Next you would check the Distribution layer, and then you would move up to the Core layer where a majority of users would be affected.

Let's take a look at Figure A.2, which shows the Cisco Campus model and its three layers.

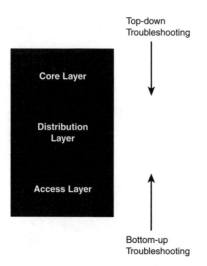

Figure A.2   The top-down and the bottom-up approach to troubleshooting using the Cisco Campus Model.

If you quickly determine that most or all of your users are affected by the problem, you would troubleshoot from the reverse direction and take a top-down troubleshooting approach. You would use this approach because the Core layer affects most of your users. The access layer would affect only localized data traffic affecting only a small percentage of users in the network.

Contacting Cisco
for Support

No one is an expert at every aspect of networking or Cisco routers and switches. There comes a time when you have to admit that you are having trouble configuring or troubleshooting your Cisco equipment. That's when you need to contact the Cisco Technical Assistance Center (TAC).

 Before you reach the point of contacting the TAC, you should be consistently preparing good documentation of your network and the troubleshooting efforts you've taken. Most problems are easy to fix, but the difficult problems require documentation of all the steps that are taken to solve the problem.

Although there is always a warranty on new equipment, it is still a good idea to keep a current Cisco maintenance contract. Different contracts cover replacement of any failed components, the configuration, and even onsite help if needed. If you don't have an existing maintenance contract, warranty, or service contract, you will be billed for TAC's services.

TAC has information about certain codes that isn't available to the general public. Cisco can access a lot of information quickly, and can save you time you'd otherwise spend in lengthy searches for the answers you need. TAC is available to you via email, fax, phone, and the Cisco Web site, Cisco Connection Online (CCO). Figure B.1 shows the Technical Support homepage of the Cisco CCO Web site.

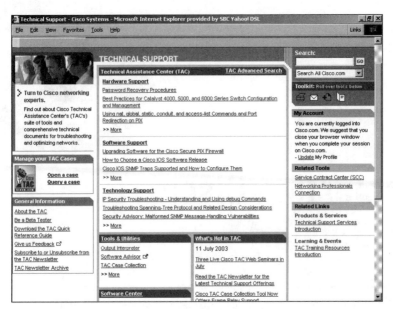

Figure B.1   The Technical Support home page on the Cisco CCO Web site.

Contacting the TAC

Before you call TAC, you should execute the show tech-support command from the problem equipment. The output of this command will provide TAC with additional information to help solve the problem. It is also a good idea to keep records of configuration changes, show or debug command output, and any other information relevant to the problem. TAC may request any of this information.

In contacting TAC, you must follow a standard process that Cisco has created when you choose not to go online and start a Cisco Support incident to receive technical service. The following are the steps you must follow to get assistance from TAC personnel:

1. When you first call TAC, the Customer Response Center will ask for the following information: name, company name, address, email address, contact name, telephone number, equipment type, equipment serial number, and a contract number, if any. At this point, the operator will assign a ticket number. It is a good idea to write down the ticket number, because it will be your reference for future contact.

2. The operator will ask for a brief description of the problem and for any additional information regarding the steps that you have taken to

resolve the problem. This is the time to describe all documentation that you have gathered. The operator will then assign a priority for your case and send it to the proper engineers. When assigning a priority, the operator uses these guidelines:

➤ Priority 1—Your production network is down or a portion of your production network is down. This priority requires a TAC engineer to stay on the phone during the entire outage or until the priority is downgraded.

➤ Priority 2—You have noticed a significant change in your network performance that is almost crippling your network.

➤ Priority 3—You have noticed that your network performance has been depleting over time and not rebounding.

➤ Priority 4—You need additional information from TAC, including answers to questions about code versions, configuration issues, and additional product information.

3. After your ticket has been routed to an engineering group, you will receive automated updates on the status of the ticket each time a change is made to the ticket's status or it is routed to another engineer. At this point, you will also be able to add any information and questions you may have regarding your problem via email or telephone.

Utilizing the Cisco CCO Site

Cisco's Web site provides a wealth of information regarding everything from new technology developments to code upgrades. For some people, it is almost too much information to gather, so carefully defining your search on the site is helpful.

The Cisco Connection Online (CCO) is designed for you to see any information regarding your equipment and any changes or "bugs" that have been found. The information pages enable you to see IOS configurations for routers and switches, along with troubleshooting tools. The CCO does provide more extensive information if you have a login account, in which case you are provided with extensive technical documents, Cisco code upgrades, detailed product information, and access to TAC.

To obtain a login account for CCO, you must be registered online as a Cisco user who has purchased a service contract from Cisco, an authorized Cisco partner, or be a Cisco Certified Internetwork Expert (CCIE).

Core Dumps

When contacting CCO, one of the troubleshooting methods they may ask you to perform is a core dump. If a router crashes, it may be useful to obtain a copy of the memory to see whether it indicates a cause for the crash. A *core dump* contains a picture of the information that is currently in the system memory. If your system memory (RAM) is very large, the core dump file also will be very large.

 Using core dump commands most likely will disrupt a production network while they are being performed. Use caution when using the commands. You should make sure that a slow down of the routers processing power will not effect the network's users.

You use the `exception` command to create a core dump. This command is used only after the router has crashed. Using the `exception` command enables you to configure a router to execute a core dump if a router has crashed. Before you use the `exception` command, you must know the IP address of a server, such as a TFTP, FTP, or RCP server. The following is an example of configuring an exception command to a TFTP server:

```
Support#
Support#config t
Enter configuration commands, one per line. End with
   CNTL/Z.
Support(config)#exception dump 207.212.78.110
Support(config)#^C
Support#
```

A TFTP server doesn't require any additional commands, whereas sending a core dump to an FTP or an RCP server requires a few additional commands to allow the transfer. The following is an example of configuring a core dump to an FTP server:

```
Support#
Support#config t
Enter configuration commands, one per line. End with
   CNTL/Z.
Support(config)#exception protocol ftp
Support(config)#ip ftp username support
Support(config)#ip ftp password ccnp
Support(config)#ip ftp source-interface serial 1
Support(config)#exception dump 207.212.78.110
Support(config)#exit
Support#
```

When a router is still on a network, you may also create a core dump from the command line. The following is an example of configuring a `write core` command:

```
Support#
Support#write core
Remote host? 207.212.78.110
Name of core file to wite [Router_A-core]?
Write file Router_A-core on host 207.212.78.110? [confirm]
Writing Router_A-core !!!!!!!!!!!!!!!!!!!!!!!!!!!!!!!!!!!!!!!!!!!!! [OK]
Support#
```

After you execute this command, the Cisco TAC personnel will be able to look at the dump and try to determine the problem the router is having. The core dump file will not be useful without the Cisco TAC personnel to interpret the source code.

When you retrieve a core dump from your router, the core dump will be in the form of a binary file. The binary file length will depend on the size of the memory in your router. After you retrieve the core dump, you must transfer the binary file to a server such as Trivial File Transfer Protocol (TFTP), File Transfer Protocol (FTP), or Remote Copy Protocol (RCP) server. At this point, you can send the file to Cisco personnel where it is then interpreted. Technical support representatives have access to the source code and memory maps to help identify the problem of the router before it crashed.

Cisco has a new Web site at **http://c2.cisco.com**. This Web site allows the Cisco technical support person helping you to use a chat feature or telnet from your local PC in to the router or switch you are working on. This feature allows you to view in real time or save a log of what the support representative does to help you.

After creating a core dump file, you may also want to include a few other files for the Cisco TAC. In the Privilege Exec Mode, the **show stacks** command will display data saved by the ROM monitor, which includes a failure type, an operand address, and a failure counter. Another good command is the **show version** command. This command shows the IOS version number, which enables the Cisco TAC personnel to make a more informed decision about how to handle the problem, since some versions of the IOS have various bugs that may contribute to the problem you are experiencing. If you're troubleshooting Ethernet, you should also include the **show interfaces** command as well.

By collecting all this information and forwarding this to the Cisco TAC, you can help in resolving your technical support issue quickly.

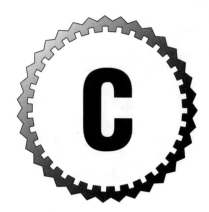

Scenario Questions

The Cisco Support exam scenario questions aren't easy. You won't be shown a picture of three routers—two of them shiny and new and the third smoking—and asked to choose which router has a problem. You may, instead, get a single description of a series of problems experienced by a very large network that connects routers and switches located across many cities. After reading the given scenario, you're asked to determine the source of the problems.

The following are three common scenarios similar to those you may encounter on the exam.

Scenario 1—Bad Subnetting

In Figure C.1, you will see a hub and spoke network. There are two subnetted IP addresses. One address is there to throw you off and is invalid. Do you know subnetting well enough to tell which link has an invalid subnet?

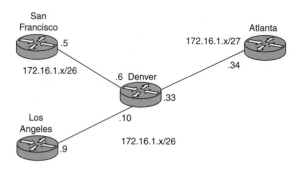

Figure C.1 A diagram showing invalid subnetting.

The link between Atlanta and Denver would be the problem link. The reason is that a /27 network is the same as stating a subnet of 255.255.255.224. If you take a magic number of 256 and subtract 224, you get 32. This means that the first network would be the .32 network, then second the .64 network. The broadcast addresses in the .32 network would be .63 and all the addresses in between would be valid. This means that if the interface in Denver was 172.16.1.33, the only valid addresses in that network would be from .34 to .62. Only those addresses could be used on the Atlanta side of the link.

Scenario 2—Utilizations

In Figure C.2, you are looking at routers in another hub and spoke network. The administrators of the routers in these four cities have recently used the show process cpu command on the routers and determined their average utilization. Looking at the utilization percentages of these four routers, which of them needs to be upgraded?

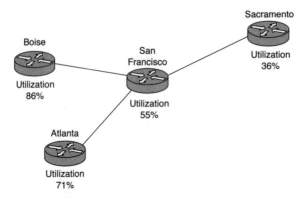

Figure C.2   The Average router utilizations from routers in four cities.

A router that is slow on its processing times is basically a better doorstop than a router in your network. Depending on the type of router, Cisco recommends that a router operating above 65 to 70 percent average utilization needs to be upgraded. If you go by the Cisco recommendations, this means that both the routers in Atlanta and Boise need to be upgraded or replaced.

Scenario 3—Determining the Probable Source

This is the type of scenario you can expect to see reflected in several questions on the exam. You should understand how ICMP works in the network as a troubleshooting tool. In Figure C.3, you see a network with five PCs on different floors. There is a connectivity issue and PCs on the first floor cannot communicate with PCs on the second floor.

The two PCs on the first floor can ping each other, but they cannot ping their own configured default gateway. The PCs on the second floor can successfully ping each other and their default gateway. The PCs on the second floor cannot ping the IP address of the first floor PCs' default gateway. What is the most likely problem?

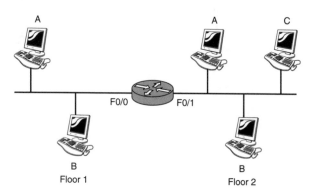

Figure C.3   A network where the first floor PCs have problems communicating with the PCs on the second floor.

In this case, the most likely problem could be narrowed down to either a misconfigured routing table on the router, an interface configuration problem , or a hardware problem with the Fast Ethernet 0/0 interface. One or more of these items would be listed as choices for correct answers on the exam.

Scenario 4—Determining the Probable Source II

For this final scenario, let's look at Figure C.3 a little differently. We already know that the first floor PCs can successfully ping themselves, but cannot ping their default gateway. What would be the most likely scenario if the PCs on the second floor could successfully ping themselves and the Fast Ethernet 0/0 interface, which is the default gateway of the PCs on the first floor?

If you know Cisco devices, you know that an address on a router interface is only successfully pingable if the interface is up and the protocols are configured correctly. This means that the Fast Ethernet 0/0 interface must be functioning and the configured address must be correct. Since the PCs can ping each other, this pretty much narrows down the possibilities to a single item. The default gateway configured on the PCs is wrong or not configured.

Conclusion

These are all scenarios you are likely to encounter on the exam. You should know subnetting and how ICMP works, as well as all the information found on the Cram Sheet at the front of the book. If you have a good understanding of all these items, as well as items taught to you throughout this book, you will pass the exam with a great score. Good luck.

What's on the CD-ROM

This appendix is a brief rundown of what you'll find on the CD-ROM that comes with this book. For a more detailed description of the PrepLogic Practice Exams, Preview Edition exam simulation software, see Appendix E, "Using PrepLogic Practice Exams, Preview Edition Software." In addition to the PrepLogic Practice Exams, Preview Edition software, the CD-ROM includes an electronic version of the book in Portable Document Format (PDF) and the source code used in the book.

PrepLogic Practice Tests, Preview Edition

PrepLogic is a leading provider of certification training tools. Trusted by certification students worldwide, PrepLogic is, we believe, the best practice exam software available. In addition to providing a means of evaluating your knowledge of the Exam Cram material, PrepLogic Practice Exams, Preview Edition features several innovations that help you to improve your mastery of the subject matter.

For example, the practice tests allow you to check your score by exam area or domain to determine which topics you need to study more. Another feature allows you to obtain immediate feedback on your responses in the form of explanations for the correct and incorrect answers.

PrepLogic Practice Exams, Preview Edition exhibits most of the full functionality of the Premium Edition but offers only a fraction of the total questions. To get the complete set of practice questions and exam functionality, visit PrepLogic.com and order the Premium Edition for this and other challenging exam titles.

Again for a more detailed description of the PrepLogic Practice Exams, Preview Edition features, see Appendix E.

An Exclusive Electronic Version of the Text

As mentioned previously, the CD-ROM that accompanies this book also contains an electronic PDF version of this book. This electronic version comes complete with all figures as they appear in the book. You can use Acrobat's handy search capability for study and review purposes.

Using PrepLogic
Practice Exams,
Preview Edition Software

This Exam Cram includes a special version of PrepLogic Practice Exams—a revolutionary test engine designed to give you the best in certification exam preparation. PrepLogic offers sample and practice exams for many of today's most in-demand and challenging technical certifications. This special Preview Edition is included with this book as a tool to use in assessing your knowledge of the Exam Cram material, while also providing you with the experience of taking an electronic exam.

This appendix describes in detail what PrepLogic Practice Exams, Preview Edition is, how it works, and what it can do to help you prepare for the exam. Note that although the Preview Edition includes all the test simulation functions of the complete, retail version, it contains only a single practice test. The Premium Edition, available at PrepLogic.com, contains the complete set of challenging practice exams designed to optimize your learning experience.

Exam Simulation

One of the main functions of PrepLogic Practice Exams, Preview Edition is exam simulation. To prepare you to take the actual vendor certification exam, PrepLogic is designed to offer the most effective exam simulation available.

Question Quality

The questions provided in the PrepLogic Practice Exams, Preview Edition are written to the highest standards of technical accuracy. The questions tap the content of the Exam Cram chapters and help you review and assess your knowledge before you take the actual exam.

Interface Design

The PrepLogic Practice Exams, Preview Edition exam simulation interface provides you with the experience of taking an electronic exam. This enables you to effectively prepare for taking the actual exam by making the test experience a familiar one. Using this test simulation can help eliminate the sense of surprise or anxiety you might experience in the testing center because you will already be acquainted with computerized testing.

Effective Learning Environment

The PrepLogic Practice Exams, Preview Edition interface provides a learning environment that not only Exams you through the computer, but also teaches the material you need to know to pass the certification exam. Each question comes with a detailed explanation of the correct answer and often provides reasons the other options are incorrect. This information helps to reinforce the knowledge you already have and also provides practical information you can us on the job.

Software Requirements

PrepLogic Practice Exams requires a computer with the following:

➤ Microsoft Windows 98, Windows Me, Windows NT 4.0, Windows 2000, or Windows XP

➤ A 166MHz or faster processor is recommended

➤ A minimum of 32MB of RAM

➤ As with any Windows application, the more memory, the better your performance

➤ 10MB of hard drive space

Installing PrepLogic Practice Exams, Preview Edition

Install PrepLogic Practice Exams, Preview Edition by running the setup program on the PrepLogic Practice Exams, Preview Edition CD. Follow these instructions to install the software on your computer.

1. Insert the CD into your CD-ROM drive. The Autorun feature of Windows should launch the software. If you have Autorun disabled, click Start and select Run. Go to the root directory of the CD and select setup.exe. Click Open, and then click OK.

2. The Installation Wizard copies the PrepLogic Practice Exams, Preview Edition files to your hard drive; adds PrepLogic Practice Exams, Preview Edition to your Desktop and Program menu; and installs test engine components to the appropriate system folders.

Removing PrepLogic Practice Exams, Preview Edition from Your Computer

If you elect to remove the PrepLogic Practice Exams, Preview Edition product from your computer, an uninstall process has been included to ensure that it is removed from your system safely and completely. Follow these instructions to remove PrepLogic Practice Exams, Preview Edition from your computer:

1. Select Start, Settings, Control Panel.

2. Double-click the Add/Remove Programs icon.

3. You are presented with a list of software installed on your computer. Select the appropriate PrepLogic Practice Exams, Preview Edition title you want to remove. Click the Add/Remove button. The software is then removed from your computer.

Using PrepLogic Practice Exams, Preview Edition

PrepLogic is designed to be user friendly and intuitive. Because the software has a smooth learning curve, your time is maximized because you start practicing almost immediately. PrepLogic Practice Exams, Preview Edition has two major modes of study: Practice Test and Flash Review.

Using Practice Test mode, you can develop your test-taking abilities as well as your knowledge through the use of the Show Answer option. While you are taking the test, you can expose the answers along with a detailed explanation of why the given answers are right or wrong. This gives you the ability to better understand the material presented.

Flash Review is designed to reinforce exam topics rather than quiz you. In this mode, you will be shown a series of questions but no answer choices. Instead, you will be given a button that reveals the correct answer to the question and a full explanation for that answer.

Starting a Practice Test Mode Session

Practice Test mode enables you to control the exam experience in ways that actual certification exams do not allow:

➤ **Enable Show Answer Button**—Activates the Show Answer button, allowing you to view the correct answer(s) and full explanation(s) for each question during the exam. When not enabled, you must wait until after your exam has been graded to view the correct answer(s) and explanation.

➤ **Enable Item Review Button**—Activates the Item Review button, allowing you to view your answer choices, marked questions, and to facilitate navigation between questions.

➤ **Randomize Choices**—Randomize answer choices from one exam session to the next. Makes memorizing question choices more difficult therefore keeping questions fresh and challenging longer.

To begin studying in Practice Test mode, click the Practice Test radio button from the main exam customization screen. This enables the options detailed in the preceding list.

To your left, you are presented with the option of selecting the preconfigured Practice Test or creating your own Custom Test. The preconfigured test has a fixed time limit and number of questions. Custom Exams allow you to configure the time limit and the number of questions in your exam.

The Preview Edition included with this book includes a single preconfigured Practice Test. Get the compete set of challenging PrepLogic Practice Exams at PrepLogic.com and make certain you're ready for the big exam.

Click the Begin Exam button to begin your exam.

Starting a Flash Review Mode Session

Flash Review mode provides you with an easy way to reinforce topics covered in the practice questions. To begin studying in Flash Review mode, click the Flash Review radio button from the main exam customization screen. Select either the preconfigured Practice Test or create your own Custom Test.

Click the Best Exam button to begin your Flash Review of the exam questions.

Standard PrepLogic Practice Exams, Preview Edition Options

The following list describes the function of each of the buttons you see. Depending on the options, some of the buttons will be grayed out and inaccessible or missing completely. Buttons that are appropriate are active. The buttons are as follows:

➤ **Exhibit**—This button is visible if an exhibit is provided to support the question. An exhibit is an image that provides supplemental information necessary to answer the question.

➤ **Item Review**—This button leaves the question window and opens the Item Review screen. From this screen you will see all questions, your answers, and your marked items. You will also see correct answers listed here when appropriate.

➤ **Show Answer**—This option displays the correct answer with an explanation of why it is correct. If you select this option, the current question is not scored.

➤ **Mark Item**—Check this box to tag a question you need to review further. You can view and navigate your Marked Items by clicking the Item Review button (if enabled). When grading your exam, you will be notified if you have marked items remaining.

➤ **Previous Item**—View the previous question.

➤ **Next Item**—View the next question.

➤ **Grade Exam**—When you have completed your exam, click to end your exam and view your detailed score report. If you have unanswered or marked items remaining, you will be asked if you would like to continue taking your exam or view your exam report.

Time Remaining

If the test is timed, the time remaining is displayed on the upper-right corner of the application screen. It counts down minutes and seconds remaining to complete the test. If you run out of time, you will be asked if you want to continue taking the test or if you want to end your exam.

Your Examination Score Report

The Examination Score Report screen appears when the Practice Test mode ends—as the result of time expiration, completion of all questions, or your decision to terminate early.

This screen provides you with a graphical display of your test score with a breakdown of scores by topic domain. The graphical display at the top of the screen compares your overall score with the PrepLogic Exam Competency Score.

The PrepLogic Exam Competency Score reflects the level of subject competency required to pass this vendor's exam. Although this score does not directly translate to a passing score, consistently matching or exceeding this score does suggest you possess the knowledge to pass the actual vendor exam.

Review Your Exam

From the Your Score Report screen, you can review the exam that you just completed by clicking on the View Items button. Navigate through the items, viewing the questions, your answers, the correct answers, and the explanations for those questions. You can return to your score report by clicking the View Items button.

Get More Exams

Each PrepLogic Practice Exams, Preview Edition that accompanies your training guide contains a single PrepLogic Practice Test. Certification students worldwide trust PrepLogic Practice Exams to help them pass their IT certification exams the first time. Purchase the Premium Edition of PrepLogic Practice Exams and get the entire set of all new challenging Practice Exams for this exam. PrepLogic Practice Exams—Because You Want to Pass the First Time.

Contacting PrepLogic

If you would like to contact PrepLogic for any reason, including information about our extensive line of certification practice Exams, we invite you to do so. Please contact us online at www.preplogic.com.

Customer Service

If you have a damaged product and need a replacement or refund, please call the following phone number:

800-858-7674

Product Suggestions and Comments

We value your input! Please email your suggestions and comments to the following address:

feedback@preplogic.com

License Agreement

YOU MUST AGREE TO THE TERMS AND CONDITIONS OUT-LINED IN THE END USER LICENSE AGREEMENT ("EULA") PRESENTED TO YOU DURING THE INSTALLATION PROCESS. IF YOU DO NOT AGREE TO THESE TERMS, DO NOT INSTALL THE SOFTWARE.

Glossary

Area Border Router (ABR)
The router running an OSPF protocol and placed on the border of one or more OSPF areas. An ABR connects the OSPF areas to the OSPF backbone.

Access layer
In the *Campus Hierarchical model*, the Access layer is where the workstation connects to the network. Hubs and switches reside here, and it's also where workgroups access the network.

access list
A security feature used with the Cisco IOS to filter traffic types as part of data routing. Access lists are also used to filter traffic between different VLAN numbers.

active monitor
Active monitor is used in Token Ring and refers to the node on a Token Ring network that is responsible for management tasks, such as preventing loops and monitoring the token's activities. A network can have multiple active monitors.

address
A set of numbers, usually expressed in binary format, that are used to identify and locate a resource or device on a network.

address filter
A way of using Layer 2 MAC addresses or switching ports to filter traffic. This process allows you to filter traffic and restrict access without the use of VLANs, and is a feature of the Cisco Catalyst 3000 Series. Although it uses a process similar to access lists on the Cisco IOS, you can apply multiple address filters to the same interface.

Address Resolution Protocol (ARP)

The protocol that is used to map an IP address to a MAC address. Described at the Internet layer of the DoD model, ARP is used to find a hardware address, given the IP address.

administrative distance

This distance is defined with a number from 0 to 225 that represents the integrity of a routing information source. This term usually refers to a particular protocol. The lower the number, the more trustworthy it is.

American National Standards Institute (ANSI)

The organization that publishes standards for communications, programming languages, and networking.

ANDing

The process of comparing the bits of an IP address with the bits in a subnet mask to determine how a packet will be handled.

anycast address

An address used in ATM for shared multiple-end systems. An anycast address allows a frame to be sent to specific groups of hosts.

AppleTalk

A group of protocols used in Macintosh computer environments. These protocols allow a network—or more than one network—to operate in more than one zone.

Application layer

The layer of the OSI model that provides support for end users and for application programs using network resources.

area

Usually used in CLNS, DECnet, or OSPF networks, an area is a logical set of segments and devices that are defined as a particular group. Routers use areas to distinguish a defined group to create a single autonomous system (AS).

Asymmetric Digital Subscriber Line (ADSL)

A service that transmits digital voice and data over existing analog phone lines.

Asynchronous Transfer Mode (ATM)

ATM is an international standard used in high-speed transmission media such as E3, SONET, and T3 for cell relay that is common in today's corporate networks. ATM guarantees throughput, minimizes delay, and can provide scalability at speeds up to many gigabits per second.

attachment unit interface (AUI)

IEEE 802.3 specification used between a multistation access unit (MAU) and an Ethernet network interface card (NIC). MAUs are typically associated with Token Ring networks; AUI ports are specific to Ethernet. This cable connects an AUI port on the Ethernet access card to an Ethernet 10Base2, 10Base5, or 10BaseFx transceiver.

attachment unit interface (AUI) connector

A 15-pin, D-type connector that is sometimes used with Ethernet connections.

attenuation

The loss of signal that is experienced as data is transmitted across network media.

autonegotiation

Allows a hub or switch and a network device to communicate their compatibilities and agree upon an optimal communication speed and/or duplex.

autonomous switching

A switching mechanism that allows Cisco routers to process packets faster by using the Ciscobus—and not the system processor—to switch packets.

autonomous system (AS)

A group of networks (defined by routers) that are running the same routing protocol. Autonomous systems are subdivided by areas and must be assigned a 16-bit number to identify the area.

backbone

A high-capacity infrastructure system that provides optimal transport on a LAN. In a LAN, the data running from router to router, switch to switch, or switch to router is typically transported through a faster physical topology than the rest of the local area or virtual LAN devices. The backbone is the physical cable.

BackboneFast

A protocol used on a switch. When initiated, a root port or blocked port receives an inferior BPDU from its designated bridge, the MaxAge timer is bypassed, and the secondary or backup port immediately changes to the forwarding mode.

backplane

The primary data/control bus located on a Cisco Catalyst switch, and similar to the motherboard in a PC. The Backplane interconnects all the modules inside the switch chassis.

bandwidth

The rated throughput capacity of a given network protocol or medium.

base bandwidth

The difference between the lowest and highest frequencies that are available for network signals. The term is also used to describe the rated throughput capacity of a given network protocol or medium.

Basic Rate Interface (BRI)

An ISDN digital communications line that consists of three independent channels: two bearer (or B) channels, each at 64Kbps; and one data (or D) channel at 16Kbps. ISDN BRI is often referred to as *2B+D*.

baseline

Refers to a network's average performance that is established using the networks historical data and routine network utilizations. A network baseline allows for accurate monitoring and measurement, and serves as an effective guide to determine network changes or faults.

binary

The base 2 numbering system, characterized by its use of ones and zeros and used in digital signaling.

binding

The process of associating a protocol and a network interface card (NIC).

bit

An electronic digit used in the binary numbering system.

blocking architecture

A condition in which the total bandwidth of the ports is greater than the capacity of the switching fabric.

bridge

A device that connects and passes packets between two network segments that use the same communications protocol. Bridges operate at the Data Link layer of the OSI reference model to filter, forward, or flood an incoming frame based on the MAC address of that frame.

Bridge Protocol Data Unit (BPDU)

A multicast frame that is generated by the switch and carries information about itself and changes in the network topology.

bridging address table

A list of MAC addresses kept by bridges and used when packets are received to determine which segment the destination address is on, before sending the packet to the next interface or dropping the packet if it is on the same segment as the sending node.

broadband

A communications strategy that uses analog signaling over multiple communications channels.

broadcast

A packet delivery system in which a copy of a packet is given to all hosts attached to the network.

broadcast domain

In a nonswitched network, all the devices that can receive a broadcast sent on the physical wire from one machine in the network. The broadcast domain is a segment that's not separated by a Layer 2 device or Layer 3 device that can filter broadcasts. On a switched network using VLANs, the broadcast domain is all the ports or collision domains that belong to the same VLAN.

broadcast storm

Occurs when broadcasts throughout the LAN become so numerous that they consume all the available bandwidth on a LAN, slowing the network to a halt.

buffer

A storage area to receive/store data while it is waiting to be processed. Buffers are mainly used by devices that receive and store data from faster processing devices, and allow the device to process the data as fast as the processing speeds allow.

bus

A path used by electrical signals to travel between the CPU and the attached hardware.

bus topology

A linear LAN architecture that uses a common cable with multipoint connections for the flow of data in a serial progression to all nodes on that network segment.

byte

A set of bits (usually eight) that operates as a unit to signify a single character.

campus

A group of buildings in a fixed geographical location, owned and controlled by an organization.

carrier access module (CAM)

A module attaching to the ATM cell switching bus. A CAM can support two port-adapter modules to provide physical ATM line ports used by end nodes. A CAM can be placed in the Cisco Catalyst 5500 in slot 9, 10, 11, or 12; it can be placed in the LS1010 in slot 0, 1, 3, or 4.

Carrier Sense Multiple Access with Collision Avoidance (CSMA/CA)

A media-access method comprised of collision-avoidance techniques used in Ethernet.

Carrier Sense Multiple Access with Collision Detection (CSMA/CD)

A media-access method involving collision detection that listens to the network to see if it is in use. If the network is clear, data is transmitted. If a collision occurs, both stations retransmit their data.

Challenge Handshake Authentication Protocol (CHAP)

Protocol used with PPP encapsulation as a security feature that identifies the remote end. After performing CHAP, the router determines whether the user is permitted access.

change control

A detailed record that documents every change made to the network.

channel

A communications path used for data transmission.

channelized T-1

A link that is separated into 23 B channels and one D channel of 64Kbps each, with the link operating at 1.544Mbps. This link can support DDR, frame relay, and X.25.

channel service unit (CSU)

A network communications device used to connect to the digital equipment lines of the common carrier, usually over a dedicated line or Frame Relay. Used in conjunction with a *data service unit (DSU)*.

checksum

A mathematical method that uses a recalculation method to compare the data sent and received to determine whether the destination is receiving the correct amount of data from the source.

Cisco Connection Online (CCO)

Cisco's Web site that offers device documentation and technical support. It also features new technology and the recent upgrades of device codes.

Cisco Discovery Protocol (CDP)

A Cisco protocol that gathers and stores information regarding other neighboring devices on the network. It can be used in Ethernet, Token Ring, Serial, and FDDI media types. All Cisco devices including hubs support CDP.

Cisco Express Forwarding (CEF)

Cisco's newest ASIC, which utilizes the Forwarding Information Base and an adjacency table to route Layer 2 and Layer 3 addresses with very high performance.

Cisco Group Management Protocol (CGMP)

A Cisco protocol used by the Catalyst switch to forward multicast frames intelligently. CGMP dynamically discovers user stations participating in multicast applications and, when receiving a multicast, forwards the multicast directly to the users instead of broadcasting it throughout the network.

Class A network

A TCP/IP network that uses addresses starting between 1 and 126; IPv4 supports up to 126 Class Anetworks with 16,777,214 unique hosts each.

Class B network

A TCP/IP network that uses addresses starting between 128 and 191; IPv4 supports up to 16,384 Class B networks with 65,534 unique hosts each.

Class C network

A TCP/IP network that uses addresses starting between 192 and 223; IPv4 supports up to 2,097,152 Class C networks with 254 unique hosts each.

Class D network

A TCP/IP network that uses addresses starting between 224.0.0.0 and 239.255.255.255. Typically reserved for experimental uses and not found in production networks.

Class E network

A TCP/IP network that uses addresses starting between 240 and 254. Typically reserved for experimental uses and not found in production networks.

classless interdomain routing (CIDR)

A technique that allows multiple addresses to be consolidated into a single entry.

Clear Header

A field (part of the 802.10 header) that copies the encrypted Protected Header for security purposes to help guarantee against tampering with the frame. Also known as the *Secure Data Exchange (SDE) Protocol Data Unit.*

client

A node that requests a service from another node on a network.

client/server networking

Networking architecture utilizing front-end demand nodes that request and process data stored by the back end or resource node.

collision

The result of two frames transmitting simultaneously. When these two frames collide in an Ethernet network, both frames are destroyed.

collision domain

All the interfaces on a single segment that can send data on the same physical wire. In a hub, all the interfaces that are connected to its ports are in their own collision domain. In the case of a switch, all the nodes connected to each individual port are in their own collision domain.

color blocking logic (CBL)

A feature of the SAMBA ASIC used to enable the EARL to make forwarding decisions. It also ensures that a tagged frame coming from a particular VLAN does not exit through a port that belongs to another VLAN. CBL also assists in placing ports in one of four different modes for the Spanning Tree Protocol: blocking, learning, listening, or forwarding.

Command-Line Interface (CLI)

Software on Cisco devices that allows you to use commands to configure and control the devices.

communication

The transfer of information among nodes on a network.

congestion

A large amount of traffic that exceeds the network's capability to process traffic in a timely manner.

connection-oriented communication

Packet transfer in which the delivery is guaranteed.

connectionless-oriented communication

Packet transfer in which the delivery is not guaranteed.

connectivity

The linking of nodes on a network so communication can take place.

Content Addressable Memory (CAM)

A table used by a bridge to make forwarding and filtering decisions. The CAM table contains MAC addresses with port addresses leading to the physical interfaces. The CAM table uses a specialized interface that is faster than RAM to make the forwarding and filtering decisions. The CAM table updates information by examining the frames it receives from a segment and then updating the table with the source MAC address from the frame.

control plane

Functions that dictate how data actually flows through the switch fabric.

convergence

The amount of time it takes for all routers on the network to update their routing tables.

Copper Distributed Data Interface (CDDI)

The implementation of the FDDI standard using electrical cable rather than optical cable.

core block

The end point for networks, requiring fast access and no policy implementation.

Core layer

In the Cisco hierarchical model, the backbone of the network, designed for high-speed data transmission.

cost

The number of hop counts it takes a transmission to reach a destination via a certain path. Routing protocols use cost to determine paths, with the premise being that the lower the cost, the better the path.

crosstalk

Electronic interference caused when two wires are too close to each other.

cut-through packet switching

A switching method that does not copy the entire packet into the switch buffers. Instead, the destination address is placed in buffers, the route to the destination node is determined, and the packet is quickly sent out the corresponding port. The switch begins forwarding the frame as soon as the first 13 bytes and MAC address are received. It relies on the receiving device to discard the frame if there is corruption. Cut-through packet switching maintains a low latency.

cyclic redundancy check (CRC)
A method used to check for errors in packets that have been transferred across a network. A computation bit is added to the packet and recalculated at the destination to determine if the entire packet contents have been transferred correctly.

D channel
The D channel is a 16Kbps (BRI) or 64Kbps (PRI) ISDN channel.

DAC
A device connected to the FDDI counter-rotating rings. The DAC serves as a hub to provide passive connections to the rings for peripheral devices.

data communications equipment (DCE)
The physical connection to the network that provides a link between a DTE and a DCE device. DCE is also used in a lab environment with DTE to simulate a WAN environment. Also defined as d*ata circuit-terminating equipment.*

data field
The field or section in a frame that contains the data.

data plane
Functions applied directly against the actual data being directed in and out of the switching fabric.

Data-Link Connection Identifier (DLCI)
The identifier of virtual circuits used in Frame Relay networks.

Data Link layer
This is Layer 2 of the OSI reference model. The Data Link layer is above the Physical layer. Data comes off the cable, through the Physical layer, and into the Data Link layer.

data service unit (DSU)
Formats and controls data for transmission over digital lines. Used in conjunction with a *channel service unit (CSU)*.

data terminal equipment (DTE)
A physical device at the user end of a user-network interface. These devices serve as a data source, a destination, or both, and include computers, protocol translators, and multiplexers. A DTE combined with a DCE also simulates a WAN environment used in a lab.

datagram
Information groupings that are transmitted as a unit at the Network layer.

debug

A CLI command that allows for detailed information or a snapshot of certain interfaces or links. This command is used in troubleshooting a problem, not for monitoring.

dedicated line

A constant connection between two points, generally used in WANs.

default gateway

Normally, a router or a multi-homed computer to which packets are sent when they are destined for a host that is not on their segment of the network.

demand node

Any end user or interface that requests and accesses network resources, such as servers or printers.

demarc

An established point between the carrier equipment and the customer premise equipment (CPE).

designated bridge

A segment forwarding a frame to the root bridge with the lowest cost.

designated root bridge

The MAC address of the root bridge.

designated root cost

The cost of the shortest path to the root bridge.

designated root port

The port that is chosen as the lowest cost to the root bridge. Routing and bridging protocols use cost to determine paths, with the premise being that the lower the cost, the better the path.

designated root priority

The priority of the root bridge. All bridges have a default priority of 32,768.

destination address

The network address where the frame is being sent. In a packet, this address is encapsulated in a field of the packet so that all nodes know where the frame is being sent.

Destination Service Access Point (DSAP)

A one-byte field in the frame that combines with the service access point (SAP) to inform the receiving host of the identity of the destination host.

dial-up line

A circuit that is established by a switched-circuit connection from the telephone company network.

dialed number identification service

The method for delivery of automatic number identification using out-of-band signaling.

diameter

A unit of measurement between the root switch and child switches, calculated from the root bridge. The root bridge counts as the first switch, and each subsequent child switch out from the root bridge is added to produce the diameter number.

dial-up networking

The connection of a remote node to a network using *POTS* or *PSTN*.

digital subscriber line (DSL)

A public network technology that delivers high bandwidth over conventional copper wiring at limited distances.

distance-vector algorithm

An algorithm for finding the shortest path to a destination. The algorithm requires each router to update its neighbors about given hop routes.

distributed switching

An implementation in which switching decisions are made at either the local port or the line module.

Distribution layer

In the Cisco hierarchical model, this layer functions as the separation point between the Core and Access layers of the network. The devices in the Distribution layer implement the policies that define how packets are to be distributed to the groups within the network.

domain

A logical grouping of interfaces in a network or intranet to identify a controlled network of nodes that are grouped as an administrative unit.

domain name system (DNS)

Used to identify host names that correspond to IP addresses.

dual attached stations (DAS)

A connection that allows a device to connect to both FDDI counter-rotating rings.

dual-homed

An FDDI end station attached to two DACs for redundancy.

Dynamic Host Configuration Protocol (DHCP)

A protocol that provides an IP address to requesting nodes on the network.

Dynamic ISL

A protocol that performs trunking negotiation and verifies that the two connected ports can become trunk links. A Dynamic ISL port can be configured in one of four modes: On, Off, Desirable, or Auto.

dynamic VLAN port

A VLAN number assigned to a certain MAC address. The node attaching to any dynamic port on the switch is a member of the VLAN assigned to the MAC address. Dynamically assigned

VLANs are configured with CiscoWorks 2000 or CiscoWorks for Switched Internetworks software.

dynamic window

A mechanism that prevents the sender of data from overwhelming the receiver. The amount of data that can be buffered in a dynamic window can vary. See also *flow control*.

electromagnetic interference (EMI)

External interference from electromagnetic signals, causing reduction of data integrity and increased error rates in a transmission medium.

Electronics Industries Association (EIA)

The group that specifies electrical transmission standards. See also *Telecommunications Industry Association*.

emulated LAN (ELAN)

A feature used by ATM LANE to perform the basic functionality of a VLAN in Token Ring or Ethernet environments. Like VLANs, ELANs require a route processor such as a router to route frames between ELANs.

encapsulation

A technique used by layered protocols in which a layer adds header information to the *protocol data unit (PDU)* from the layer above.

Encoded Address Recognition Logic (EARL) ASIC

An *ASIC* located on the Catalyst 5000 family of switches that sees all the frames that cross the bus and performs a task similar to that of the content addressable memory (CAM). The ASIC is responsible for making switching decisions based on the MAC address and the source VLAN. It's also responsible for updating the address table.

encryption

The modification of data for security purposes prior to transmission, so that it is not readable without the proper decoding method.

end-to-end VLAN

A *VLAN* in which users (or groups of users) who utilize a common set of security requirements are grouped independently of the physical location. The port becomes a member of the VLAN assigned to the user, or MAC address of the user's machine. This type of VLAN is beneficial for networks whose resource nodes are not centralized in one common area. Users moving around the campus network remain in the same VLAN.

Enhanced Interior Gateway Routing Protocol (EIGRP)

A Cisco protocol containing link-state and distance-vector protocols to create a more efficient routing protocol.

Enterprise Services
Services that involve crossing the backbone to achieve access. These services are typically located on a subnet that is separate from the rest of the network devices.

EtherChannel
A connection used on the Catalyst 3000 family or Kalpana switches. It can utilize half- or full-duplex links and allows as many as seven Ethernet links to be bundled and load-balanced frame by frame to provide up to 140Mps of bandwidth.

ethernet interface processor (EIP)
An interface processor card found in the Cisco 7000 supporting Ethernet, via 10Mbps AUI ports, allowing a path to other interfaces.

extended IP access list
An access list that allows the extended filtering of packets based on address, protocol, traffic, or port.

extended ping
This option is available in the Privileged Mode of a router, allowing a defined number of ICMP requests sent to a destination.

Fast EtherChannel
A connection used on the Catalyst 5000 family of switches that allows as many as seven Ethernet links to be bundled and load-balanced frame by frame to provide up to 800Mbps of bandwidth.

Fast Ethernet
The IEEE 802.3 specification allowing for data transfers of up to 100Mbps. See also *100BaseT*.

fault tolerance
A theoretical concept defined as a resistance to failure. It is not an absolute and can be defined only in degrees.

fiber (or fibre) channel
A technology that defines full giga-bit-per-second (Gps) data transfer over fiber-optic cable.

Fiber Distributed Data Interface (FDDI)
A high-speed, data-transfer technology that is designed to extend the capabilities of existing LANs using a dual rotating-ring technology similar to Token Ring.

File Transfer Protocol (FTP)
The set of standards or protocols that allows you to transfer complete files between different computer hosts.

firewall
A device or group of devices configured with access lists and other mechanisms to stop unwanted traffic from entering a specific portion of a network.

flash memory
A type of memory that holds its contents (usually the operating system) when the power is cycled off.

flow control

A method used to control the amount of data that is transmitted within a given period of time. There are different types of flow control. See also *dynamic window* and *static window*.

Forwarding Engine (FE)

A major component of ASIC; part of the ClearChannel architecture on the Cisco Catalyst Series 1900 and 2820 switches. FE is responsible for learning addresses, allocating buffer space in the shared memory space, frame queuing, forwarding decisions, and maintaining statistics.

Forwarding Information Based Switching (FIB)

Similar to a routing table or information base, FIB is a mirror image of the routing information contained in the IP routing table. It updates this information and recalculates the next-hop information whenever the network's routing or topology changes. FIB, used with *CEF ASIC*, maintains a list of all known routes and eliminates the need for the route cache maintenance that is associated with fast switching or optimum switching.

fragment-free switching

A fast packet-switching method that reads the first 64 bytes of the frame to determine whether the frame is corrupted. If this first part is intact, the frame is forwarded. Also known as *runtless switching*.

frame

The grouping of information that is transmitted as a unit across the network at the Data Link layer.

Frame Check Sequence

This field performs a cyclic redundancy check (CRC) to ensure that all of the frame's data arrives intact.

frame filtering

This process uses a filtering table to drop frames based on a certain value contained in any one of the many fields in the data frame, such as the source or destination address. As part of normal operations, switches share filter tables. The frame's contents are compared to the filter table in the switch, thereby increasing the latency of the switch. Although frame filtering is useful for VLANs, it is not used in the Cisco Catalyst 5000 or 6000 family of switches to implement VLANs.

Frame Length

In a data frame, this field specifies the length of a frame. The maximum length for an 802.3 frame is 1,518 bytes.

Frame Relay

A switching protocol on the Data Link layer that is used across multiple virtual circuits of a common carrier, giving the user the appearance of a dedicated line.

frame tagging

A VLAN implementation method used to add VLAN information to data frames. A frame is tagged with VLAN information when it enters the switch, and the frame retains this information through the switch fabric. The tagging is removed before the frame exits the switch port with the attached destination interface. The entire process is transparent to the sending and receiving interfaces.

Frame Type

In a data frame, this field names the protocol that is being sent in the frame.

full duplex

Transmission method in which the sending and receiving (Rx and Tx) channels are separate, thus preventing collisions. Data is transmitted in two directions simultaneously on separate physical wires.

gateway

A hardware and software solution that enables communication between two dissimilar networking systems or protocols. Gateways usually operate at the upper layers of the OSI protocol stack, above the Transport layer.

Get Nearest Server (GNS)

Used on an IPX network, NetWare-enabled devices send a request packet to locate the nearest active server of a given type. GNS is part of IPX and SAP.

gigabit (Gb)

One billion bits or one thousand megabits.

Gigabit Ethernet

The IEEE specification for transfer rates up to one gigabit per second. See also *1000BaseX*.

half duplex

A circuit designed for data transmission in both directions, but not simultaneously.

head-of-line blocking

A situation in which congestion on an outbound port limits throughput to uncongested ports. Head-of-line blocking is completely different from *oversubscription*, in that physical data from another source device blocks the data of the sending device.

high-level data link compression (HDLC)

A Layer 2 serial encapsulation method that is used by PPP to transfer data over serial point-to-point links. HDLC is a bit-oriented protocol that uses frames and checksums to transfer the data.

hop

A recorded movement between two network nodes.

host

Any system on a network. In the Unix world, any device that is assigned an IP address.

host ID

A unique identifier for a client or resource on a network.

hostname

The NetBIOS name of the computer or node, given to the first element of the Internet domain name. It must be unique on your network.

Hot Standby Routing Protocol (HSRP)

A Cisco protocol that provides redundancy. Should a link fail, another can be configured to take its place.

hub

A hardware device that connects multiple independent nodes. Also known as a *concentrator* or *multiport repeater*.

Hypertext Transfer Protocol (HTTP)

The protocol used by Web browsers to transfer pages and files from a remote node to your computer.

input/output (I/O)

Any operation in which data either enters a node or is sent out of a node.

Institute of Electrical and Electronics Engineers (IEEE)

A professional organization that develops standards for networking and communications.

Integrated Local Management Interface (ILMI)

A protocol created by the ATM forum to allow any ATM switch and ATM device to communicate using the Simple Network Management Protocol (SNMP).

Integrated Services Digital Network (ISDN)

An internationally adopted standard for end-to-end digital communications over Public Switched Telephone Network (PSTN) that permits telephone networks to carry data, voice, and other source traffic.

intelligent hubs

Hubs that contain some management or monitoring capability.

Interior Gateway Routing Protocol (IGRP)

A Cisco protocol using a distance-vector algorithm to calculate the best path using the factors of load, bandwidth, delay, the MTU, and reliability.

internal IPX address

A unique eight-digit number that is used to identify a server. This address is usually generated at random when the server is installed.

internal loopback address

Used for testing with TCP/IP. This address—127.0.0.1—allows a test packet to reflect back into the sending adapter to determine whether it is functioning properly.

International Organization for Standardization (ISO)

A volunteer organization, founded in 1946, which is responsible for creating international standards in many areas, including communications and computers.

Internet Control Message Protocol (ICMP)

The Network-layer Internet protocol, documented in RFC 792, that reports errors and provides other information relevant to IP packet processing.

Internet Engineering Task Force (IETF)

A group of research volunteers responsible for specifying the protocols used on the Internet and for specifying the architecture of the Internet.

Internet Group Management Protocol (IGMP)

The protocol responsible for managing and reporting IP multicast group memberships.

Internet layer

In the TCP/IP architectural model, this layer is responsible for the addressing, packaging, and routing functions. Protocols operating at this layer of the model are responsible for encapsulating packets into Internet datagrams. All necessary routing algorithms are run here.

Internet Protocol (IP)

The Network-layer protocol, documented in RFC 791, that offers a connectionless internetwork service. IP provides features for addressing, packet fragmentation and reassembly, type-of-service specification, and security.

Internet Research Task Force (IRTF)

The research arm of the *Internet Architecture Board*. This group performs research in areas of Internet protocols, applications, architecture, and technology.

internetwork

A group of networks that are connected by routers or other connectivity devices so that the networks function as one network.

Internetwork Operating System (IOS)

Cisco's proprietary operating system used in its routers and switches.

Internetwork Packet Exchange (IPX)

The Network-layer protocol generally used by Novell's NetWare network operating system. IPX provides connectionless communication, supporting packet up to 64K in size.

Internetwork Packet Exchange/Sequenced Packet Exchange (IPX/SPX)

This protocol is the default used in NetWare networks, and it is a combination of the IPX protocol (to provide addressing) and SPX (to provide guaranteed delivery for IPX). It's similar in nature to its counterpart, TCP/IP.

Inter-Switch Link (ISL)

A special Cisco proprietary Ethernet protocol that assigns a 26-byte header to an encapsulated frame and a four-byte checksum, sometimes referred to as the *FCS* or the *CRC*.

IPCONFIG

A Windows command that displays IP information for all interfaces on the local host. This includes IP addresses, subnet masks, DNS servers, DHCP information, and some NetBIOS information.

IPSec

A protocol designed for virtual private networks (VPNs). Used to provide strong security standards for encryption and authentication.

IPX address

The unique address that identifies a node in the network.

LAN Emulation (LANE)

A standard created by the ATM forum to govern the connections of ATM endstations to either Ethernet or Token Ring devices.

LAN Module ASIC (LMA)

An ASIC part of the Cisco Catalyst 3000 Series switch that provides frame buffering, address learning, bus arbitration, and switching decisions for Ethernet ports.

latency

The time used to forward a packet in and out of a device. Commonly used in reference to routing and switching.

Layer 2 Forwarding Protocol (L2F)

A dial-up VPN protocol designed to work in conjunction with PPP to support authentication standards, such as TACACS+ and RADIUS, for secure transmissions over the Internet.

Layer 2 Tunneling Protocol (L2TP)

A dial-up VPN protocol that defines its own tunneling protocol and works with the advanced security methods of IPSec. L2TP allows PPP sessions to be tunneled across an arbitrary medium to a home gateway at an ISP or corporation.

learning bridge

A bridge that builds its own bridging address table rather than requiring you to enter information manually. Also known as a *smart bridge*.

line module communication processor (LCP)

Located on each line module, the LCP is responsible for providing communications for the MCP located on the supervisor engine.

Link Accessed Procedure Balanced (LAPB)

This is a bit-oriented, Data Link layer protocol for the X.25 protocol stack. It is a derivative of HDLC.

Link Access Procedure on the D Channel (LAPD)

A Data Link layer protocol for ISDN that is used specifically for the D channel on ISDN. LAPD was created from LAPB for signaling requirements of ISDN.

link-state routing algorithm

An algorithm that waits for each router to broadcast its location and the cost of reaching the router and its neighbors.

local-area network (LAN)

A group of connected computers that are located in a geographic area—usually a building or campus—and that share data and services.

local target logic (LTL)

A feature of some line modules that assists the EARL in making forwarding decisions.

local VLAN

Beneficial for networks whose resources are centralized and in one geographical location. The VLAN can span one switch or many switches within the same floor or building.

logical addressing scheme

The addressing method used in providing manually assigned node addressing.

Logical Link Control (LLC)

A sublayer of the Data Link layer of the OSI reference model that provides an interface for the Network-layer protocols and the Media Access Control (MAC) sublayer, which is also part of the Data Link layer.

loop

A continuous circle through a series of nodes in a network that a packet travels until it eventually times out. Without a protocol such as STP to detect loops, the data could continuously circle the network if no life cycle is assigned to the packet.

loopback plug

A device used for loopback testing.

loopback testing

A troubleshooting method in which the output and input wires are crossed or shorted in a manner that allows all outgoing data to be routed back into the card.

management
Fault, capacity, accounting, performance, and security control for a network.

Management Information Base (MIB)
An MIB is a database of managed objects running on a device which gathers information from the device and sends it to a central location using SNMP management software.

master communication processor (MCP)
A feature of the supervisor engine that takes commands from the network management processor (NCP) and forwards them to the correct line module communication processor (LCP). MCP is also responsible for testing, configuring, and controlling the local ports using LTL and CBL, and performing diagnostics on the memory, SAINT ASICs, LTL, and CBL. MCP is also responsible for downloading software to the line modules.

Media Access Control (MAC) address
A six-octet number that uniquely identifies a host on a network. It is a unique number that is burned into the network interface card, so it cannot be changed.

Media Access Control (MAC) layer
In the OSI model, the lower of the two sublayers of the Data Link layer. Defined by the IEEE as responsible for interaction with the Physical layer.

media access unit (MAU)
The IEEE 802.3 specification that refers to a transceiver. Not to be confused with a Token Ring MAU (multistation access unit), which is sometimes abbreviated *MSAU*.

megabit (Mb or Mbit)
One million bits. This term is used to rate transmission transfer speeds (not to be confused with *megabyte*).

megabyte (MB)
One million bytes. This term is usually used to refer to file size.

multicast
A single-packet transmission from one sender to a specific group of destination nodes.

multilayer switches
A switch with the ability to perform Layer 1, 2, and 3 switching and routing decisions. Newer switches can perform at layer 4 and 5.

multiprocessor
A single machine capable of supporting multiple processors.

multistation access unit (MAU or MSAU)

A concentrator or hub used in a Token Ring network. It organizes the connected nodes into an internal ring and uses the RI (ring in) and RO (ring out) connectors to expand to other MAUs on the network.

netflow switching

A feature incorporated into the MSM, NFFC, and NFFC II that allows for transparent switching in hardware while incorporating Quality of Service (QoS) features, including security, multicast forwarding, multilayer switching, NetFlow data exporting, and packet filtering at Layer 3 and Layer 4 application ports.

NetWare Core Protocol (NCP)

The NetWare protocol that provides a method for hosts to make calls to a NetWare server for services and network resources.

network address translation (NAT)

An algorithm to allow translation of a network address from one network to a foreign network so it can be used on the foreign network.

network analyzer

A device, also called a *protocol analyzer*, that collects and analyzes data to see a particular protocol or address packet to aid in troubleshooting.

network diameter

The cabling distance between the two farthest points in the network.

network down

Describes the situation in which the clients are unable to use the network. This can be administrative, scheduled downtime for upgrades or maintenance, or it can be the result of a serious error.

Network Driver Interface Specification (NDIS)

A Microsoft-proprietary specification or standard for a protocol-independent device driver. These drivers allow the NIC to bind multiple protocols to the same NIC, allowing the card to be used by multiple operating systems. Similar to *Open Data-Link Interface (ODI)*.

network ID

The part of the TCP/IP address that specifies the network portion of the IP address. It is determined by the class of the address, which is determined by the subnet mask used.

network interface card (NIC)

The hardware component that serves as the interface, or connecting component, between your network and the node. It has a transceiver, a MAC address, and a physical connector for the network cable. Also known as a *network adapter*.

Network Interface layer

The bottom layer of the TCP/IP architectural model; it's responsible for sending and receiving frames.

Network layer

The third layer of the OSI reference model, where routing based on node addresses (IP or IPX addresses) occurs.

network management processor (NMP)

A feature of the Catalyst supervisor engine that is responsible for general control and some management functions of the switch. It is responsible for executing the system's configuration changes, the CLI, and running diagnostics on boot components as well as new additional components.

Network Management Systems (NMS)

A complete package of hardware and software for monitoring a network and gathering information such as performance and security.

network monitor

A software-based tool that monitors a network using SNMP or ICMP to gather statistical data and to determine a baseline.

Network Time Protocol (NTP)

A protocol that allows all network equipment to synchronize the date and time on the private or internetwork environment.

nonblocking

A condition in which the fabric contains more bandwidth than the sum total of all the ports' bandwidth combined.

nonvolatile RAM (NVRAM)

Static memory similar to that of the flash. Memory stored in NVRAM does not get lost when the power is turned off. On a switch, the NVRAM stores the VLAN configuration, system configuration, SNMP parameters, STP configuration, and configuration of each port.

Novell Directory Services (NDS)

The user, group, and security information database of network resources that is used in a NetWare 4.x and/or NetWare 5.x internetwork. NDS is now called eDirectory for version 6.X of NetWare.

Open Shortest Path First (OSPF)

A link-state protocol that uses factors such as load balancing and least-cost routing to determine the shortest path.

Open Systems Interconnection (OSI) Model

A seven-layer model created by the ISO to standardize and explain the interactions of networking protocols.

optical time domain reflector (OTDR)

An advanced cable tester that analyzes fiber by sending pulses.

oversubscription

A condition in which the total bandwidth of the ports is greater than the capacity of the switching fabric. Also referred to as a *blocking architecture*.

Packet Internet Groper (PING)

A TCP/IP protocol-stack utility that works with the Internet Control Message Protocol to test connectivity to other systems by using an echo request and reply.

password

A set of characters that is used with a username to authenticate a user on the network and to provide the user with rights and permissions to files and resources.

permanent virtual circuit (PVC)

A logical path established in packet-switching networks between two locations. Similar to a dedicated leased line. Also known as a *permanent virtual connection* in ATM terminology (but not to be confused with *private virtual circuit*, which is also known as a *PVC*).

permissions

The authorization that is provided to users, allowing them to access objects on the network. The network administrators generally assign permissions. Slightly different from—but often used interchangeably with—the term *rights*.

physical addressing scheme

Refers to the MAC address on every network card manufactured.

Physical layer

The bottom layer (Layer 1) of the OSI reference model, where all physical connectivity is defined.

plain old telephone system (POTS)

The current analog public telephone system. Also known as the *PSTN*.

plug-and-play

Architecture designed to allow hardware devices to be detected by the operating system and for the driver to be automatically loaded.

Point-To-Point Protocol (PPP)

A common dial-up networking protocol that includes provisions for security and protocol negotiation and provides host-to-network and switch-to-switch connections for one or more user sessions. PPP is the common modem connection used for Internet dial-up.

Point-To-Point Tunneling Protocol (PPTP)

A protocol that encapsulates private network data in IP packets. These packets are transmitted over synchronous and asynchronous circuits to hide the underlying routing and switching infrastructure of the Internet from both senders and receivers.

polling

The media-access method for transmitting data, in which a controlling device is used to contact each node to determine if it has data to send.

port adapter modules

Modules attached to the carrier access modules on the LS1010 ATM and Catalyst 5500 Series ATM bus that provide physical ATM line ports for the user stations.

Port Aggregation Protocol (PAgP)

Manages the Fast EtherChannel bundles and aids in the automatic creation of Fast EtherChannel links.

PortFast

A protocol that forces an STP port to enter the forwarding state immediately after startup for a single workstation or server connected to a switch port.

power-on self-test (POST)

A series of tests that automatically run on a Cisco Catalyst switch when the power is turned on. The POST tests the hardware, memory, processors, ports, and ASICs to verify that they are functioning properly.

Presentation layer

Layer 6 of the OSI reference model. Prepares information to be used by the Application layer.

primary rate interface (PRI)

A higher-level network interface standard for use with ISDN. Defined at the rate of 1.544Mbps, it consists of a single 64Kbps D channel plus 23 (T1) or 30 (E1) B channels for voice or data.

priority queuing

A priority-based configuration that allows certain types of traffic to be routed before others based upon the level of priority configured for that type of traffic. You can configure a priority based on the particular traffic type, packet size, protocol, or interface.

proprietary

A standard or specification that is created by a manufacturer, vendor, or other private enterprise and is not always a recognized standard.

Proprietary Fat Pipe ASIC (PFPA)

An ASIC utilized on the Catalyst 3000 Series switches that use non-10BaseT ports such as Fast Ethernet, 100VG/AnyLAN, ATM, or the Stackport of the Stack Port Matrix. The PFPA is functionally the same as the LMA.

protocol

A set of rules that govern network communications among networks, computers, peripherals, and operating systems.

protocol analyzer

A device that collects and analyzes network data traffic to aid in troubleshooting. Also called a *network analyzer*.

Protocol Identification

In a frame, this five-byte field identifies and communicates to the destination node the protocol that is being used in the data transmission.

protocol stack

Two or more protocols that work together (such as TCP and IP, or IPX and SPX). Also known as a *protocol suite*.

public switched telephone network (PSTN)

All the telephone networks and services in the world. The same as POTS, PSTN refers to the world's collection of interconnected public telephone networks that are either commercial or government owned. PSTN is a digital network, with the exception of the connection between local exchanges and customers, which remains analog.

q.921

Resides on the D channel of ISDN as a Layer 2 protocol to provide protocol connectivity from the central office switch to the router.

q.931

Resides on ISDN as a Layer 3 protocol to provide a snapshot of messages of ISDN connections.

quality of service (QoS)

A guarantee of a particular level of service for a connection. QoS uses queuing and other methods to guarantee that bandwidth is available for a certain protocol, application, or address. QoS is important for implementing applications such as voice and video.

queuing

A method of providing QoS by the use of buffering and priority control mechanisms to control data congestion on the network.

read/writes

The counting of packets on the ingress (read) as well as the egress (write) from the switching fabric.

redistribution

Allowing a protocol to be integrated in a network using a different protocol.

resource node

Any interface on the network that provides a service for a demand node. Resource nodes can be such things as servers and printers. Incorrect placement of your resource nodes can have terrible effects on your network.

Remote Network Monitoring (RMON)

An Internet Engineering Task Force (IETF) standard that defines how devices gather and share the network monitoring information that is sent to an SNMP Management Station. RMON gathers Layer 2 information concerning bandwidth use, collisions, and errors.

remote node

A node or computer that is connected to the network through a dial-up connection. Dialing in to the Internet from home is a perfect and common example of the concept.

remote services

Services in which the device that supplies the services resides on a separate subnet from the device that requests the services.

repeater

A device that regenerates and retransmits the signal on a network. Generally used to strengthen signals going long distances.

resource node

An interface on the network that provides a service for a demand node. Resource nodes can be items such as servers and printers. The incorrect placement of your resource nodes can also have terrible effects on your network.

Reverse Address Resolution Protocol (RARP)

The protocol that allows a MAC address to be mapped or correlated to identify the IP address of the device. Opposite of ARP.

rights

Authorization provided to users, allowing them to perform certain tasks. The network administrators generally assign rights. Slightly different from—but often used interchangeably with—the term *permissions*.

ring in (RI)

A connector used in an IBM Token Ring network on a multistation access unit (MSAU) to expand to other MSAUs on the network. Counterpart to the RO (ring out), the RI connector on the MSAU connects to the media to accept the token from the ring.

ring topology

A network structure that is physically and logically organized in a ring formation with devices connected to the ring.

ring out (RO)

A connector used in an IBM Token Ring network on a multistation access unit (MSAU) to expand to other MSAUs on the network. A counterpart to the RI (ring in), the RO connector on the MAU connects to the media to send the token out to the ring.

root bridge

The bridge or switch that is most centrally located in the network and provides the shortest path to other links on the network. Unlike other bridges, the root bridge always forwards frames out over all of its ports.

root timers

The timers received from the root bridge.

Routing Information Field (RIF)

A field on Source Route Bridge Token Ring frames that contains information regarding the rings and bridges that the frame must travel to the destination interface.

Routing Information Protocol (RIP)

Protocol that uses hop counts as a routing metric to control the direction and flow of packets between routers and switches on an inter-network.

runtless switching

A switching method in which the switch reads the first 64 bytes to verify that there is no corruption of the packet. If the packet is corrupt-ed, a preset maximum of errors changes the switching type from cut-through switching to store-and-forward switching. Also known as *fragment-free switching*.

Security Association Identifier (SAID)

One of the three values that make up a Clear Header on the FDDI frame type. It is used for security for the Clear Header, which con-tains a SAID, LSAP, and the Management Defined Field (MDF).

Sequenced Packet Exchange (SPX)

Protocol used in conjunction with IPX when connection-oriented delivery is required. It is used mainly in NetWare network envi-ronments.

server

A resource node that fulfills service requests for demand nodes. Usually referred to by the type of service it performs, such as file server, email server, or print server.

service access point (SAP)

A field in a frame that instructs the receiving host which protocol the frame is intended for.

Service Advertising Protocol (SAP)

NetWare protocol used on an IPX network. SAP maintains server information tables, listing each service that has been advertised to it, and provides this information to any nodes attempting to locate a service.

Service Advertising Protocol agent (SAP agent)

Router or other node on an IPX network that maintains a server information table. Such a table lists each service that has been adver-tised to it and provides this infor-mation to any nodes that are attempting to locate a service.

Service Profile Identifier (SPID)

This number is assigned by the service provider and network administrators and identifies a BRI port and services provided to the number. Although ISDN uses SPIDS in North America to access the service provider, it is optional in other areas.

Session
The dialog that exists between two computers.

Session layer
This fifth layer of the OSI reference model establishes, manages, and terminates sessions between applications on different nodes.

shared systems
The infrastructure component routed directly into the backbone of an internetwork for optimal systems access. Provides connectivity to servers and other shared systems.

shielded twisted pair (STP)
Twisted-pair network cable that uses shielding to insulate the cable from electromagnetic interference.

Simple Network Management Protocol (SNMP)
A protocol used in TCP/IP networks to provide network devices with a method to monitor and control network devices. It is used to manage configurations, statistics collection, performance, and security, and to report network management information to a management console that is a member of the same community.

Simple Network Management Protocol (SNMP) trap
An SNMP protocol utility that sends out an alarm in an identified community, notifying its members that some network activity differs from the established threshold, as defined by the administrator.

single attached station (SAS)
A FDDI device that has a single connection to a single DAC.

socket
A logical interprocess communications mechanism through which a program communicates with another program or with a network.

socket identifier
An eight-bit number that is used to identify the socket. Developers and designers of services and protocols usually assign socket identifiers. Also known as a *socket number*.

source address
The address of the host who sent the frame. The source address is contained in the frame so that the destination node knows who sent the data.

source route bridging (SRB)
A type of bridging that is used to segment Token Ring networks. Requires all rings and bridges to have a unique number.

source route switching (SRS)
A type of bridging that combines SRB and SRT. Developed to allow more physical rings on the network. It allows for increasing bandwidth needs while preserving the benefits of SRB.

source route translational bridging (SR/TLB)

A type of bridging that bridges a Token Ring segment to another physical media type such as Ethernet or FDDI. It is transparent to the source and destination interfaces.

source route transparent bridging (SRT)

A type of bridging that combines SRB and TB. Using SRT, the bridge places a RIF into a frame traveling from the TB to the SRB side. It then strips the RIF when the frame travels from the SRB port to the TB port.

Source Service Access Point (SSAP)

A one-byte field in the frame that combines with the SAP to tell the receiving host the identity of the source or sending host.

Spanning Tree Algorithm (STA)

Defined by IEEE 802.1 as part of the Spanning Tree Protocol to eliminate loops in an internetwork with multiple paths. The Spanning Tree Algorithm is responsible for performing Spanning Tree Protocol topology recalculations when a switch is powered up and when a topology change occurs.

Spanning Tree Protocol (STP)

Defined by IEEE 802.1, STP was developed to eliminate the loops caused by the multiple paths in an internetwork. STP communicates

topology changes from switch to switch with the use of bridge protocol data units (BPDUs). See also *color blocking logic*.

split-horizon

Routing mechanism that inquires about routes to prevent information from using the same interface through which the information was received, therefore preventing a loop.

standard IP access list

An access list that only filters based on the source address.

star topology

A logical network topology with end points that join at a common area using point-to-point links.

static IP addresses

IP addresses that are assigned to each network device individually. Often referred to as *hard-coded*.

static VLAN port

A port on a switch manually assigned a VLAN number. Any node or interface connected to the port automatically becomes a member of the assigned VLAN.

static window

A mechanism used in flow control to prevents a data sender from overwhelming the receiver. Only a set amount of data can be buffered in a static window. See also *flow control*.

station IPX address

A 12-digit number that is used to uniquely identify each device on an IPX network.

storage area network

A subnetwork of storage devices, usually found on high-speed networks and shared by all servers on the network.

store-and-forward

A fast packet-switching method that produces a higher latency than other switching methods, because the switch waits for the entire packet to arrive before checking the CRC. It then forwards or discards the packet.

subinterface

A virtual interface that can be configured on an interface.

subnet mask

A 32-bit address that is used to mask or screen a portion of the IP address to differentiate the part of the address that designates the network from the part that designates the host.

subnetting

The process of dividing your assigned IP address range into smaller clusters of hosts.

switch

A Layer 2 networking device that forwards frames based on destination addresses.

switch block

Switching devices located in wiring closets, requiring high-speed uplinks and redundancy.

switched port analyzer (SPAN)

A port at which traffic from another port or group of ports is attached to a protocol analyzer or probe device. The SPAN aids in the diagnoses of problems that are related to traffic patterns on the network.

switched virtual circuit

A virtual circuit that is established dynamically on demand to form a dedicated link and is then broken when transmission is complete. Also known as a *switched virtual connection* in ATM terminology.

switching fabric

A term used to describe the "highway" that the data travels to get from the input port on a switch to the output port.

Synchronous Data Link Control (SDLC)

A bit-oriented serial protocol for the Data Link layer of SNA. SDLC created the basics for HDLC and LAPB protocols.

synchronous transmission

A digital signal transmission method that uses a precise clocking method and a predefined number of bits sent at a constant rate.

syslog

Messages sent to a remote machine regarding the switch system configuration, such as software and configuration changes.

T1

Digital WAN carrier facility that transmits DS-1-formatted data at rates of up to 1.544Mbps through the telephone switching network, using AMI or B8ZS coding.

T3

Digital WAN carrier facility that transmits DS-3 formatted data at rates of up to 44.763Mbps.

TACACS+

A security feature that uses an MD5-encrypted algorithm to enforce strict authentication controls. It requires both a user name and a password, thus allowing administrators to better track network usage and changes based on user accounts.

TCP/IP

See *Transmission Control Protocol/Internet Protocol*.

Telecommunications Industry Association (TIA)

An organization that develops standards with the *EIA (Electronics Industries Association)* for telecommunications technologies.

Telnet

Standard terminal-emulation protocol in the TCP/IP protocol used to perform terminal emulation over TCP/IP via remote terminal connections, enabling users to log in to remote systems and use their resources as if the users were locally on that system.

thicknet coax

Thick cable (approximately 0.375 inches in diameter) most commonly found in the backbone of a coaxial network.

thinnet coax

Cable thinner than thicknet (approximately 0.25 inches in diameter), commonly used in older bus topologies to connect the nodes to the network.

time domain reflectors (TDRs)

An advanced cable tester that can isolate a cable fault within a few feet of the actual problem on the wire.

time-to-live (TTL)

Indicator of how long a packet remains alive on the network.

token

A frame that provides controlling information. In a Token Ring network, the node that possesses the token is the one that is allowed to transmit next.

Token Ring

An IBM proprietary, token-passing, LAN topology defined by the IEEE 802.5 standard. Token Ring operates at either 4Mbps or 16Mbps in a star topology.

topology

The shape or layout of a physical network and the flow of data through the network.

trace

Also referred to as *traceroute*. A command used to send ECMO ECHO messaged to track the path of a packet from a source to a destination.

Transmission Control Protocol (TCP)

Part of the TCP/IP protocol stack. A connection-oriented, reliable, data-transmission communication service that operates at the OSI Transport layer.

Transmission Control Protocol/Internet Protocol (TCP/IP)

The suite of protocols combining TCP and IP, developed to support the construction of worldwide internetworks. See also *Transmission Control Protocol* and *Internet Protocol*.

Transmission Control Protocol/Internet Protocol (TCP/IP) socket

A *socket*, or connection to an endpoint, that is used in TCP/IP communication transmissions.

transmit

The process of sending data using light, electronic, or electric signals. In networking, this is usually done in the form of digital signals that are composed of bits.

Transparent Bridging (TB)

A bridging type that uses the MAC address to make forwarding and filtering decisions transparent to the sender and receiver interfaces. Used in Ethernet.

Transport layer

Layer 4 of the OSI reference model. Controls the flow of information.

Trivial File Transfer Protocol (TFTP)

A simplified version of FTP that allows files to be transferred over a network from one computer to another. Also used to install the Cisco IOS on an IOS-based switch, router, or GSR.

troubleshooting model

A series of guidelines to be used as an aid in the troubleshooting process to resolve network issues.

trunk link

A special type of VLAN connections. Unlike a user port, trunk links expect the device at the other end of the connection to understand the inserted frame tags. Standard Ethernet and Token Ring cards do not understand frame tags.

twisted pair

A type of cable that uses multiple twisted pairs of copper wire.

unicast

A frame in which the destination MAC address specifies the single computer of destination. Summarized as direct network traffic between two individual nodes.

unshielded twisted pair (UTP)

A type of cable that uses multiple twisted pairs of copper wire in a casing that does not provide much protection from EMI. UTP is rated in five categories and is the most common cable in Ethernet networks.

UplinkFast

Provides a protocol to aid in fast convergence after an STP topology change and achieves load balancing between redundant links.

User Datagram Protocol (UDP)

Operating at the Transport layer of the OSI model, this communications protocol provides connectionless and unreliable communications services. It requires a transmission protocol such as IP to guide it to the destination host.

virtual LAN (VLAN)

Allows a network administrator to divide a bridged network into several broadcast domains. Each VLAN is considered its own separate subnet, and Layer 3 routing is still required to route between VLANs. VLANs can be based on the port identifier of the switch, the MAC address, Layer 3 addressing, directory information, or application information. VLANs can be implemented on different media types such as Ethernet, FDDI, Token Ring, or ATM. The benefits of VLANs are limited broadcast domains, added security, and redundancy.

virtual private network (VPN)

A network that uses a public network (such as the Internet) as a backbone to connect two or more private networks. VPN provides users with the equivalent of a private network in terms of security.

VLAN Trunking Protocol (VTP)

A protocol used to enhance and configure the extension of broadcast domains across multiple switches. VTP dynamically reports the addition of VLANs throughout the switched network, thus creating a consistent switched network.

VLAN Trunking Protocol (VTP) pruning

A protocol used to reduce the number of switches participating in VTP by removing switches from the database that do not have certain VLANs assigned to numbered ports. If VTP pruning were not enabled on a trunk port, all VLAN traffic would travel through the trunk links to all the switches whether they had destination ports or not.

wide-area network (WAN)

This data communications network serves users across a broad geographical area. WANs often use transmission devices such as modems and channel service units/data service units (CSU/DSU) to carry signals over leased lines or common carrier lines.

window flow control

A flow-control method in which the receiving host buffers the data it receives and holds it in the buffer until it can be processed. After it is processed, an acknowledgment is sent to the sender.

WINIPCFG

A Windows 95 or 98 command utility that brings up a graphical user interface (GUI) to display DHCP-obtained IP information settings. This utility allows you to release, renew, or view the DHCP settings for the local hosts adapters.

Index

. . . .

M

MAC (Media Access Control), 17

magic number (256), determining hosts in subnets, 65

management
configuration/fault (Physical layer), 172-177
connections, 433
CWSI, 194
ICMP, 70-73
nslookup command, 106-111
password recovery, 196-197
remote connections
telnet command, 118-119
troubleshooting tools, 193
VTP, 229-231
advertisements, 231-232
assigning VLAN memberhips, 240-242
configuring VLANs, 234-240
enabling VLAN on 1900 EN series switches, 242-243
inter-VLAN routing, 232-234, 243-246
pruning, 240
show vtp domain command, 249-250
troubleshooting inter-VLAN routing, 247-248

Management Defined Field (MDF), 227

manual binding, 84

maps
dialer map command, 328-329
IP addresses, 116
process, 19

MDF (Management Defined Field), 227

Media Access Control (MAC), 17

memberships, 1900 series switches, 240-242

messages, types, 339

MIDI (Musical Instrument Digital Interface), 15

misconfigured provider switches, troubleshooting, 334

models
Cisco Campus, 422-423
Cisco Hierarchical, 22
Access layer, 24
Core layer, 23-24
Distribution layer, 24
Internetworking Troubleshooting, 18-19, 22
networks, 12

monitors
Cisco NMS software, 177
networks, 173-176
RMON, 195

MPEG (Motion Picture Experts Group), 15

MSAU (multistation access unit), 44

multicasting
Ethernet, 41-42
VTP advertisements, 231-232

multiple DNS servers, adding, 68-69

multiplexing
ATM, 42
ISL, 227-229

multistation access unit (MSAU), 44

Musical Instrument Digital Interface (MIDI), 15

N

names (DNS), 68
caching, 69-70
configuring, 68-69
nslookup command, 106-111
routers, 68
servers, 106

narrowband, 38

netstat command (Windows), 112-116

NetWare
encapsulation, 127-128
IPX/SPX, 126
access lists, 138-140
encapsulation, 127-128

How can we make this index more useful? Email us at indexes@quepublishing.com

trunking
  IEEE 802.1Q, 247
  ISL, 246
  VLANs, 226
    IEEE 802.10, 227
    IEEE 802.1Q, 227
    ISL, 227-229
    LANE, 229
  VTP, 229-231
    advertisements, 231-232
    assigning VLAN memberships,
      240-242
    configuring VLANs, 234-240
    enabling VLAN on 1900 EN series
      switches, 242-243
    inter-VLAN routing, 232-234,
      243-246
    pruning, 240
    show vtp domain command, 249-250
    troubleshooting inter-VLAN rout-
      ing, 247-248
type field, 37
types
  of messages, 339
  of switches (ISDN), 341

U

UDP (User Datagram Protocol), 15, 58
unicast forwarding, 192
Unicast transmissions, Ethernet, 41-42
Unshielded Twisted Pair (UTP), 18
updates, triggered, 299
User Datagram Protocol. See UDP, 15
utilities. *See also* show commands;
  troubleshooting
    arp command, 116
    basic cable testers, 153
    ftp command, 117-118
    netstat command, 112-116
    network monitors, 173-176
    nslookup command, 106-111
    OTDRs, 154
    ping command, 71-73
    protocol analyzers, 155

RPC, 15
TDRs, 154
telnet command, 118-119
troubleshooting software, 193-194
utilization of routers, 432
UTP (Unshielded Twisted Pair), 18

V

viewing
  HILI, 36
  IP addresses, 67
  MIDI, 15
  PrepLogic, 438
  shutdown state, 264
  speed, 264
  TCP/IP, 94-98
  troubleshooting interfaces, 263
  X.25, 287
virtual circuits, SAP, 131-132
VLAN Trunking Protocol (VTP), 226-231
  advertisements, 231-232
  inter-VLAN routing, 232-234, 243-248
  pruning, 240
  show vtp domain command, 249-250
  VLAN
    assigning memberships to 1900 series
      switches, 240-242
    configuring, 234-240
    enabling on 1900 EN series switches,
      242-243
VLANs (Virtual LANs), 226
  configuring, 234-240
    assigning memberships to 1900 series
      switches, 240-242
    enabling on 1900 EN series switches,
      242-243
  ISL, 246
  trunking, 226
    IEEE 802.10, 227
    IEEE 802.1Q, 227

informIT